Encyclopedia of Heavy Metal Music

Encyclopedia of Heavy Metal Music

WILLIAM PHILLIPS AND BRIAN COGAN

GREENWOOD PRESS
Westport, Connecticut • London

Library of Congress Cataloging-in-Publication Data

Phillips, William, 1961–
　　Encyclopedia of heavy metal music / William Phillips and Brian Cogan.
　　　　p. cm.
　　Includes bibliographical references and index.
　　ISBN 978-0-313-34800-6 (alk. paper)
　　1. Heavy metal (Music)—Encyclopedias. 2. Heavy metal (Music)—Bio-bibliography—
Dictionaries. I. Cogan, Brian, 1967– II. Title.
　　ML102.R6P54　2009
　　781.66—dc22　　2008034199

British Library Cataloguing in Publication Data is available.

Library of Congress Catalog Card Number: 2008034199
ISBN: 978-0-313-34800-6

First published in 2009

Greenwood Press, 88 Post Road West, Westport, CT 06881
An imprint of Greenwood Publishing Group, Inc.
www.greenwood.com

Printed in the United States of America

The paper used in this book complies with the
Permanent Paper Standard issued by the National
Information Standards Organization (Z39.48-1984).

10　9　8　7　6　5　4　3　2　1

Contents

List of Entries   vii

Guide to Related Topics   xiii

Preface   xix

Acknowledgments   xxiii

The Encyclopedia   1

Heavy Metal Music: An Introduction   3

Entries A–Z   10

Selected Bibliography   271

Index   275

List of Entries

Accept

AC/DC

Aerosmith

Agalloch

Airheads

Alabama Thunder Pussy

Alcatrazz

Alcohol

Alice Cooper

Alice in Chains

The Amboy Dukes

Amon Amarth

Amps

Anaal Nathrakh

Angel Witch

Anthrax

Anvil

April Wine

Arch Enemy

Armored Saint

Asphalt Ballet

At the Gates

Autograph

Avenged Sevenfold

Badlands

Bad News

Bang Tango

Bathory

Beatallica

Behemoth

Biohazard

Black Label Society

Black Metal

Black Sabbath

Blitzkreig

Bloodstock

Blue Cheer

Blue Murder

Blue Öyster Cult

Body Count

Tommy Bolin

Bolt Thrower

Bon Jovi

Boris

Britny Fox

Buckcherry

Budgie

Bullet Boys

Burning Witch

William S. Burroughs

Burzum

Cacophony

Candlemass

Cannibal Corpse

Carcass

Cathedral

Celtic Frost

Cinderella

Circus of Power

Cirith Ungol

"Cookie Monster" vocal style

Corpsepaint

Corrosion of Conformity

Crossover

Crowbar

Crumbsuckers

Cryptic Slaughter

The Cult

Cult of Luna

Danzig

Dark Angel

The Darkness

Darkthrone

Dead Horse

Death

Death Metal

Decline of Western Civilization, Part II: The Metal Years

Deep Purple

Def Leppard

Deftones

Deicide

Demos

Dethklok

Dimmu Borgir

Dio

Ronnie James Dio

Discharge

Dismember

Dissection

Disturbed

Dokken

Dream Theater

DRI

Dusk

Dust

Eagles of Death Metal

Earache Records

Electric Guitars

Elf

Emperor

English Dogs

Enslaved

Europe

Exodus

Extreme

Faith No More

Fargo Rock City

Fashion and Metal

Faster Pussycat

Fates Warning

Festivals

Filter

Firehouse

Flotsam & Jetsam

Foghat

Lita Ford

Fu Manchu

Funeral

Girlschool

Goatsnake

Goblin Cock

God Dethroned

Godflesh

Godsmack

Gorgoroth

Great White

Grim Reaper

Grindcore

Dave Grohl

Grunge

Guitar Hero

Guns N' Roses

GWAR

Hanoi Rocks
Hardcore (Punk)
Hatebreed
Headbanging
Heaven and Hell
Heavy Metal Kids
Heavy Metal Parking Lot
Hellhammer
Helloween
High on Fire
Holocaust
The Horns
Immortal
Incubus
Infectious Grooves
Insane Clown Posse
Iron Butterfly
Iron Maiden
Isis
Jackyl
Jethro Tull and the Grammys
Judas Priest
Juggalos
Jen Kajzer
Diane Kamikaze
Kat
Kid Rock
Killswitch Engage
King Diamond
King's X
Kiss
Kittie
Kix
Korn
Kreator
Krokus
Kyuss
Lamb of God
L'Amours
Leather
Led Zeppelin
Leng Tch'e

Lez Zeppelin
Limp Bizkit
Living Colour
Lord of the Rings
Lords of Chaos
Machine Head
Yngwie Malmsteen
Manowar
Marilyn Manson
Masters of Reality
Mastodon
Mayhem
Megadeth
Melvins
Mercyful Fate
Meshuggah
Metal Blade
Metal Church
"Metal Up Your Ass"
Metalheads
Metallica
Misfits
M.O.D.
Monster Magnet
Montrose
Moonsorrow
Morbid Angel
Moshing
Mötley Crüe
Motorhead
Mr. Big
Mudvayne
Mushroom Head
Napalm Death
Nashville Pussy
Neurosis
New York Dolls
Nickelback
Night Ranger
Nile
Norwegian Black Metal
Ted Nugent

Om

Orgy

Ozzy Osbourne

Overdose

Overkill

Pariah

John Peel

Pentagram

Piercings

Pig Destroyer

The Pit

Poison

Poison the Well

Possessed

Power Mad

Powerman 5000

Primus

Probot

Prong

Queens of the Stone Age

Queensrÿche

Quiet Riot

Racer X

Rage Against the Machine

Raging Slab

Rainbow

Rammstein

Ratt

Raven

Riot

Roadrunner Records

The Rods

The Runaways

Running Wild

Rush

Sacred Reich

Saigon Kick

Samson

Sarcófago

Satanicide

Satanic Rock

Joe Satriani

Savatage

Scatterbrain

Scorpions

Sepultura

Shock Rock

Shotgun Messiah

Sir Lord Baltimore

Skid Row

Slaughter

Slayer

Sleep

Slipknot

Smokewagon

Andy Sneap

S.O.D.

Sodom

Soilent Green

Soulfly

Soundgarden

Southern Lord Records

Speed Metal

Speedcore

Spikes

Spinal Tap

Spread Eagle

Static X

Steve Stevens

Stryper

Studs

St. Vitus

Suicidal Tendencies

Sunn O)))

The Sword

Tad

Tesla

Testament

Thin Lizzy

Thor

Thrash Metal

Tora Tora

Tribute Bands

Triumph

Trixter

Trouble

Eddie Trunk

TSOL

Twisted Sister

Type O Negative

UFO

Upper Crust

Uriah Heep

Steve Vai

Vandenberg

Van Halen

Venom

Vinnie Vincent

Virtuosity in Heavy Metal

Vision of Disorder

Vixen

Voivod

Warrant

W.A.S.P.

Watain

White Lion

Whitesnake

White Zombie

Wino

Wishbone Ash

Woodstock 1999

Wykyd Sceptre

Zolar X

Rob Zombie

Guide to Related Entries

BANDS

Accept

AC/DC

Aerosmith

Agalloch

Alabama Thunder Pussy

Alcatrazz

Alice Cooper

Alice in Chains

The Amboy Dukes

Amon Amarth

Anaal Nathrakh

Angel Witch

Anthrax Anvil

April Wine

Arch Enemy

Armored Saint

Asphalt Ballet

At the Gates

Autograph

Avenged Sevenfold

Badlands

Bad News

Bang Tango

Bathory

Beatallica

Behemoth

Biohazard

Black Label Society

Black Sabbath

Blitzkreig

Blue Cheer

Blue Öyster Cult

Body Count

Bolt Thrower

Bon Jovi

Boris

Britny Fox

Buckcherry

Budgie

Bullet Boys

Burning Witch

Burzum

Candlemass

Cannibal Corpse

Carcass

Cathedral

Celtic Frost

Cinderella

Circus of Power

Cirith Ungol

Corpsepaint

Corrosion of Conformity

Crowbar

Crumbsuckers

Cryptic Slaughter

The Cult

Cult of Luna

Danzig

Dark Angel

The Darkness

Darkthrone

Dead Horse

Death

Deep Purple

Def Leppard

Deftones

Deicide

Dethklok

Dimmu Borgir

Dio

Discharge

Dismember

Dissection

Disturbed

Dokken

Dream Theater

DRI

Dusk

Dust

Eagles of Death Metal

Elf

Emperor

English Dogs

Enslaved

Europe

Exodus

Extreme

Faith No More

Faster Pussycat

Fates Warning

Filter

Firehouse

Flotsam & Jetsam

Foghat

Lita Ford

Fu Manchu

Funeral

Girlschool

Goblin Cock

God Dethroned

Godflesh

Goatsnake

Godsmack

Gorgoroth

Great White

Grim Reaper

Dave Grohl

Guns N' Roses

GWAR

Hanoi Rocks

Hatebreed

Heaven and Hell

Heavy Metal Kids

Hellhammer

Helloween

High on Fire

Holocaust

The Horns

Immortal

Incubus

Infectious Grooves

Insane Clown Posse

Iron Butterfly

Iron Maiden

Isis

Jackyl

Jethro Tull and the Grammys

Judas Priest

Kat

Killswitch Engage

King Diamond

King's X

Kiss

Kix

Korn

Kreator

Krokus

Kyuss

Lamb of God

Led Zeppelin

Leng Tch'e

Lez Zeppelin

Limp Bizkit

Living Colour

Machine Head

Yngwie Malmsteen

Manowar

Marilyn Manson

Masters of Reality

Mastodon

Mayhem

Megadeth

Melvins

Mercyful Fate

Meshuggah

Metal Church

Metallica

Misfits

M.O.D. (Method of Destruction)

Monster Magnet

Montrose

Morbid Angel

Moonsorrow

Mötley Crüe

Motorhead

Mr. Big

Mudvayne

Mushroom Head

Napalm Death

Nashville Pussy

Neurosis

New York Dolls

Nickelback

Night Ranger

Nile

Om

Orgy

Overdose

Overkill

Ozzy Osbourne

Pariah

Pig Destroyer

Poison

Poison the Well

Possessed

Power Mad

Powerman 5000

Prong

Queens of the Stone Age

Queensrÿche

Quiet Riot

Racer X

Rage Against the Machine

Raging Slab

Rainbow

Rammstein

Ratt

Raven

Riot

The Rods

The Runaways

Running Wild

Rush

Sacred Reich

Saigon Kick

Samson

Sarcófago

Satan

Satanicide

Savatage

Scatterbrain

Scorpions

Sepultura

Shotgun Messiah

Sir Lord Baltimore

Skid Row

Slaughter

Slayer

Sleep

Slipknot

Smokewagon

S.O.D.

Sodom

Soilent Green

Soulfly

Soundgarden

Spinal Tap

Spread Eagle

Static X

Stryper

St. Vitus

Suicidal Tendencies

Sunn O)))

The Sword

Tad

Tesla

Testament

Thin Lizzy

Thor

Tora Tora

Triumph

Trixter

Trouble

TSOL

Twisted Sister

Type O Negative

UFO

Upper Crust

Uriah Heep

Vandenberg

Van Halen

Venom

Vision of Disorder

Vixen

Voivod

Warrant

W.A.S.P.

Watain

White Lion

Whitesnake

White Zombie

Wino

Wishbone Ash

Wykyd Sceptre

Zolar X

PERSONALITIES/SOLO PERFORMERS

Tommy Bolin

William S. Burroughs

Ronnie James Dio

Lita Ford

Dave Grohl

Jen Kajzer

Diane Kamikaze

Kat

Kid Rock

Yngwie Malmsteen

Marilyn Manson

Ted Nugent

Ozzy Osbourne

John Peel

Joe Satriani

Sir Lord Baltimore

Andy Sneap

Steve Stevens

Eddie Trunk

Steve Vai

Vinnie Vincent

Rob Zombie

BOOKS/FILMS/LABELS/FESTIVALS

Airheads

Bloodstock (festival)

Decline of Western Civilization, Part II: The Metal Years

Earache Records

Fargo Rock City

Heavy Metal Parking Lot

Lord of the Rings
Lords of Chaos
Metal Blade Records
Roadrunner Records
Southern Lord Records
Woodstock 1999

SUB-GENRES

Black Metal
Crossover
Death Metal
Grindcore
Grunge
Hardcore (Punk)
Norwegian Black Metal
Satanic Rock
Shock Rock
Speed Metal
Speedcore
Thrash Metal

HEAVY METAL CULTURE

Alcohol
Amps

"Cookie Monster" vocal style
Demos
Electric Guitars
Fashion and Metal
Festivals
Guitar Hero
Headbanging
Jethro Tull and the Grammys
Juggalos
Leather
"Metal Up Your Ass"
metalheads
Moshing
Pentagram
Piercings
The Pit
Scatterbrain
Spikes
Studs
Tribute bands
Virtuosity in Heavy Metal

Preface

The Encyclopedia of Heavy Metal Music was a daunting but enjoyable endeavor for a multitude of reasons. First of all it must be stated at the outset that within the heavy metal community there is a constant debate about the parameters of metal and what consists of true and false metal. There are not only controversies about what bands are metal, but what makes a band metal and what makes a band not metal. The intersection between the terms *hard rock* and *heavy metal*, for example, is problematic at best, and the purpose of the authors was not to be the sole arbiters of taste, but to be as broadly inclusive as possible. We did not set ourselves up in some metal Valhalla, drinking mead and making dark sacrifices to the metal gods to decide. Instead, we carefully analyzed the difficulty inherent in setting categories in terms of music, especially one with as vibrant and active an audience as is the metal audience.

In writing about heavy metal certain limitations and contradictions must be considered, especially since almost no two scholars or metal fans agree on the following issues:

- An exact definition of the term (or who first coined the term or used it as a reference for a musical genre);
- When metal began (Start with Black Sabbath and Led Zeppelin? Or trace it back further to Blue Cheer or Iron Butterfly, or any of the other bands that sounded vaguely metallic during the early to mid-sixties?);
- Does "true" heavy metal currently exist or is current metal simply an imitation of a dead art form?

These are legitimate questions, and music scholars and magazines have been debating them for years, with little or no consensus. (For more details on this, see the essay preceding the A-Z entries: "Heavy Metal: An Introduction.") While we do not wish to add fuel to the fire or to fuel the ire of those in the metal community who believe that to write about heavy metal for public consumption is an act of selling out and only of benefit to those who aren't "true" fans to begin with, we nonetheless believe that this book will provide a necessary resource for historians, students, and others who share our fascination with heavy metal and its various subcultures.

This encyclopedia, with nearly 350 entries, examines the huge scope of heavy metal and is not so much an effort to be the definitive work on the genre (we would need another ten volumes just to be complete about American metal!), but instead to provide a guide to the vast expanse of work that has been labeled heavy metal and to serve as an entry point and reference to those who want to know more about this music and its subcultures. There are many who argue over the scope of "when" metal was at its heyday, and indeed if new metal bands are still true to the roots of metal or are simply playing a new hybrid containing elements of metal. We do not regard heavy metal as static and unchanging but as a genre in a constant state of evolution, not only because of innovative new musicians, but also because of fan participation and "ownership" of the music. The *Encyclopedia of Heavy Metal Music* examines this form in all its complexity, contradictions, inconsistency, and power.

WHAT IS INCLUDED IN THIS ENCYCLOPEDIA

To determine which bands were to be included in this encyclopedia, we have tried to be as broad and inclusive as possible. Therefore, because of the active nature of the metal audience, and the proprietary way in which many metal fans regard the genre, there are inclusions and exclusions that may disappoint some fans. As an example, after vigorous debate, the authors have decided to include several bands, such as Limp Bizkit, not considered to be "true metal" by some in the metal community, because we believe that if a major band is considered metal by many and has been considered metal by a large numbers in the community, it deserves inclusion. This also applies to the category of "hair metal," where we were faced with many difficult decisions about inclusion and eventually decided to err on the side (for the most part) on inclusion rather than exclusion. We must state, however, that, because of reasons of space and time, not every band that was ever considered a metal band is included here. Because we feel that it is better to highlight some lesser-known but praiseworthy bands in this encyclopedia, we feel that if we have erred, it is on the side of writing about bands that will be appreciated by the novice, as opposed to listing every band from every time period.

Another key issue we had to consider in writing this encyclopedia was defining when metal began. To some whom we discussed this project with, metal culture can be traced back not merely to the sixties, but some have argued that metal began with Wagner, Aleister Crowley, or even Dracula. While it is true that there are many seminal influences on metal music, we have argued previously that two key bands laid the foundations for heavy metal and that to try and work in any elements of "heaviness" throughout history would be futile.

Was "You Really Got Me" by the Kinks the first metal song? Was the use of feedback on a song enough to make it heavy? Was "Helter Skelter" by the Beatles metal? All of these are interesting questions for barroom debate; they are ultimately not the main question. In our view, two key bands started metal: First, Black Sabbath, with guitarist Tony Iommi's tuned-down guitar, leaden pace, and wail of Ozzy Osbourne, along with Geezer Butler's lyrics that dealt with the occult, provided building blocks for the construction of the template of metal. Second, Led Zeppelin, with the technical virtuosity of Jimmy Page, John Bonham's ferocious attack on the drums, and Robert Plant's rock god persona, also filled in the outline for the thousands of bands that came after them. These bands possessed not only the prerequisite ability to play ferociously, but also the *intentionality* to play that way, a key factor in determining (in retrospect for the two bands in particular) what is or is not metal.

Metal is not just about playing well, but playing with the intention to *be* a heavy metal band. A metal band, and members of the subculture, need to understand that to live metal is to dress metal, to talk metal, to follow associated metal rituals and to understand the symbols and signs of metal. To be a heavy metal fan or band is to try and live metal in the most authentic way possible. A casual fan can get by without knowing the canon of metal back and forth, but for fans who want to be considered part of the metal community, understanding the value of metal cultural capital means understanding the history of metal, and being able to articulate a position on what constitutes true or false metal. To metal bands, the nature of metal performance, with liveness and virtuosity an agreed-on standard for almost every aspect of the various metal subcultures, demands a level of detail and understanding of metal conventions, which many bands dismissed as "false metal" simply do not understand. In order to be a metal fan, or to be a credible metal fan, one must "get" metal.

Acknowledgments

This book has been a joy to produce, and the authors have seldom undertaken a task this broad and difficult with as much enthusiasm or sense of fun in quite some time. We would like to thank the following individuals, without whom this work would not have been possible. In terms of research, John Lisa and Ken Wohlrob have been indispensable sources of guidance and wisdom in terms of metal history and the succession of metal waves and new movements within the genre, and we thank them for their time and patience. Gwenn Morreale was also an invaluable research aid in terms of gathering raw material and data for this book. For her constantly inspiring radio show on WFMU, Diane Kamikaze deserves special thanks for her efforts at publicizing some of the most extreme bands in metal today. Joe Cogan (our resident Uriah Heep expert) and Rick Ventura, our resident expert on, and ex-member of, Riot were also a huge help. We would like to thank the following as well for their consistent help in conversations about music and fandom: John Pilarella, Chris Geiser, Michael Grabowski, Laura Tropp, Sue Collins, MJ Robinson, Marion Wrenn, Lila Bauman, Devon Powers, and Tony Kelso. Brian would also like to thank his family, wife Lisa, parents Joseph and Ann Cogan, brother Joe and sister-in-law Amy, and brother Sean, sister-in-law Diane, and nephews Cara and Gavin. Brian would like to thank Bill Phillips for all of his wisdom and patience. Bill would like to thank Brian Cogan for his inspiration and humor in the course of this project, and Sue Collins for her support and camaraderie. Thanks also to Joel Lanigan, Angus Nesbit, and John Bush, for their friendship and shared fandom of music throughout the years which has helped to inform this project, and finally my deepest appreciation to my loving father and mother, William and Mary Phillips, and sisters Nancy McKechnie and Meg Callaway, all of whom have supported my musical passions throughout my life. And to my amazing nieces and nephews whose love of music continues to inspire my own. Brian and Bill would like to thank Kristi Ward, our editor at Greenwood, for her dedication and inspiration over the course of this project. To Kristi, Brian promises never again to work on two publications at the same time, unless Greenwood decides to put out two books on dub reggae and Dr. Who at the same time, then he is ready and willing.

Encyclopedia of Heavy Metal Music

Heavy Metal Music: An Introduction

Heavy metal, often just referred to by the phrase "metal," is a musical subgenre of rock and roll and an explicit subculture with its own rules, rituals, conflicting sets of ideologies, and fashion. The genre is generally agreed to have started in the mid- to late 1960s, depending on which band one takes as the starting point. While many critics and scholars look at bands such as Blue Cheer, Iron Butterfly, MC5, and Steppenwolf as metal, these bands can more properly be classified as proto-metal. The emergence of two major bands helped to define the style—Black Sabbath and Led Zeppelin—and they are properly known as the first metal bands. They helped set the template for the metal bands that followed, especially in terms of musicianship, but also in fashion, attitude, and style. Heavy metal fashion and style, however, just like the music, are constantly transforming and evolving into distinct subgenres and subcultures with their own evolving rules and rituals. The term *metal* is often used because the contraction of the full term is a code used by fans to indicate that they obviously know that the band being mentioned is a "heavy" band or that the genre of music they listen to could not be described as soft or weak in any way. It seems as though this term is primarily used by masculine fans of the genre, as the sexist presumption among many members of the community is that women are attracted to less-heavy music and more to power ballads.

ORIGINS

The Term *Heavy Metal*

The origin of the term *heavy metal* is often disputed. Most scholars believe that the term was first used outside of the scientific community in the early sixties in the books *The Soft Machine* and *Nova Express* by the acclaimed Beatnik writer William S. Burroughs, who introduced the character of Uranium Willy, "the heavy metal kid," although it is clear in this context that heavy metal refers to a drug addiction as opposed to a musical genre. Music is mentioned in the line, "With their diseases and orgasm drugs and their sexless parasite life forms—Heavy Metal People of Uranus wrapped in cool blue mist of vaporized bank notes—And the Insect People of Minraud with metal music" (Burroughs, 112).

American journalist Sandy Pearlman has claimed to have coined the term in 1968 in a review of the Byrds song "Artificial Energy" on the *Notorious Byrd Brothers* album in *Crawdaddy* magazine, although it is difficult to find a citation for this claim. Lester Bangs had likewise claimed to have originated the term to describe the music of Detroit's the MC5. The term also appears in the Steppenwolf song "Born To Be Wild," where the lyrics relate "I like smoke and lightning/Heavy Metal thunder," which also is not a direct reference to music, at least not explicitly. Other critics have claimed that the term was first used in a review of the band Sir Lord Baltimore in the May 1971 edition of *Creem* magazine by "metal" mike saunders, who wrote: "This album is a far cry from the currently prevalent Grand Funk sludge, because Sir Lord Baltimore seems to have down pat most all the best heavy metal tricks in the book. Precisely, they sound like a mix between the up tempo noise blasts of Led Zeppelin (instrumentally) and singing that's like an unending Johnny Winter shriek: they have it all down cold, including medium or up tempo blasts a la LZ, a perfect carbon of early cataclysmic MC5" (Heavy Metal).

Regardless of which critic first used the term or introduced it to common parlance, it was clearly in use by the early seventies and soon became widely accepted as a name for the new genre of "heavier" music produced by bands such as Black Sabbath and Led Zeppelin, as referenced by Saunders. The term soon became widely accepted, although as we note in this work, it rapidly became divided into various subgenres and metal subcultures such as thrash metal, and especially black metal and death metal.

Metal Music Beginnings

Can a genre truly exist until it is named? Some movements are named during their time period and other musical genres are named after they are gone. In the academic study of music, the terms "proto" and "post" are used as devices that situate a particular movement in time. An example of this would be calling Blue Cheer a "proto-metal band," because they existed and played a musical form similar to metal in a time period before most critics used the term heavy metal, or calling a band like Messuggah or Om "Post-metal," because they play music that has clearly evolved beyond the parameters of heavy metal.

For the purposes of this book, we have set a timeline as to when metal was "founded" and argue that the true founding fathers of heavy metal are Black Sabbath and Led Zeppelin, respectively, and that bands that came before them such as Blue Cheer are proto-metal because they lacked some elements of heavy metal. In terms of the "post-" prefix, that is a more difficult question. We argue in this book that metal did not simply exist and then cease to be, but instead split into smaller subcultures; we instead use the term "post-metal" only when the band considers itself to be playing in the post-metal genre. We also have attempted in this book to properly categorize each band according to the genre that they most identify.

While there are many similarities between some metal subgenres and subcultures, such as black metal and death metal, many bands that fall into either camp are extremely specific about what kind of music they play and would not consider themselves to be in the other camp, no matter how similar they appear to spectators outside the metal community. As Stanley Fish in his work on interpretive communities has speculated, fans feel a sense of ownership over particular bands, and they would find offense if we labeled Venom, for example, as a doom metal band, instead of a black metal band. Fans are notoriously possessive about metal to the point where the most minute distinction or error is seized on as indicative of someone not having sufficient knowledge of metal or one of its subgenres. This sense of ownership has led to heavy metal fans becoming one of the most vocal groups of fans in contemporary music, at live events, in online discussions, and in virtual communities. Many in the metal communities have strict definitions as to what constitutes true metal and what music is simply pop music dressed up in metal outfits playing "false metal," also a subgenre.

To many in the metal community, the distinction between what can be considered "true" or "false" metal is a key way of identifying who is a fan and who is simply a poseur pretending to be a fan. The band Manowar was obsessed for years with the idea of what bands played true or false metal. According to bassist Joey Demaio, a metal band can be called authentic based on what they bring to the table not only on records, but what they bring live as well. To Demaio, "The whole purpose of playing live is to blow people's heads off. That's what we do; that's the energy of this band, we're out to kick ass. We're out to turn our gear on and blast. We're out there to kill. That's what metal is. Anyone saying otherwise is not playing heavy metal" (Hunter, 11). To Demaio and to the metal fan community, metal means commitment and dedication, not only to a killer live show, but to living a life that evokes metal, to feel as though one is not merely doing it for the money, but living metal as a way of life.

HEAVY METAL AND THEORY

One of the most daunting tasks in writing this work was analyzing heavy metal not simply from a fan's perspective or to explain which bands "rock" and which ones do not, but to also conceptualize the movement in terms of academic theory about music. As a subculture, and one that has grown to encompass a legion of smaller subsets and subcultures within subcultures, it is clear that there is a distinct heavy metal audience, one with its own rituals and signifiers of meaning, and that to understand heavy metal, one must understand the metal audience.

The Heavy Metal Audience

One of the main questions to examine in studying heavy metal is not only what musicians create while playing metal but also how the audience engages with the music and what meanings they create from the music. Pierre Bourdieu in his book *Distinctions* argues that common sense of meanings and sometimes values are shared by audiences with what can be called cultural, or subcultural, capital. An example of this is the painted back of a denim jacket in the late seventies and early eighties with the re-creation of the Iron Maiden *Number of the Beast* album cover. This would indicate to other fans not just an aesthetic approval of the contents of the album, but also a shared kinship and value system based on mutually shared taste. Liking Iron Maiden enough to have an album cover painted on your jacket

Some typical metal fans celebrating their individuality. (REX USA)

means not only a shared enthusiasm for the band, but also a shared allegiance to the idea of heavy metal as a subculture with shared values and meanings.

To metal fans, heavy metal is not just a genre of music to listen to; it is also akin to a way of life, one that provides a sense of belonging and meaning. Furthermore, engaging the music from the perspective of one of metals subgenres, such as black metal or death metal, is a further form of self-expression in which one indicates that taste has become a dividing line even to some others in the metal community. As Manowar argued the song "Black Arrows," "Let each note I now play be a black arrow of death sent straight to the hearts of all those who play false metal," many metal bands (and fans) dislike the commercialization of metal, and many were angered by the proliferation of what they considered to be "false metal," in which bands used pop hooks to sell their music, as opposed to either superb virtuosity or adherence to what would be considered less commercial, and, thus, more pure metal values.

According to Seb Hunter, "Heavy metal is essentially a club, a gang with an allegiance to a musical and social set of values. It might be frowned upon by society at large, but that's something that binds metal even more tightly" (Hunter, 15). Some critics make assumptions about the insular nature of the metal audience or criticize it for its apparent lack of diversity, its propensity for homophobia, or its misogyny.

Certain aspects of the criticism are accurate. Unlike other genres such as dance music, there are few minority members of the metal scene, few female bands, and few openly gay members of the scene. Misogyny is certainly a problem in the scene, and homophobia, especially in the black and death metal scenes, has led to several high-profile murders. But to assume that this is true of all aspects of the metal scene is reductionist at best. To many metal fans, the true definition of what constitutes a metal fan is not so much about what metal excludes, but what it includes, especially on a technical level, namely what kind of metal one listens to, true or false metal.

The problem with this is that there is not one set definition of what heavy metal is or what can be considered "true" metal. While metal fans are obsessed with the idea of authenticity, the definitions vary widely among them. Because of the difficulties that are associated with any means of defining a subculture, many, even within the metal community, disagree, often quite angrily, on what is actually metal and what is not. Even using technical terms or defining metal based on instrumentation or virtuosity on an instrument such as a guitar is difficult to use as an arbiter of true metal. An example is a band such as the Who, who clearly possessed a guitarist skilled enough to be accepted by metal fans, but for some qualities, either tangible or intangible, are not considered metal by fans of heavy metal (even ones who are also fans of the Who).

Musical Roots of Heavy Metal

The two most significant musical influences on the development of heavy metal have been blues and classical music. These seemingly disparate genres have each contributed important elements to heavy metal's characteristic sound.

The Blues. With its simple, yet soulful, 12-bar form, and its own roots in African music, the blues has provided the foundation for all rock music, and, as heavy metal is in some ways merely the heaviest and most powerful of rock music, it shares those deep roots in the blues. Beyond that basic connection, however, the earliest forms of metal owe a bit more to the blues.

As rock music continued to evolve in the mid to late sixties, the influence of blues was particularly profound, as British artists in particular took inspiration from earlier American blues musicians such as Muddy Waters and Howling Wolf. These British musicians, like Eric Clapton and Jeff Beck, began emulating the earlier American blues, but at higher volumes, and with increasingly distorted guitars. Clapton, with Cream, and Beck with his Jeff Beck Group, in particular, played their blues at much higher volumes, and with much greater guitar amp distortion, two key characteristics that would make their way into heavy metal. In Cream, Eric Clapton and bassist Jack Bruce specialized in playing heavy unison blues riffs, as in "Sunshine of Your Love," for instance, laying down another metal trope, one that would be picked up by Black Sabbath in particular.

The primary chord form in blues music and most rock is a barre or power chord, meaning a chord whose voicing is composed of the I (the root) and the V (fifth) with an octave of the root often added. This power chord is so named for the powerful and simple sound it produces. It also sounds particularly good when played with amp distortion since it lacks the other chord tones such as sixths, sevenths, and others that would produce more dissonance with a distorted tone. While the sound of distorted power chords may be found in numerous idioms of rock music, that sound itself is perhaps the sonic focus of heavy metal.

As the early blues rock groups grew in volume with the emergence of bigger, more powerful amplifiers by makers like Marshall and other companies, drummers moved from playing basic blues shuffles to playing more muscular beats, and using kits with larger and more drums in an attempt to match and better complement the rising din of guitar amplifiers. Vocalists, for their part, began refining their technique, using more powerful deliveries and increasingly relying more upon amplification to be heard in the louder context of the music. All of these developments, of course, set the stage for the powerful sound of heavy metal.

By the time Led Zeppelin released its first album in 1969, titled *Led Zeppelin*, all of these developments were in place, and part of the reason that the group is often cited as one of the first metal groups, if not *the* first, is that it went further in introducing the elements of Robert Plant's particularly high and powerful vocal range, John Bonham's huge-sounding drums and technically advanced playing, and Jimmy Page's guitar heroics. All of which became new standard elements in heavy metal and made the group a prototype for bands of the genre.

In terms of the songs Zeppelin played, much of its repertoire, especially on the first two albums, consisted of the blues covers of the era, which they played at increasingly high decibel levels, like their peers, Cream, Mountain, Blue Cheer, Jeff Beck's group, and others. While groups like Judas Priest would eventually strip out much of the blues influence, as they refined what would come to be called heavy metal, it's clear that, historically speaking, the earliest sonic architects of heavy metal were in fact largely playing heavy bluesrock.

As heavy rock evolved, the sonic elements of loud and distorted guitar, thundering drums, and wailing vocals became as central to its personality as the actual music that was played, and Black Sabbath was one of the first groups to move away from explicitly playing blues-influenced music as they found their unique way to utilize these elements. Sabbath instead pioneered the playing of loud, ponderous riffs (riffs being the term for patterns of notes repeated in the same manner, "ostinato" in classical music terms). The riffs were tuned down a half-step or more from standard guitar tuning, giving them a darker, more ominous timbre.

Part of the reason for this move was the result of an otherwise tragic circumstance, as guitarist Tony Iommi had only a few years earlier had lost the tips of two of his main fretting fingers in an industrial accident. Consequently finding more complex chords difficult to play with the artificial fingertips that he had managed to fashion, he evolved a somewhat simpler approach that focused on heavy single-string riffs and power chords, tuned down since the reduced tension of the strings was easier to play. These features of Iommi's personal guitar style gave Sabbath much of its signature sound and went a long way toward refining the unique style of heavy metal. While many of Sabbath's songs had riffs that were derived from the minor pentatonic scale of blues music, they increasingly departed from stock blues licks and played on the strengths of the heavy *sounds* of the guitar and band, evolving a new and darker sounding music, which in part derived from the lower register of Iommi and bassist Geezer Butler's instruments.

Black Sabbath was probably the first band to actively exploit the sound of these instrumental changes for their own sake, not merely as a vehicle for the blues-based music that preceded them. And as they did, they helped to open up new possibilities for music that would use the new heavy sounds, essentially leading the way to what we now call heavy metal. As they and later groups like Judas Priest continued to strip out the blues elements, they brought us closer to metal.

Classical Influences. While blues music may be seen as a foundational influence that has heavily influenced the evolution of heavy metal, the classical influence is much less so, and in fact has functioned as an influence that most often is overlaid upon the music as opposed to providing a foundation for it. The Beatles are most often noted as the first rock band to introduce classical elements into rock, most notably with their *Sergeant Pepper's Lonely Hearts Club Band* album in 1967. Following some of their experiments, classically trained musicians such as keyboardists Keith Emerson and Rick Wakeman of the groups Emerson, Lake, and Palmer, and Yes, respectively, were important innovators in progressive rock, bringing much more classical ideas into rock and fusing them into the hybrid that progressive rock represents.

Ritchie Blackmore and Jon Lord of Deep Purple were some of the very first musicians to bring some of these classical ideas into heavy rock, and consequently, into heavy metal. An excellent example is in the song "Highway Star" from the band's *Machine Head* album; while the song remains a high-energy rocker built roughly on a blues-derived progression, the extended solos of both Lord (on organ) and Blackmore (on guitar) feature classical motifs and scale patterns. These early experiments would influence such later artists as Scorpions' guitarist Uli Jon Roth and Ozzy Osbourne guitarist Randy Rhoads, who would both go on to incorporate classical motifs into their soloing, Roth in a more improvisational sense and Rhoads more compositionally. Their forays into classical would be superseded by those of Yngwie Malmsteen, whose technical mastery of the guitar was steeped not only in the work of Blackmore (which combined a blues feel and vibrato technique) but also in the compositions of Mozart, Bach, and Beethoven, and more particularly in the compositions of the violinist-composer Niccolò Paganini, whose own legendary feats of improvisation and flamboyant stage performances inspired those of the Swedish guitarist.

Malmsteen in particular was extremely influential in his integration of classical elements into rock guitar playing and helped to spur the subgenre of neoclassical rock and metal, a genre characterized by classical scales and arpeggios played at blindingly fast tempos and with incredible precision. Robert Walser (1993) suggests that in their appropriation of classical virtuosic elements in their playing, musicians like Malmsteen and Rhoads may actually be closer to the classical tradition than we might otherwise suspect. While our contemporary experience of classical music is largely in a recorded form and studiously performed in a carefully preserved tradition, many classical composers were in fact live performers who also incorporated improvisation into their performances, a tradition that musicians like Malmsteen and Rhoads may have done more to carry on than many contemporary classical musicians who may feel more bound by more conservative classical performance traditions.

While the classical tradition has given heavy metal much to work with in terms of musical influences, it should be noted that the incorporation of classical element into rock has also been somewhat superficial, with the use of classical scales, arpeggios, and motifs, but rarely with the depth or experimentation of classical composers.

A

ACCEPT (1979–97). Udo Dirkschneider (vocals), Wolf Hoffmann (guitars), Jorge Fisher (guitars), Peter Baltes (bass), Stefan Kaufman (drums).

Formed in Solingen, Germany, in the early seventies, Accept were the first German metal band after the Scorpions to make a dent in the American and European markets. Featuring the caterwauling vocalist Udo Dirkschneider and the dual-guitar (often harmonizing) assault of guitarists Wolf Hoffmann and Jorge Fisher (on matching Flying V guitars!), as well as bassist Peter Baltes and drummer Stefan Kaufman, the band combined the power and precision of the Scorpions but with a harder edge that would be an important influence on the thrash metal that would follow.

While their first two albums, *Accept* (1979) and *I'm a Rebel* (1980), did little to distinguish the band, their third album, *Breaker* (1981), marked the emergence of the Accept style—a streamlined aggressive approach matching precision playing and classic, somewhat Judas Priest–style guitars with Udo's inimitable wail over the top of their luscious sonic din. Songs like "Starlight," the title track, and "Son of a Bitch" (the last track written about a record company) were tightly crafted blasts of metal that complemented the contemporary style of the new wave of British Heavy Metal that was evolving at the time. Another factor in the album's favor was the contributions of producer Michael Wagener—who would go on to work with a veritable "Who's Who" of hard rock and heavy metal such as Mötley Crüe, Skid Row, and Ozzy Osbourne. Wagener's studio prowess gave the band a sonic punch and polish that did much to put it into the big leagues of heavy metal and helped the band garner the attention it had lacked in the American market.

Accept's follow-up *Restless and Wild* in 1982 was their breakthrough. The songs and Wagener's production were first-rate and original, showing the band's capacity to innovate and energize the genre. The song "Fast as a Shark" in particular served as a template for thrash metal bands like Slayer and Anthrax who would come later.

The band's next album, 1983's *Balls to the Wall,* was even more successful commercially, and featured the headbanging title track that became a hit MTV video, featuring Udo's unique vocalizing and stage presence and not a little homoerotic imagery. Accept helped promote the album with their first American tour supporting Kiss.

With 1985's *Metal Heart* Accept attempted to build on their growing success in the States. Hiring Dieter Dirks, the Scorpion's long-time producer, they also wrote more melodic material and toned down their lyrical sexual overtones, replacing them with more mainstream themes. These efforts led the band closer to mainstream success but at the expense of previous diehard fans who had supported their heavier approach.

1986 saw the release of the live *Kaizoku-Ban* and their return to the studio to work with Michael Wagener. The resulting album, *Russian Roulette,* was an attempt to go back to their more aggressive style, but the move led to tensions in the band over Accept's continuing direction. Ultimately, the band took a bit of a break, with Udo releasing the solo album *Animal House* under the band name U.D.O. (with his Accept band members backing him in the studio).

When Udo put together his own group and released his second solo album, *Mean Machine*, in 1988, the rest of Accept sought a new frontman for the group and settled on American David Reese. The subsequent album, *Eat the Heat* (1989), was in a much mellower direction for Accept. Despite some airplay for the video "Generation Clash," the album was a disappointment from both a creative and commercial standpoint, and the group disbanded shortly thereafter.

After a few years of dormancy, the band members (minus Jorge Fisher) reunited in 1992, releasing the album *Objection Overruled*. Something of a return to form for the band, the album did well in Europe but failed to generate much interest in the States, where the rise of grunge had fairly well decimated the commercial potential of most metal bands. Accept would record and tour sporadically over the next decade, releasing the albums *Death Row* (1995) and *Predator* (1997), officially calling it quits in 1997. In 2005, Accept reconvened briefly for a one-shot commemorative European tour performing most notably at the Monsters of Rock festival in Kavarna, Bulgaria.

Discography: *Accept* (Razor, 1979); *I'm a Rebel* (Passport, 1980); *Breaker* (Universal/ Brain, 1981); *Restless and Wild* (Portrait, 1983); *Balls to the Wall* (Portrait, 1984); *Rest of Accept* (Brain, 1985); *Metal Heart* (Portrait, 1985); *Metal Masters* (Razor, 1985); *Kaizoku-Ban* (Portrait, 1986); *Russian Roulette* (Portrait, 1986); *Eat the Heat* (Epic, 1989); *Staying a Life* [live] (Epic, 1990); *Objection Overruled* (CMC, 1993); *No Substitutes* (Sony, 1995); *Death Row* (Pavement, 1995); *Predator* (Sweat Shop, 1997); *All Areas—Worldwide* (Pure Metal, 1998); *Rich & Famous* (Drakkar, 2003).

AC/DC (1973–PRESENT). Malcolm Young (guitar), Angus Young (guitar), Bon Scott (vocals, 1974–79), Brian Johnson (vocals, 1979-present), Cliff Williams (bass), Phil Rudd (drums).

One of the most influential hard rock bands of all time, AC/DC have built their reputation on a less-is-more approach, doing more with three (or four) chords than most groups could do with many more and influencing scores of imitators during their three-decade-plus reign.

Unique among hard rock/heavy metal bands is the fact that the group eschews overreliance upon power chords and heavily distorted guitars, instead favoring a less-distorted (yet still mightily crunchy!) guitar tone, and the use of "open"

AC/DC performs in the 1980s. Shown from left: Malcolm Young, Brian Johnson, Phil Rudd, Angus Young, and Cliff Williams. (Atlantic/Photofest)

chords, which combine to give the band its signature ringing guitar sound behind its anthemic classic songs.

The band got its start in 1973, when guitarist Malcolm Young and younger brother Angus (whose signature schoolboy uniform became his stage outfit when he joined the band at 15) started the band in Sydney, Australia. After releasing a single, "Can I Sit Next to You," which was produced by their brother George Young and his partner Harry Vanda (both ex of the Easybeats).

In 1974 the band moved to Melbourne, where they enlisted drummer Phil Rudd, bassist Mark Evans, and a roadie named Bon Scott. When original vocalist Dave Evans refused to take the stage, Scott happily volunteered and the band's classic lineup was largely set. Scott's mischievous sense of humor and characteristic caterwaul complemented the band's style, and his streetwise pedigree (with numerous misdemeanor convictions to his credit) added to the band's nascent bad-boy image, which they would exploit throughout their long career. Later that year the band's first full-length album, *High Voltage,* was released in Australia.

1975 saw the release of *TNT,* and in 1975, an adapted version of *High Voltage* (featuring material from *TNT* as well) was given broader release in both the U.K. and the U.S. with the band touring Britain and the States for the first time. Later that year, the band released *Dirty Deeds Done Dirt Cheap.*

In 1977, the band recorded *Let There Be Rock,* with new bassist Cliff Williams. The band was beginning to experience a new level of success with their heavy touring schedule, and *Let There Be Rock* became their first album to do well in the American charts.

For the next couple of years, the band worked diligently, both in the studio and on the concert trail, slowly but surely building a loyal and ardent fan base. Subsequent albums such as *Powerage*, and the live *If You Want Blood You've Got It*, cemented a rocking reputation as a no-holds-barred live act, and set the stage for their breakthrough album, *Highway to Hell*, released in 1980. Thanks to the title track, and the wide radio play it received, the album got to 17 on the U.S. charts (8 in the U.K.), and was the band's first platinum (million-plus sales) release.

Unfortunately, it was at this fortuitous time that the hard-charging, hard-living Scott found his own limits. He was found dead in his car of alcohol poisoning, after an all-night binge (Engleheart & Durieux, 2008). Devastated, the band took time to mourn and assess their situation. Most of their next album had been largely recorded with producer Robert "Mutt" Lange, but without the band's longtime frontman, the band was at a standstill. Once the band decided to soldier on, however, they recruited ex-Georgie vocalist Brian Johnson. In retrospect, Johnson was a natural choice, given his raspy caterwaul and working-class demeanor. At the same time, however, his six-foot-plus frame and cap-wearing image presented quite a contrast to Scott's (and the Young brothers') diminutive stature.

With Johnson at the vocal mic, AC/DC finished work on *Highway*'s follow-up, the suitably titled *Back in Black*. Arguably the band's finest work both in terms of writing and production quality, the album became the band's best-selling album, has gone on to sell over 42 million copies, and helped to confirm the band's status as one of the world's greatest hard rock acts.

The band stayed on a roll for the next few years. With *For Those About to Rock We Salute You*, the band stayed on the charts. However, after the recording of *Flick of the Switch* (1983), drummer Phil Rudd was sacked from the band. Rudd had taken Scott's death hard and was experiencing a growing conflict with Malcolm, the band's leader. Rudd was replaced by Simon Wright, who first appeared in the early MTV videos "Flick of the Switch" and "Nervous Shakedown."

Flick of the Switch marked the end of the band's working relationship with producer Mutt Lange, who had shepherded the band's breakthrough albums. With *Flick*, the band had produced themselves, attempting to bring the band's sound back to its basics. In that they largely succeeded, and the album was in some ways a return to their rougher Scott days. Nonetheless, the album did less well than its predecessors, and the band began to experience a bit of a commercial decline, although they still sold well in the record stores and on tour. Even so, their subsequent eighties albums, *Fly on the Wall* (1985), *Who Made Who* (1986), *Blow Up Your Video* (1988), and *The Razor's Edge* (1990), marked a period of less impressive, though still decent quality work from the band.

Producer and longtime fan Rick Rubin stepped in in 1995 to produce *Ballbreaker*, which proved to be something of a return to form for the band, both performance-wise and commercially. Rubin's stripped-down aesthetic fit the band well, and their erstwhile drummer Phil Rudd had been brought back into the fold, marking the first time that the *Back in Black* lineup had recorded together in a dozen years. Upon its release, *Ballbreaker* went platinum within the year and went as high as number four on the U.S. album chart.

The band has since slowed its work schedule considerably, releasing *Stiff Upper Lip* in 2000. 2008 found them in the studio with renowned producer Brendan O'Brien working on their seventeenth studio album, *Black Ice*, which was released in October of that year.

Discography: *TNT* (EMI, 1975); *High Voltage* (Epic, 1976); *Dirty Deeds Done Dirt Cheap* (Epic, 1976); *Let There Be Rock* (Epic, 1977); *Powerage* (Epic, 1978); *If You Want Blood You've Got It* [live] (Epic, 1978); *Highway to Hell* (Epic, 1979); *Back in Black* (Epic, 1980); *For Those About to Rock We Salute You* (Epic, 1981); *Flick of the Switch* (Epic, 1983); *Fly on the Wall* (Epic, 1985); *Who Made Who* (Epic, 1986); *Blow Up Your Video* (Epic, 1988); *The Razor's Edge* (Epic, 1990); *AC/DC Live* (Atco, 1992); *Ballbreaker* (East West, 1995); *Live in Madrid* (Atlantic, 1997); *Stiff Upper Lip* (East West, 2000); *Black Ice* (Columbia, 2008).

AEROSMITH (1973–PRESENT). Steven Tyler (vocals), Joe Perry (guitar), Brad Whitford (guitar), Joey Kramer (drums), Tom Hamilton (bass).

Perhaps the single most important hard rock band to come from the U.S., and one of the most popular of the seventies, Aerosmith had their roots in the blues-influenced British bands that dominated the rock scene during the late sixties and early seventies. Drawing much of their inspiration from Cream, Led Zeppelin, the first Jeff Beck Group, as well as the Rolling Stones (whose frontmen Mick Jagger and Keith Richards Aerosmith's Tyler and Perry emulated imagewise), Aerosmith took the blues-based rock form and translated it into a quintessentially American version of often sleazy and catchy bluesrock. After a drug-induced low-point in the early eighties (at which point both Perry and Whitford had left the band), the group came back to their full commercial, if not creative, strength.

The band's roots were in the vacation town of Sunapee, New Hampshire, where Tyler, Perry, and Hamilton originally met while vacationing with their families. Perry and Hamilton had played for four summers in the Jam Band, playing the blues-based rock of their day—Jeff Beck Group, Led Zeppelin—when they met Tyler, who was fronting another local band. After graduating from high school, Perry and Hamilton moved to Boston and hooked up with Tyler. Drummer Joey Kramer was soon enlisted, and the band started gigging around the Boston area. After working a while with rhythm guitarist Ray Tabano, the band caught a performance by the band Justin Thyme featuring guitarist Brad Whitford. Impressed by Whitford's accomplished playing style, the band invited him to join them, which he did.

After polishing their act in the clubs and colleges of Beantown, the band secured a record deal with Columbia, who issued *Aerosmith* in 1973. Recorded quickly with producer Adrian Barber, *Aerosmith* was a serviceable if raw debut, but gave little indication of what the band would ultimately be capable of. Nonetheless, songs like "Mama Kin," "Somebody," and "One Way Street" were solid rockers with their roots in the blues, and Tyler's raspy vocal approach, along with Perry and Whitford's riffing guitars, made for a unique take on the British bluesrock that the band had cut their teeth on. While the album failed to chart initially, it contained what would later become their first radio hit, the ballad "Dream On."

Following their debut, they began touring, supporting such stalwarts as Mott the Hoople and Bad Company, and began to get a reputation as a dynamic live act, based on Tyler and Perry's charisma, as well as the band's increasingly tight performances.

For the band's second album, 1974's *Get Your Wings*, the band hooked up with producer Jack Douglas, who helped to polish their studio chops and deliver an album that delivered on their live reputation. The album was a strong one and featured what would become some of the band's best-loved tracks, including "Same

Old Song and Dance" and the band's cover of "Train Kept a Rollin'." Although "Train" sounds like a live recording, it was actually a studio recording that Douglas added an audience track to in order to emulate the excitement of a live show. He also went so far as to run speakers out to the studio building's stairwell and played the track at full volume. He then rerecorded the echoing sound back onto the track to simulate the sound of a concert arena. In a move that must have been difficult for the band's guitarists, he also enlisted A-list rock session and touring guitarists Steve Hunter and Dick Wagner (of Alice Cooper and Lou Reed's touring bands) to play the incendiary lead breaks (uncredited) that punctuate the tune. The result was the hottest live track the band never recorded live. Nonetheless, "Train" and the rest of *Get Your Wings* went a long way to building Aerosmith's reputation as one of the best rock bands in the U.S. Supported with relentless touring, the album spent over a year on the charts.

1975 saw the release of perhaps the best album of Aerosmith's career, *Toys in the Attic*. If *Wings* had kicked the band up a few notches from their debut, *Toys* certainly kicked it up a few more again. Douglas's production was polished, yet didn't sacrifice the band's raw sensual power. The title track was a powerhouse rocker, and "Adam's Apple" might well be one of the coolest guitar riffs ever devised. And tracks like "Walk This Way" and "Sweet Emotion" would be some of the best hard rock that would make it onto Top 40 radio. The album peaked at number 11 on the charts and prompted the re-release of "Dream On," which went into the top ten. *Toys* was the band's commercial breakthrough and one of their creative high points. It is for the most part devoid of filler and continues to be one of Aerosmith's most popular albums.

With *Rocks* in 1976, the band continued their winning streak with another collection of great songs and performances. The album's title worked with its cover art (which depicted five diamonds, i.e., "rocks") to convey a bit of a pun. And rock Aerosmith did. If anything, *Rocks* was overall a heavier album than its predecessor, and while there were no Top 40 hits to be had, the album made it to number three on the charts, and provided some of the band's heaviest tunes and a number of what would become live chestnuts: "Back in the Saddle" with its air of gunslinger bravado, and Whitford's classic riffed "Lost Child," with its deft melding of rock power and funk groove. Other tracks, such as "Rats in the Cellar," "Lick and a Promise," and "Nobody's Fault" contributed to making *Rocks* one of Aerosmith's most enduring and rocking albums and clearly a major influence on bands such as Guns N' Roses who would appear in the following decade.

With *Toys* and *Rocks*, Aerosmith had hit the big time and were experiencing both the prizes and the perils of stardom. Drugs were one problem, and no one in the band seemed immune. All the hard work that the band had put into pursuing success was paying off, and they were enjoying that success, but at the same time, having difficulty in maintaining the touring and recording schedule that they were being held to. As a result, tensions between band members, especially between Tyler and Perry, became strained. All the same, the band marched on. *Draw the Line* was released in 1977 and was the first album that failed to match its predecessor in its general quality or in sales. The album's title track and "Kings and Queens" were the standout tracks and received airplay, but the album was generally less inspired and indicated that the band were as well. Around the same time, the band also participated in the ill-advised movie version of the Beatles' *Sergeant Pepper's* album, which also featured Peter Frampton and the Bee Gees. The band portrayed heavies in the film and performed a version of "Come Together," which received airplay as a single.

Live Bootleg was released in 1978 and charted at number 13. By the time the band's next studio album, *Night in the Ruts,* was released in 1979, Perry had exited the band to form the Joe Perry Project. After considering numerous guitarists, including Michael Schenker and Derringer's Danny Johnson, the band selected Jimmy Crespo to take Perry's place. The band toured in support of *Night,* but its success—peaking at number 14 and selling half a million copies—paled in comparison with the band's earlier albums, and after the tour, guitarist Whitford had left and would form the Whitford-St. Holmes Band with Derek St. Holmes, former vocalist and guitarist with Ted Nugent.

The band continued on, hiring guitarist Rick Dufay to replace Whitford and recording the 1982 album *Rock in a Hard Place.* The album only got as high as number 32, failing to even match the sales of *Night in the Ruts.* At the same time, rumors were flying that the band members were dealing with various addictions to drugs and alcohol.

After two years, both Perry and Whitford had rejoined the band, and Aerosmith began an attempt to win back their reputation and status. Their first attempt was *Done With Mirrors,* which was the first for their new label, Geffen Records. Featuring a questionable reworking of Perry's solo tune "Let the Music Do the Talking," the album was serviceable, but not quite the return to form that the band and Geffen were after. And when Tyler passed out on stage during the subsequent tour, concerns were raised about the band's ability to beat their addictions.

Fortunately, the band had allies in new manager Tim Kelly and their Geffen A&R man, John Kalodner. Under their guidance Tyler, Perry, and eventually all of the band underwent rehab programs. In 1986, Tyler and Perry appeared on the recording and video for Run-DMC's cover of "Walk This Way." The video exposed a new generation to Aerosmith and set the stage for *Done With Mirrors'* follow-up. The band then began collaborating with a number of outside songwriters, most notably Desmond Child and Holly Knight. The new songs that appeared on the album *Permanent Vacation* tweaked the old Aerosmith sound in a more melodic, radio-friendly direction, and on the album's release in 1988 helped it to sell over three million copies and reach number 11 on the charts. At the same time, the singles "Dude (Looks Like a Lady)," "Rag Doll," and "Angel" became hits, in part, thanks to a series of highly stylized videos that helped the band to craft a new image in the public eye.

Permanent Vacation's follow-up, *Pump,* released in 1989, continued the band's comeback success, with hit singles and accompanying videos for the songs "Love in an Elevator," "Janie's Got a Gun," and "What it Takes," helping the album to sell four million copies and peak at number 5 on the album charts. Likewise, 1993's *Get a Grip* replicated Aerosmith's new formula for success.

While some fans of the band missed the raw immediacy of the group's classic seventies work, there was no doubt that the input of professional songwriters had helped the band to find new commercial success, even as it somewhat dulled the band's former hard rock edge. And it was difficult sometimes to see the band attempt to retain their visual image of their halcyon days while moving further and further away from the blues rock riffing that had built their reputation. But a new day had dawned, and the band had traded their rags for riches and weren't about to trade them back again.

In 1990, at the height of their comeback, the band had signed a multimillion-dollar deal with their former label, Columbia, and in 1997, after their obligations to Geffen were fulfilled, the band released *Nine Lives*, their first new album for Columbia. The album's recording had been difficult, and an earlier version of the album had been scratched before the band tried again with producer Kevin Shirley. Keenly anticipated, the album debuted at number 1, but failed to stay there, quickly dropping off. 1998 saw the release of the live album *A Little South of Sanity*.

In 2001, the band got a big shot of publicity when they took out their old war-horse "Walk This Way" for an appearance at the Super Bowl halftime show, along with pop and rap stars Britney Spears, Mary J. Blige, and 'N Sync, setting the stage for the release of *Just Push Play*. In something of a concession to fans of their earlier work and to themselves, the band reunited with their former producer Jack Douglas to record an album largely comprised of blues-infused covers strangely entitled *Honkin' on Bobo* (a reference to playing a blues harmonica). *Bobo* was released in 2004, along with a live CD, *Rockin' the Joint*, and a DVD, *You Gotta Move*, both of which included a healthy helping of their seventies-era material, along with more recent fare. 2006 saw a new hits package in *Devil's Got a New Disguise*.

Discography: *Aerosmith* (Columbia, 1973); *Get Your Wings* (Columbia, 1974); *Toys in the Attic* (Columbia, 1975); *Rocks* (Columbia, 1976); *Draw the Line* (Columbia, 1977); *Live Bootleg* (Columbia, 1979); *Night in the Ruts* (Columbia, 1978); *Rock in a Hard Place* (Columbia, 1982); *Done with Mirrors* (Geffen, 1985); *Permanent Vacation* (Geffen, 1987); *Pump* (Geffen, 1989); *Get a Grip* (Geffen, 1993); *Nine Lives* (Columbia, 1997); *A Little South of Sanity* [live] (Geffen, 1998); *Just Push Play* (Columbia, 2001); *Honkin' on Bobo* (Columbia, 2004); *Rockin' the Joint* [live] (Columbia, 2005); *Live in Philadelphia* (Immortal, 2008).

AGALLOCH (1995–PRESENT). John Haughm (vocals/guitar), Don Anderson (guitar), Jason William Walton (bass), Chris Green (drums, replaced by Aesop Dekker).

Agalloch is regarded by many as Portland, Oregon's, finest black metal band, although there is not much competition. The band's combination of caustic guitars, progressive elements, and traditional black metal sets them apart from most bands in the genre and has led some critics to put them in the "post-rock" genre, as some of their more recent music has been relatively hard to categorize. *Ashes Against the Grain* (2006), their most recent full-length album, is a fascinating blend of folk and heavy progressive black metal and one of the strangest metal albums ever released.

Discography: *Pale Folklore* (The End, 1999); *The Mantle* (The End, 2002); *Ashes Against the Grain* (The End, 2006); *The White [EP]* (The End, 2008).

AIRHEADS. "Airheads" (1994) is a fictional film about a heavy metal band that starred Brendan Fraser, Steve Buscemi, and Adam Sandler as a bad heavy metal band known as the Lone Rangers, who inexplicably take over a radio station in an effort to air their music to the general public. Of course wackiness ensues, and the band is not particularly talented (or that much metal), but the film does discuss the issue of why metal is not played frequently on many radio stations and also has a cameo by Lemmy and music from White Zombie, so overall it stands as a particularly minor film about heavy metal.

ALABAMA THUNDER PUSSY (1996–PRESENT). Johnny Throckmorton (vocals, replaced by Johnny Weils, replaced by Kyle Thomas), Aseich "Cleetus Leroque" Bogden (guitar), Erik Larson (guitar), Bill Storms (bass, replaced by Sam Krivenac, replaced by Mike Bryant), Brian Cox (drums).

Alabama Thunder Pussy are a country-tinged metal band from Richmond, Virginia, who mix a dose of southern rock, punk, and skuzzy and sleazy metal for a mixture not unlike the similarly named Nashville Pussy. The band has gone through various members over the years, including three lead vocalists. Many bands try and rock old-school metal with southern style, but somehow Alabama Thunder Pussy pulls it off. *River City Revival* is the key record for fans new to the band. ATP demonstrate that the south has a lot to offer to the contemporary metal scene.

Discography: *Rise Again* (Man's Ruin, 1998); *River City Revival* (Man's Ruin, 1999); *Constellation* (Man's Ruin, 2000); *Half Way to Gone* (Game Two, 2000); *Staring at the Divine* (Man's Ruin, 2001); *Fulton Hill* (Relapse, 2004); *Open Fire* (Relapse, 2007).

ALCATRAZZ (1982–87; 2007–PRESENT). Classic lineup: Graham Bonnet (vocals), Yngwie Malmsteen (guitar, 1982–83), Jimmy Waldo (keyboards), Gary Shea (bass), Jan Uvena (drums), Steve Vai (guitar, 1984–85), Danny Johnson (guitar, 1985–86).

Alcatrazz is perhaps best remembered as the group that launched shredmeister Yngwie Malmsteen into international prominence. Formed in 1982, the band featured ex-Rainbow and Michael Schenker vocalist Graham Bonnet, bassist Gary Shea, and keyboardist Jimmy Waldo—both formerly of the band New England, and drummer Jan Uvena, along with Malmsteen, who had been playing with the L.A. band Steeler. Their debut album, *No Parole from Rock 'n' Roll*, released in 1983, was similar in style to the music of Bonnet's former group Rainbow, guitar-driven melodic hard rock featuring keyboards and occasional classical touches, albeit with a more high energy approach. The album was a solid affair, combining the classical overtones of Rainbow and Malmsteen's primary inspiration, Ritchie Blackmore, and proved an apt vehicle for the establishment of the Swedish guitarist's reputation. Songs such as "Hiroshima Mon Amour" and the scorcher "Jet to Jet" established the band as a formidable contender in the sweepstakes of rock, and Bonnet and Malmsteen as an effective songwriting team. Unfortunately, the album itself performed poorly, and after a hastily released live album, Malmsteen departed for a solo career.

The band next hired ex-Frank Zappa guitarist Steve Vai in 1984, who quite ably filled Malmsteem's shredding shoes and went on to play up a storm on 1985's *Disturbing the Peace*. Missing, however, was the songwriting element, and the album soon tanked, with Vai departing shortly after.

The band soldiered on with ex-Derringer and Axis guitarist Danny Johnson taking over guitar duties. Unfortunately, the resulting album, *Dangerous Games* (1986), did no better than its predecessors, and the band packed it in after a short tour.

In 2007, vocalist Bonnet put together a new lineup under the Alcatrazz banner and toured Japan, and were said to be recording a new album.

Discography: *Live Sentence* (Grand Slamm, 1984); *No Parole from Rock 'n' Roll* (Grand Slamm, 1984); *Disturbing the Peace* (Capitol, 1985); *Dangerous Games* (Capitol, 1986); *Best of Alcatrazz* (Tokuma, 2007).

ALCOHOL. Alcohol has long been one of the defining elements of the debauched side of heavy metal music and, along with drugs, is tied into rituals of acceptance and masculinity both in many metal bands and in the general fandom. The use of alcohol is widespread in the metal community, which does not contain a large number of straight-edge subcultures as the punk community does. While there are numerous metal bands and personalities who do not drink (Ted Nugent being the most prominent case) or who used to and have tried to quit (Ozzy Osbourne being another prime example), the frequent use of alcohol in the heavy metal community is the consequence of a variety of different factors.

Alchohol and Songwriting/Performing. One aspect of this relationship is the fact that there is a tradition in performance of hypermasculinity and staying in control, or being able to hold one's own while drinking. One of the typical lead-singer poses is to chug from a bottle of Jack Daniel's whiskey or wine onstage as a sign that the lead singer (and sometimes the rest of the band) can drink and remain proficient at their music. In certain ways drinking is seen to also add virility and superior musicianship, despite scientific evidence to the contrary. This masculine pose is well established in metal, and outside of drug casualties there are also numerous well-known metal stars who reportedly died from alcohol consumption or cirrhosis of the liver, such as John Bonham of Led Zeppelin, Phil Lynott of Thin Lizzy, Bon Scott of AC/DC, and David Byron of Uriah Heep. In the movie *The Decline of Western Civilization, Part II: The Metal Years*, Chris Holmes of W.A.S.P. is shown in a famous scene lounging in a swimming pool at night drinking copious amounts of vodka and even pouring the drink all over his face while his mother sits alongside the pool watching his antics. The film demonstrated that alcohol was an integral part of the metal scene on the Sunset Strip and that many musicians who thought they were using alcohol for recreation were, in fact, alcoholics with serious problems. Drugs were also certainly a major factor, especially in bands such as Guns N' Roses and Mötley Crüe, whose members notoriously struggled with both problems for years as documented in Nikki Sixx's *Heroin Diaries* and Slash's book *Slash*.

In addition, many bands have songs that either mention alcohol or celebrate the virtues of heavy drinking (and in many cases drug use as well). At a Kiss concert, one of the most eagerly anticipated songs is "Cold Gin," which at best is ambivalent about alcohol consumption and the band is ironically well-known for the continued sobriety of two of its key members, Gene Simmons and Paul Stanley.

Sammy Hagar, late of Van Halen and his own prodigious solo career, often praises the virtues of his own brand of tequila, Cabo Wabo, in his song "Mas Tequila." Other bands that extol the virtues of alcohol include Guns N' Roses, who were for a time a walking ad for Jack Daniel's, as well as Metallica, who were widely known as "alcohollica" for many years due to the excessive drinking habits of the band (James Hetfield later spent considerable time in rehab attempting to fight his longtime addiction to alcohol, as noted by Weiderhorn).

While many artists have a long and troubled history with alcohol, some new bands, such as Until the End, are straight edge or do not actively consume alcohol, and others in numerous bands have gone through rehab (such as Slash and Duff, formerly from Guns N' Roses) and now espouse the virtues of clean living and abstinence. Most famously, Ted Nugent, one of the most opinionated men in music today and a metal icon, has for decades espoused a life free of drugs and alcohol (along with the inclusion of plenty of hunting and meat eating). Nugent was a major influence on the punk straight-edge movement, which later went on to influence some newer metal bands and many bands who were considered punk, such as Earth Crisis, who sounded like a metal band and espouses a militant version of straight edge. Ozzy Osbourne, who also struggled with addictions for most of his career, is also well known for writing the infamously misinterpreted anti-alcohol song "Suicide Solution" as well as the less subtle "Demon Alcohol."

Alcohol and fandom. One pre-show ritual of many metal fans is to get as loaded as possible. This is due, in part, to the overall rock-and-roll involvement with alcohol (and drugs), as well as to several factors that are unique to heavy metal. The idea of binge drinking before shows is not just a way in which fans prepare to enjoy a show more, but it is also a rite of passage in terms of masculinity, where fans can prove not just their ability to get wasted, but also to demonstrate their tolerance for alcohol consumption (and in many cases drugs as well). The aim of this practice is to enhance the pleasure of the show (much in the way that fans of the Grateful Dead and other jam bands try and plan their consumption of drugs to peak moments in the music). Metal fans want to enjoy the show more, and by drinking, even to excess, not only has a point been proven about masculinity, but the show is presumably exponentially better due to alcohol consumption.

This is not to suggest that female heavy metal fans do not consume alcohol. Many female metal fans can drink as much or sometimes more than male fans, but in terms of body weight and consumption, most women are physically incapable of consuming as much alcohol as men. Also, many women do not drink the same kinds of drinks as men, such as the omnipresent beer readily available both in the parking lot of many events and often at the venue too, but prefer wine and other drinks. Heavy metal fans do not differ radically from fans of other genres such as hard rock, but the reputation of many bands as having a fan base who are heavy drinkers, such as Motorhead, may encourage binge drinking or other forms of mass consumption around organized rituals such as concerts. Overall, the connection between heavy metal and fan consumption of alcohol is one that bears further investigation.

Source: Weinstein, Deena. *Heavy Metal: The Music and Its Culture.* New York: Da Capo Press, 2000.

ALICE COOPER (1968–PRESENT). Alice Cooper (vocals), Mike Bruce (guitar, later replaced by many others), Glen Buxton (later replaced by many others), Dennis Dunaway (bass, later Prakash John, followed by many others), Neal Smith (drums, later Penti Glan, and others).

Alice Cooper started out as a hard rock band formed by high school friends in Phoenix, Arizona, under such names as The Earwigs, The Spiders, and The Nazz. A few years later, in 1969, using the Alice Cooper name, they settled in Detroit. With elements including outrageous drag outfits early on and an impressive stage show that eventually labeled them as "shock rock," Alice Cooper—led by lead singer Vincent Furnier, who eventually absorbed the Alice Cooper moniker as his stage name—have been one of the most successful hard rock/heavy metal bands and have been active now for four decades. The band started out as an avant garde band playing stripped-down rock and roll. The early records reflect the group's songwriting process that suited the band best, especially on the third record *Love it to Death*, which featured the quintessential Alice Cooper track, "I'm Eighteen," as well as other classic hard rock tracks such as "Long Way to Go." *Killer* continued the trend and the *School's Out* record yielded the title track, much beloved by stoner high school students to this day.

For the *Welcome to My Nightmare* record, Cooper added ace guitarists Dick Wagner and Steve Hunter and came up with what was arguably his last classic record. The title track in particular found Alice Cooper in a compellingly creepy vibe, and the cameo by Vincent Price on "The Black Widow" cemented both Alice's reputation as a proto-goth, as well as his movement toward crowd-pleasing moments. Cooper continued to work in show business as well as rock, appearing memorably on *The Muppet Show* as himself (not to mention appearances on *Tony Orlando and Dawn* or the *Soupy Sales* show) working to try have the Muppets sign contracts with the devil.

The basic Alice Cooper sound became formulaic at the end of the seventies as Cooper's battle with alcoholism reportedly escalated (Ernst 2007).

During the mid-eighties, Cooper decided to go in a more conventional eighties metal direction, imitating some of the very bands that had imitated his sound and look in the first place, gaining him a later period top ten hit and much-played video with "Poison" in 1989. The rest of the nineties saw Cooper floundering in the commercial wilderness, but still a successful live act where his over-the-top theatrics, snakes, and blood went over well with metal audiences, although they must look somewhat tame today compared with GWAR or Marilyn Manson. Cooper continues to make cameo appearances on film and TV (including a notable cameo in *Wayne's World*) and to concentrate on his game of golf, and remains an elder statesman of metal to this day, one of the true innovators not just in sounds but in metal fashion and showmanship as well. Cooper is also an unacknowledged influence on the death and black metal scenes, as well as the punk and goth scenes, all of which he predated.

Discography: *Pretties for You* (Warner Brothers, 1969); *Easy Action* (Warner Brothers, 1970); *Love It to Death* (Warner Brothers, 1971); *Killer* (Warner Brothers, 1971); *School's Out* (Warner Brothers, 1972); *Billion Dollar Babies* (Warner Brothers, 1972); *Muscle of Love* (Warner Brothers, 1974); *Alice Cooper's Greatest Hits* (Warner Brothers, 1974); *Welcome to My Nightmare* (Warner Brothers, 1975); *Alice Cooper Goes to Hell* (Warner Brothers, 1976); *Lace and Whiskey* (Warner Brothers, 1977); *The Alice Cooper Show* (Warner Brothers, 1977); *From the Inside* (Warner Brothers, 1978); *Flush the Fashion* (Warner Brothers, 1980); *Special Forces* (Warner Brothers, 1981); *Dada* (Warner Brothers, 1982); *Zipper Catches Skin* (Warner Brothers, 1982); *Constrictor* (MCA, 1986); *Raise Your Fist and Yell* (MCA, 1987); *Trash* (Epic, 1989); *Hey Stoopid* (Epic, 1991); *The Last Temptation* (Epic, 1994); *A Fist Full of Alice Live* (Capital, 1997); *Alice Cooper Live* (Delta, 2001); *Take 2* (WEA International, 2001); *Dragonfire* (Spitfire, 2001); *The Eyes of Alice Cooper* (Eagle, 2003); *Dirty Diamonds* (New West, 2005); *Live at Cabo Wabo 96* (Emi, 2005); *Live at Montraux* (Rajon, 2005); *Live at Toronto* (Kala, 2006); *Nobody Like Alice Cooper ... Live* (Cedar, 2006).

ALICE IN CHAINS (1987–2002). Jerry Cantrell (guitar), Layne Staley (vocals), Mike Starr (bass, 1987–92), Sean Kinney (drums), Mike Inez (bass, 1992-present).

One of the most successful heavy bands in the era of grunge, Seattle's Alice in Chains was perhaps the best answer to the question, "What happened to metal after grunge came to town?" Hailing from Seattle, the birthplace of grunge, Alice in Chains had one foot in the post-punk grunge camp and another in that of heavy metal, with their unapologetically heavy guitars and unique harmonies giving them more traditionally mainstream appeal than many of their Seattle-based brethren. This split personality also signified different musical orientations within the group and would ultimately lead to tensions that kept the band from developing to their full commercial and creative potential.

The impetus for the group went back to Staley's high school days when he had a group called Alice n Chains. After graduation, Staley hooked up with guitarist Cantrell in 1987 to form a new incarnation of the band, now called Alice in Chains. Bassist Starr and drummer Sean Kinney joined shortly thereafter. After a period of playing clubs in the Northwest, the band was signed by Columbia Records in 1989. The band was marketed as a metal band, and following their debut album, *Facelift*, went on the road as a support band for Van Halen, Iggy Pop, and Poison. The album became a hit, earning gold status within a year of its release. Shortly thereafter, the band released its *Sap* EP, which was also well-received.

Before the release of the band's sophomore album, the cataclysmic event that was Nirvana's juggernaut *Nevermind* album hit the music world. Nirvana's immense success signaled a sea change in popular music and triggered the wholesale removal of metal bands (especially "MTV" hair metal bands) from the Billboard charts and their placement on the endangered genres list. Seattle subsequently became a magnet for record companies looking for the next Nirvana, and the capital of what would soon be called grunge.

Seeing the writing on the wall, Columbia changed their game plan for Alice in Chains, and began marketing the group as an alternative band. The band had a new song, "Would," placed in the Seattle-set film *Singles*, which built anticipation for their forthcoming second album, *Dirt*. *Dirt* was released in the fall of 1992 and was well received, ultimately selling three million copies. Its bleak lyrics didn't seem to hinder its sales and in fact fit well into the aesthetic of the alternative scene. Nonetheless, the album's expression of the bleak existence of drug addiction, especially in the songs "God Smack," "Junkhead," and "Hate to Feel," gave rise to the rumors—ultimately proven true—that Staley was dealing with drug addiction. The band denied the rumors and toured in support of the album, most notably as part of the third Lollapalooza tour in 1993. Bassist Starr quit the band during this period, citing exhaustion from touring and the desire to spend more time with his family. He was replaced by Mike Inez.

Despite the drug rumors (and reality) Alice in Chains was doing well commercially, with *Dirt* going three times platinum. In 1994 the band released their *Jar of Flies* EP which was the first EP to dominate the album charts. The band returned with their third full-length album in 1995, simply entitled *Alice in Chains*. Although the album debuted at number one, the band declined to tour behind it, giving rise to more rumors of Staley's addiction, which proved to be true. In 1996, the band managed to deliver a live performance on *MTV Unplugged*, which was released as an album later that year.

Cantrell later released a solo album, *Boggy Depot*, in 1998, and later explained that he did so since he wasn't able to get Staley to work on Alice in Chains material. The band would remain dormant for the next several years, even as their label, Columbia, put out a box set, a live album, and greatest hits collection of the band's material.

Finally, the other shoe fell, and it was announced in April of 2002 that Layne Staley had been found dead in his apartment, the result of an overdose of cocaine and heroin (Bogdanov, et al. 2002).

Discography: *Facelift* (Columbia, 1990); *Dirt* (Columbia, 1992); *Jar of Flies* (Columbia, 1994); *Alice in Chains* (Columbia, 1995); *Unplugged* [live] (Columbia, 1996); *Live* (Columbia, 2000); *Nothing Safe* (Columbia, 1999).

THE AMBOY DUKES (1965–75). Bob Lenhert (vocals, replaced by John Drake, Rusty Day), Ron Medeiros (guitar, replaced by Ted Nugent), Gary Hicks (guitar, replaced by Steve Farmer), Dick Treat (bass, replaced by Bill White, Greg Arama), Gail Uptadale (drums, replaced by Dave Palmer), Rick Lober (keyboards, replaced by Andy Soloman).

The Amboy Dukes were a psychedelic rock group from Detroit, Michigan, that pioneered a proto-metal and psychedelic combination. They are perhaps best known as being the first band to give exposure to young guitarist Ted Nugent, who chafed under the restrictions of the band. The Nuge, who did not partake in the drinking, drugging, and chemical abuse of the band, nevertheless was able to translate the band's chemically fueled leaning into spectacular solos on epic guitar workout, such as "Journey to the Center of Your Mind," where Nugent cut loose on a psychedelic metal solo that would have made the British band Hawkwind proud. After fights over musical direction with Farmer (who wrote the lyrics, while Nugent wrote the music) the band members left one by one, and for several years Ted Nugent kept the band going as "Ted Nugent and the Amboy Dukes" to diminishing returns, before he retired the name and released his first solo record in 1975. The Amboy Dukes will be remembered primarily for being the birth caul of Ted Nugent, but their better and harder rocking songs such as "Journey" and "Why is a Carrot More Orange than an Orange?" are psychedelic classics. There are also many bootlegs and compilations available not listed here on various record companies, usually of questionable quality, and Nugent fans are urged to find the earlier releases.

Discography: As the Amboy Dukes: *The Amboy Dukes* (Repertoire, 1967); *Journey to the Center of the Mind* (Repertoire, 1968); *Migration* (Repertoire, 1969); As Ted Nugent and the Amboy Dukes: *Survival of the Fittest Live at the Eastown Theater Detroit* (Polydor, 1971); *Call of the Wild* (Discreet, 1973); *Totoh, Fang & Claw* (DiscReet, 1974).

AMON AMARTH (1992–PRESENT). Johan Hegg (vocals), Olavvi Mikkonen (guitar), Johan Soderberg (guitar), Ted Lumdstrom (bass), Martin Lopez (drums, replaced by Fredrik Andersson).

Amon Amarth is a death metal/Viking metal band from Stockholm. The band started in 1992 in Tumba, a small suburb of southern Stockholm where apparently something in the water leads to majestic and killer Viking metal. The band is essentially a death metal band (with some black metal tinges) that has turned their attention to Norse mythology and themes of Viking sagas and epics. For those put off by the Viking outfits in the promotional pictures, the band is actually quite amazing in an epic way, reminiscent of Cookie Monster singing for Mastodon on a longboat set aflame after a particularly costly raid on a distant castle. Also lead singer Johan Hegg has one of the best beards in metal. Signs that the band may have a sense of humor about the Viking image is evident in the title of the 2006 record *With Odin on Our Side*.

Discography: *Shemhamforash* (Witchhunt, 1996); *Sorrow Throat the Nine Worlds* (Pulverized, 1996); *Once Sent From the Golden Hall* (Metal Blade, 1998); *Avenger* (Metal Blade, 1999); *The Crusher* (Metal Blade, 2001); *Versus the World* (Metal Blade, 2002); *Fate of Norns* (Metal Blade, 2004); *With Odin on Our Side* (Metal Blade, 2006).

AMPS. Of all the characteristics that "define" heavy metal as a musical genre, perhaps none is as crucial as the technology of amplification, the sonic appliance that amplifies electric guitars and gives them their trademark volume and tone and lends the music and its culture the "sturm and drang" that differentiate it from the more polite musical forms of civil society.

Guitar amplifiers were invented in the aftermath of radio's introduction in the 1920s and were first applied to the challenge of getting the volumes of jazz guitarists above the din of big band swing ensembles. By the early 1960s amplifier technology had advanced to a sufficient level that country-western, pop, and jazz guitarists could amplify their instruments to a satisfactory volume and achieve the tonal characteristics they sought from the Fender, Vox, and other amps that were available at the time. These amps were commonly one-piece compact units featuring one or two 12-inch speakers, although one, two, or even four 10-inch speaker models were common as well. Their electronics generally produced from 15 to 40 "watts" (a measure of electrical power).

In England a former drummer-turned-music-shop-owner named James Marshall had begun to manufacture guitar amplifiers. Using Fender's 4-by-10-inch Bassman as his inspiration, he designed an amp with a separate 30-watt head (electronics section) and speaker cabinet. Instead of the Fender's open-backed, 4x10 design, Marshall used four 12-inch speakers in a closed-back cabinet. This cabinet design gave the Marshall a fuller, more powerful sound and more low-end energy. In addition, the electronic components that Marshall used—in particular the KT66, and later, EL34 power tubes—gave the amp a more aggressive, "growling" tone than the Fenders of the day, especially when cranked.

The Marshall amp quickly became quite popular with British rock guitarists. Among these was Pete Townshend of the Who. As the Who's live performances became louder and more raucous, Townshend and bassist John Entwhistle requested more powerful amplifiers. Marshall complied, but in order to handle the increased wattage (100 watts) he doubled the size of the cabinet to hold eight 12-inch speakers. The resulting amps provided an imposing presence and gave the group the sound they were looking for. However, the six-foot-high speaker cabinets were difficult to transport, so Townshend asked if they could be cut in half. Marshall's response was to redesign two complementary 4-by-12-inch cabinets that could be "stacked" for the desired 8-by-12-inch effect. The resulting Marshall "stack" has become one of the most iconic features of hard rock and heavy metal stages ever since. Similar amplifier stacks were subsequently offered by other amp companies such as Hiwatt, Laney, and Sunn, and even today are a mainstay offering of contemporary amplifier manufacturers like Mesa, Bogner, and Diesel, among many others. While there have been innumerable advances in amplifier technology, the general appearance of the amplifier "stack" has changed little in the last forty years. And in their size and configuration, particularly their slant/straight cabinet design, today's amp stacks show their debt to Jim Marshall's original design.

As central as the look of amplifiers have been to the iconography of heavy metal, the sound of guitar amplifiers is even more central to the signature sound of the music. That sound of course is one of *distortion*. Initially, guitar amplifiers were designed to cleanly reproduce the sound of the electric guitar. This was certainly desired for the early jazz guitarists of the thirties and forties, and for those working in country music. As the rock genre evolved, however, and rock bands began to play at louder volume levels and in a more aggressive style, guitarists began to experiment with more aggressive tones. One legend has it that Keith Richards achieved his buzz-saw tone on "Satisfaction" by slicing the speakers in his amp. Whether this is true or not, guitarists increasingly sought methods and devices that would give them a "dirtier" tone through their amps.

One of the touchstones in this evolution came when Eric Clapton purchased a Marshall JTM45 2-by-12-inch combo amp to record his debut with John Mayall's Bluesbreakers, the legendary "Beano" album (so named for the Beano comic book that Clapton is seen reading on the album's cover. Clapton so enjoyed the over-driven tone of his Gibson Les Paul guitar through the amp when it was "cranked" that he went against the low volume conventions of 1960s recording practices and insisted on recording the amp at high volumes. While the recording engineers ini-tially protested, Clapton prevailed and the Beano album, with its groundbreaking Les Paul and Marshall tones, heralded a new paradigm in rock guitar tones, and made Clapton a star at the same time.

The tone that Clapton introduced on the album was aggressive yet sweet—an in-dication of the paradox of distorted guitar tones. While the sound of overdriving tubes is indeed a powerful and aggressive one, it is also quite pleasing to the ear since it emphasizes the odd order harmonics and overtones that are generally con-sonant to the ear. The tone allows chords—especially 1-5-1 voicings (known as "power chords")—to sound massive and full, and as Clapton and others, such as Pete Townshend, Jimi Hendrix, and Jimmy Page, continued pioneering heavy rock sounds, the amplifiers, particularly those of Marshall, became bigger and more ca-pable of delivering distortion sounds that became the foundation of the sound of heavy metal. With the big and full sound of the amps, single note riffs themselves became as full sounding as chords and became part of the lexicon of heavy rock, especially via the works of bands like Black Sabbath, many of whose songs were explicitly riff-based.

To a great extent, the choice of amplifier and tone that a guitarist chooses deter-mines (along with playing style) the "sound" of the band. Thus the sounds of Van Halen, AC/DC, Pantera, and other heavy metal bands are often very closely associ-ated with their guitarist's choice of amplifier.

At this point in the evolution of amplifier technology, there are a multitude of different amplifiers that provide a variety of different distortion tones, and guita-rists have more choices than ever before. One constant that remains, however, is that for any band to be considered "heavy metal," there must be a distorted ampli-fier at the center of their sound.

ANAAL NATHRAKH (1999–PRESENT). Dave Hunt (vocals), Michael Kenny (guitar/other instruments).

This death/black metal band from England who play part time (the band has only two full-time members) and dress in normal street clothing still play a fero-cious and horrifically loud brand of fast metal. The band was started in 1999 as a way of combining industrial with black metal and is named after the spell Merlin uses to create magic in the film *Excalibur*. The band started the way most metal bands do, through word of mouth and demos. Two of their demos, the Anaal Nathrakh and the Total Fucking Necro, came to the attention of Earache Records, who then signed the band in 2002. Because of the limited two-man lineup the band rarely tours, but they do play the festival circuit from time to time. Despite the limited number of musicians in the band, Anaal Nathrakh is one of the most brutal and powerful bands in the extreme music genre.

Discography: *The Codex Necro* (Earache, 2001); *Total Fucking Necro* (Earache, 2002); *When Fire Rains Down from the Sky, Mankind Will Reap As It Has Sown* (Earache, 2003); *Domine Non Es Dignus* (Season of Mist, 2004); *Eschaton* (Season of Mist, 2005); *Hell Is Empty and All the Devils Are Here* (Feto Records, 2007).

ANGEL WITCH (1980–PRESENT). Kevin Heybourne (vocals/guitar), Grant Dennison (guitar, 1989), Kevin "Skids" Riddles (bass, replaced in 1989 by Peter Gordelier), Dave Hogg (drums, replaced in 1989 by Spencer Holman).

Angel Witch were a minor but entertaining band from the New Wave of British heavy metal. The band was formed initially in 1977, but finally gelled as a lineup in 1980, led by Heybourne. Through the years numerous members have come and gone, leaving Heybourne the one constant. "Baphomet" is their one killer song from the band's self-titled debut, but it would not be a bad idea to pick up one of the many compilations available on various record labels.

Discography: *Angel Witch* (Bronze, 1980); *Screamin' & Bleedin* (Killerwatt, 1985); *Frontal Assault* (N/A, 1986); *Live* (Capitol, 1990); *Resurrection* (Crook'd, 2000); *2000: Live at LA2* (Zoom Club/Windsor, 2001); *82 Revisited* (Thunderbolt, 2002); *Death Angel: Live at East Anglia Rock Festival* (Mausoleum, 2006).

ANTHRAX (1981–PRESENT). Neil Turbin (vocals, replaced by Joey Belladonna, John Bush, Dan Nelson), Scott Ian (guitar), Dan Spitz (guitar), Dan Lilker (bass, replaced by Frank Bello), Charlie Benante (drums).

One of the key thrash metal bands who introduced numerous metal fans to both punk rock and rap and helped pioneer the rap/metal crossover sound with both their collaboration with Public Enemy on the cover of *Bring the Noise* (1987) as well as their own rap song "I'm the Man" (1991). The band started out in Queens in 1981 led by guitarist Scott Ian, who has fired numerous members of the band over the years, leaving him and drummer Charlie Benante as the only original members. In 1984 they released their classic first record, *Fist Full of Metal*, a quintessential thrash album. Shortly after Lilker was fired, Turbin left and was replaced by the far more mainstream-sounding Joey Belladonna, who proved to be the main Anthrax vocalist for several crucial records including the brilliant *Among the Living* record, which spawned the pit classic "Caught in a Mosh," an anthem of sorts for many metal heads. They became well known early on, especially guitarist and leader Scott Ian, for championing new music, particularly rap. Rap group Public Enemy responded by giving a shout out to Anthrax on the song "Bring the Noise," in which they rap that "wax is for Anthrax, still they can rock the bells." Anthrax returned the favor by recording their own version of "Bring the Noise," one of the first rap/metal crossover singles. By 1992, tensions in the band forced Belladonna's departure and his replacement by ex-Armored Saint singer John Bush, who added a harder edge to the band than Belladonna was capable of. Ironically, this led to a long fallow period for Anthrax.

Although the band has not been prolific in recent years, and even pondered changing their name after the anthrax poisonings following 9/11/2001, the band continues to tour to this day with new singer Dan Nelson, after a brief detour back to Joey Belladonna from 2005 to 2007. Despite their numerous personnel changes, Anthrax, along with Slayer, Metallica, and Megadeth, is one of the key architects of the thrash sound, and one of the most open minded in recording nonmetal (the band even covered Joe Jackson's "Got the Time" on the *Persistence of Time* album) influences and the first to pioneer the rap/rock crossover.

Discography: *Fistful of Metal* (Megaforce, 1984); *Armed and Dangerous EP* (Megaforce, 1985); *Spreading the Disease* (Megaforce/Island, 1985); *Among the Living* (Megaforce/Island, 1987); *I'm the Man* [EP] (Megaforce/Island, 1987); *State of Euphoria* (Megaforce/Island, 1988); *Persistence of Time* (Megaforce/Island, 1990); *Attack of the Killer B's* (Megaforce/Island, 1991); *Sound of White Noise* (Elektra, 1993); *Live: The Island Years* (Megaforce/Island, 1994); *Stomp 442* (Elektra, 1995) *Volume 8: The Threat Is Real* (Tommy Boy, 1998); *We've Come for You All* (Beyond, 2003); *Music of Mass Destruction: Live from Chicago* (Sanctuary, 2004); *Alive 2: The Music Is* (Sanctuary, 2005).

ANVIL (1981–PRESENT). Steve "Lips" Kulow (lead vocals, lead guitar), Ian Dickson (bass), Robb Reiner (drums), Dave Allison (rhythm guitar).

An early influence on the development of speed metal, Canadian band Anvil got their start in the late 1970s. Fronted by guitarist vocalist Steve "Lips" Kulow, and including bassist Ian Dickson, drummer Robb Reiner, and rhythm guitarist Dave Allison, the band first went by the name Lips, and released their first album *Hard 'n' Heavy* independently in 1981. Gaining the attention of Attic records, the label re-released this album after the band changed its name to Anvil. Playing a technically advanced variation of metal, the band broke ground for the speed metal genre with a series of subsequent albums, *Metal on Metal* (1982), *Forged in Fire* (1983), *Backwaxed* (1985), and *Pound for Pound* (1987), that paved the way for such bands as Megadeth and Metallica. Ultimately, Anvil would never see the same level of commercial success as those bands they helped influence. The band has continued to record and play live, most recently releasing *This is Thirteen* in 2007. In 2008 the band received some overdue recognition when a documentary by filmmaker Sacha Gervasi (an old friend and former roadie for the band), *Anvil: The Story of Anvil,* was screened at the Sundance Film Festival.

Discography: *Hard 'n' Heavy* (Attic, 1981); *Metal on Metal* (Attic, 1982); *Forged in Fire* (Attic, 1983); *Backwaxed* (Viper, 1985); *Pound for Pound* (Capitol, 1987); *Strength of Steel* (Metal Blade, 1987); *Worth the Weight* (Metal Blade, 1991); *Plugged in Permanent* (Metal Blade, 1997); *Speed of Sound* (Hypnotic, 2000); *Plenty of Power* (Hypnotic, 2001); *Absolutely No Alternative* (Import, 2002); *Back to Basics* (New Media Studios, 2004); *This Is Thirteen* (Independent, 2007).

APRIL WINE (1971–PRESENT). Myles Goodwyn (lead vocals and guitar), Gary Moffet (guitar), Brian Greenway (guitar), Steve Lang (bass), Jerry Mercer (drums).

Along with Rush and Heart, April Wine was one of the few hard rock bands to emerge from Canada in the 1970s to make a commercial impact in the United States. Combining powerful songwriting with strong guitar-heavy arrangements, the band had a commanding presence on concert stages and FM radio throughout the 1980s.

The band had their first hit with "Fast Train" in 1971. "You Could Have Been a Lady" in 1972 was the band's first Canadian number 1. By 1978's *First Glance*, the band had developed a harder-edged rock sound. Building on this foundation, the band released *Harder ... Faster* in 1979. The album featured new addition Brian Greenway (making for a three-guitar lineup). *Nature of the Beast* followed in 1981 and featured the band's biggest U.S. hit, "Just Between You and Me." After 1982's *Power Play* and its subsequent tour, Goodwin relocated to the Bahamas, and the band went on an extended hiatus. After a series of reformations, recordings, and tours, the band continues to tour occasionally and release recordings, though their salad days are behind them.

Discography: *April Wine* (Big Tree, 1972); *Electric Jewels* (Aquarius, 1973); *Live* (Aquarius, 1974); *On Record* (Aquarius, 1974); *Stand Back* (Big Tree, 1975); *Forever for Now* (Aquarius, 1976); *The Whole World's Goin' Crazy* (London, 1976); *Live at the El Mocambo* (London, 1977); *First Glance* (Capitol, 1979); *Unreleased Live* (Capitol, 1979); *Harder ... Faster* (Capitol, 1980); *Nature of the Beast* (Capitol, 1981); *Summer Tour 1981* [live] (Capitol, 1981); *Power Play* (Capitol, 1982); *Animal Grace* (Capitol, 1984); *Walking through Fire* (Capitol, 1988); *Attitude* (Fre, 1993); *Frigate* (Fre, 1994); *Oowatanite* (Aquarius, 1998); *King Biscuit Flower Hour* [live] (King Biscuit, 1999); *Back to the Mansion* (Civilian, 2001); *Greatest Hits Live* (King Biscuit Flower Hour, 2003); *From the Front Row Live* (Silverline, 2003); *Roughly Speaking* (April Wine, 2006); *Rock 'n' Roll Is a Vicious Game* (Capitol, 2003).

ARCH ENEMY (1995–PRESENT). Johan Liiva (bass and vocals, replaced by Angela Gossow), Michael Amott (guitar), Christopher Amott (guitar, replaced by Fredrik Akesson), Daniel Erlandsson (drums).

Arch Enemy are a Swedish death metal band with the unusual advantage of being fronted by a female lead singer, Angela Gossow, who has a natural range far beyond most male vocalists in the death metal scene. The band was started by legendary guitarist Michael Amott (ex Carnage, Carcass, Candlemass) along with his brother Christopher Amott, ex-Carnage bassist, and Johan Liiva on bass and vocals, and drummer Daniel Erlandsson. After several personnel changes, the band took the unusual step of hiring a female vocalist in 2001 (not the most common occurrence in a straightforward death metal band), namely, Angela Gossow for the *Wages of Sin* record. Although Christopher Amott left after the *Doomsday Machine* record, new guitarist Fredrik Akesson, formerly of Tiamat, ably filled the guitar slot. Arch Enemy continue to be one of the more innovative and successful death metal bands touring today, and vocalist Gossow is known for giving as well as she gets when insulted by unruly fans who are unable to accept a female vocalist fronting a band as heavy as Arch Enemy.

Discography: *Black Earth* (Wrong, 1996); *Stigmata* (Century Media, 1998); *Burning Bridges* (Century Media, 1999); *Wages of Sin* (Century Media, 2001); *Anthems of Rebellion* (Toys Factory, 2003); *Dead Eyes See No Future* (2004); *Doomsday Machine* (Century Media, 2006); *Rise of the Tyrant* (CMA, 2007).

ARMORED SAINT (1982–92, 1998–2001, 2006). John Bush (vocals), David Pritchard (guitar, replaced after he died from leukemia by Jeff Duncan in 1990), Phil Sandoval (guitar), Joey Vera (bass), and Gonzo (drums, brother of Phil Sandoval).

Armored Saint were a fairly pedestrian heavy metal band best known for the vocal stylings of lead singer John Bush. Bush later went on to sing for Anthrax for several years before returning to reform Armored Saint until the band finally ran out of steam in 2006.

Discography: *Armored Saint* (Metal Blade, 1983); *March of the Saint* (Chrysalis, 1984); *Delirious Nomad* (Chrysalis, 1985); *Raising Fear* (Chrysalis, 1987); *Saints Will Conquer* (Restless, 1988); *Symbol of Salvation* (Metal Blade, 1991); *Revelation* (Metal Blade, 2000); *Nod to the Old School* (Metal Blade, 2001).

ASPHALT BALLET (1988–93). Gary Jefferies (vocals), Danny Clarke (guitar), Julius J. Ulrich (guitar), Terry Phillips (bass), Mikki Kiner (drums).

A contender for the L.A. hair metal sweepstakes in the late eighties, Asphalt Ballet's tough melodic rock never quite had a chance given their late entry on the scene. While 1991's self-titled album showed a lot of promise, it arrived a bit late to the party, as musical tastes were moving toward alternative rock, and despite the band's loyal L.A. following, the album fared poorly. 1993's *Pigs* sealed the deal, and the band split shortly thereafter.

Discography: *Asphalt Ballet* (Virgin, 1991); *Pigs* (Capitol, 1993).

AT THE GATES (1990–96, 2006–PRESENT). Tomas Lindberg (vocals), Anders Bjoler (guitar), Martin Larsson (guitar), Jonas Bjoler (bass), Adrian Erlandsson (drums).

At the Gates was one of the quintessential black metal bands of the nineties as epitomized on classic records such as *Slaughter of the Soul*. Founded in Gothenburg, Sweden, along with fellow band In Flames, At the Gates is known for their brutal assault, which was sadly cut off when the band broke up in 1996. Luckily for metal purists, the band reunited in 2006, and pretty much picked up right where they left off.

Discography: *Gardens of Grief* [EP] (Dolores, 1990); *The Red in the Sky is Ours* (Century Media, 1992); *With Fear I Kiss the Burning Darkness* (Deaf, 1993); *Terminal Spirit Disease* (Futurist, 1994); *Slaughter of the Soul* (Earache, 1995).

AUTOGRAPH (1983–88). Steve Plunkett (lead vocals/guitars), Steve Lynch (lead guitar), Randy Rand (bass), Steven Isham (keyboards), Keni Richards (drums).

Emerging from L.A.'s pop-metal scene in the early eighties, Autograph hit it big in the mid-eighties with their hit single and MTV video "Turn Up the Radio" from their first album, 1984's *Sign in Please*. Their second album, *That's the Stuff*, released the following year featured the MTV hit "Blondes in Black Cars." While the band's music was tuneful, it was also woefully generic sounding, ironically the source of their mainstream success and their lack of staying power. Although the band exuded a likeable "guys next door in spandex" appeal, it wasn't enough for them to compete with the big boys, and their final album in 1987 made that *Loud and Clear.*

Discography: *Sign in Please* (RCA, 1984); *That's the Stuff* (RCA, 1985); *Loud and Clear* (RCA, 1987); *Missing Pieces* (Pavement, 1997); *More Missing Pieces* (Point, 2004).

AVENGED SEVENFOLD (2001–PRESENT). M. Shadows (vocals), Zacky Vengeance (guitar), Synyster Gates (guitar), Johnny Christ (bass), The Reverend (drums).

Featuring an aggressive punk metal style, Avenged Sevenfold first came together as high school students in Huntington Beach, California, and consist of vocalist

M. Shadows, guitarists Zacky Vengeance and Synyster Gates, bassist Johnny Christ, and drummer The Reverend. After a series of albums for independent labels, 2001's *Sounding the Seventh Trumpet* (Good Life), and 2003's *Waking the Fallen* (Hopeless), the band got the attention of Warner Brothers Records, who released *City of Evil* in 2005. On the strength of the single "Bat Country" and its video, which received heavy rotation on MTV, the album made it to number 30 on the Billboard album chart. Their self-produced sophomore album, *Avenged Sevenfold*, was released in 2007.

Discography: *Sounding the Seventh Trumpet* (Good Life, 2001); *Waking the Fallen* (Hopeless, 2003); *City of Evil* (Warner Bros., 2005); *Avenged Sevenfold* (Warner Bros., 2007).

B

BADLANDS (1989–92). Jake E. Lee (guitar), Ray Gillen (vocals), Greg Chaisson (bass), Eric Singer (drums).

Formed around ex-Ozzy Osbourne guitarist Jake E. Lee and latter-day Black Sabbath vocalist Ray Gillen, Badlands were to a large extent a band out of time. Toward the end of the hair band era, the group looked more to the early seventies hard rock of Free and Led Zeppelin for musical inspiration, and their gritty back to basics approach in some ways presaged the coming of grunge, which similarly sought to strip hard rock and metal of its more pretentious elements. But the band never really took off since they weren't really embraced by pop/hair metal fans and didn't really fit in with the post-punk grunge aesthetic that was just around the corner. After a promising debut and follow-up, internal disputes about the band's musical direction led to a falling out between Lee and Gillen, and the singer left the band. While the band attempted to soldier on with new singer John West, the band was dropped by their label (Atlantic) and went their separate ways shortly thereafter.

Discography: *Badlands* (Atlantic, 1989); *Voodoo Highway* (Atlantic, 1991); *Dusk* (Pony Canyon, 1999).

BAD NEWS. Bad News was a mock heavy metal band created by Rick Mayall, Nigel Planer, and Adrian Edmondson (of the popular British program *Young Ones*). They debuted on the Channel 4 television show *The Comic Strip Presents* in 1983 and were active around the same time that *This Is Spinal Tap* (1984) was in production. Apparently heavy metal is so full of clichés that it can stand more than one parody band. The band performed on stage several times in the eighties, including special guest appearances by Jimmy Page and Brian May.

BANG TANGO (1986–94). Joe Lesté (vocals), Kyle Stevens (guitar), Mark Knight (guitar), Kyle Kyle (bass), Tigg Ketler (drums).

With a sound that sometimes had more in common with acts like Billy Idol or the Cult, Bang Tango was nonetheless lumped into the pop metal category that most of their Sunset Strip contemporaries inhabited. Although they experienced some local L.A. success and won a contract with MCA after releasing an independent live album in the late eighties, their studio debut *Psycho Café*, released in 1989, despite some video airplay on MTV, failed to generate much interest in the larger rock market. Subsequent albums in the early nineties failed to find the band a larger audience, and they broke up shortly after their last album, *Love After Death*, was released in 1994, as grunge and alternative rock took over the airwaves.

Discography: *Live Injection* (World Of Hurt, 1987); *Psycho Café* (Mechanic, 1989); *Dancin' on Coals* (MCA, 1991); *Love After Death* (Music For Nations, 1994); *United and Live* (Cleopatra, 1999); *Ready to Go* (Shrapnel, 2004); *Big Bangs and Live Explosions* (Mausoleum, 2006); *From the Hip* (Perris, 2006); *Live* (Deadline, 1998); *Greatest Tricks* (Deadline, 1999); *The Ultimate Bang Tango: Rockers and Thieves* (Lemon, 2004).

BATHORY (1983–2004). Quorthon (vocals/guitar/other instruments), Freddan (bass, replaced by Ktohar), Jonas Akerlund Vvorth (drums).

Bathory were one of the most pagan of the black metal scene and helped to introduce the worship of the Norse gods as part of the black metal pantheon. Many also consider Bathory's signature gloomy sound to be the foundation of the black metal sound. The band typically also dressed on album covers in traditional Viking outfits complete with copious amounts of spikes and swords. The band also veered into fascist and pro-Aryan ideology that marred their output as Bathory (mostly the work of Quorthon, who eventually played all the instruments in the band, which declined to play live gigs). The band ended with the death of Quorthon of heart failure in 2004, but his influence on the black metal scene is considerable.

Discography: *Bathory* (Black Mark, 1984); *The Return of Darkness and Evil* (Black Mark, 1985); *Under the Sign of the Black Mark* (New Renaissance, 1987); *Blood Fire Death* (Maze/Kraze, 1988); *Hammerheart* (Noise, 1990); *Twilight of the Gods* (Black Mark, 1991); *Requiem* (Black Mark, 1994); *Octagon* (Black Mark, 1995); *Blood on Ice* (Black Mark, 1996); *Destroyer of Worlds* (Black Mark, 2001); *Nordland I* (Black Mark, 2003); *Nordland II* (Black Mark, 2004).

BEATALLICA (2001–PRESENT). James Lennfield (vocals/guitar), Greg Hammetson (guitar/vocals), Kiff McBurtney (bass/vocals), Ringo Lars (drums).

Beatallica are a faux heavy metal cover band that perform Beatles songs in the style of Metallica. While the concept may sound silly or strained, the mixture actually seems to make sense on songs such as "Sandman," a Metallica-esque cover of "Taxman," "... And Justice for All My Lovin'," and especially on the hilarious "Ktulu" ("He's So Heavy"). The band may be a bit of a joke band, but as far as innovative tribute bands go, Beatallica has one of the best gimmicks outside of Mini-Kiss.

See also the section on tribute bands.

Discography: *Sgt. Hetfield's Motor Breath Pub Band* (Oglio, 2007).

BEHEMOTH (1991–PRESENT). Nergal (vocals/guitar), Seth (guitar), Orion (bass), Inferno (drums).

Behemoth are one of the most legendary of the death metal bands to come from Poland in the mid-nineties. The band is led by singer/guitarist Nergal, who has been the one constant in the band's history. His consistent vision for the band was what kept them going through a dizzying array of lineup changes; although initially labeled a death metal band, by the late nineties, the band had evolved into more of a hybrid of black and death metal.

Discography: *Sventevith (Storming Near the Baltic)* (Last Episode, 1995); *Grom* (Metal mind, 1996); *Pandemonic incantations* (Season of Mist, 1998); *Satanica* (Import, 1999); *Thelema 6* (Olympic, 2000); *Zos Kia cultus (Here and Beyond)* (Olympic, 2002); *Demigod* (Regain, 2004); *The Apostasy* (Act, 2007).

BIOHAZARD (1988–2005). Evan Seinfeld (vocals, bass), Billy Graziadei (vocals, guitar), Bobby Hambel (guitar, replaced by Rob Echeverria, replaced by Leo Curley, replaced by Carmine Vincent, replaced by Scott Roberts), Danny Schuler (drums).

Biohazard were one of the few metal bands, along with Anthrax, to posses a keen appreciation for rap music as well as crunchy metal riffs. Unlike Anthrax, Biohazard were more willing to commit themselves to incorporating rap more regularly into their sound. The band came across as a bunch of Brooklyn street toughs who would almost rather rob you than play for you. But this added a gritty edge to the band that incorporated hip hop beats with heavy vocals, going so far as to even do their own version of the Anthrax/Public Enemy duet, with their collaboration with the rap groups Onyx on the metal version of that group's hit "Slam" (which was a fairly hard song to begin with). They also played together on the quintessential rap/rock hybrid movie soundtrack "Judgment Night," which showcased the in-concert ferocity for which the group had become revered. *New World Disorder* in 1995 was probably the peak of the band's career.

Evan Seinfeld went into an unjustly deserved purgatory, when he joined the VH1 "Supergroup" show, along with Scott Ian of Anthrax and Ted Nugent. Still, at their peak, Biohazard were one of the hardest, hippest, and most urban of the rap/metal hybrid bands. Seinfeld, a metal punk legend, also made notable appearances on the gritty HBO prison drama "Oz." It seems as though Biohazard were too left field at the time for many bands that preferred the simulated rap metal of groups such as Limp Bizkit as opposed to bands who actually walked the walk and talked the talk.

Discography: *Biohazard* (Maze, 1990); *Urban Discipline* (Roadrunner Records, 1992); *State of the World Address* (Warner Music Group, 1994); *Mata Leao* (Warner Music Group, 1996); *No Holds Barred [Live in Europe]* (Roadrunner, 1997); *New World Disorder* (Mercury, 1999); *Tales from the B-Side* (Orchard, 2001); *Uncivilization* (Sanctuary Records, 2001); *Kill or Be Killed* (Sanctuary Records, 2003); *Means to an End* (SPV, 2005); *Live in San Francisco* (2BI, 2007).

BLACK LABEL SOCIETY (1999–PRESENT). Zakk Wylde aka Jeffrey Phillip Wielandt (vocals, guitar, bass, piano), Nick "Evil Twin" Cantanese (guitar*)*, Steve "S.O.B." Gibb (bass, replaced by Mike Inez, replaced by Robert Trujillo, replaced by James LoMenzo, replaced by John "JD" DeServio), Phil "Philth" Ondich (drums, replaced by Craig Nunenmacher).

Black Label Society is the brainchild of ace guitarist (and buddy of catcher Mike Piazza) Zakk Wylde. The band started in 1999 after Wylde left Ozzy Osbourne's band and started out on his own. After several failed solo records, Wilde tried again, essentially still solo, but with drummer Phil Ondich, and Wylde on guitar, drums, and bass as well as lead vocals. Black Label Society differed from Wylde's solo career by being less country-tinged and more balls to the walls metal. Wylde has also subsequently made up with Ozzy and has played on Ozzfest, as well as a tour in Japan. Wylde also appeared in the Mark Wahlberg film *Rock Star* as a guitarist for the fictional band Steel Dragon based on Judas Priest. To many, Wylde is one of the definitive metal guitarists and part of a new generation of shredders. The acoustic *Hangover Music* record is just bizarre, but the others are worth buying for students of serious fretwork.

Discography: *Sonic Brew* (Spitfire, 1999); *Stronger Than Death* (Spitfire, 2000); *Alcohol Fueled Brewtality Live!* (Spitfire, 2001); *1919 Eternal* (Spitfire, 2002); *Blessed Hellride* (Spitfire, 2003); *Hangover Music, Vol. 6* (Spitfire, 2004); *Kings of Damnation* (Spitfire, 2005); *Mafia* (Artemis, 2005); *Shot to Hell* (Roadrunner, 2006).

BLACK METAL. Black metal is a subgenre of heavy metal that involves thrash style musicianship and lyrical invocations of the occult, Satanism, allegiance to the old religions of Norway, or sometimes associations with white power and Aryan pride movements. The first band to be labeled black metal was the English band Venom in the early eighties, whose second record, *Black Metal*, included several odes to Satanism. Subsequent bands such as Bathory and Burzum also recorded in their style (although many bands who have flirted with this type of imagery are not considered black metal, such as Led Zeppelin and Black Sabbath).

The roots of the genre start with Venom, who were the first to play in a style that is today considered to be the authentic black metal musical and lyrical standard, and it may have been Venom, who many deride as not being technically proficient, who led to the signature low-fi or cheaply recorded sounds of many black metal bands such as Darkthrone.

While most performers in the scene are not expected to be cannibals or murderers in real life, many in the black metal scene such as members of Mayhem, Dissection, and Emperor have all been arrested for crimes ranging from church burnings, such as the Fantoft church burning in June 1992, to murder (such as the murder of a gay man by Bard Eithun of Emperor in August 1992), as noted by Moynihan and Soderland (1998). While some bands seem to be more tongue in cheek than others, many clearly take their views seriously, such as Quorthorn of Bathory who ardently wished for a revival of the old Norse religion in the early eighties.

Church Burning. During the nineties, especially in Norway and Sweden, there were several notorious church burnings attributed to black metal adherents. While there were certainly fewer church burnings than the media made it out to be, the trend was nonetheless disturbing and an indication of exactly how far certain members of the black metal and Odin revivalist scene were willing to go in the name of their beliefs. (This is not to be confused with racist church burning in the United States in the south and to the present; although some of the black metal fans who burned churches in Norway and Sweden were racist or fascist, the burnings in the United States had no connection to the scenes across the ocean.)

Church burning began in earnest in the eighties and continued for several years. The major damage was horrific, and it was almost impossible to put a monetary value on the churches that were damaged or destroyed, as many of them had been in operation for hundreds of years and were invaluable parts of the community and its history.

The rationale behind the church burnings is mixed up in varying degrees of twisted ideologies, genuine allegiance to pagan religions, a mixture of white power and fascist ideology, and some visceral thrill-seeking by metal bands, who were increasingly challenged by their fans to take things to the next level and prove their claims of being evil. However, the end result was not to shake the foundations of Christianity but instead to destroy buildings of great historical significance, especially the Norwegian state churches that were burned, some of which dated back five or six centuries and were considered priceless.

See also Mayhem, Venom, and Bathory.

BLACK SABBATH (1969–PRESENT). Ozzy Osbourne (vocals, replaced by Ronnie James Dio and too many to count, see below) Tony Iommi (guitar), Geezer Butler (bass, replaced by many, now Geezer Butler), Bill Ward (drums, replaced by Vinnie Appice, many others, now Bill Ward).

To many fans, Black Sabbath invented metal. It is as simple as that. The only other major contender is Led Zeppelin (or earlier proto-metal bands such as Blue Cheer and Iron Butterfly, if we are to count bands from the pre-metal era), but most metal fans will argue in the direction of Sabbath, if only for the signature metal sound pioneered by Sabbath guitarist Tony Iommi.

The band originally formed as Earth in 1968, a more blues-based band featuring guitarist Tony Iommi, bassist Geezer Butler, drummer Bill Ward, and helium-sounding vocalist John "Ozzy" Osbourne. The band toured for a while as Earth mostly doing covers of popular contemporary bands and blues songs, until Iommi briefly decamped for Jethro Tull, which was only to last a few months before he retuned to the band. They then changed their name to the far more aggressive-sounding Black Sabbath.

Sabbath from the start was a groundbreaking band. Due to an industrial accident in which he lost the tips of his fretting fingers, guitarist Tony Iommi improvised and added downtuned guitars, giving the band a creepy feeling sonically from the start. As metal expert John Lisa notes, downtuning involved "taking the strings and literally lowering the tuning so the E string sounds more like a D string, lower with more bottom and doomier sounding" (Lisa, 2008). This made the strings less tense and thus easier for Iommi to play, and also resulted in a unique sound that numerous bands were to copy for the next four decades. (Although some metal scholars have suggested that Blue Cheer was the first band to downtune, this has been disputed by others.)

Bassist and early lyricist Butler also brought a sense of the macabre and a vision of the occult to the band. Their groundbreaking first album, *Black Sabbath*, was released in 1970, and was unlike almost anything else out on a major label at that

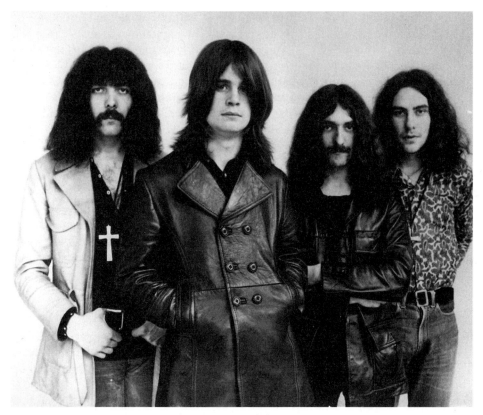

Black Sabbath, pictured here in 1969, were the parents of the heavy metal sound.
(Pictorial Press Ltd / Alamy)

time. Songs such as "The Wizard" (one of the few metal songs with a harmonica as a key instrument), "NIB," and the classic title song. This first record led to a string of five records in a row that all redefined the boundaries of metal, from slow to fast, but always downtuned, even on sped-up songs such as "Paranoid" or maniacal shriekers such as "Sabbath, Bloody Sabbath." Sabbath is also responsible for the creation of the heavy metal "power ballad" on the song "Changes" from *Volume 4*.

However, after the first five or six records, a series of lackluster albums (by early Sabbath standards) emerged, and with Ozzy's drinking getting out of control, it was decided by Iommi in 1979 that Sabbath needed fresh blood if they were going to continue.

After Ozzy left the band in 1979, Sabbath stabilized with the introduction of lead singer Ronnie James Dio for the reinvigorated albums *Heaven and Hell*, *Live Evil*, and *The Mob Rules* (Dio would later return after a decade to record a fourth album with the band, *Dehumanizer*). Drummer Ward had eventually found himself beset with drug and alcohol problems and was uneasy with the new singer, so he departed the band after the *Heaven and Hell* record, to be replaced by Vinnie Appice (the brother of Carmine Appice from Vanilla Fudge) on drums.

The relative stability was not to last and eventually tensions grew between Dio and Iommi, leading eventually to a revolving door of singers who included at last count: Ozzy Osbourne, David Walker (never recorded), Ronnie James Dio, Ian

Gillian, David Donato, Glenn Hughes, Ray Gillen, Tony Martin, Dio again, Martin again, Ozzy again, and now Ozzy *and* Dio in two different versions of Sabbath. There have also been numerous other bassists, drummers, and occasional keyboard players who have come and gone from Sabbath over the years, but the two most consistent lineups are with Osbourne singing and Ward on drums, or with Dio singing and Vinnie Appice on drums.

To this day, fans are split with many fans preferring Ozzy as Black Sabbath lead singer, even with the limitations of his voice at his age, while many other partisans of the Dio years follow the alternate version of Sabbath known as Heaven and Hell. Either way, Black Sabbath counts as the band that definitively established the distinct metal sound and, along with Led Zeppelin, are the key templates that almost every metal band has followed since their inception.

At this point it looks as though both versions of Black Sabbath will continue to tour and put out new music sporadically, at least until someone gets into a fight with Tony Iommi, that is ...

Discography: *Black Sabbath* (Warner Bros., 1970); *Paranoid* (Warner Bros., 1971); *Master of Reality* (Warner Bros., 1971); *Black Sabbath Vol. 4* (Warner Bros., 1972*)*; *Sabbath, Bloody Sabbath* (Warner Bros., 1973); *Sabotage* (Warner Bros., 1975); *Technical Ecstasy* (Warner Bros., 1976); *Never Say Die* (Warner Bros., 1978*)*; *Heaven and Hell* (Warner Bros., 1980); *Live at Last* (Nems, 1980); *The Mob Rules* (Warner Bros., 1981); *Live Evil* (Vertigo, 1983); *Born Again* (Warner Bros., 1983); *Seventh Star* (Warner Bros., 1986); *The Eternal Idol* (Warner Bros., 1987); *Headless Cross* (IRS, 1989); *TYR* (IRS, 1990); *Dehumanizer* (IRS, 1992); *Cross Purposes* (IRS, 1994); *Forbidden* (EMI, 1995); *Greatest Hits* (ESM, 1996); *Past Lives* (Sanctuary, 2002*)*; *The Dio Years* (Warner Bros., 2007).

BLITZKREIG (1980–81, 1984–91, 1992–94, 1996–99, 2001–PRESENT). Brian Ross (vocals), Jim Sirtoto (guitar, replaced by John Antcliffe, replaced by Sirtoto, replaced by Chris Beard, replaced by Glenn S. Howe, replaced by Paul Nesbitt (1992), replaced by Sirtoto (1995), replaced by Phil Millar (1996), replaced by Glenn S. Howes (1996–99), replaced by Paul Nesbitt (1998–2006), replaced by Guy Laverick (2007–)); Ian Jones (1980–81) (guitar, replaced by Mick Proctor (1984–86), replaced by JD Binnie (1986–87), replaced by Steve Robertson (1988–89), replaced by Tony J. Liddle (1989–96), replaced by Martin Richardson (1996–98), replaced by Tony J. Liddle (2001–2), replaced by Ken Johnson (2004–)).

Steve English (1980–81) (bass, replaced by Mick Moore (1981, 1984–86), replaced by Darren Parnaby (1986–87), replaced by Robbie Robertson (1988–89), replaced by Glenn Carey (1989–90), replaced by Mick Moore (1991), replaced by Dave Anderson (1992–94), replaced by Steve Ireland (1996), replaced by Gav Gray (1996–99), replaced by Andy Galloway (2001–4), replaced by Paul Brewis (2005–)); Steve Abbey (drums, replaced by Sean Taylor (1984–86, 1991–94), replaced by Sean Wilkinson (1986–87), replaced by Kyle Gibson (1988–89), replaced by Gary Young (1989–90), replaced by Sean Taylor (1991–94), replaced by Paul Ward (1996), replaced by Paul "Sid" White (1996), replaced by Niel Nattrass (1996), replaced by Mark Hancock (1996–98), replaced by Mark Wyndebank (1998–99), replaced by Phil Brewis (2001–)).

Blitzkreig is a long-running, often broken up and reformed band who matched Spinal Tap for members who came and left in the band. Blitzkrieg has broken up and reformed no fewer than four different times and had at least 32 different lineup changes since 1981. Despite the fact of the astounding number of personnel changes, the band has been regarded as a cult favorite by numerous British fans, who are apparently more tolerant of frequent lineup changes than most fans of the genre. The band started in 1981 as part of the New Wave of British heavy metal (NWOBHM) and soon had moderate success with the classic "Buried Alive" single, which brought them to the attention of the British public, just in time for them to break up and several members to go off and join Satan (the NWOBHM band, not the prerequisite deal with the devil, although ...). After a few years Ross decided to reform the band again, this time with a different lineup and produced music in the mid-eighties and then again in the nineties. After that it was endless tours in Eastern Europe, Russia, and other regions still starved for real metal a decade after the fall of the iron curtain. The band continues to this day with a new lineup of Brian Ross and a rotating cast of new musicians and will probably be a force in metal long after the original lineup is dead and gone. To their credit, "Buried Alive" was a great single.

Discography: *Time of Changes* (Castle, 1994); *Unholy Trinity* (Neat, 1984); *Blitzkrieg* (Feel The Power, 1996); *Ten* (Neat Metal, 1997); *Mists of Avalon* (Import, 1998); *A Time of Changes-Phase I* (Castle, 2003); *Absolute Power* (Edgy, 2003); *Back to No Future* (Step 1, 2003); *Absolutely Live* (Metal Nation, 2004); *Gathering Storm* (Street Anthem, 2005); *Sins and Greed* (Metal Nation, 2005); *Theatre of the Damned* (Armageddon, 2007).

BLOODSTOCK (2001–PRESENT). Bloodstock is a British open air heavy metal festival dedicated, according to its promoters, to "bring a wider choice of heavy metal bands to the UK" and to provide a forum for true metal heads to see a wide range of genre-defying acts (bloodstock.uk.com). The three-day festival brings a wide and diverse array of major and smaller acts together, leaning in 2008 towards some of the more experimental new bands such as Opeth, alongside heavyweights such as Dimmu Borgir, At the Gates, and classic acts such as Helloween. Other bands that have appeared over the years include Saxon, Children of Bodom, Metal Church, and Arch Enemy. While there have been touring festivals for metal for years (such as the Monsters of Rock tour, Ozzfest, etc.), there have been relatively few festivals dedicated to exclusively cutting-edge metal bands, and Bloodstock is a sign that if promoted correctly, fans will come to camp, drink, and listen to ferocious metal for three days on end.

BLUE CHEER (1968–PRESENT). Classic lineup: Dickie Peterson (vocals/bass), Leigh Stephens (guitar), Paul Whaley (drums).

One of the seminal proto-metal groups that helped to give birth to the genre of heavy metal, Blue Cheer helped define the notion of a "power trio" as a three-piece band that made up for its lack of members with a loud and aggressive approach to the somewhat psychedelic heavy blues rock that they played. While the band is still remembered as being one of the very first to have what is now recognized as a heavy metal approach and are widely acknowledged as progenitors in the field, they never experienced much in the way of commercial success and are perhaps one of the most important one-hit-wonders, given the significance of that one hit, a cover of Eddie Cochran's "Summertime Blues" that hit the charts in 1968. While the song was a bona fide hit, hitting number 14 on the Billboard charts, it would in fact be the band's only such hit. Formed in the San Francisco Bay area, the band was originally comprised of bassist/vocalist Dickie Peterson, guitarist Leigh Stephens, and drummer Paul Whaley.

After the release of their 1968 *Vincebus Eruptum* album (which featured "Summertime Blues"), the band released four more albums, none of which made much commercial impact, and after a variety of personnel changes, the band broke up in 1971. In the years following their split, the band was increasingly recognized for their innovations in heavy rock. In the late 1980s Peterson put together a new lineup, mainly for the purposes of touring in Europe. In 1989 Blue Cheer released the live album *Blitzkrieg over Nüremberg*, on which Peterson was accompanied by guitarist Duck McDonald and drummer Dave Salce. In 1990, the band—now with original drummer Paul Whaley back in the fold—released *Highlights & Lowlives*, their first studio album in almost twenty years. Another studio album, *Dining with Sharks*, followed in 1991, and saw McDonald replaced by Dieter Saller on guitar. In 2007, the band released yet another studio album, *Whatever Doesn't Kill You ...* which featured Duck McDonald back on guitar duties.

Discography: *Vincebus Eruptum* (Polygram, 1968); *Outsideinside* (Polygram, 1968); *New! Improved! Blue Cheer* (Philips, 1969); *Blue Cheer* (Philips, 1969); *The Original Human Being* (Philips, 1970); *Oh! Pleasant Hope* (Philips, 1971); *Blitzkrieg Over Nüremberg* (Magnum, 1989); *Dining with the Sharks* (Nibelung, 1991); *Highlights & Low Lives* (Thunderbolt, 1996); *Live in Japan* (Track, 2003); *Live Bootleg: London* (Hamburg Rockview, 2005); *What Doesn't Kill You ...* (Rainman, 2007); *Hello Tokyo Bye Bye Osaka* (Blue Cheer, 2007).

BLUE MURDER (1989–94). Classic lineup: John Sykes (guitar/vocals), Tony Franklin (bass), Carmine Appice (drums).

In a number of respects, Blue Murder's self-titled debut was a more appropriate (and more inspired) follow-up to Whitesnake's phenomenally successful 1987 *Whitesnake* album than Whitesnake's own *Slip of the Tongue*, released the same year (1989). This is because of John Sykes, whose virtuosic guitar and writing were critical elements in the success of Whitesnake's commercial breakthrough. Having been fired from Whitesnake shortly before the release of their self-titled album, Sykes went on to form Blue Murder, which released its debut in 1989. Joining him on the album are bassist Tony Franklin (ex-The Firm), and veteran drummer Carmine Appice (Vanilla Fudge, Cactus, Rod Stewart). After searching for a lead vocalist, Sykes ended up singing himself. He sounds very much like David Coverdale, with remarkable range and power, although perhaps a shade less bluesy.

The writing on the album is similar to Whitesnake, with blues-based hard rock influences manifesting themselves in epic arena rock soundscapes and rockers. Franklin's fretless bass adds some unusual ambience to the mix, while Appice's thundering drums anchor the band effectively, in a style reminiscent of his contemporary and friend John Bonham. The key sonic element here though is Sykes' explosive guitar sound, which provides the glue that holds the record together, much as it did in the 1987 *Whitesnake* album. It's a sound at once raw and refined and full of power and belies the group's power trio configuration. Sykes' writing too, while missing some of the more obvious hooks of his work with Whitesnake, is in a number of ways more interesting. Tracks like "Valley of the Kings" and "Ptolemy" tap into historical and mythical imagery in their lyrics, giving the album its own unique flavor.

While "Valley of the Kings" did well as an MTV video and the album was moderately successful, Blue Murder was not able to match the success of Sykes' former group. And while Sykes returned with a new and expanded lineup for a follow-up in 1993, the market for his style of melodic metal had shrunken considerably. Sykes has nonetheless maintained a successful solo career and has also toured consistently with the re-formed, post-Phil Lynott Thin Lizzy, of whom he was a latter-day member.

Discography: *Blue Murder* (Geffen, 1989); *Nothin' But Trouble* (Geffen, 1993); *Screaming* (Alex, 1994); *Live in Japan* (Import, 1994).

BLUE ÖYSTER CULT (1967–PRESENT). Eric Bloom (lead vocals/guitar), Donald Roeser, aka Buck Dharma (lead guitar), Allen Lanier (keyboards), Albert Bouchard (drums), Joe Bouchard (bass).

One of the most important heavy metal bands that followed the first wave of innovators—Sabbath, Zeppelin, Deep Purple—Blue Öyster Cult are perhaps best known for their sci-fi lyrical themes and epic live performances that featured some of the first uses of laser light shows. In a twist, BOC was initially masterminded by two writers and rock critics—Sandy Pearlman and Richard Meltzer, when they were college students at Stony Brook College in New York in 1967. Originally named Soft White Underbelly, Pearlman and Meltzer were the primary songwriters, while Pearlman served as the group's manager. After a bad gig review, Pearlman had the band drop their name and adopt the mantle Blue Öyster Cult. By this time, the band was made up of guitarist Donald Roeser (aka Buck Dharma), keyboardist Allen Lanier, Albert Bouchard on drums, his brother Joe Bouchard on bass, and Eric Bloom on lead vocals and guitar.

Signed by Columbia Records, the band released its debut album in 1972 which featured the heavily riffing "Cities on Flame with Rock and Roll." Their second album, *Tyranny & Mutation,* came in 1973. *Secret Treaties* in 1974, featuring the band's classic "Dominance and Submission," became their first album to chart, breaking the top 100. Regular touring and a tight live show were making the band a favorite on the concert scene. Columbia capitalized on the band's live reputation with the classic double-live album *On Your Feet or On Your Knees* in 1975. The band's big commercial breakthrough came in 1976 with the release of *Agents of Fortune,* which featured the band's hit "Don't Fear the Reaper," and became their first gold (and subsequently platinum) album. BOC continued to enjoy a run of commercial success with a string of albums and occasional hit single, culminating with *Cultosaurus Erectus* in 1981 which featured the single "Burnin' for You."

That same year, drummer Albert Bouchard left the band and was replaced by Rick Downey. And in 1984 keyboardist Lanier left. The band continued on with various personnel changes, putting out their final Columbia release, *Imaginos,* in 1988. Although the band's releases have become significantly less frequent, they have continued to tour regularly, with Dharma and Bloom being the remaining original members.

Discography: *Blue Öyster Cult* (Columbia, 1972); *Tyranny and Mutation* (Columbia, 1973); *Secret Treaties* (Columbia, 1974); *On Your Feet or on Your Knees* [live] (Columbia, 1975); *Agents of Fortune* (Columbia, 1976); *Spectres* (Columbia, 1977); *Some Enchanted Evening* (Columbia, 1978); *Mirrors* (Columbia, 1979); *Cultosaurus Erectus* (Columbia, 1980); *Fire of Unknown Origin* (Columbia, 1981); *Extraterrestrial Live* (Columbia, 1982);

Blue Öyster Cult Live (Columbia, 1982); *The Revolution by Night* (Columbia, 1983); *Club Ninja* (Koch International, 1986); *Imaginos* (Columbia, 1988); *Bad Channels* (Moonstone, 1992); *Live 1976* (Gopaco, 1994); *Heaven Forbid* (CMC International, 1998); *Champions of Rock* (EMI, 1998); *The Curse of the Hidden Mirror* (CMC International, 2001); *A Long Day's Night* [live] (Sanctuary, 2002).

BODY COUNT (1989–PRESENT). Ice-T (vocals), Ernie C (guitar), D-Roc (guitar), Mooseman (bass), Beatmaster V (drums).

Body Count is a metal/punk hybrid band led by rapper/actor Ice-T, who decided to emulate the punk rock and metal he found himself increasingly drawn to during the late eighties and early nineties. The band features Ernie C on guitar, Mooseman on bass, and Ice-T on vocals. From the beginning the band was surprisingly good with sometimes ridiculous and over-the-top lyrics, such as "KKK Bitch" and "Body Count" that featured Ice-T's humorously twisted view on race relations.

The band would become infamous in 1992 for the song "Cop Killer" that polarized politicians across the country. Sample lyrics include "Cop Killer/Better you than me, Cop Killer," "Fuck police brutality," and a final chant of "Fuck the police!"). This aroused the ire of police organizations and provoked denouncements by various politicians across the country. Although Ice-T defended the song as a response to police harassment of the African-American community, record company Time Warner eventually grew nervous and reacted to the controversy by re-releasing the album without the offending track, instead including a spoken word piece by Jello Biafra of the Dead Kennedys abut free speech. The band was inactive for many years as Ice-T spent his time releasing sporadic rap albums and acting, most notably on the television show *Law & Order: Special Victims Unit* where, ironically, he plays a cop. In recent years the band was re-formed by surviving members Ice-T and guitarist Ernie C, along with new members Bendrix on rhythm guitar, Vincent Price on bass, and TO on drums. Although Body Count was not the most popular metal band of their time, their style of punk/metal crossover was a major label alternative to the relatively safe rock and roll of the time, and despite the controversy of "Cop Killer," the band will also be remembered for their dynamic live shows.

Discography: *Body Count* (Sire, 1992); *Born Dead* (Virgin, 1994); *Violent Demise: Last Days* (Virgin, 1997); *Live in L.A.* (New Media Studio, 2005); *Murder for Hire* (Escape Music, 2006).

TOMMY BOLIN (1951–76). One of the greatest losses of the 1970s was the passing of guitarist Tommy Bolin, not so much due to what he had accomplished in his musical career, so much as what it seemed he was about to accomplish.

Beginning his career with the band Zephyr in the early seventies, the young, charismatic guitarist began playing fusion as well as rock in the band Energy, and as a result, came to the attention of superstar drummer Billy Cobham (of the Mahavishnu Orchestra), who tapped Bolin to play on his seminal 1973 solo album, *Spectrum*. Bolin established the beginning of his reputation with the album, tearing it up on tracks like "Red Baron," "Quadrant Four," and "Stratus." The album was an important step in fusion's bridging of rock and jazz and was a particularly influential work that encouraged Jeff Beck to embark on his own fusion efforts in the early 1970s.

Soon, Bolin found himself replacing Joe Walsh in the James Gang, at the latter's recommendation. Bolin went on to record a pair of albums with the band, *Bang* and *Miami,* in 1973 and 1974, respectively. His next gig was replacing Ritchie Blackmore in Deep Purple, a gig that gave him his greatest visibility. Bolin played on Purple's *Come Taste the Band* in 1975 and toured with the group. Unfortunately, it was also at this time that it became apparent that Bolin was dealing with a serious addiction to heavy drugs. But as his longtime girlfriend Karen Ulibarri noted after his death, "The only person who could tell Tommy to cool it was Tommy" (Young).

It was after leaving Purple that expectations for Bolin really began to rise. Having released his outstanding solo debut *Teaser* in 1975, the album had brilliantly showcased the performer's breadth and depth with an eclectic collection of inspired performances from Bolin on both guitar and vocals, on songs that ranged from hard rock to reggae and fusion to funk. Bolin had put together a crack band including ex-Frank Zappa saxophonist Norma Jean Bell and was touring in support of his second solo album, *Private Eyes.* On December 4, 1976, the day after the last night of a tour supporting Jeff Beck, Bolin was found dead of a heroin overdose. The guitarist was 25 years old.

Discography: *Teaser* (Nemperor, 1975); *Private Eyes* (Columbia, 1976); *Naked, Vol. 2* (Tommy Bolin Archives, 2007); *The Ultimate: The Best of Tommy Bolin* (Geffen, 1989); *Live!* (Tommy Bolin Lives, 1994); *From the Archives, Vol. 1* (Rhino, 1996); *Live at Ebbets Field 1974* [1999] (Zebra, 1997); *Live at Northern Lights Recording Studios 9/22/76* (Tommy Bolin Archives, 1997); *Live at Ebbets Field 1976* (Tommy Bolin Archives, 1997); *Bottom Shelf* (Tommy Bolin Archives, 1997); *From the Archives, Vol. 2* (Zebra, 1998); *Come Taste the Man* (Tommy Bolin Archives, 1999); *Snapshot* (Tommy Bolin Archives/ Purple Pyramid, 2000); *Energy* (Tommy Bolin Archives, 2000); *Naked* (Tommy Bolin Archives, 2002); *Albany, NY 9/20/76* [live] (Tommy Bolin Archives, 2004); *Live at the Jet Bar* (Tommy Bolin Archives, 2004); *Bolin* (Lemon, 2004); *Whips and Roses* (Steamhammer/ SPV, 2006); *Whips and Roses II* (SPV, 2006); *The Glen Holly Jams/After Hours* (Tommy Bolin Archives, 2006); *The Jet Bar* (Tommy Bolin Arcives, 2006); *The Bottom Shelf Volume 1* (Tommy Bolin Archives, 2006); *Ultimate: Redux* (Friday, 2008).

BOLT THROWER (1986–PRESENT). Alan West (vocals, replaced by Karl Willets, then Martin VanDrunen, Dave Ingram, now Willets again), Gavin Ward (guitar), Barry Thompson (guitar), Jo Bench (bass), Andy Whale (drums, replaced by Alex Thomas, then Martin Kearns).

Bolt Thrower is a long-running English death metal band who have refined and perfected one of the most distinctive and aggressive styles of the subgenre. The band started in Birmingham, which, due to its depressed economic conditions and unusually gloomy weather, has inspired countless metal bands. Bolt Thrower is unique in that their lyrical themes are not so much about rotting corpses with words taken straight from a medical dictionary but they have concentrated their lyrics more on battles, armies, and warfare (including a unique bit of metal product placement, where the band teamed with the company behind the Realm of Chaos game, leading to the *Warhammer* record where most songs were about events in the game). Like Napalm Death, John Peel, always looking out for aggressive music, helped discover the band and featured them on his radio program on BBC1 and helped them record a Peel Sessions record. Bolt Thrower also have the distinction of having one of the few women in death metal, Jo Bench on bass. The band has evolved gradually away from the completely sped-up style of the early death metal sound to use more dynamics and slower parts when necessary, backed by Willets's bearlike growl.

The band floundered a bit in the late nineties when Willets and original drummer Whale departed, but after a series of less-than-stellar tours and records, Willets returned in 2004 and the band has continued to tour with the renewed lineup since then. The band's website is also well worth checking out, not just for the usual news and lyrics, but also for the band members' profiles, where each member is ranked according to battle honors and tours of duty. Bolt Thrower may be one of the most consistent bands in death metal history and certainly is one of the most fascinating bands in that genre.

Discography: *In Battle There Is No Law* (Future Shock, 1988); *Realm of Chaos* (Combat, 1989); *Warmaster* (Combat, 1991); *The IVth Crusade* (Combat, 1993); *Who Dares Wins* (Combat, 1994); *... For Victory* (Earache, 1995); *Mercenary* (Metal Blade, 1998); *Realm of Chaos* (Earache, 1999); *Honor Valor Pride* (Metal Blade, 2002); *Those Once Loyal* (Metal Blade, 2005).

BON JOVI (1983–PRESENT). Jon Bon Jovi (vocals), Ritchie Sambora (guitar), David Bryan (keyboards), Tico Torres (drums).

One of the most successful groups from the "hair metal" era of the 1980s, Bon Jovi's particular blend of pop sensibility and working-class lyrical themes, along with a string of MTV videos showcasing Jon Bon Jovi's good looks, gave them a wider appeal and longer career life than almost any of their direct peers, to the extent that they have continued to enjoy a viable career into the new millennium.

Jon Bongiovi (his real name) got his start through his cousin Tony Bongiovi, who owned the famous New York City recording studio The Power Station. After recording a series of demos at the studio, one of them, "Runaway," became a local hit on New Jersey radio. Bongiovi subsequently put together a band featuring his longtime friend keyboardist David Rashbaum, drummer Tico Torres, bassist Alec John Such, and guitarist Dave Sabo. The band soon became the object of an intense bidding war between a number of record labels. Ultimately, the band signed with Polygram in 1983. Before the release of the band's debut, Bongiovi changed his name to Bon Jovi, Rashbaum changed his to Bryan (his middle name), and Richie Sambora replaced Dave Sabo (who would later go on to success with Skid Row).

Released in 1984, *Bon Jovi* was a success with "Runaway" replicating its previous success as a hit single on a national scale. Unfortunately, Tony Bongiovi sued the band, claiming that he had served to develop their successful sound. The suit was ultimately settled out of court. The band's sophomore album, *7800° Fahrenheit*, released in 1985, also did well. Seeking a higher level of success, the band hired professional songwriter Desmond Child to collaborate on new material, which was subsequently test marketed to teens in the New York/New Jersey area. All of Bon Jovi's R&D paid off with the 1986 album *Slippery When Wet*, which would go on to sell over nine million copies. Aided by a series of lush performance-oriented videos on MTV, the album made the band superstars. Featuring two number 1 hits in "You Give Love a Bad Name" and "Livin' on a Prayer," and the top ten "Wanted Dead or Alive," the album became the quintessential album of the pop-metal/hair band era.

Bon Jovi (Photofest)

New Jersey (1988) utilized the same production template and achieved almost the same level of success, giving the band five more top ten hits, including the two number 1 hits "Bad Medicine" and "I'll Be There for You." The album sold over five million copies and was supported by more MTV videos and an 18-month-long tour. After the tour, the band went on hiatus, during which Jon Bon Jovi provided the soundtrack to *Young Guns II*. The soundtrack, released in 1990 as *Blaze of Glory*, produced two hit singles, and its western imagery only cemented the band's all-American appeal.

By the early nineties, the shelf-life of hair bands was ebbing, and grunge would soon come to dominate the music scene. Nonetheless, such was Bon Jovi's appeal that *Keep the Faith*, released in 1992, was a commercial success and showed that the band had staying power, and a loyal following. As the band continued recording and touring into the nineties, they gradually eschewed the trappings of heavy metal, trimmed their hair and focused on songwriting that tapped into the heartland themes that were the cornerstones of their lyrics. 1995 saw the release of *These Days*. Branching out, Jon Bon Jovi began a part-time acting career, appearing in the film *Moonlight and Valentino* in 1996. A year later, his debut solo album was released.

In the year 2000 the band released *Crush*, which featured the hits "It's My Life" and "Thank You for Loving Me," and ultimately sold eight million copies. The band continued to perform well throughout most of the decade, releasing the albums *Bounce* (2002), *This Left Feels Right* (2003)—featuring rerecordings of many of their previous hits—and the box CD/DVD set *100,000,000 Bon Jovi Fans Can't Be Wrong* (2004). *Have a Nice Day* followed in 2005, and featured the song "Who Says You Can't Go Home," which was subsequently released as a duet with country singer Jennifer Nettles from the band Sugarland. The single became a hit on the country charts, and hinted at Bon Jovi's country crossover appeal, ultimately winning a Grammy Award for Country Performance with Vocals.

In 2007 the band took their mainstream crossover appeal into a country direction, releasing the Nashville-inspired *Lost Highways*, which featured duets with LeAnn Rimes and Big & Rich. The album debuted at number 1, becoming the band's third number 1 album.

Discography: *Bon Jovi* (Mercury, 1984); *7800° Fahrenheit* (Mercury, 1985); *Slippery When Wet* (Mercury, 1986); *New Jersey* (Mercury, 1988); *Keep the Faith* (Mercury, 1992); *Live* (Mercury, 1993); *These Days* (Mercury, 1995); *Crush* (Island, 2000); *Bounce* (Island, 2002); *This Left Feels Right* (Island, 2003); *Have a Nice Day* (Island, 2005); *Live from the Have a Nice Day Tour* (Island Def Jam, 2006); *Lost Highway* (Island, 2007); *Cross Road* (Mercury, 2007).

BORIS (1994–PRESENT). Wata (guitar), Takeshi (bass), Atsuko (drums/vocals).

Boris are a Japanese metal/punk/garage/noise band that have experimented wildly with styles and genres across their many albums. The band has also collaborated with drone metal band Sunn O))). Boris was formed in 1994 and immediately looked as though they were a walking identity crisis, never quite sure what style or genre they wanted to embrace from album to album, or sometimes within the same album. Their collaboration with drone metal pioneers Sunn O))) led to the album *Altar*, which managed to combine the best of both groups, Boris' experimentation with the long drawn-out chords of Sunn O))) to create a new hybrid sound that mixes the drone and doom metal of Sunn O))) with the dynamics of Boris. The mixture of the two bands is particularly effective in tracks such as "N.L.T.," in which Atsuko plays bowed cymbal and gong along with guest star Bill Herzog on bass, or "Etna" and "Bloodswamp" in which both bands play together on all tracks. This breaks new ground in avant garde metal in which there is no real resemblance to traditional metal song structure, but more of a resemblance of the experiments of Tony Conrad and Steve Recih, along with some of Sunn O)))'s best. The latest record, the live collaboration with Japanese noise king Merzbow is a glorious reinvention of older Boris songs such as "Pink."

Discography: *Absolutego* [Special Low Frequency Version] (Southern Lord, 2001); *Amplifier Worship* (Man's Ruin, 2001); *Megatone* (Vivid Sound, 2002); *Akuma No Uta* (Southern Lord, 2005); *Mabuta No Ura* (3D, 2005); *Boris at Last-Feedbacker* (Conspiracy, 2005); *Sun Baked Snow Cave* (Hydra Head, 2005); *Flood* (Sony International, 2005); *Archive Volume One: Live 96–98* (Archive, 2005); *Archive Volume Two: Drumless Shows* [Live] (Archive, 2005); *Pink* (Southern Lord, 2006); *Vein* (Important, 2006); *Final* (3D, 2006); *Dronevil: Final* (Inoxia, 2006); *Rainbow* (Drag City, 2007); *Rock Dream* [Live] (Southern Lord, 2007); *Archive Volume Three: 2 Long Songs* [Live] (Archive, 2007) *Boris with Merzbow Rock Dream* (Southern Lord, 2008).

BRITNY FOX (1986–92; 1993–PRESENT). Dizzy Dean Davidson (lead vocals/guitar, 1986–90), Michael Kelly Smith (lead guitar), Billy Childs (bass), Tommy Paris (lead vocals/guitar, 1991–92).

Bearing a superficial resemblance to their fellow Philly chums in Cinderella (the boys shared hairdressers and vocal teachers), Britny Fox were the Slade to Cinderella's Aerosmith—not a fair fight, really. Still, singer/guitarist Dizzy Dean Davidson had a good screaming voice and a knack for writing straightforward hooky rockers. Having relocated to L.A. from Philly, the band hooked up with former Cinderella guitarist Michael Kelly Smith. After securing a deal with Columbia, through their fairy godmothers in Cinderella the band released their debut, *Britny Fox*, in 1988. Supported by its MTV video, the single "Long Way to Love" helped the album to a charting position, but the follow-up "Girlschool" failed to generate much excitement.

Diminishing the glam influence on the following year's *Boys in Heat* did little to expand the band's fan base, and singer Dizzy left the band for parts unknown. Returning with new singer Tommy Paris, the band released *Bite Down Hard*, but even with guest appearances by such excellent spellers as Poison's Rikki Rocket and guitarist Zakk Wylde, the band couldn't energize the faithful, and split up shortly thereafter.

In recent years, various incarnations of the band have reunited for limited touring, most recently a lineup assembled by original bassist Billy Childs.

Discography: *Britny Fox* (Columbia, 1988); *Boys in Heat* (Columbia, 1989); *Bite Down Hard* (East West, 1991); *Long Way to Live!* (Spitfire, 2000); *Springhead Motorshark* (Spitfire, 2003); *Live at Froggy's* (Paradise Media Partners, 2005); *The Best of Britny Fox* (Sony, 2001); *The Bite Down Hard Demo Sessions* (Paradise Musicwerks, 2005).

BUCKCHERRY (1999–2002; 2006–PRESENT). Josh Todd (vocals), Keith Nelson (guitar), Stevie D. (Dacanay, guitars), Jimmy Ashhurst (bass), Xavier Muriel (drums).

Emerging in the mid-nineties in L.A., Buckcherry played an AC/DC-flavored brand of old-school rock. The band was formed when guitarist Keith Nelson and vocalist Josh Todd were introduced, as legend would have it, by their mutual tattoo artist. After winning a contract with Dreamworks Records, their debut self-titled album was released in 1999 and featured the hits "Lit Up" and "Check Your Head," which helped to make the album a success. After the follow-up *Time Bomb* failed to match the success of its predecessor, the band members went their separate ways.

Deciding to try again three years later, Nelson and Todd put together a new lineup and put out the album *15*, comprised of fifteen tracks that they had recorded in fifteen days. Hitting the road behind the album, they reinvigorated their fan base and tapped into a legion of fans who still appreciated the old-school, AC/DC and Guns N' Roses–influenced rock and roll that the band did so well. On the basis of tracks like the vulgar yet funky stripper favorite "Crazy Bitch," and the more radio-friendly "Everything" and "Sorry," the album went platinum, and set the stage for the follow-up *Black Butterfly* in 2008.

Discography: *Buckcherry* (DreamWorks, 1999); *Time Bomb* (DreamWorks, 2001); *Time Bomb* [Japan Bonus Track] (Dreamworks, 2002); *15* (Eleven Seven, 2006); *Black Butterfly* (Atlantic, 2008).

BUDGIE (1971–85). Classic lineup: Burke Shelley (vocals, bass), Tony Bourge (guitar), Raymond Phillips (drums).

Welsh proto-metal group Budgie enjoyed success in the UK but never really hit international stardom, though they influenced many groups that would follow, due to their riff-ready songs and singer/bassist Burke Shelley's piercing vocals. Coming together in Cardiff, Wales, in 1967, the band, consisting of Shelley, guitarist Tony Bourge, and drummer Raymond Phillips, released their self-titled debut in 1971 on MCA records. Along with their two follow-up recordings, 1972's *Squawk* and 1973's *Never Turn Your Back on a Friend,* the band purveyed a Sabbath-like set of riff-oriented songs that soon built them a sizeable European following.

With Phillips leaving in 1974, a series of lineup changes occurred over the years, with Shelley the only remaining original. The band would continue under Shelley's leadership, releasing albums regularly until the mid-eighties when it finally split up.

Discography: *Budgie* (Roadrunner, 1971); *Squawk* (Roadrunner, 1972); *Never Turn Your Back on a Friend* (MCA, 1973); *In for the Kill!* (Repertoire, 1974); *Bandolier* (A&M, 1975); *If I Were Brittania I'd Waive the Rules* (Repertoire, 1976); *Impeckable* (Repertoire, 1978); *Power Supply* (Active, 1980); *Nightflight* (RCA, 1981); *Deliver Us from Evil* (RCA, 1982); *Life in San Antonio* [Live] (Noteworthy, 2002); *You're All Living in Cuckooland* (Noteworthy, 2006); *Definitive Anthology* (Alex, 1996); *An Ecstasy of Fumbling: The Definitive Anthology* (Repertoire, 1996); *The Very Best of Budgie* (MCA International, 1998); *Heavier Than Air: Live on the BBC* (Griffin, 1998); *We Came We Saw* (*Live on the BBC*) (Pilot, 1998); *The Last Stage* (Noteworthy, 2004); *Out of the Cage into the Vault* (Pilot, 2004); *Radio Sessions 1974 & 1978* (Noteworthy, 2006); *The BBC Recordings* [Live] (Noteworthy, 2006).

BULLET BOYS (1988–2000). Marq Torien (vocals), Mick Sweda (guitar), Lonnie Vincent (bass), and Jimmy d'Anda (drums).

A somewhat bluesy-sounding L.A. metal band, Bullet Boys emerged on the national scene with Van Halen–like buzz that started with the fact that they shared producer Ted Templeman and ended with the superficial similarities between blond-haired frontman Marq Torien and David Lee Roth. Riding the last wave of the L.A. hair metal scene, the band's stock in trade was sleazy rock, perhaps best displayed in such songs as "Do Me Raw" and "Smooth Up (In Ya)." After an initial splash on MTV, the band's fortunes declined, and while they moved in a bluesier direction (even covering bluesman Robben Ford's "Talk to Your Daughter"), they quickly faded from the national spotlight.

Discography: *Bulletboys* (Warner Bros., 1988); *Freakshow* (Warner Bros., 1991); *Za-Za* (Warner Bros., 1993); *Acid Monkey* (Swordholio, 1995); *Burning Cats and Amputees* (Cleopatra, 2000); *Sophie* (2003); *Smooth Up in Ya: The Best of the Bulletboys* (Cleopatra, 2006); *Behind the Orange Curtain* [Live] (Crash, 2007); *Freakshow/Za-Za* (Wounded Bird, 2005); *Greatest Hits* (Lemon, 2005).

BURNING WITCH (1996–98). Edgy59 (vocals, guitar), G. Stuart Dahlquist (subharmonics), Jamie Boggy Sykes (battledrums, replaced by B.R.A.D. on war drums).

Burning Witch was one of the key new metal bands of the eighties that combined both a serious appreciation for metal as an artform, with dark and satanic lyrics, as well as new and innovative styles of drone-based music (not unlike the early Velvet Underground or the experiments of Indian-influenced composer Lamonte Young). While Burning Witch was not active for that long, they did manage to record two highly acclaimed but difficult to find records, the *Towers* EP and the *Rift.Canyon.Dream* EP, both of which highlighted the ultra-heavy sound the band was aiming for. According to the Southern Lord biography of the band, they created "ultra-heavy dark minimalist riffs, bombastic bass and plodding war drums collided with vocals which alter between a nasal melodic singing voice and a brutal tortured demented scream/shriek" (Southern Lord). Members of the band went on to join Asva and Savant, as well as a little unknown band called Sunn O))) who managed to revitalize metal almost all by themselves.

Discography: *Towers ...* (Slap a Ham Records, 1998); *Rift.Canyon.Dream* [EP] (Merciles records, 1998); *Crippled Lucifer* (Southern Lord, 1998, reissue 2008).

WILLIAM S. BURROUGHS (1914–97). William S. Burroughs was one of the most influential experimental writers of the twentieth century and a key writer from the Beat Generation who amazed audiences with his cut and paste style in books such as *Naked Lunch*. Burroughs was also one of the most ground-breaking American authors in terms of trying to experiment with words and definitions and may have been one of the inadvertent creators of the term *heavy metal*. Burroughs was not the inventor of the term in its current sense, but he may have been among the first to use it in his book *The Soft Machine*, where a character named Uranium Willy is also known as the "Heavy Metal Kid"—in this case using the term to refer to drugs or drug addiction. It is unclear if later writers such as Sandy Pearlman borrowed the term to describe music or simply came up with it on their own (see also the introduction). Although Burroughs was not much a fan of contemporary music, he may have been amused that his term was used to describe a genre of music that included some of the most twisted and dark music currently being made. Burroughs would also have no doubt admired the copious use of drugs, particularly heroin, by many in the metal community.

BURZUM (1991–PRESENT). Varg (Kristian) Vikernes (vocals/guitar/bass/keyboards/drums).

In the realm of black metal, Burzum is one of the key bands who helped to establish the parameters of both music and in living the lifestyle. Burzum was the unholy brainchild of murderous ex-Mayhem bassist Varg Vikernes (aka Count Grishnakh). Vikernes developed Burzum as an ongoing project where he played all the instruments. The band served as a vehicle not only for Vikernes' idea about expanding the parameters of black metal but also for articulating his own twisted philosophy. While much of black metal is particularly brutal, much of the work of Burzum is actually more like ambient trance music, only designed to allow the listener to experience the particular version of "magick" that Vikernes has encoded in the songs. Vikernes has been in jail for almost a decade now for murdering Euronymous of Mayhem, and, after an escape attempt several years ago, it is unclear if he will be released any time soon. Vikernes was also a Tolkien aficionado, and the name Count Grishnakh is taken from an orc in the J. R. R. Tolkien book *The Two Towers*, and the name Burzum is a word used by Tolkien on the inscription of the one ring.

Discography: *Det Som engang Var* (Mysanthropy, 1993); *Hvis lysetTar Oss* (Mysanthropy, 1994); *Filosofem* (Fereal House, 1996); *Balder's Dod* (Mysanthropy, 1997); *Daudi Baldrs* (Mysanthropy, 1997); *Hlidskjalf* (Misanthropy, 1999).

C

CACOPHONY (1986–90). Peter Marrino (vocals), Marty Friedman (guitar), Jason Becker (guitar, bass, drums).

Cacophony was a virtuoso metal band with actual songs and melodies unlike other artists such as Yngwie Malmsteen. Cacophony was started in 1986, and their first record, *Speed Metal Symphony*, was a combination of classic metal riffs along with classical flourishes that showed that alongside the great Kat's example, classical music and metal made a natural fit. The second record did not sell nearly as well as the first, and the band, discouraged by the lack of sales despite their virtuosity of the two axe men, soon fell apart. Friedman later joined Megadeth and Becker briefly played in the solo records of David Lee Roth. Becker retired from performing when he was diagnosed with Lou Gehrig's Disease (ALS) in 1990, but continues to work on music and has worked with other musicians to bring his ideas to life.

Discography: *Speed Metal Symphony* (Shrapnel, 1987); *Go Off!* (Shrapnel, 1989); *Transmission* (Sestinas, 2006).

CANDLEMASS (1985–PRESENT). John Lanquist (vocals, replaced by Messiah Marcolin, Tomas Vikstrom, Bjorn Fklodkvist, Messiah, Robert Lowe), Mats Bjorkman (guitar, other instruments), Lars Johansson (guitar, other instruments), Leif Edling (bass), Matz Ekstroem (drums, replaced by Jan Lindh).

Candelemass is a Swedish doom metal band, who play slow and lumbering Sabbath–type riffs along with the King Diamond meets Klaus Nomi–esque operatic vocals of lead singer Messiah Marcolin (who had a habit of wearing a monk's robe on stage). With Marcolin's departure after the *Live* record, the band recruited new singer Tomas Vikstrom and recorded the *Chapter VI* record, which saw the band in disarray, and the law of diminishing returns took over, leading to the band's demise in 1994. An ill-advised reunion in 1998 with new vocalist Bjorn Fklodkvist and a completely new lineup except of bassist Edling went nowhere slow. After going nowhere, the band finally called it quits in 1999. However, the band's classic lineup reconvened for a reunion in 2002 and 2004. Sadly, following this Messiah departed the band yet again, and the band rather pointlessly carried on with Edling Lindh and yet another new lineup. In their prime (the Messiah years) Candlemass proved that a metal band could be slow and evil, without having to go into lyrical flights of fancy. This band would be enjoyed by fans of early Black Sabbath or St. Vitus.

Discography: *Epicus Doomicus Mettalicus* (Leviathan, 1986); *Nightfall* (Restless, 1987); *Ancient Dream* (Capital, 1988); *Tales of Creation* (Capital, 1989); *Live* (Metal Blade, 1991); *Chapter VI* (Import, 1995); *Dactylis Glomerata* (MFN, 1998); *From the 13th Sun* (Music for Nations, 1999); *Doomed for Live Reunion 2002* (Powerline, 2003); *Diamonds of Doom* (Powerline, 2003); *Candlemass* (Nuclear Blast, 2005); *King of the Grey Islands* (Nuclear Blast, 2007).

CANNIBAL CORPSE (1988–PRESENT). Chris Barnes (vocals, replaced by George "Corpsegrinder" Fischer), Pat O'Brien (guitar, replaced by several), Bob Rusay (guitar, replaced by Rob Barrett, Jack Owen, then Rob Barrett), Alex Webster (bass), Paul Mazurkiewicz (drums).

Cannibal Corpse are one of the most brutal and gruesome of all the death metal bands, and along with the band Death and Carcass, they were also one of the key bands to embrace the extremely complex medical terms that became common to that genre. Not for the faint of heart, or anyone who thinks that bands like Limp Bizkit and Korn are "too heavy," the band practically invented the limitless potential of death metal by making the most obscene and perverse music ever made in the genre. A brutal assault of noise, shrieking solos, and lyrics about necrophilia and being skinned alive, the band is brilliant in their own way.

Discography: *Eaten Back to Life* (Metal Blade, 1990); *Butchered at Birth* (Metal Blade, 1991); *Tomb of the Mutilated* (Metal Blade, 1992); *The Bleeding* (Metal Blade, 1994); *Vile* (Metal Blade, 1996); *Gallery of Suicide* (1998); *Bloodthirst* (Metal Blade, 1999); *Live Cannibalism* (Metal Blade, 2000); *Gore Obsessed* (Metal Blade, 2002); *The Wretched Spawn* (Metal Blade, 2004); *Kill* (Metal Blade, 2006).

CARCASS (1985–95, 2007–PRESENT). Sanjiv (vocals, replaced by Bill Steer, Jeffrey Walker, Bill Steer), Michael Amott (guitar), Jeff Walker (bass), Ken Owen (drums, replaced by Daniel Erlandsson).

Carcass were one of the earliest and most important of the new generation of grindcore/death metal bands. The band was started by Steer, Owen, and Walker in 1984 and was quickly hailed for the brutal power of their live shows and the uncompromising power of their first record, the classic *Reek of Putrefaction*.

Influential British DJ and taste maker John Peel was an early fan, who featured some of their work on his radio show on BBC One. When anxious listeners called in to complain, an undeterred Peel continued to champion the band, featuring them on one of his Peel Sessions shows, which was later released as a live EP. The band couldn't carry on long, due to the fact that one could only get so fast and extreme without becoming a parody of oneself. The band broke up seemingly for good in 1995. (All the band members had gone to other projects—the most successful was Amott who joined the Swedish death metal band Arch Enemy), but in 2007, the band surprised many in the death metal community by reuniting with almost all the original members (drummer Ken Owen, who had been a crucial part of the band's sound since its inception, was too ill to take part).

The band are touring to this day and re-releasing their old material on Earache Records. It seems that a new generation raised on emo bands and the national retail store chain Hot Topic may be ready to embrace a more extreme and brutal form of music than they were force-fed by the radio and MTV.

Discography: *Reek of Putrefaction* (UK Earache, 1988); *Symphonies of Sickness* (UK Earache, 1989, Earache/Relativity, 1990); *The Peel Sessions* [EP] (UK Strange Fruit, 1989).

CATHEDRAL (1990–PRESENT). Lee Dorian (vocals), Adam Lehan (guitar), Gary Jennings (guitar), Mark Griffiths (bass), Ben Mochrie (drums).

Cathedral were a reaction to the grindcore scene led by former Napalm Death lead singer Lee Dorian. They played incredibly slow, almost dirge-like death metal. After Dorian was unceremoniously booted from Napalm Death, perhaps one of the most innovative bands of the grindcore era, he soon found common cause with Griffiths and Jennings who shared his fascination with early Black Sabbath and the slow-as-all-hell riffage of the Melvins to create one of the ultimate slow doom metal bands. The band soon signed to Earache and released numerous records of slow metal. Highly recommended for fans of Sabbath, or curious Napalm Death fans wondering what it would sound like if the formula was inverted.

Discography: *Echoes of Dirges Into the Naves* [EP] (Mex. MM/PPR, 1990); *Forest of Equilibrium* (Earache/Relativity, 1992); *Soul Sacrifice* [EP] (Earache/Columbia, 1992); *The Ethereal Mirror* (Earache/Columbia, 1993); *Cosmic Requiem* [EP](Earache/Columbia, 1994); *In Memorium* ([EP] (UK Rough Trade, 1994); *Statik Majik* [EP] (UK Earache, 1994); *Carnival Bizarre* (Earache, 1995); *Supernatural Birth Machine* (Earache, 1996); *Caravan Beyond Redemption* (Earache, 1998); *Endtyme* (Earache, 2001); *The VIIth Coming* (Spitfire, 2002); *The Garden of Earthly Delights* (Nuclear Blast, 2006); *Ensemble for the Midevil* (Black Magic/Journess, 2006); *The Bridge* (Cathedral, 2007).

CELTIC FROST (1984–96, 2002–PRESENT). Tom Warrior (vocals/guitar), Oliver Amberg (guitar), Martin Eric Ain (bass, replaced by Dominic Steiner, Curt Bryant, Ain again), Reed St. Mark (drums, replaced by Stephen Priestly).

Celtic Frost are a classic Swiss black metal band with symphonic touches, and among the most important bands in modern metal. The band started out as the influential Hellhammer, which grew to prominence on demo tapes and word of mouth before slowing down the pace and changing its name to the more mysterious Celtic Frost. Since inception the band has been led by Tom Warrior (Thomas Fischer), who has a unique vision and blend of Norse mythology and Satanism.

The best of Celtic Frost is both majestic and frightening, such as classic records *To Mega Therion* and *Into the Pandemonium*, but the band was increasingly unstable and after a new lineup, the band made the awful *Cold Lake* record. They then dissolved in shame when the comeback record *Vanity/Nemesis* was not enough to bring back the faithful (even with Ain back in the fold) who felt betrayed by the pop and glam of *Cold Lake*. The band reformed in 2006 to release the utterly brutal, beautiful, evocative, and scary *Monotheist*, which demonstrated to fans that Fischer, along with Ain, could still deliver the goods.

Despite their relatively limited output (not counting the Hellhammer work), Celtic Frost have been an enormously influential band on the black metal scene as well as to any new bands that try for a combination of the macabre and the heavy. Few bands have gone to the places that Celtic Frost have gone to and survived, and most likely very few bands should even try. Avoid *Cold Lake* like the plague, though; it is the quintessential "sellout" record with little input from Warrior and a disastrous attempt at mainstream recognition. The rest of the catalog is indispensable.

Discography: *Morbid Tales* (Metal Blade, 1984); *To Mega Therion* (Noise, 1985); *Into the Pandemonium* (Noise, 1987); *Cold Lake* (Noise, 1988); *Vanity/Nemesis* (RCA, 1989); *Tragic Serenades* [EP] (Combat, 1990); *Morbid Tales/Emperor's Return* (Noise, 1997); *Monotheist* (Century Media, 2006).

CINDERELLA (1983–PRESENT). Tom Keifer (vocals/guitar), Eric Brittingham (bass), Jeff LaBar (guitar), Fred Coury (drums).

An early winner in the hair metal sweepstakes of the 1980s, Cinderella did well, with a series of best-selling albums and MTV videos but should have had a more successful career due to their solid blues-rock roots and general songwriting talents of lead vocalist/guitarist Tom Keifer. With a style that combined the bluesy swagger of Humble Pie and AC/DC with a more pop-oriented sense of melody, the band had significant mainstream appeal. And in frontman Tom Keifer Cinderella had the best of Aerosmith's Steven Tyler *and* Joe Perry, a situation that was aptly demonstrated in concert and videos when the guitar-less singer would dramatically catch a guitar thrown by a roadie just in time to play a lead break without missing a beat.

Cinderella came together in 1983 in Philadelphia, Pennsylvania, and developed an all-original act with Keifer as the main songwriter. In 1985 they were spotted performing in a nightclub by none other than Jon Bon Jovi, who told his A&R person about the band. The band was subsequently signed to Mercury Records and veteran producer/engineer Andy Johns was brought on board to produce the album. While session drummer Jody Cortez performed on the debut album, the band's new permanent drummer, Fred Coury, joined in time to appear on the album jacket and to tour with the band. The album, *Night Songs*, was released in June of 1986. After a slow start, the album began to chart after the band had toured as a supporting act and had videos for "Shake Me" and "Nobody's Fool" in rotation on MTV, and the album earned platinum status by the year's end.

The band's second album, *Long Cold Winter*, was released in July of 1988, and largely replicated the success of the band's debut. Featuring the power ballad "Don't Know What You've Got (Till It's Gone)" and the rockers "Gypsy Road" and "The Last Mile," the band continued to demonstrate a flair for melding seventies hard rock sensibility with eighties flash.

After taking a year off to record their third album, *Heartbreak Station* was released in November 1990. The album found the band expanding their sound by going further back into the seventies for inspiration and coming back with a somewhat rootsier sound. The lead-off single "Shelter Me" was a Stones-like rocker, from its title (reminiscent of "Gimme Shelter") and intro of dobro slide guitar to the black female backup singers and honking sax solo. While the album initially did well, achieving gold status fairly quickly, it failed to reach the platinum status of its predecessors. Internally, the band faced its own set of problems, first when drummer Coury quit the band, and more seriously when Keifer suffered problems with his vocal cords that necessitated surgery and therapy.

By the time the band's fourth album, *Still Climbing*, was released in late 1994, the grunge movement was in full swing, and the band's style had gone out of fashion. After the album failed to chart significantly, Mercury dropped the band. In the aftermath, Keifer relocated to Nashville to work as a songwriter, managing to place songs with Lynyrd Skynyrd and Andy Griggs. Through the years, Cinderella has periodically re-formed to tour as part of package tours, most significantly in 2006 when they teamed with Poison for a tour to celebrate the 20-year anniversary of their respective debut albums.

Discography: *Night Songs* (Mercury, 1986); *Long Cold Winter* (Mercury, 1988); *Heartbreak Station* (Mercury, 1990); *Live* (Alex, 1991); *Still Climbing* (Mercury, 1994); *Live at the Key Club* (Cleopatra, 1999); *In Concert* (Cleopatra, 2004).

CIRCUS OF POWER (1988–94). Alex Mitchell (vocals), Ryan Maher (drums), Rickey Beck Maler (guitar), Gary Sunshine (guitar), Zowie (bass).

New York City's Circus of Power played a rough and ready brand of hard rock that emulated the streetwise gutter rock of Guns N' Roses while tapping into a particularly New York sense of the street. While both Guns N' Roses and Circus of Power marked a departure from the "pretty boy" images of the pop/hair metal of the late eighties, it might be argued that part of GNR's appeal was that, under the veneer of dirt, they could clean up pretty well. Circus of Power offered no such illusions. And while they offered some satisfying heavy rock ("Motor," "Mama Tequila"), they never had the instrumental chops or songwriting skills to compete on GNR's level.

After playing the New York club scene in the late eighties, the band signed with RCA Records, releasing their self-titled debut in 1988. The album established the band's heavy blues-based approach to sleazy rock and roll. *Still Alive* followed the same format in 1989. In 1990 the band released their third album, *Vices*, and brought new bassist Zowie into the band while Gary Sunshine moved to second guitar. After *Vices* RCA dropped the band from their roster. Columbia, however, took a chance on the group, releasing their fourth album, *Magic & Madness*, in 1993. *Magic & Madness* failed to stir much excitement, however, in part due to the fact that the band's brand of sleaze rock was quickly going out of fashion. After Columbia dropped the band they officially disbanded, although they have occasionally reunited for one-off shows.

Discography: *Circus of Power* (RCA, 1988); *Still Alive* (RCA, 1989); *Vices* (RCA, 1990); *Magic & Madness* (Columbia, 1993).

CIRITH UNGOL (1972–92). Tim Baker (vocals), Greg Lindstrom (guitar, replaced by Jerry Fogle, replaced by Jim Baraza), Michael Flint (bass, replaced by Vernon Green), Robert Garvin (drums).

Cirith Ungol are an American band from Los Angeles who played a type of hard rock mixed with metal originally, but eventually evolved into a dark progressive band. Their name came from a tower under the dominion of Sauron in J. R. R. Tolkien's *Lord of the Rings* trilogy. The band played a metal style similar to the New Wave of British metal early on, although the original band predated that scene by almost a decade. Because of their name, they flirted with some sword and sorcery themed songs, and to further make sure that they never reached the charts, Cirith Ungol developed progressive leanings thrown in for good measure towards the end of their career. Despite the ardent desire of many fans, the band has not indicated any plans to reunite to tour or record. While unknown to many modern metal fans their work is worth finding, especially the first two records.

Discography: *Frost & Fire* (One Way, 1981); *King of the Dead* (Enigma, 1984); *One Foto in Hell* (Metal Blade, 1986); *Paradise Lost* (Restless, 1991).

"COOKIE MONSTER" VOCAL STYLE. Despite his seemingly benign appearance, the cookie-addicted muppet has inspired a legion of metal singers to try and emulate his gravely voice. Since the start of the grindcore and death metal movements, the "Cookie Monster" vocals of bands such as Napalm Death, Death, Kreator, and countless others have made the unintelligible growl the new vocal de rigueur trick of the day (although many singers also go back and forth between singing and growling like Cookie Monster).

It is ironic to think that when the creators of *Sesame Street* envisioned this muppet, they never thought he would one day become the inspiration for countless heavy metal singers and a force in the black and death metal scenes. In recent years, Cookie Monster has even changed his image to become a "healthy monster" in an attempt to make kids aware of the dangers of obesity. What some believe is that this made Cookie Monster even *more* relevant as he now mirrors the vegetarian stances of bands such as Napalm Death and Carcass. It would be interesting to consider which other muppets will eventually become heavy metal icons. Certainly Kermit seems like a strong contender, but one must never count out the power of Elmo.

CORPSEPAINT. Corpsepaint is the name for a variety of make-up styles used by black metal bands (and some death metal bands) in order to whiten their faces to look more corpselike, or possibly more demonic, depending on the band and their intentions. Numerous bands have used corpsepaint ever since the trend was started by black metal bands in the eighties and is still used today by bands such as Darkthrone and Immmortal. While it is tempting to look at Kiss as an inspiration (especially for King Diamond), most metal fans would dismiss Kiss as too mainstream rock and roll to be an influence on a practice that was supposed to be more dark and intricate and used in the name of personal expression as opposed to rocking all night and partying every day. Bands such as Darkthrone, along with many others, have performed constantly in corpsepaint and many fans, in an effort to demonstrate their devotion, often wear corpsepaint to shows, as well.

CORROSION OF CONFORMITY (1982–PRESENT). Mike Dean (bass/vocals, replaced for several years by Phil Swisher, returned 1993), Woody Weatherman (guitar/vocals), Reed Mullin (drums, replaced by others, now Jason Patterson).

This punk metal crossover band originally started in Raleigh, North Carolina, in 1982. The band's first record, *Eye for an Eye,* is a standard thrash record, but subsequent records and new vocalists saw the band evolving in a more metal and then Southern rock direction. The band continues to this day with a lineup of Reed,

Patterson, and Dean. COC will long be remembered for being one of three key punk bands to cross over and do so in a hard and fast direction, maintaining their integrity while trying to open up the palette of the punk scene to accept more diversity. Although some of the later records veer in more of a Southern rock direction, fans to metal/punk crossover cannot go wrong by picking up *Animosity, Technocracy* or *Blind*.

Discography: *Eye for an Eye* (Caroline, 1983, 1990); *Animosity* (Combat, 1985; Metal Blade, 1994); *Technocracy* (Combat, 1987; remastered, Sony, 1995); *Blind* (Combat, 1991; extra tracks and remastered, Sony, 1995); *Vote with a Bullet* (Relativity, 1992); *Deliverance* (Sony, 1994); *Wiseblood* (Sony, 1996); *America's Volume Dealer* (Sanctuary, 2000); *Live Volume* (Sanctuary, 2001); *In the Arms of God* (Sanctuary, 2005).

CROSSOVER. The term *crossover* refers to music that blurs the line between heavy metal and punk, especially hardcore during the early to late eighties. Early on in the punk movement, many fans saw punk and metal as being mutually exclusive with metalheads deriding the perceived ineptness of punk musicians, while many punks despised what they saw as the pomposity and self-seriousness of heavy metal. After the acceptance of Motorhead by the punk community, the tide began to turn and many punks realized that some trappings of metal, such as better musicianship, were to be admired, and many metalheads began to emulate the raw aggression and speed of hardcore punk. The rise of the thrash and speed metal scenes, as well as bands such as Sacred Reich and the Crumbsuckers that blurred the boundaries between punk and metal, led to a distinct style. This was

Punk and metal fans (© Barry Lewis / Alamy)

epitomized by the formerly punk band DRI, who released the *Crossover* record (for once, a case of truth in advertising) in 1987. Today the term has fallen into disuse and many bands that identify as metal these days are actually post-hardcore punk bands, and many punks who listen to bands such as Earth Crisis and Lamb of God find almost no difference other than haircuts and perhaps being straight edge between the two bands. The best part of the crossover scene was the fact that many subcultures, despite apparent differences, were actually quite similar and shared common values (well, maybe not straight edge ...).

CROWBAR (1992–2000). Original lineup: Kirk Windstein (vocals and guitars), Matt Thomas (guitars), Todd Strange (bass), and Craig Numenmacher (drums).

Often compared to Pantera and the Melvins, New Orleans' Crowbar became known for playing a slow and grinding version of sludge metal and also gained notoriety for their physical weight, with a number of members tipping the scales at 300 pounds. Their first album was 1992's *Obedience Thru Suffering*. Their second album, 1993's *Crowbar*, was produced by Pantera frontman Phil Anselmo, a friend of the band. Anselmo's involvement led to appearances on MTV's *Headbanger's Ball* and video airplay for the songs "All I Had (I Gave)" and "Existence" on the TV show *Beavis & Butthead*. The band also went on tour supporting Pantera. After 1995's *Time Heals Nothing*, drummer Numenmacher left the band and was replaced by Jimmy Bower, guitarist for Eyehategod. 1996's *Broken Glass* saw the departure of guitarist Thomas and the arrival of his replacement Sammy Pierre Duet. Sid Montz joined the band for *Equilibrium* in 2000, replacing Bower, but was soon replaced himself by original drummer Numenmacher. Bassist Todd Strange left later the same year.

Discography: *Obedience Thru Suffering* (Grind Core Int., 1992); *Crowbar* (Zoo, 1993); *Live + 1* (Pavement, 1994); *Time Heals Nothing* (Pavement/Zoo, 1995); *Broken Glass* (Pavement, 1996); *Odd Fellows Rest* (Mayhem, 1998); *Equilibrium* (Spitfire, 2000); *Sonic Excess in Its Purest Form* (Spitfire, 2001); *Lifesblood for the Downtrodden* (Candlelight, 2005).

CRUMBSUCKERS (1985–89). Dave Brady on demos, then Chris Notaro (vocals) Dave Wynn (guitar), Chris Lenihan (guitar), Gary Meskil (bass), Dan Richardson (drums).

Crumbsuckers were a metal/punk crossover band from the late eighties who recorded relatively little but were influential on the crossover scene. Like bands such as Cryptic Slaughter, Corrosion of Conformity, and DRI, the Crumbsuckers ushered in a new wave of music, one that broke boundary lines that only a few years ago had seemed as solid as the then-imposing Berlin Wall. They were, for a while, one of the most interesting bands in the New York hardcore scene, but were quickly becoming more enamored of technical proficiency and the more melodic songs of contemporary heavy metal. The first record is a bit of a classic, mostly hardcore with metallic solos, but by the second record the band had evolved into a speed metal band and were not as interesting as they had been during the earlier period when they had been more of a genuine mixture of the two. Crumbsuckers broke up in 1989 but there have been sporadic reunions, most recently in 2007.

Discography: *Life of Dreams* (Combat Core, 1986); *Beast on My Back* (Combat, 1988).

CRYPTIC SLAUGHTER (1984–88, 1990, 2003–PRESENT). Bill Crooks (vocals/bass), Les Evans (guitar), Adam Scott (guitar), Scott Peterson (drums), and Ron Nicholson (bass).

This hardcore punk/thrash crossover band from Santa Monica formed in the mid-eighties and helped pioneer the crossover sound, blending metal with hardcore punk to help create a new sound reminiscent of bands such as DRI, Discharge, and Corrosion of Conformity. They were a rare beast in the crossover speedcore scene, bringing punk's antiestablishment politics into the usually apolitical field of metal and influencing a whole new wave of music. The first three records, particularly *Money Talks* and *Convicted*, are ultra-fast slabs of pure aggression and well worth seeking out. However, don't be conned into buying the *Speak Your Peace* album, as it is a Cryptic Slaughter record in name only, with only Evans remaining a constant from the first record and with much less compelling new vocalist Dave Hollingsworth.

After years of inactivity and a growing new legion of fans who sought out the old material, the band is apparently back together with Crooks once again on vocals, and Evans, Peterson, and Nicholson once again in the band. Although there were many contestants in the contest to blend hardcore punk and metal together into one seamless package, out of the American bands that created the new movement, Cryptic Slaughter remain one of the best.

Discography: *Convicted* (Restless, 1986); *Money Talks* (Metal Blade, 1987); *Stream of Consciousness* (Enigma, 1988); *Speak Your Peace* (Restless, 1990).

THE CULT (1983–95, 1998–PRESENT). Ian Astbury (vocals) Billy Duffy (guitar), Jamie Stewart (bass, moved to rhythm guitar, replaced by Kid Chaos then Stewart again, Charlie Drayton, Kinley Wolf, Craig Adams, Martyn LeNoble, Billy Morrison, Craig Adams, others), Raymond Smith (drums, replaced by Nigel Preston, Mark Brzezicki, Les Warner, Micky Curry, Michael Lee, Matt Sorum, Scott Garrett, John Tempesta, others).

The Cult started out as Southern Death Cult, a goth band with Native American trappings led by Ian Astbury, before morphing into the slightly more accessible Death Cult and finally simply the Cult. Although the Cult's first proper album as the Cult, *Dreamtime* is a psychedelic blend of goth and hippie noise mixed together with a little post-punk. It also indicated, particularly through Astbury's wailing vocals and Duffy's tasteful yet provocative solos, that more was to come. Their breakthrough record in 1985, *Love*, provided the band with several hits, including "Rain" and the dynamic "She Sells Sanctuary." These singles were still indicative of the band's love for sixties psychedelia over hard rock. After more personnel changes, the band went into the studio for their next production and soon began to record more aggressive material. Dissatisfied with the sound they were getting, the band decamped to Los Angeles where they met with producer Rick Rubin, who ended up producing their new record after making the band re-record what he considered "inferior" versions of the band's new songs.

When the new record *Electric* was released, Astbury and guitarist Billy Duffy had fully grown out their hair and morphed into a power metal band, much to the surprise of their original audience. *Electric* was a massive crossover hit, containing the powerful crunch of "Love Removal Machine," an AC/DC-style metal song, albeit with Astbury's sonic shriek wailing over the top. While "Love Removal

Machine" was essentially the same song as the band's last big single "Rain," it didn't seem to disturb fans. The next album provided yet another rewrite, "Fire Woman," which proved conclusively that the same melody can be repeated at least three times before it gets old. *Sonic Temple* was as good a raw metal album as any put out that year, and Bob Rock's production was certainly sympathetic to the band's strengths, but the formula was wearing thin, and the Cult began to flounder on the next two records, *Ceremony* and *The Cult*, neither of which repeated the success of *Electric* or *Sonic Temple*. The band soon went on hiatus for several years after friction between Astbury and Duffy became too much for the band. During the hiatus, Astbury took part in a much-maligned reunion of the Doors with Ray Manzarek and Robby Krieger (drummer John Densmore sat out the tours and sued the band), which did as much to besmirch the memory of that band as anything else.

After several years of inactivity, Astbury and Duffy reformed the Cult and are currently on tour with a new rhythm section. Drummer Matt Sorum went on to drum for both Guns N' Roses and later Velvet Revolver. The Cult's metal legacy is dependent on the two "metal" records they released at the end of the eighties, and despite the band's tendency towards pretension, they are two ultimately listenable records and highly recommended. Unfortunately, recent releases are essentially retreads, and metal fans who wish to go beyond the two metal albums should probably seek out *Love* to hear the band at their most experimental.

Discography: *Dreamtime* (Beggar's Banquet, 1984); *Love* (Beggar's Banquet, 1985); *Electric* (Beggar's Banquet, 1987); *Sonic Temple* (Beggar's Banquet, 1989); *Ceremony* (Beggar's Banquet, 1991); *The Cult* (Beggar's Banquet, 1994); *Beyond Good and Evil* (Atlantic, 2001); *Born Into This* (Roadrunner, 2007).

CULT OF LUNA (2000–PRESENT). Klas Rydberg (vocals), Erik Oloffson (guitar), Johannes Peterson (guitar), Magnus Lindberg (keyboards), Andreas Johansson (bass), Marco Hilden (drums, replaced by Thomas Hedland), Adders Tegland (samples).

Cult of Luna are a dark and moody but almost progressive Swedish band who have been one of the most consistently interesting metal bands of the past few decades. The band incorporates soundscapes and samples into its drearily dark music that makes them hard to fit into one metal subgenre. The band at times is reminiscent of Neurosis and has developed the idea of moody and dark metal to a true artform. For fans of experimental metal or avant-garde music, drone or doom metal, or even Sigur Ros. *The Beyond* is the best record for new listeners to start, although all of their records come highly recommended.

Discography: *Cult of Luna* (Earache, 2003); *The Beyond* (Earache, 2003); *Salvation* (Earache, 2004); *Somewhere Along the Highway* (Earache, 2006).

D

DANZIG (1987–PRESENT). Glenn Danzig (vocals), John Christ (guitar, replaced by Tommy Victor, Todd Youth, Robert Benkovic), Eerie Von (bass, replaced by Josh Lazie, Howie Pyro, Steve Zing), Chuck Biscuits (drums, replaced by Joey Castillo, Bevan Davies, Johnny Kelly).

Glenn Danzig is one of the most polarizing figures in music, first on the punk and more recently on the metal scene, where his brilliance was almost outshown by his arrogance and ego. His bands—the Misfits, Samhain, and Danzig—are legendary for their music, but Danzig himself, a bodybuilder with an Elvis-like voice, who is just as likely to compose dark symphonic music as muscular punk—tinged metal, remains an enigma to many in the punk and metal communities who wonder why Danzig the band still fails to live up to its initial promise.

After splitting from the Misfits and forming the more goth and doom rock oriented Samhain, Danzig began to take more seriously (at least on the surface) the satanic leanings of the Misfits, along with an interest in the new wave of thrash metal that was then sweeping America. In 1987 Danzig took Samhain member Eerie Von with him to found Danzig along with guitarist John Christ and drumming wizard Chuck Biscuits (from DOA and the Circle Jerks). The band found themselves with a surprising hit with the song "Mother" in 1988 on the *Danzig* record.

Subsequent records were less successful, and eventually Danzig's ego got in the way of his strategy. As band members were dumped left and right, the band became more of a pet project than a real band. Several tours where Doyle from the Misfits appeared for some songs were highlights of the last few years, but other than that, Danzig has been a lost cause. Danzig took some of the Misfits sound and image and toned it down while bringing to the surface some of the more explicit satanic imagery. The early band was just as good as most metal bands of the time, albeit with Danzig's powerful set of pipes that set them aside from most other bands in the dark and heavy genre. Sadly, Glenn Danzig is an example of how a singer's ego can get in the way of the potential musical innovation that was the hallmark of Glenn Danzig for most of his career.

Discography: *Danzig* (American, 1988); *Danzig II: Lucifuge* [live] (American, 1990); *Danzig III: How the Gods Kill* (American, 1992); *Danzig IV* (American, 1994); *Blackacidevil* (E-Magine, 1996); *6:66 Satan's Child* (E-Magine, 1999); *Live on the Black Hand Side* (Restless, 2001); *I Luciferi* (Spitfire, 2002); *Circle of Snakes* (Evilive, 2004); *The Lost Tracks of Danzig* (Evilive, 2007).

DARK ANGEL (1983–91). Dan Doty (vocals, replaced by Ron Rhinehart), Eric Meyer (guitar), Jim Durkin (guitar, replaced by Brett Erickson), Rob Yahn (bass, replaced by Mike Gonzalez), Jack Schwartz (drums, replaced by Gene Hoglan).

Dark Angel were a thrash metal band from Los Angeles that helped found the sound of extreme thrash. Their second record, *Darkness Descends,* is the group at their best, although *Leave Scars* is also a worthy testament to the band's abilities. The group floundered for a time, and when second vocalist Rhinehart left in 1991, the band dissolved. There are few metal bands where the drummer is the most adept instrumentalist, but Hoglan was clearly one of the best in the industry, and he went on to a legendary stint in the band Death.

Discography: *We Have Arrived* (Metalstorm, 1984); *Darkness Descends* (Combat, 1986); *Leave Scars* (Combat, 1989); *Live Scars* (Combat, 1990); *Time Does Not Heal* (Combat, 1991).

THE DARKNESS (2000–6). Justin Hawkins (vocals, guitar, keyboards), Dan Hawkins (guitar), Frankie Poullain (bass, replaced by Richie Edwards), Ed Graham (drums).

The Darkness were a hilarious modern English metal band with a wicked sense of humor that recalled the excesses of seventies heavy metal and especially the band Queen. They were sadly derailed after two records. The band was led by over-the-top vocalist Justin Hawkins, who could reach a high falsetto with ease, his brother Dan on guitar, and a stellar rhythm section of Frankie Poullain on bass (replaced after the first album by Richie Edwards) and Ed Graham on drums.

While the Darkness were not conceived as a band trying to emulate the style of Queen, it is interesting to note that the band's formation was based on how well Justin Hawkins had done singing "Bohemian Rhapsody" at karaoke on New Year's Eve. The band's first record, *Permission to Land,* was a surprising success in their native England. The band made in-roads in the United States with the single "I Believe in a Thing Called Love," which was a surprising minor hit and allowed the band to play various festivals almost to the size they did in their native England. Other key tracks off the first record include the classic "Get Your Hands Off of My Woman" (unplayable on the radio for its "mother fucker" reference) and the comedy songs "Growing on Me" (which was about a venereal disease) and "Love on the Rocks With No Ice."

After the success of the first album, internal tension led to the departure of original bassist Frankie Poullain, and his replacement by Richie Edwards in time for the second record, *One Way Ticket to Hell ... and Back.* The album followed allegations in the British press of drug abuse by the Darkness, including lead singer Hawkins' alleged propensity for cocaine (Hamilton 2006). This was mocked on the new album's opening track, "One Way Ticket," which opens up with pan pipes playing followed by the sound of someone snorting drugs and laughter.

The new record was also produced by classic metal producer Roy Thomas Baker, who had previously worked with Queen. The influence of Thomas was clear as the band added multi-tracked elaborate backing harmonies that echoed classic Queen so much that Brian May could have contemplated a plagiarism lawsuit. Despite the presence of several good tracks, including the dumb-joke "Knockers" and the Queen-esque "English Country Garden," the band was running out of steam, and lead singer Hawkins ended up in rehab again. After his release, he disbanded the Darkness, announcing that he was not physically or mentally prepared for the temptation of touring again. Despite their relatively short life span, the Darkness were one of the more interesting of the revivalist bands of the new decade, and it seems as though they were cut short too soon—before they could forge their own identity outside of the joke songs and references to classic metal. After Justin Hawkins' departure, Dan Hawkins decided to continue in a heavier direction and promoted bassist Richie Edwards to lead vocals, along with drummer Ed Graham. They recruited new bassist Toby MacFarlaine from the new band Stone Gods. Justin Hawkins has been planning a solo career for some time and has contributed backing vocals to bands such as Def Leppard and others since the dissolution of the Darkness.

Discography: *Permission to Land* (Atlantic, 2003); *One Way Ticket to Hell … and Back* (Atlantic, 2005).

DARKTHRONE (1988–PRESENT). Nocturno Culto (vocals/guitar/bass), Anders Risberget (guitar), Ivar Enger (guitar), Dag Nilsen (bass), Fenriz, aka Glyve Nagel (drums).

Darkthrone are a Norwegian black metal band (former death metal) with punk and crust influences, who have been one of the most consistently interesting black metal bands of the past two decades. The band was formed in 1988 by drummer and lyricist Fenriz as a five piece, but as members left eventually Darkthrone were reduced to a duo of Nocturno Culto and Fenriz. Fenriz later curated the ultimate black metal compilation, *Fenriz Presents … the Best of Old School Black Metal*, on Peaceville Records in 2004. While many were fans of Darkthrone for their music, others preferred the occult-driven lyrics, which is no surprise as the band was also notorious for its association with Mayhem.

Darkthrone were also one of the key first bands to wear corpsepaint, the death-like pallor that became a trademark with black metal and some death metal bands as time went on.

Discography: *Soulsie Journey* (Peaceville, 1990); *Ablaze in the Northern Sky* (Peaceville, 1991); *Under a Funeral Moon* (Peaceville, 1993); *Panzerfaust* (Peaceville, 1994); *Transylvanian Hunger* (Peaceville, 1994); *Total Death* (MoonFog, 1995); *Goatlord* (MoonFog, 1997); *Tribute* (Premium, 1999); *Plaguewielder* (End, 2001); *Darkthrone Holy Darkthrone* (Tatra, 2002); *Hate Them* (The End, 2003); *Sardonic Wrath* (MoonFog, 2005); *Ravishing Grimness* (The End, 2006); *The Cult Is Alive* (Peaceville/Tyrant, 2006); *F.O.A.D* (Peaceville, 2007); *Live from the Past* (Conquer, 2008); *Frostland Tapes* (Peaceville/Snapper, 2008); *New Wave of Black Heavy Metal* (Snapper, 2008).

DEAD HORSE (1987–96). Greg Martin (vocals/guitar), Michael Hagaa (guitar, replaced by Scott Sevall), Allen Price (bass), Ronny Guytoe (drums).

Dead Horse were a Texas-based death metal band and one of the most underappreciated American death metal bands. The band started in 1987 and lasted more or less till the late nineties. Sadly, they only released two records in their career, but both records are well worth seeking out.

Discography: *Peaceful; Death and Pretty Flowers* (Big Chief, 1991); *Horsecore* (Relapse, 1999).

DEATH (1983–2001). Chuck Schuldiner (vocals/guitar), Shannon Hamm (guitar), Scott Clendenin (bass), Richard Christy (drums).

Death were one of the earliest and most influential death metal bands. The band originally started as Mantas (named after the stage name of guitarist Jeff Dunn of Venom) led by guitarist and band mainstay Chuck Schuldiner. After hearing early death metal band Possessed, the band moved away from a black metal direction toward more of a straightforward death metal sound. After an aborted attempt to make this type of music work in Florida, Schuldiner moved to the more active San Francisco scene. There he recruited like-minded drummer Chris Reifert to record the quintessential *Scream Bloody Gore* record, which was among the heaviest and most shocking death metal records of its time.

By the time of the 1990 release *Spiritual Healing*, Death was selling over 50,000 copies of their records, a high point for a band in the underground extreme metal scene. Numerous personnel changes began to take their toll in the mid-nineties and by the late nineties, Death had changed musical directions (as had most of the other early death metal bands) and was playing in a more progressive, but still sped-up, direction. After a lackluster final album, *The Sound of Perseverance*, the band went on hiatus and Schuldiner concentrated on his side project, the even more progressive-oriented Control Denied, before succumbing to cancer in December of 2001. Their legacy lives on in the recorded output, and the first three records in particular are highly recommended for those wanting to get a taste of the rawest of the death metal sound. Not for the timid or faint of heart.

Discography: *Scream Bloody Gore* (Combat, 1987); *Leprosy* (Combat, 1988); *Spiritual Healing* (Combat, 1990); *Human* (Combat, 1991); *Individual Thought Patterns* (Combat, 1993); *Symbolic* (Roadrunner, 1995); *Sound of Perseverance* (Nuclear Blast, 1998); *Vinyl Collection* (Combat, 2000); *Live in L.A.: Death & Raw* (Nuclear Blast, 2001); *Live at Eindhoven* (Nuclear Blast, 2002).

DEATH METAL. Death metal is a sub-genre of heavy metal that evolved out of thrash metal in the early eighties. It largely retains the speed, intensity, and often the complexity of thrash metal, but takes a much more morbid turn in its lyrics, which generally feature grisly, macabre themes of suffering and violence. Musically, it features heavily de-tuned guitars, fast and challenging rhythm riffs, and rapid drum riffs, with plenty of virtuosic double bass-drum figures. While the music usually comes on like a brutal wall of noise, it can often be quite atmospheric at the same time.

Death metal emerged and was popularized in the mid-1980s, and was pioneered by such British and American acts as Napalm Death and Possessed, with the latter being among the first to use the term on their song "Death Metal," which was featured on their 1984 demo, itself entitled *Death Metal*, and also on the band's 1985

Seven Churches album, released the following year. The term soon caught on as a way to describe the genre, which, although it sometimes used occult imagery, concentrated more on shocking and graphic descriptions of violence, degradation, torture, and slaughter of the innocents.

As the musical genre grew, the use of the Cookie Monster vocal style—long guttural growls instead of actually singing, became more and more common. One of the key death metal bands was Cannibal Corpse, who have pushed the envelope since their emergence in the early 1990s more than most with their graphic album cover art and lyric imagery. While the genre peaked in the early 1990s with the relative commercial success of such death metal bands as Morbid and Cannibal Corpse, it remains an influential and popular sub-genre of heavy metal.

DECLINE OF WESTERN CIVILIZATION, PART II: THE METAL YEARS. After creating the defining film illustrating the Los Angeles punk scene during its prime (and decline) in 1979–80, filmmaker Penelope Spheeris then turned her camera to the burgeoning metal scene on the Sunset Strip in the mid-eighties. In her second film analyzing the musical and social scenes surrounding a new movement, Spheeris wisely decided to once again let her subjects speak, illustrating their genius, decadence, or descent into alcoholism and addiction.

In notable scenes, Ozzy Osbourne tried to cook breakfast with hands shaking so badly that he could barely hold a plate. Most notoriously, in a scene that would be replayed over and over in documentaries, W.A.S.P. guitarist Chris Holmes is shown floating in his pool, alternately drinking vodka straight out of a bottle and pouring it over his head as he talks about his career and not caring about life, with his mother sitting stoically on a chair in the background.

The Metal Years is a stunning document of the logical excess that unsupervised wealth and power had on the metal scene of the eighties, and although it will probably be remembered primarily as a document of unbridled excess, the live performances and interviews will give even the most casual viewer a good idea of why the Sunset Strip metal scene was so important and so successful at the time, and also why many modern metal bands still seek to live the dream as epitomized in the film, despite the fact that it demonstrates conclusively that the boundary between dream and nightmare is tenuous at best.

DEEP PURPLE (1968–PRESENT). Classic lineup: Ian Gillan (vocals), Ritchie Blackmore (guitar), Jon Lord (keyboards), Roger Glover (bass), Ian Paice (drums).

One of the first wave of classic heavy rock bands (along with Black Sabbath and Led Zeppelin) to find massive commercial success with heavy music, Deep Purple were unique in their prominent use of keyboards, and related to this, in their incorporation of classical elements in their songwriting, which would later prove to be influential in progressive rock.

In a career spanning forty years, the band has experienced a variety of personnel changes and a handful of "versions" of the band. First forming in 1968 in Hertfordshire, England, the band initially featured guitarist Ritchie Blackmore, vocalist Rod Evans, bassist Nick Simper, keyboardist Jon Lord, and drummer Ian Paice. This first version of the band (Deep Purple I to their fans) was the most pop-oriented, and their first album, *Shades of Deep Purple*, released in 1968, yielded a hit single in a remake of Joe South's "Hush." Their second album, 1969's *The*

Deep Purple were a lot more than simply "Smoke on the Water." (Rex Features)

Book of Taliesyn, similarly produced a hit of a cover, this time "Kentucky Woman," written by Neil Diamond.

As the band sought to develop their own musical personality, they began to experiment more with classical elements, bringing Jon Lord's keyboards (particularly organ) to the fore on the band's eponymous third album, *Deep Purple,* released in 1969. Further seeking to reinvigorate the band, Evans and Simper were fired and replaced by vocalist Ian Gillan and bassist Roger Glover. Gillan was a skilled rock vocalist and gave the band a much more aggressive vocal style. The band's first outing with the newest version of the group (Deep Purple II if you're keeping score), was the Lord-penned *Concerto for Group and Orchestra* of 1970, which found the band playing the original work along with the Royal Philharmonic Orchestra. While not commercially successful, it represented the group's sincere desire to fuse rock and classical sensibilities.

Seeking a more aggressive sound, guitarist Blackmore began to dominate the group, evolving a heavier, guitar-based sound, that combined a highly original guitar sound with Lord's classical organ themes. Around this time, Blackmore began playing Fender Stratocaster guitars instead of the smoother-sounding Gibsons he had favored previously. The sound of the Fender played through cranked Marshall amplifiers gave Blackmore—and Purple—a distinct rock guitar sound, one that was powerful yet retained a level of definition that was unusual in heavy rock, and that would be highly influential to Yngwie Malmsteen and others who would follow.

The fruits of Blackmore's influence were first heard on 1970's *In Rock,* which was the first Deep Purple album to deliver what would come to be the classic Deep Purple sound: high energy, classically influenced melodic compositions, delivered with virtuosic instrumental precision and soulful, aggressive vocals. Featuring the tracks "Speed King" and "Child in Time," the album was a solid hit, selling over a million copies, and signaled the beginning of the band's most creative and commercially rewarding era. The follow-up *Fireball* continued both the band's formula and its success.

For the band's next album they had planned to record at the Casino in Montreaux, Switzerland, using the Rolling Stones' mobile recording unit. As it happens, the venue burned down just before their arrival, an event chronicled in the band's classic "Smoke on the Water." Finding another venue, the band proceeded to record perhaps their best-known album, *Machine Head*, in Montreaux. The album was a multi-platinum smash featuring not only "Smoke" but also other classic tracks such as "Space Truckin'" and the burning rocker "Highway Star." With *Machine Head*, the band entered the top ranks of rock stardom. The 1973 follow-up, *Who Do We Think We Are?*, featured the hit "Woman From Tokyo" and consolidated the band's success.

Long-simmering tensions in the group came to a head, however, and vocalist Gillan and bassist Glover were forced out, as Blackmore sought to reinvigorate the band. Bassist/vocalist Glenn Hughes was the first to be brought on board. Formerly of the band Trapeze, Hughes was not only an excellent bass player, but was a distinctive vocalist with unique funk influences. After a long search, the band settled on lead vocalist David Coverdale. Coverdale, an art student and part-time vocalist wore glasses and was somewhat overweight—at least for a rock star—and the band set about rectifying the situation by getting him contacts and diet pills.

With the new lineup settled, the band turned to recording the first album with the newest lineup (Deep Purple III). The resulting album, *Burn*, released in 1974 was much more blues-influenced than its predecessors, which fitted Coverdale's style. In particular, the track "Mistreated" was a slow, heavy blues that burned with intensity. Another factor in the band's new sound related to the fact that the band now had two outstanding vocalists, and tracks like "Burn," "Lay Down, Stay Down," and "You Fool No One" took full advantage of the fact, and featured Coverdale and Hughes trading vocals in a dynamic and unique way. *Burn* was another enormous hit for the band and they followed it up with major tours of Europe and the U.S.

After *Stormbringer* released later that same year, Blackmore, ever restless, left Purple to form Rainbow with vocalist Ronnie James Dio. The band brought in former James Gang guitarist Tommy Bolin to take his place. Bolin had come to the attention of the band via his appearance on drummer Billy Cobham's classic fusion album *Spectrum*. The first and only album by this version of the band (Deep Purple IV, anyone?) was 1975's *Come Taste the Band*. The constant personnel changes and the lack of a true leader for the band were damaging, though, and the band had broken up by 1976, with Coverdale eventually forming Whitesnake, and Bolin going on to a promising solo career that was cut short by his death of a heroin overdose a year later (Young).

After Blackmore's Rainbow finished its run, the band's classic *Machine Head* lineup reunited for 1984's *Perfect Strangers* album, which was a solid hit for the band, and featured the successful single "Knocking at Your Back Door." 1987 saw the release of *The House of Blue Light*, but relations between band members soured again, and Gillan left, to be replaced by Joe Lynn Turner (formerly of Rainbow) on *Slaves and Masters* in 1990. Gillan was back for 1992's *The Battle Rages On*, but Blackmore himself quit the band while on tour for the album and had to be temporarily replaced by guitarist Joe Satriani.

1994 marked the beginning of a relatively stable and tranquil period as former Dixie Dregs guitarist Steve Morse joined the band. A unique and virtuosic player and innovative composer, Morse brought an influx of new energy into the group, and the success of *Purpendicular* in 1996 (Deep Purple version V) marked the acceptance of a Purple without Blackmore. The group has continued to release studio albums at regular intervals, along with a variety of archival releases and box sets, fitting the band's legacy. John Lord officially retired in 2002 (replaced by veteran keyboardist Don Airey), leaving drummer Ian Paice as the sole founding member still on board.

Discography: *Shades of Deep Purple* (Tetragrammaton, 1968); *Concerto for Group and Orchestra* (Warner Bros., 1969); *Deep Purple* (Tetragrammaton, 1969); *The Book of Taliesyn* (Spitfire, 1969); *Deep Purple in Rock* (Warner Bros., 1970); *Fireball* (Warner Bros., 1971); *Made in Japan* [live] (PSP, 1972); *Machine Head* (Warner Bros., 1972); *Who Do We Think We Are* (Warner Bros., 1973); *Burn* (Warner Bros., 1974); *Stormbringer* (Warner Bros., 1974); *Come Taste the Band* (Warner Bros., 1975); *Made in Europe* (Warner Bros., 1976); *Last Concert in Japan* [live] (Purple, 1977); *In Concert* [live] (Harvest, 1980); *Deep Purple in Concert* [live] (Portrait, 1981); *Live in London* (Harvest, 1982); *Perfect Strangers* (Mercury, 1984); *Fireworks* (EMI, 1985); *The House of Blue Light* (Mercury, 1987); *Nobody's Perfect* [live] (Mercury, 1988); *Slaves and Masters* (RCA, 1990); *The Battle Rages On ...* (Giant, 1992); *Live and Rare* (Combat, 1992); *Come Hell or High Water* [live] (BMG, 1994); *Live '85* (European Import, 1994); *King Biscuit Flower Hour* [live] (King Biscuit Flower, 1996); *Purpendicular* (Prominent, 1996); *Live at the Olympia '96* (Thames, 1997); *The Gemini Suite* (Cleopatra, 1998); *Abandon* (CMC International, 1998); *Child in Time* (Karussell, 1998); *Live at the Royal Albert Hall* (Spitfire, 2000); *Days May Come and Days May Go: The 1975 California Rehearsals* (Purple, 2000); *This Time Around: Live in Tokyo '75* (CMC International, 2001); *Under the Gun* (Polygram International, 2001); *Royal Philharmonic Orchestra* (Japanese Import, 2002); *Gemini Suite Live 1970* (Vap, 2003); *California Jam 1974* [live] (Japanese Import, 2003); *Bananas* (EMI, 2003); *The Best & Live* (BMG, 2004); *Rapture of the Deep* (Eagle, 2005); *Live at Montreux 2006* (Eagle Rock, 2007); *The Friends and Relatives Album* (Elap, 2007).

DEF LEPPARD (1978–PRESENT). Joe Elliot (vocals), Phil Collen (guitar), Vivian Campbell (guitar), Rick Savage (bass), Rick Allen (drums).

Along with Bon Jovi, Def Leppard were the quintessential rock band of the 1980s. Emerging initially as part of the New Wave of British heavy metal, and with roots in glam metal, the band eventually traded in their more aggressive AC/DC-influenced sound for a more polished, pop-informed sound. This is somewhat ironic since the polish came largely from their association with uber-producer Mutt Lange, who was perhaps best known for his work with AC/DC. The band ultimately became one of the most successful hard rock bands of the era, selling over 65 million records worldwide.

The band first came together as students of the Tapton School in Sheffield, England, when bassist Rick Savage, guitarist Pete Willis, and drummer Tony Kenning started a band in 1977 called Atomic Mass. Vocalist Joe Elliot auditioned as a guitarist for the band but had soon taken over lead vocal duties. It was Elliot who contributed the name Deaf Leopard, which was soon given its well-known misspelling, Def Leppard. After adding second guitarist Steve Clark in 1978, the band worked on developing their sound. By the time they recorded their debut three-song EP, drummer Kenning had left, to be replaced by fifteen-year-old Rick Allen.

Leppard's burgeoning career got off to a good start when the song "Rocks Off" was played extensively on BBC radio. In addition, the band began to develop a British following by playing the club scene, eventually gaining the attention of AC/DC manager Peter Mensch, who took them on, helping to secure a recording contract with Phonogram/Mercury records. The band's first album, *On Through the Night*, was released in March of 1980 and helped to establish their individual style, which was as rooted in the glam rock of Mott the Hoople and T-Rex as it was in the hard rock of AC/DC and Led Zeppelin. The album helped to solidify the band's following and to establish them as one of the foremost bands of what became known as the New Wave of British heavy metal.

At the beginning, however, the band's aims at superstardom were off-putting to some British fans, who saw the track "Hello America" and the band's subsequent American touring priorities as offensive. And this displeasure marred their performance at the Reading Festival in the summer of 1980 when audience members pelted the band with garbage and verbal insults. Such unpleasantries notwithstanding, however, the band was off to a running start and the album charted in the top 15 of the UK charts.

Before long the band had attracted the attention of producer Mutt Lange, who had recently helped AC/DC to superstar status with their *Back in Black* album. Working with Lange on their second album, *High 'N' Dry*, Def Leppard was able to realize their vision for the band, and Lange's meticulous attention to detail helped them to craft an album that gave their rock-style power a more precise and radio-ready polish. Released in July of 1981, *High 'N' Dry* also benefited from the presence of the new music channel MTV, and their video for "Bringin' on the Heartache" was one of the first metal videos aired and was given heavy rotation. The band also toured heavily, winning opening slots on tours with Ozzy Osbourne and Blackfoot.

Going into the studio to follow up on the success of *High 'N' Dry*, the band faced the unpleasant task of firing founding guitarist Pete Willis, whose excessive drinking was affecting his performance (Berelian). Guitarist Phil Collen, formerly of the band Girl, stepped in to take his place.

With 1983's *Pyromania* (and with the help of producer Lange), the band's formula of strong, hook-laden songs with larger-than-life production hit its stride. And with help again from MTV, the band became worldwide superstars and their songs became ubiquitous on the radio. "Photograph" was the album's first single and became the most requested video on MTV. The song also dominated the U.S. rock charts for six weeks, and crossed over to the pop charts rising as high as number 12. It was followed by the singles "Rock of Ages" and "Foolin'," which ultimately helped the album to sell six million copies in 1983 alone.

In preparation for *Pyromania*'s follow-up, Def Leppard relocated to Dublin (for tax purposes) and began working again with Mutt Lange. However, the overworked Lange backed out of songwriting sessions due to exhaustion, and songwriter/producer Jim Steinman (of Meatloaf fame) was temporarily brought in to help out. Toward the end of the year, the band faced its most trying moment when drummer Rick Allen lost his left arm when his Corvette hit a stone wall at a high rate of speed. During Allen's recovery, he was determined to try to continue drumming and practiced using his right hand, combining it with his feet. Ultimately, the rest of the band supported his efforts, and Allen contracted the Simmons electronic drum company to customize an electronic kit for him. When the band went back on tour, drummer Jeff Rich was initially hired to augment Allen, but was soon let go since Allen proved able to handle the job on his own.

Shortly after Allen's recovery Lange returned and the band resumed work on *Pyromania's* follow-up. *Hysteria* was finally released in August of 1987. The album proved a blockbuster for the band, and ultimately produced a record seven singles that made it into the U.S. singles charts. Led by the singles "Animal," "Pour Some Sugar on Me," and "Armageddon It," the album ended up selling over 18 million copies. Def Leppard also embarked on a hugely successful 15-month tour and cemented their position as the most commercially successful rock band of the era.

After the success of *Hysteria*, the band began work on their fifth album. Tragically, however, guitarist Steve Clark, who had been on leave from the band to deal with issues related to his alcoholism, died when he accidentally mixed alcohol and prescription drugs.

Instead of replacing the guitarist, the band resolved to complete the album as a four-piece. The resulting album, *Adrenalize*, despite debuting at number 1 and featuring a number of hit singles, ultimately failed to generate the sales or excitement of its predecessors. Prior to touring for the album, ex-Dio and Whitesnake guitarist Vivian Campbell was added to the fold.

In something of a concession to popular tastes, the band issued *Slang* in 1996, which featured a sparer sound and alternative rock feel. But despite generally positive critical reviews of the album, it failed to attract many new fans while somewhat alienating their old fans.

1999's *Euphoria* marked a return to their previous arena rock style and to commercial success, albeit on a more moderate level. Several successful albums have followed. Like Bon Jovi, even after the emergence of grunge and alternative rock signaled changes in the public's taste, Def Leppard's fan base has been so large and loyal that they have been able to sustain their career even as their album sales have decreased from their eighties peak.

Discography: *On Through the Night* (Mercury, 1980); *High 'N' Dry* (Mercury, 1981); *Pyromania* (Mercury, 1983); *Hysteria* (Mercury, 1987); *Adrenalize* (Mercury, 1992); *Slang* (Mercury, 1996); *Euphoria* (Mercury, 1999); *X* (Universal, 2002); *Yeah!* (Bludgeon Riffola/Island, 2006); *Songs from the Sparkle Lounge* (Bludgeon Riffola/Island, 2008).

DEFTONES (1995–PRESENT). Chino Moreno (vocals), Stephen Carpenter (guitar), Chi Cheng (bass), Abe Cunningham (drums).

Playing in a style not unlike that of their contemporaries Korn and Limp Bizkit, the Deftones have been parlaying their brand of metal since 1988 when they first formed in Sacramento, California, featuring vocalist Chino Moreno, guitarist Stephen Carpenter, bassist Chi Cheng, and drummer Abe Cunningham. Beginning in a more conventional style, the band drew influence from such bands as Tool and Rage Against the Machine and developed a more original take on heavy music, being one of the first metal bands to incorporate more ethereal breaks into their otherwise furious onslaught. The band signed with Madonna's Maverick Records in 1994, releasing their debut album, *Adrenaline*, the following year. Produced by Soundgarden and Pantera veteran Terry Date, the album sold some 200,000 copies largely on the strength of the band's live act and word of mouth. Tours with Ozzy Osbourne and Korn followed the album's release.

Around the Fur, released in October of 1997, delivered on the band's initial promise and sales were helped by the band's MTV videos for "My Own Summer (Shove It)" and "Be Quiet and Drive (Far Away)." Around the same time the band added turntablist Frank Delgado to expand their live sound and re-create some of the new aural textures they had added in the studio.

The band continued to experiment with their sound and released *White Pony* in June of 2000. The album, debuting at number 3, showed a band continuing to evolve and innovate beyond the limits of the metal genre, and such tracks as "Rx Queen," "Teenager," and "Change (In the House of Flies)" were indicative of their willingness to incorporate previous influences like the Smiths and the Cure into their sound.

The Deftones followed in 2003, again produced by Terry Date, and rose to number 2 on the U.S. album charts. After tours with Linkin Park and Metallica, the band took an extended break. They returned with *Saturday Night Wrist* in 2006.

Discography: *Adrenaline* (Maverick, 1995); *Around the Fur* (Maverick/Warner Bros., 1997); *White Pony* (Maverick, 2000); *Deftones* (Maverick, 2003); *School of Brilliant Things* (United States of Distribution, 2006); *Saturday Night Wrist* (Maverick, 2006); *Live Tracks* (Maverick, 1999); *B–Sides & Rarities* (Maverick, 2005).

DEICIDE (1987–PRESENT). Glen Benton (vocals/bass), Brian Hoffman (guitar, replaced by Dave Suzuki), Eric Hoffman (guitar, replaced by Ralph Sanotlla), Steve Ashiem (drums).

This death metal band's hatred of God and Christianity is notably demonstrated by the inverted cross branded into the forehead of lead singer Glen Benton. The band was formed in Florida in the mid-eighties by Benton, the two Hoffman brothers, and drummer Ashiem. They quickly became well-known on the black and death metal circuits, where their relentless commitment to the destruction of Christianity gained them many followers. In 2004, the Hoffman brothers were unceremoniously sacked from the band, allegedly over their insistence on being paid the same for songwriting royalties, but the Hoffman brothers claimed that Benton was not really a Satanist and not committed enough to Deicide. The band continues to this day, touring on the death metal circuit.

Discography: *Deicide* (Roadrunner, 1990); *Legion* (Roadrunner, 1992); *Once Upon the Cross* (Roadrunner, 1992); *Serpents of the Light* (Roadrunner, 1997); *When Satan Lives* (Roadrunner, 1998); *Insineratehymn* (Roadrunner, 2000); *In Torment, in Hell* (Roadrunner, 2001); *Scars of the Crucifix* (Earache, 2004); and *Stench of Redemption* (Earache, 2006).

DEMOS. For many in the underground metal scene, demos are now and have long been an important way to not only try to get the music into the hands of major labels but also for truly underground music to circulate. This was especially prevalent in the black metal and death metal scenes in the eighties where bands such as Behemoth, Carcass, and Vader all were well known outside of their own countries due to the prevalent underground demo swapping scene. Fans in different countries would circulate tapes, essentially establishing a fanbase for a band before they could get a record contract or tour.

Several demos were extremely influential in the death metal scene, with bands such as Napalm Death and Carcass making influential demos that could be taped for friends, building excitement for the band and a tour. Even a stoner rock band such as Sleep was able to secure a record contract with Earache, who received the completed demo tape for Sleep's *Holy Mountain* release, which they agreed to put out without any overdubs. In terms of fan participation, demos also gave fans a sense that the few people who were lucky enough to find a demo of a new band were granted insider knowledge and therefore were more in tune with the underground metal scene than people who merely read metal magazines such as *Kerrang* or *Circus* to find out information about new music. Fans who found the demos also made sure to copy them for select groups of fans, and thereby maintain their insider status.

Today, tape trading is almost nonexistent, largely as a result of the Internet and cheap file-sharing programs and social networks such as MySpace and Facebook, where bands can cheaply post demos for the world to hear. While some of the mystique of hearing about an underground band from Sweden or Norway has been lost in the age of the Worldwide Web, at least many new bands are gaining valuable exposure that they would not have had in the eighties or nineties.

DETHKLOK (2007–PRESENT). Nathan Explosion (vocals), Toki Wartotoh (rhythm guitar), Skwisgaar Skwigelf (lead guitar), Murderface (bass), Pickles (drums).

Dethklok are the fictional death/black metal band in the cartoon network series *Metalocalypse* created by Brendan Small and Tommy Blacha. In the series, the group of moronic metal lords causes constant chaos and mayhem wherever they go and are also the most successful heavy metal band in the world, with an annual income that ranks as the twelfth largest GNP economy in the world (next to the home of the waffle, Belgium, which usually ranks at number 13). The plots of most of the series involve Dethklok trying (usually unsuccessfully) to put on a concert or write songs, observed constantly by a mysterious shadowy cabal of financiers' politicians, generals, and bishops who gravely discuss the implications of the band's idiotic (and usually deadly) stage sets and endorsement deals. The band is a cross between death metal and black metal styles, with guitarists from Sweden and Norway (the definitive home of black metal) and a drummer who appears to have been in a Guns N' Roses-style L.A. metal band, Snakes N' Barrels. The band is one of the most brutally accurate and honest portrayals of a heavy metal band ever seen on television, in cartoon form or otherwise.

On the official Dethklok album release, creator Brendan Small played bass, guitar and sang, and classic death metal drummer Gene Hoglan (Death/Dark Angel) supplied some suitably authentic death metal drums.

DIMMU BORGIR (1993–PRESENT). Shagrath (vocals/guitar/bass/keyboards), Silenoz (guitar), Brynjard Tristen (bass, replaced by Nagash, ICS Vortex), Stian Aarstad (keyboards, replaced by Mustis), Tjodaly (drums, replaced by Nicholas Barker Hellhammer, Tony Laureano).

Dimmu Borgir are one of the key black metal bands from Norway. They formed in the early nineties (the first EPs and first album are sung in Norwegian). The band broke overseas with *Enthrone Darkness Triumphant,* which made them a favorite of American fans who liked the relatively melodic black metal sound of the band. Frequent personnel changes marred Dimmu Borgir's stability for many years, but they kept coming out with increasingly ambitious records, including *Death Cult Armageddon*, which was recorded with the Prague Philharmonic and strangely enough meshed well with Dimmu Borgir's already orchestral wall of sound. The band is so well-known in death metal circles that they were parodied on the Cartoon Network show *Metalocalypse* as "Dimmu Burger," a death metal burger shop. Dimmu Borgir is one of the most beloved black metal bands in the world and certainly one of the most adventurous. Drummer Hellhammer (also in Mayhem) has apparently had to leave the band recently due to an arm injury.

Discography: *For All Tid* (Nuclear Blast, 1994); *StormBlast* (Cacaphonous, 1996); *Enthrone Darkness Triumphant* (Nuclear Blast, 1997); *Godless Savage Garden* (Nuclear Blast, 1998); *Spiritual Black Dimensions* (Nuclear Blast, 1999); *Devil's Path/In the Shades of Life* (Hammerheart, 1999); *Puritanical Euphoric Misanthropia* (Nuclear Blast, 2001); *Alive in Torment* (Nuclear Blast, 2002); *Death Cult Armageddon* (Nuclear Blast, 2003); *Sons of Satan Gather for Attack* (Candlelight, 2004); *In Sorti Diablo* (Nuclear Blast, 2007).

DIO (1982–PRESENT).   Ronnie James Dio (vocals), Vivian Campbell (guitar), Jimmy Bain (bass), Vinnie Appice (drums).

Dio is the primary solo band for Ronnie James Dio, former lead singer of numerous classic heavy metal bands, including Black Sabbath, Elf, Rainbow and Heaven and Hell. Although Ronnie James Dio had been in the music industry sporadically for almost two decades, Dio had been primarily known as frontman in bands dominated by various strong guitar players who believed that the lead singer played second fiddle, as in Dio's involvement in Rainbow and Black Sabbath.

When Ronnie James Dio and Sabbath drummer Vinnie Appice acrimoniously departed from Black Sabbath in 1982, Dio decided that he had had enough of the interpersonal conflicts and formed a band that played up to his image with Sabbath and Rainbow. Basing his themes primarily on the typical Black Sabbath themes of the unknown, the occult, and the medieval, Dio found a slightly more contemporary formula and had instant success with his first record that featured, along with Dio and Appice, the killer combination of ex–Rainbow bassist Jimmy Bain and guitarist Vivian Campbell.

For the next record, Dio expanded the sound with the addition of keyboard player Claude Schell, who helped give eerie background atmospherics to the next Dio record, *The Last in Line*, which proved to be even more successful than the first offering. Dio's fantasy-tinged videos were soon all over MTV, where Dio's height and hair problems somehow turned out not to be problems, as metal fans anxiously ate up Dio's sound in an era where Black Sabbath was going through a very fallow period. By the next record, *Sacred Heart*, the usual personnel differences had begun to rear their ugly head, leading to the departure of guitarist Campbell and his replacement by Craig Goldy (formerly of Giuffria), but the rot had set in and by 1990 Dio had replaced the entire band. A revolving cast of characters went in and out for the next decade, and Dio was sometimes distracted by Black Sabbath, which he rejoined in 1992 and in 2006 for tours and recording.

Currently Dio is touring with the reunited Sabbath under the name Heaven and Hell. Despite the corny theatrics and medieval/occult theme that Dio has been associated with for most of his career, his vocals have remained incredibly agile for a man his age and he remains a fan favorite when he gets the band back together for frequent tours.

Ronnie James Dio with the late eighties lineup of his band (© Pictorial Press Ltd / Alamy)

Discography: *Holy Diver* (Reprise, 1983); *The Last in Line* (Warner Brothers, 1984); *Sacred Heart* (Warner Brothers, 1985); *Dream Evil* (Reprise, 1987); *Lock up the Wolves* (Reprise, 1990); *Strange Highways* (Reprise, 1994); *Angry Machines* (Mayhem, 1996); *Inferno: Last in Live* (Mayhem, 1998); *Magica* (Spitfire, 2000); *Killing the Dragon* (Spitfire, 2002); *Master of the Moon* (Sanctuary, 2004); *Evil or Divine Live* (Spitfire, 2005); *Holy Diver Live* (Eagle, 2006).

RONNIE JAMES DIO (1949–). Vocalist Ronnie James Dio (Ronald Padavona) has been a fixture of the heavy metal scene for over four decades (his musical career goes back even further to older rockabilly recordings from the late fifties). He was notable for playing off and on with numerous influential bands such as Elf, Rainbow, Black Sabbath, Dio, and Heaven and Hell (the reformed Dio fronted a version of Black Sabbath that toured in 2006 and 2007 under the name Heaven and Hell, allegedly because Sharon Osbourne, Ozzy's wife and manager, would not let them tour under the name Black Sabbath). Dio has one of the most consistent and remarkable voices for a heavy metal frontman, and his legacy as one of the key vocalists for three of metal's most enduring acts cements his place in metal history.

Dio started out in the progressive group Elf (1970–75), who played considerably less heavy than Dio would in his subsequent bands. After having Roger Glover produce one of the Elf records, Dio was introduced to dissatisfied Deep Purple guitarist Ritchie Blackmore's new project, Rainbow. After a few years, Dio and Blackmore found themselves increasingly at odds and Dio's fantasy-laden lyrics and grandiose themes caused friction between Dio and Blackmore, leading to Dio's departure to join Black Sabbath in 1979.

Ronnie James Dio with the other members of Dio. (© Pictorial Press Ltd / Alamy)

For several years the new singer led Sabbath through a career renaissance, but eventually the tensions between Iommi and Dio grew and he departed the band acrimoniously in 1982. Ronnie James Dio then commenced a long and successful solo career with his new band, Dio. Dio has also come back to Black Sabbath on two different occasions, first in 1992 for the *Dehumanizer* album, and later in 2006 for the collection of Dio-era Sabbath and a subsequent successful tour with the Sabbath (under the name Heaven and Hell for legal reasons), which is ongoing at this writing.

Dio's charitable side also shown through in the eighties when he organized the "Hear n' Aid" benefit in 1985 (released in 1986) featuring numerous metal luminaries such as Rob Halford of Judas Priest and Eric Bloom of Blue Öyster Cult. Dio also has a good claim to inventing or at least popularizing the "horns" or "devil sign" thrown by numerous rock stars through the eighties, although others, notably Kiss, claim to have come up with the idea first. Dio, who reputedly is said to have learned it from his Italian grandmother, has a good claim on not only one of metal's most remarkable vocals, but also on one of its most enduring symbols. To this day Ronnie James Dio is one of the most influential vocalists in metal history.

DISCHARGE (1977–87, 1991–93, 2001–PRESENT). Terry "Tezz" Roberts (vocals, replaced by Kelvin "Cal" Morris in 1979), Tony "Bones" Roberts (guitar, replaced by Peter Pyrtle, Les Hunt, then Stephen Brooks), Roy "Rainy" Wainwright (bass), Hacko (drums, replaced by Terry Roberts, Gary Maloney, then Nick Haymaker).

Discharge is a hardcore band active primarily during the early to late eighties who pioneered the hardcore/thrash crossover sound in England, eventually adding elements typical of metal such as prolonged soloing and metallic-style vocals. The ultra-crunchy guitar sound of records such as the 1982 *Hear Nothing, See Nothing, Say Nothing* is one of the best known of all the hardcore/punk crossover records. The band formed in 1977 and broke up originally in 1993, and then again in 1997.

The original lineup included Terry "Tezz" Roberts on vocals (replaced by Cal in 1979), Tony "Bones" Roberts on guitar (replaced by Peter Pyrtle, then Les Hunt, then Stephen Brooks; Bones returned for the 1997 reunion), Roy "Rainy" Wainright on bass, and Hacko on drums (replaced by Terry Roberts, then Gary Maloney, then Nick Haymaker, then Roberts returned for the 1997 reunion.) The band broke up again for several years, but now tours without original vocalist Cal (who apparently cannot be found—several rumors have him either dead or in the army) with new vocalist Rat from classic English hardcore band the Varukers. The legacy of Discharge, and what was called the D-core sound, is measured directly not only in their influence on the crossover between punk and metal, but also in their direct influence on the grindcore sound, where bands like Napalm Death were directly inspired by Discharge to not only play that fast but to even up the ante. Ironically, it was when Discharge went most "metal" that they began to lose fans not only in the punk community, but in the metal community as well. Their albums such as *Massacre*, with faux metal vocals, were much less popular than the hard, fast, and brutal records such as *Why* and *Hear Nothing, See Nothing, Say Nothing*.

Discography: *Realities of War* [EP] (Clay, 1980); *Fight Back* [EP] (Clay, 1981); *Decontrol* [EP] (Clay, 1981); *Why* (Clay, 1981; Castle, 2003); *Hear Nothing, See Nothing, Say Nothing* (Clay 1982; Castle, 2003); *Never Again* (Clay, 1984; Castle, 2003); *Grave New World* (Profile, 1986); *Massacre Divine* (Clay, 1991; 1995); *Shooting Up the World* (Clay, 1991, 1995); *Live at City Gardens, NJ* (Clay, 1995); *Clay Punk Singles Collection* (Clay, 1995); *Live Nightmare Continues* (Clay, 1996); *Protest & Survive 1980–84* (Clay, 1996); *Vision of War* (Recall, 1998); *Hardcore Hits* (Cleopatra, 1999); *Discharge* (Sanctuary, 2002); *Decontrol: The Singles* (Castle, 2002); *Society's Victims* [box set] (Castle, 2004); *Anthology Free Speech* (Castle, 2004); *Born Immortal* (Rebellion, 2005).

DISMEMBER (1988–PRESENT). Robert Sennback (vocals/bass), Richard Cabeza (bass, later Sharlee d'Angelo), David Blomqvist (guitars), Fred Estby (drums).

Dismember are a long-running Swedish death metal band who have been grinding out the real death sound since their inception. The band started as a power trio, but after some personal turmoil, which included Sennback leaving the band for a while, the band regrouped in 1991 with new bassist Cabeza and Sennback handling vocals. The promise of the first releases was realized on the *Indecent & Obscene* record, which found the band getting on an even keel and developing the style that would carry them forward for the next twenty years. For fans of real Swedish death metal.

Discography: *Like an Ever Flowing Stream* (Nuclear Blast, 1991); *Indecent & Obscene* (Nuclear Blast, 1993); *Massive Killing Capacity* (Nuclear Blast, 1995); *Death Metal* (Nuclear Blast, 1997); *Hate Campaign* (Nuclear Blast, 2000); *Where Iron Crosses Grow* (Candlelight, 2004); *God that Never Was* (Candlelight, 2006); *Dismember* (Regain Us, 2008).

DISSECTION (1989–2006). Jon Nodtveidt (vocals/guitar), John Zwetsloot (guitar, replaced by Johan Norman, finally Set Tietan), Peter Palmdahl (bass, replaced by Bruce Leclercq), Ole Ohman (drums, replaced by Tomas Asklund).

Dissection were a Swedish black metal band formed by guitarist and vocalist Jon Nodtveidt in 1989. The band was controversial for its dark lyrics and Nodtveidt later espousing of satanic and Aryan pride sentiments. The first record is fairly tame by black metal standards, but the follow-up *Storm of the Lights Bane* is a classic brutally heavy and monstrously evil black metal record. However, as was the case in many bands in the genre, Dissection was forced to take an unscheduled detour, thanks to Nodtveidt's idiocy. The band (actually an all-new band featuring only original member Nodtveidt) came back strong with the cryptic and occult-obsessed *Reinkaos* album following Nodtveidt's stint in prison. (Nodtveidt was convicted in the extremely brutal killing of a 38-year-old homosexual man, one that in a less-lenient country would have gotten him life behind bars.) Plans for a tour of the United States were postponed first by the troubles the band encountered in getting a visa to enter the United States, and then further postponed when Nodtveidt killed himself on August 16, 2006. Ultimately, Dissection will be remembered by their fans for their uncompromising philosophical and ideological stance, as well as their sheer brutality, and also by the inventively clever and often beautiful music they created when at their best. For outsiders, Dissection is another example of how twisted those in the black metal community have become and how unaccepting of homosexuality many in the metal community can be. The last record is a fitting final statement for the band, but it remains uncertain if fans of black metal should excuse the abhorrent personal behavior of members of their favorite bands.

Discography: *The Somberlain* (No Fashion, 1993); *Storm of the Lights Bane* (Nuclear Blast, 1996); *The Past Is Alive* (Necropolis, 2000); *Live Legacy* (Nuclear Blast, 2003); *Reinkaos* (The End Records, 2006).

DISTURBED (1996–PRESENT). Dave Drainman (vocals), Dan Donegan (guitar), Fuzz (bass), Mike Wengren (drums).

Disturbed are a heavy metal band with a debt to early metal and mainstream thrash-like bands such as Pantera. The band started out in Chicago in the late nineties. Drainman's unique vocal style helped gain them a huge following in the Midwest, eventually getting them signed in 2000 to the small Giant label, who released their first album, *The Sickness*. While the first album is a relatively good low-budget affair, the band had access to a larger production budget once they moved over to music giant Warner Brothers, and the second record is miles above *The Sickness* with payer and liberation" proving that Donegan is a first-rate metal guitarist and that Drainman's "I gargled with broken glass before this song" and then suddenly clear singing voice knows how to work a song. The band even manages to end the record with the power ballad "Darkness" that manages to be spooky instead of cheesy.

The next two records seemed a bit less focused (*Ten Thousand Fists* in particular) and seem almost as though the band, in trying some electronic touches, was becoming a bit more concerned with mainstream airplay, or at least interested in creating downloadable ringtones for emo metal kids. Although Disturbed was often lumped into the new metal field by critics, their music was actually much heavier than one would assume. The first two records in particular are well worth investigating.

Discography: *The Sickness* (Giant, 2000); *Believe* (Warner Brothers, 2002); *Ten Thousand Fists* (Warner Brothers, 2005); *Indestructible* (Reprise, 2008).

DOKKEN (1982–PRESENT). Classic lineup: Don Dokken (vocals), George Lynch (guitar), Jeff Pilson (bass), Mick Brown (drums).

One of the stalwarts of the hair metal scene of the 1980s, Dokken rose to prominence on the basis of strong songwriting and the presence of a bona fide guitar hero in guitarist George Lynch. With their rockers and power ballads, the band was a fixture on MTV in the eighties and enjoyed a string of best-selling albums through the decade.

Rising from the L.A. metal scene, the band was initially formed by vocalist Don Dokken in 1976 and featured drummer Mick Brown. In the late seventies George Lynch and future Ratt bassist Juan Croucier came on board and recorded *Breaking the Chains* for the European label Carerre Records, eventually released in 1983. After some success in Europe, Electra Records released the album in the U.S., and bassist Jeff Pilson joined the group. The band's first album featuring the new lineup was *Tooth and Nail*, released in 1984. Featuring "Just Got Lucky," "Into the Fire," and the power ballad "Alone Again," the album was highly successful, and the band became a fixture on radio, and, more importantly, on the burgeoning MTV. The album sold over a million copies and established Dokken's signature sound, which combined Don Dokken's relatively high and clear vocals with Lynch's hard-edged rhythms and technically impressive yet melodic leads. In addition, the band's general melodicism, especially evident on their power ballads, helped them appeal as much to female fans as to males.

After a successful tour supporting the Scorpions, the band returned in 1985 with the album *Under Lock and Key* and was similarly successful and featured the hits "In My Dreams" and "It's Not Love." Again, MTV exposure helped the band, and the video for "It's Not Love" featured them performing on a flatbed truck as it cruised through the L.A. scenery.

Back for the Attack followed in 1987 and continued the band's successful run, as the "hair metal" era reached its peak. The album contained the track "Dream Warriors," which had been featured earlier in the film *Nightmare on Elm Street III: Dream Warriors*. The song and its video helped to give the band their third consecutive platinum album.

After the release of the live album, *Beast From the East*, the growing tensions between Don Dokken and George Lynch that had been brewing through most of their collaboration came to a head, and the guitarist exited the group in 1988. The band subsequently folded, with Lynch forming the band Lynch Mob with drummer Brown, and Don Dokken forming his own short-lived solo group.

Dokken and Lynch collaborated in the writing of the song "We Don't Own This World," which appeared on Lynch's 1993 solo album *Sacred Groove*. Later that year came the official reunion of the band. Signing with Columbia Records, they released the album *Dysfunctional* in 1995. Unfortunately, the album was poorly received by both critics and fans. Soldiering on, the band released the live acoustic album *One Live Night* on CMC Records in 1996. The studio album *Shadowlife* followed the next year, but none of these efforts stirred much enthusiasm among fans or critics. Finally, with Lynch leaving to reform Lynch Mob, the band hired ex-Winger guitarist Reb Beach and recorded *Erase the Slate*, released in 1999. Though Beach left the band in 2001, the band has continued to record and tour, though not at the levels of success that they had previously enjoyed.

Discography: *Breaking the Chains* (Elektra, 1982); *Tooth and Nail* (Elektra, 1984); *Under Lock and Key* (Elektra, 1985); *Back for the Attack* (Elektra, 1987); *Beast from the East* (Elektra, 1988); *Dysfunctional* (Columbia, 1995); *One Live Night* (Alex, 1995); *Shadowlife* (CMC International, 1997); *Erase the Slate* (CMC International, 1999); *Long Way Home* (Sanctuary, 2002); *Japan Live '95* (CMC International/Sanctuary, 2003); *Hell to Pay* (Sanctuary, 2004); *From Conception: Live 1981* (Rhino, 2007); *Lightning Strikes Again* (King, 2007); *The Very Best of Dokken* (Rhino, 1999).

DREAM THEATER (1985–PRESENT). Chris Collins (vocals, replaced by Charles Dominici, replaced by Kevin James LaBrie), John Petrucci (guitars), John Myung (bass), Kevin Moore (keyboards, replaced by Derek Sherinian, replaced by Jordan Rudess), Mike Portnoy (drums).

Dream Theater are a heavy progressive/art metal band whose rabid fan base are among the most vocal and loyal in metal. The band was started by music students from Berklee College: guitarist John Petrucci, John Myung on bass, drummer Mike Portnoy, and vocalist Chris Collins, who soon left and was replaced by Charles Dominici. However, this lineup was not stable, and by 1991 Dominici was gone. He was replaced by Kevin James LaBrie to form the "classic" Dream Theater lineup that produced the majority of their best material, although keyboard player Kevin Moore eventually retired for a solo career, to be replaced by the able Derek Sherinian.

After several records of progressive bliss and lengthy songs, Dream Theater became a rare metal band that fans recorded live and actively looked to trade bootleg tapes, making them the metal analogy of a jam band. To many fans, Dream Theater is worth flying around the world to catch their live shows, which demonstrate the true potential of their material.

Discography: *When Dream and Day Unite* (One Way Records, 1989); *Images and Words* (WEA, 1992); *Live at the Marquee* (WEA International, 1993); *Awake* (Elektra, 1994); *A Change of Seasons* [EP] (EastWest America, 1995); *Falling Into Infinity* (Elektra, 1997); *Once in a LIVEtime* (Elektra, 1998); *Scenes from a Memory* (Elektra, 1999); *Live Scenes from New York* (Elektra, 2001); *Live Metropolis, Pt. 2* (East West Japan, 2001); *Six Degrees of Inner Turbulence* (Elektra, 2002); *Train of Thought* (Elektra, 2003); *Live at Budokan* (Atlantic, 2004); *Octavarium* (Atlantic, 2005); *Systematic Chaos* (Roadrunner, 2007); *Greatest Hit (… And 21 Other Pretty Cool Songs)* (Rhino, 2008).

DRI (1982–PRESENT). Kurt Brecht (vocals), Spike Cassidy (guitar); Dennis Johnson (bass, later replaced by Josh Pappe, John Menor, then Chumly Porter, then Harald Oimen), Eric Brecht (drums, later replaced by Felix Griffin, then Rom Rampy).

DRI (Dirty Rotten Imbeciles) were one of the first punk/metal crossover bands and for a time were among the most successful. DRI started out in Houston, Texas, in 1982 with a unique blurry sound where hyperfast songs sped by in the course of a minute, or often well under. As the eighties progressed, many punk bands, particularly hardcore bands, began to tire of the scene's inner politics, its inherent limited sound where soloing was looked upon as excess, and where poverty was the norm. At the same time in England, where bands like Discharge were pioneering a unique fusion of punk and metal, bands like DRI were also learning the intricacies of longer songs and guitar parts, and although things had begun to move in a more metal direction by the *Dealing With It* album, they fully crossed over into a punk/metal fusion with the release of the extremely influential *Crossover* record in 1987. The band continued in this vein and toured relentlessly, bringing skate punks to metal shows and vice versa although the band continues to this day after multiple personnel changes, the last few releases have lacked the sheer power of DRI, but the band's legacy and contribution to the punk/metal crossover is undeniable.

Discography: *Dirty Rotten* (Rotten, 1982); *Violent Pacification* EP (Rotten, 1984); *Dealing with It!* (Death/Metal Blade/Enigma, 1985; Rotten, 1991); *Crossover* (Metal Blade/Enigma, 1987; Rotten, 1995); *4 of a Kind* (Metal Blade/Enigma, 1988; Restless, 1993); *Thrash Zone* (Metal Blade/Enigma, 1989); *Dirty Rotten LP/Violent Pacification* (Rotten, 1991); *Definition* (Rotten, 1992); *D.R.I. Live* (Rotten, 1995); *Full Speed Ahead* (Rotten, 1995); *Dirty Rotten Imbeciles* (Cleopatra, 2001); *Father, Son, and Holy Shit.*

DUSK (1994–98). Steve Crane (vocals/bass), Steve Gross (guitar/keyboards), Tim Beyer (guitar), Ron Heemstra (drums).

Dusk was an influential but very short-lived Wisconsin death metal band. The early stuff is magnificently doom-laden, brilliant, and evocative. However, the band were not around long enough to make a real impact on the scene.

Discography: *Majestic, Thou in Ruin* (self-released, 1995); *Atmospherea* (Freakadelic, 1999); *Dusk* (Phi Acoustic, 2001); *Dedications and Dreams* (Phi Acoustics, 2003); *Deathgate* (Twilight, 2007); *Pray for Death* (Twilight, 2007).

DUST (1968–73). Richie Wise (vocals/guitar), Kenny Aranson (bass), Marky Bell (drums).

Dust were an early proto-metal band from New York City that featured a young Mark Bell, who would then go on to join two classic punk bands, Richard Hell's backing band the Voidoids and then later the Ramones, where he would drum for most of that band's career. Bassist Kenny Aranson went on to do session work. The band is a footnote, but the two albums are well worth hunting down for fans of hard rock and early metal.

Discography: *Dust* (Performance, 1971); *Hard Attack* (OneWay, 1972).

E

EAGLES OF DEATH METAL (1998–PRESENT). Jesse Hughes (guitar/vocals), Josh Homme (drums).

Eagles of Death Metal (EoDM) are a hard rock band side project of Queens of the Stone Age leader Joshe Homme, who drums. The Eagles of Death Metal are one of the new wave of American heavy metal bands who challenge the orthodoxy of major label metal and are trying to create a new skuzzier style of metal unconstrained by radio standards. However, the name is a misnomer. The band is more of a standard skuzzy hard rock/metal band, and certainly not death metal, despite the band name's claim to the contrary.

Discography: *Peace, Love, Death Metal* (Ant Acid Audio, 2004); *Death by Sexy* (Downtown, 2008).

EARACHE RECORDS (1985–PRESENT). Earache is one of the key metal labels of the last two decades and has released numerous crucial metal albums by bands such as Deicide, the Accused, Napalm Death, Cadaver, Carcass, Cathedral, Morbid Angel, Pitchshifter, Vader, and Sleep. The label was started in 1985 to release material of the early grindcore scene and to try and put out music that was much harder and more aggressive than anything coming from the UK punk or metal scene. The first and most notorious Earache releases were the first Napalm Death album, *Scum* (released in 1987), along with the Heresy/Concrete Sox *Split* album. Soon the label was releasing music from a new darker genre pioneered by American and European bands, and in 1988 they released the influential *Reek of Putrefication* record by Carcass, now regarded as one of the quintessential early death metal records. The streak of consistently new and brutally innovative movement kept up for Earache in 1989 with the release of the Morbid Angel's *Altars of Madness* album, as well as the *Mentally Murdered* EP from Napalm Death.

As Earache grew, they began to expand their repertoire and released classic, mostly death metal records from a variety of bands, such as Terrorizer, Entombed,

Bolt Thrower, Brutal Truth, **At the Gates**, and Decapitated. The label was initially reluctant to have anything to do with the black metal scene, largely because of an unpleasant encounter with Varg Vikernes of Burzum (and Mayhem), whose racist and fascist rejoinders during conversations convinced the label not to touch him with a ten-foot pole (Mudrian 2004, 220). The label began to struggle as many of their key bands, such as Napalm Death, left for better deals elsewhere, and later the fight between various bands, especially Napalm Death, and Earache became legendary for the vitriol they spewed between them. Eventually as Earache and Napalm Death's popularity waned, the band approved of a greatest hits compilation, *Noise of Music's Sake*, released in 2003 on Earache. Today the label still exists, releasing new material from bands such as At the Gates, Deicide, and Municipal Waste.

ELECTRIC GUITARS. While there are three main instruments that comprise the instrumental foundation of all heavy metal music—guitar, bass, and drums—the guitar is of paramount importance and central to the "sound" associated with

Tony Iommi lost the tips of his fingers in an industrial accident, and created a new way of playing guitar. (LEG/Rex Features)

Eddie Van Halen redefined virtuosity. (© Pictorial Press Ltd / Alamy)

the genre. (Vocals are of course a critical element of the genre, and keyboards are sometimes present, although never a critically necessary element.)

In general, the tone and timbre of a heavily distorted electric guitar is the defining sonic characteristic that denotes heavy metal, although it must ultimately be accompanied by heavy drums and bass, the two instruments often referred to as the "rhythm section." As the technology of the electric guitar and amplification evolved, it made the genre of heavy rock and heavy metal possible.

Setting aside the question of amplification for a moment (see the entry on amps for more on this topic), we can chart some of the more important points in the development of the electric guitar and how it has contributed to the unique characteristics of heavy metal.

Guitars first became electrified during the jazz era of the 1930s and 1940s when swing bands grew in size and the relatively low volume of arch-top (acoustic) guitars was insufficient to cut through as a solo instrument. After some early experimentation by guitarist Les Paul and others, the electromagnetic pickup was invented. This technology involves an electrified set of magnets that pick up the vibrations of the guitar's steel strings and convert them into an electrical signal that can then be amplified. Jazz guitarist Charlie Christian was probably the first famous electric guitarist and was a pioneering soloist in the jazz context. Christian's guitar, like all early electrics, were hollow-body instruments with a pickup or set of two pickups mounted on the top.

In the late forties and early fifties a variety of inventors began experimenting with the concept of a solid-body electric guitar. Since the pickup could produce all of the sound necessary, there was little intrinsic need for the guitar to be hollow. Les Paul was again one of the first to realize this and his guitar, nicknamed "the Log," was a case in point. The guitar had started out as an acoustic instrument, but Paul had cut the body in half, inserting a 4-inch-by-4-inch block of wood in the middle of the body, on which he had mounted a pickup. It was a radical way of showing the feasibility of a solid body electric guitar. After bringing his instrument to the Gibson guitar company, Paul was politely shown the door. Around the same time, however, Leo Fender was starting up the Fender guitar company, and pioneered the mass-production of solid-body guitars. One of Fender's innovations was the use of a modular design in which the neck and bodies of the instruments were screwed together rather than glued, an innovation that drastically reduced the time and cost of labor, and helped Fender to make the electric guitar quite affordable, an innovation that would be important if rock music was to take off. Fender's affordable yet quality electric guitars first became available in 1951, just as blues and country were coming together to form the earliest precursors of rock music.

Seeing Fender's success and their virtual monopoly of the solid-body market, Gibson got to work designing their own. After getting input from Les Paul, they introduced the Les Paul model Gibson in 1952, which was a fancier instrument than that which Fender offered. The guitar featured a mahogany neck and body, with a half-inch-thick maple cap on the body elegantly carved with an arched top (because Fender had no carving equipment). The Gibson was a deeper-sounding instrument than the Fender and provided some difference in sound.

A more important development occurred in 1957 when the first "hum-bucking" pickup was introduced on the Les Paul and other models of that year. Invented by Gibson designer Seth Lover, the humbucking pickup would be a critical element in the technology of heavy metal. The earliest pickups were single-coiled, that is, they utilized a single coil of wire that was wound around the magnet of the pickup. These pickups created sound effectively but tended to have a lot of high end (treble) in their sound, and had a tendency to hum or buzz, especially around lights or any other electrical interference. Working on the problem of reducing pickup noise, Lover hit on the idea of using two coils that would cancel out the inherent hum of the pickup, thereby "bucking" the hum. Lover's hum-bucking pickup was a great success, and was featured in a number of Gibson's guitars. In addition to the humbucking pickup being quieter, it was also a smoother and more powerful pickup, and was much more effective at overdriving amplifier circuits, helping to produce a very pleasing overdriven tone. This feature would go a long way toward providing guitarists with a tone that would help them create the distorted tones that we associate with rock, and later on, with heavy metal.

After Eric Clapton's and others' experiments with distorted amp tones in the late 1960s (see entry on "amps" for more information), guitarists increasingly sought to replicate these distorted tones, and the Les Pauls that had been underappreciated in the fifties were increasingly sought out for their humbucking pickups and smooth tonal characteristics. Of course, other manufacturers also began to offer similar guitars, and the humbucking pickup became a standard component for obtaining overdriven rock tones.

Body Shapes and the Aesthetics of Rock Guitar. The year after Gibson had introduced the humbucker saw them introduce two electric guitars that would have a lasting influence on heavy metal guitar designs. In 1958, inspired by the space race that had yielded Cadillac tailfins and the Fender Stratocaster, Gibson introduced two space-age model guitars, the Flying V and the Explorer. The Flying V featured a "V" or arrow-shaped design and a triangular headstock shape. The Explorer, for its part, had an offset body and that was radical in its own way with a wedge-shaped body and a jutting fin-shaped lower cutaway, and an elegantly drooped headstock shape that followed Fender's style of putting all six tuning machines on the same side. Both of these models are now considered among the most elegant of electric guitars ever designed, yet at the time, they found few fans, and for the most part hung unpurchased in guitar stores. However, in ten years' time, as rock styles evolved and humbuckers found favor, guitarists started to appreciate the Flying V and Explorer models, and a number of early heavy metal guitarists, in particular K.K. Downing of Judas Priest and Michael Schenker of UFO began to play the dramatic-looking instruments, and Gibson reintroduced the models to meet new demand. These designs from the fifties began a new tradition in heavy metal for guitars with radical body shapes that has continued to the present day, although the two Gibson designs have retained much of their popularity.

Eddie Van Halen and the Super Strat of the 1980s. Another important technological development in heavy metal guitar began in 1978. This was with the release of Van Halen's debut album. On the album, Eddie Van Halen introduced one of the all-time classic guitar sounds with his trademark "brown" sound, a harmonically rich, overdriven Marshall tone that has ever since been the envy of many a rock guitarist. Along with this tone, and his remarkable technique, Van Halen also pioneered the radical use of the tremelo bar, which allowed him to emulate the sounds of divebombing planes and all manner of sonic effects related to radically raising or lowering the pitches of his notes or harmonics. The tremelo was an early invention of Leo Fender and was featured on Fender's Stratocaster model. However, prior to Van Halen's use, the tremelo was a politely used device that was usually used to simulate finger vibrato (although guitarists such as Jeff Beck and David Gilmour had incorporated a creative use of the bar into their individual styles). Also, since the device was traditionally available on the Strat with its single-coil pickup, it hadn't been associated with heavy rock.

Van Halen was unique in that when he was dissatisfied with the Strat's sound for his band's music, he replaced the single-coil pickup in the guitar's bridge position with a humbucking pickup from one of his Gibsons. This provided Van Halen with the heavy tone that he sought and allowed him to utilize the tremelo's potential with that tone. With a huge distorted tone, Van Halen would use the bar to make his guitar swoop and wail in ways that had never been heard before. Although Van Halen would initially be upset with the legions of guitarist who would imitate his style, he irrevocably changed the course of rock guitar, and introduced a new standard in guitar design with his use of a strat-styled guitar that featured a hum-bucking pickup. Although other guitarist had used humbuckers in strats before, Van Halen popularized it to such an extent that in the decade after his debut, the dominant guitar style was largely that of what has since been called the super Strat, featuring a Strat-shaped body, a tremelo unit, and one or two hum-buckers. As these designs were further refined, it became increasingly common for the headstocks to depart from Fender's original design and take a "pointier" shape, more akin to Gibson's Explorer headstock. Van Halen's own guitar that he later developed with the Kramer guitar company was one of the first examples of these.

Many of these super Strats would also eventually feature the Floyd Rose locking tremelo. Since the radical raising and lowering of pitch with the tremelo bar would often quickly put the guitar out of tune, Rose developed a system whereby the strings were essentially locked in tune at the nut of the guitar and at the bridge, and could be fine-tuned at the bridge once locked. As a result, the player could be as radical as he or she wanted with the tremelo (often referred to as the "whammy bar") and still stay in perfect tune. With the Floyd Rose trem, the super Strat was the most ubiquitous design of the eighties and was very much associated with the era of hair and pop-metal bands.

Slash and the Return of the Les Paul. With the emergence in 1989 of Guns N' Roses and their blues-influenced guitar slinger Slash, there began a return to blues-influenced rock, and just as important, a new and growing appreciation for the Gibson Les Paul that Slash played and was associated with. Ironically, Slash's main Les Paul, which he played on Guns N' Roses' breakout album, *Appetite for Destruction* (1989), was a replica of a 1959 Les Paul built by luthier Chris Derrig that had been purchased for Slash by his manager Alan Niven when the guitarist had been having a hard time getting a good sound in the studio. In the age of super Strats, Slash was the first high-profile contemporary player who made the Les Paul his main axe, and his use of the guitar has been pivotal in the instrument's resurgence in popularity. Since the late eighties, Gibson has attempted to bring back much of the legend of the Les Paul and in 1993 began their current historic line of reissues of many of their classic Les Paul models. Many heavy metal guitarists, including Ozzy Osbourne guitarists Randy Rhoads (one of the few Les Paul users in the eighties) and Zakk Wylde as well as Whitesnake's John Sykes, have made the Les Paul their heavy metal weapon of choice, and the model remains one of the most popular even today.

Tuning Down: How Low Can You Go? One of the most widespread trends in heavy metal guitar of the last ten or more years has to do with the tuning of the instrument itself. While Tony Iommi was one of the first to tune his instrument down lower than standard pitch, and groups like Van Halen, Ratt, and Guns N' Roses regularly tuned down a half-step from standard pitch (which often helped vocalists more easily hit their higher notes), it wasn't until the 1990s that metal groups began to regularly tune their guitars (and basses) down a step or more from standard pitch, leading to a new standard guitar sound which was deeper, lower, and more guttural, almost moving into the range of the bass guitar. To better facilitate playing detuned guitars, many players have taken to utilizing seven-string guitars, such as the one that Steve Vai designed with Ibanez guitars. This model allows for a low B string in addition to the low E string and allows the playing of notes and chords a full two and a half steps below standard pitch. Such guitars usually utilize considerably heavier string gauges to maintain adequate string tension when tuned down. Another option for detuned players is to merely tune down a standard guitar with heavier strings or employ a "baritone" guitar that features a longer scale length especially for lower tunings. No matter which approach one favors, these detuned monsters are at the center of many metal bands' sounds, especially the nu-metal bands like Korn (who use seven strings) and any others who require the lowest, bowel-rattling tones possible.

ELF (1970–75). Ronnie James Dio (vocals/bass), David Feinstein (guitar), Mickey Lee Sould (guitar/keyboards), Gary Driscoll (drums).

Elf was one of the early bands that future **Black Sabbath, Rainbow,** and **Dio** singer Ronnie James Dio toiled in before he hit the limelight. The band started in 1970 and played a lighter, more progressive sound than Dio would later pioneer with Rainbow, Sabbath, and eventually Dio. The band consisted of Dio (who also played bass) as well as keyboard/guitarist Mickey Lee Sould, guitarist David Feinstein, and drummer Gary Driscoll. In 1975 most of the band, including Dio, left to form **Rainbow** with **Deep Purple** guitarist Ritchie Blackmore. While Elf were not the best known of Dio's many bands, they demonstrated the potential of Dio as a frontman and also helped pave the way for the regular use of fantasy-related lyrics common to the metal lyrical lexicon (outside of Sabbath and **Led Zeppelin**).

Discography: *Elf* (Epic, 1972); *LA./59* (MGM, 1974); *Trying to Burn the Sun* (MGM, 1975); *The Gargantuan* (Safari, 1978); *Carolina County Ball* (Safari, 1994).

EMPEROR (1992–2001; 2005–PRESENT). Ihsahn, real name Vegard Sverre Tveitan (vocals, guitar, keyboards); Samtoh, real name Tomas Thormodsæther Haugen (guitar, drums, replaced by Bard Faust, replaced by Trym Torson, aka Kai Johnny Mosaker); and Mortiis, real name Håvard Ellefsen (bass, replaced by Tchort, replaced by Jonas Alver, replaced by Tyr, aka Jan-Erik Torgersen, replaced by Sechtdaemon "Odd Tony"), Charmand Grimloch, real name Joachim Rygg (keyboards, replaced by Einar Solberg).

Emperor is one of the best-known and most respected black metal bands since the creation of the movement. The band was founded in 1992 by Samtoh and Ihsahn, and soon became one of the more popular and atmospheric black metal bands in Norway. Sadly, they also demonstrated black metal's intolerance, and in 1992 drummer Faust stabbed a gay man to death after declining his advances. Samtoh also went to jail for helping to burn down priceless churches in Norway (as noted by Moynihan and Soderlind 1998). Despite the controversy, the band's music, often well-done black metal, is worth a listen, even if the band members are not worth speaking to in person.

Discography: *In the Nightside Eclipse* (Candlelight, 1994); *Anthems to the Welkin at Dusk* (Candlelight, 1997); *IX Equilibrium* (Candlelight, 1999); *Emperial Live Ceremony* (Candlelight, 2000); *Prometheus: The Discipline of Fire & Demise* (Candlelight, 2000); *Scattered Ashes: A Decade of Emperial Wrath* (Candlelight, 2003).

ENGLISH DOGS (1982–87, 1994–96, 2003, 2007–PRESENT). Pete "Wakie" Wakfield (vocals, replaced by Troy McDonald, Adrian Bailey, Wakie, Stu Pid, Gizz), Jon Murray (guitar, replaced by Jamie Martin, Jon Murray, Swapan, Nandi), Gizz Butt (guitar), Mark "Wattie" Watson (bass), Andrew Pinching (drums, replaced by Spikey Smith).

English Dogs were one of the first British hardcore bands, pioneering the punk and metal crossover style in the U.K. alongside such bands as Exploited and **Discharge**. English Dogs may have started out as a hardcore punk band, but by the time of their first album, they had started incorporating longer metal-style solos. When guitarist Gizz had joined the band in time for the *To the Ends of the Earth* EP, the sound began to harden. The release of the landmark *Forward into Battle* EP marked one of the earliest crossover records where metallic riffs and guitars are matched with hardcore drums and bass. The addition of higher-pitched singer Adrian Bailey for the crossover record *Forward into Battle* cemented the band's reputation as one of the few early punk bands to crossover into metal territory. Unfortunately, the albums started to get more overblown and overproduced, which made the record sound like the soundtrack to a bad game of Dungeons and Dragons. The band then splintered apart and would not get together until reuniting with Wakie, Wattie, Gizz, Pinch, and Jon for the *Bow to None* record, a fairly good return to the earlier sound, but of course the band split again. In 2003 a version of the band reunited and at this point the band consists of Wakie, Wattie, Jon, and Stu on drums, playing the earlier pre-thrash material. Pinch currently plays with classic punk act the Damned.

Discography: *Mad Punx and English Dogs* [EP] (Clay, 1983); *Invasion of the Porky Men* (Caly, 1984); *To the* Ends *of the Earth* [EP] (Rto, 1984); *Forward into Battle* (Rto, 1985); *Metamorphisis* [EP] (Under one Flag, 1986); *Where Legend Began* (Under One Flag, 1986); *Bow to None* (Century Media, 1994); *I've Gotta Run* (Retch, 2001); *This is Not War* (Retch, 2002).

ENSLAVED (1991–PRESENT). Ivar (Tvar) Bjornson (vocals/guitar), Kronheim (guitar), Grutle Kgellson (bass), Dirge Rep (drums).

Enslaved are a long-running Norwegian band who gradually evolved their style from black metal to Viking metal to almost progressive. The band originally sang in Icelandic (they felt it was closer linguistically to ancient Norse) and dabbled in the usual black metal and Viking clichés before becoming more progressive but no less extreme after the landmark *Monumension* record in 2001. In that record they began to pay less attention to the trappings of extreme music and expand their palette. Recently the band have collaborated with the electronic group Fe-Mail for the Trincarcia project, sponsored by the Norwegian Ministry of Culture and Church Affairs, which is ironic considering the band started out as an ardent black metal band who produced a split album with Emperor.

Discography: *Frost* (Osmose, 1994); *Vikingligr Veldi* (Anti Mosh, 1994); *Eld* (Osmose, 1997); *Blodhemn* (Osmose, 1999); *Mardraum* (Necropolis, 2000); *Monumension* (Osmose, 2001); *Enslaved* (Import, 2002); *Below the Lights* (The End, 2003); *Isa* (Candlelight, 2005); *Ruun* (Candlelight USA, 2006).

EUROPE (1983–PRESENT). Joey Tempest (vocals), John Norum (guitar), John Leven (bass), Michael Michaeli (keyboards), Ian Haughland (drums).

Best known for their pretentiously dramatic, *Rocky*-like hit, "The Final Countdown," and their particularly photogenic countenances, Europe's classic sound featured keyboards and was a combination of prog-rock and pop influences. The group's roots were in their native Sweden where founding members Joey Tempest (vocals), John Norum (guitars), and John Leven (bass) were in the group Force, which won a national talent contest and a record contract in the early 1980s. After changing their name to Europe and releasing a pair of albums *in* Europe (1993's *Europe* and 1984's *Wings of Tomorrow*), the band inked record deal with Epic Records. At this point the lineup of the band included keyboardist Michael Michaeli and drummer Ian Haughland. The band's next album was their breakthrough. Released in 1986, *The Final Countdown* featured a more keyboard-oriented sound, largely a consequence of producer Kevin Elson's mix and production. Before the album's release, guitarist Norum left the band. Kee Marcelo replaced him. *The Final Countdown* was a major hit for the band, and the video for the title track was in heavy rotation.

Out of This World followed in 1988. It was successful, but not at the level of its predecessor. By the time *Prisoners in Paradise* was released in 1991, musical fashions had shifted and the band disbanded shortly thereafter. 2000 saw the band reunite (featuring both Norum and Marcelo on guitars) for a single New Year's Eve concert, and in 2003 the *Final Countdown* lineup, with Norum on guitar, officially reunited, releasing *Startform the Dark*. *Secret Society* followed in 2006.

Discography: *Europe* (Epic, 1983); *Wings of Tomorrow* (Epic, 1984); *The Final Countdown* (Epic, 1986); *Out of This World* (Epic, 1988); *Prisoners in Paradise* (Epic, 1991); *Gotta Have Face* (JVC Victor, 2004); *Startform the Dark* (T&T, 2004); *Collections* (Sony/BMG, 2006); *Secret Society* (T&T, 2006).

EXODUS (1981–92, 1997–PRESENT). Paul Baloff (vocals, replaced by Steve Souza), Gary Holt (guitar), Kirk Hammett (guitar, replaced by Rick Hunolt), Geoff Andrews (bass, replaced by Rob Mckillop), Tom Hunting (drums, replaced by John Tempesta).

Exodus were one of the most influential thrash metal bands of the eighties. The band formed in San Francisco in 1981 and soon established themselves as one of the most ferocious of the new thrash bands, but the band lost major momentum when guitarist Hammett defected to Metallica. Still, their stunning *Bonded by Blood* debut, although released later than it should have been, is a mixture of punk ferocity and speed with metal bombast that clearly demonstrated that Exodus were true thrash pioneers.

Exodus was one of the first American bands to be influenced not only by the New Wave of British metal but also by the ferocity of hardcore and those bands that straddled both genres such as the Misfits and Motorhead, which led them to help develop thrash, but they were not as quick to record as other bands such as Metallica, so they are generally regarded as coming in the second wave of thrash, despite their being present at its conception. They could not maintain a consistent lineup. When Baloff was ousted in favor of Steve Souza (Testament) and Hunting was forced to leave for medical reasons, the band had recycled all the original members except for Holt, and the quality went downhill over a series of lackluster albums (*Fabulous Disaster* more than lived up to its title).

At this point, Exodus seemed as though they were just going through the motions and by the early nineties the band wisely decided to call it quits. A promising reunion with original singer Baloff was working well until his tragic death from a stroke in 2002. The band continued with the return of Souza, along with the "classic" lineup of Holt, Mckillop, Hunolt, and Hunting. They continue to record to this day, making some of the best music of their career, although many purists still prefer the Baloff years. Exodus are rightly regarded as one of the pioneers of thrash, although they are rarely credited as such.

Discography: *Bonded by Blood* (Combat, 1985); *Pleasure of the Flesh* (Combat, 1987); *Fabulous Disaster* (Combat, 1989); *Impact is Imminent* (Capital, 1990); *The Lesson in Violence* (Relativity, 1991); *Force of Habit* (Capital, 1991); *Another Lesson in Violence Live* (Century Media, 1997); *Tempo of the Damned* (Nuclear Blast, 2004); *Shovel Headed Killing Machine* (Nuclear Blast, 2005); *The Atrocity Exhibition* (Nuclear Blast, 2007).

EXTREME (1989–95). Gary Cherone (vocals), Nuno Bettencourt (guitar), Pat Badger (bass), Paul Geary (drums)

Emerging initially as a Van Halen–like power metal band that featured Aerosmith–like funk grooves into their metal mix, Extreme would go on to mine a more laidback and melodic vein, enjoying a string of hits before fading from the scene in the 1990s. Extreme had its roots in the Boston club scene in a band called the Dream. When the CBS network had plans for a television program with a similar title, the Dream sold off their rights to the name and changed their name to Extreme—ex-Dream—get it? With the new name also came a new guitarist, wunderkind Nuno Bettencourt, who joined vocalist Gary Cherone, bassist Pat Badger, and drummer Paul Geary in time for the band's eponymous debut in 1989.

While not an immediate hit, the band's supertight rhythm section and Bettencourt's virtuosic guitar playing—which combined a refined sense of rhythm and melody with the technical dexterity of Yngwie Malmsteen—went a long way toward establishing their credentials with hard rock fans. The band also began to receive limited airplay of their video for the song "Kid Ego" on MTV.

Their breakthrough came with their second album, *Pornograffitti*, in 1990. The album was more diverse than the band's debut. While they retained their patented "funky metal" approach to some extent (most notably on the first single, "Get the Funk Out"), they began to incorporate more of their mellower influences. In particular, the second single, "More Than Words," was acoustic-based and incorporated more jazz-oriented chords. After overcoming record company objections, "More Than Words" became a huge crossover hit for the band, getting to number 1 on the singles chart. The similarly acoustic-based follow-up "Hole-Hearted" got to number 4.

Unfortunately, the band's success was to be short-lived. After the band's ambitious *III Sides to Every Story* (1992) failed to live up to fans' or critics' expectations, the band released *Waiting for the Punchline* in 1995. This album, too, failed commercially, and the band disbanded, with Bettencourt going on to a solo career, and Cherone briefly joining Van Halen for 1998's *Van Halen III*.

Discography: *Extreme* (A&M, 1989); *Extreme II: Pornograffitt* (A&M, 1990); *III Sides to Every Story* (A&M, 1992); *Waiting for the Punchline* (A&M, 1995); *An Accidental Collision of Atoms: The Best of Extreme* (A&M, 2000); *20th Century Masters—The Millennium Collection: The Best of Extreme* (Universal, 2002); *Best of Extreme* (A&M, 2007).

F

FAITH NO MORE (1982–98). Various, then Chuck Mosley (vocals, replaced by Mike Patton); various, then Jim Martin (guitar, replaced by Trey Spruance, Dean Manta, John Hudson); Roddy Bottum (keyboards); Billy Gould (bass); Mike Bordin (drums).

Faith No More was an avant-garde mixture of punk, funk, and metal, along with avant jazz. They are best known for their two defining anthems, "We Care a Lot" and "Epic," both with different vocalists. The band started in 1982 with the core group of keyboardist Bottum, bassist Gould, and drummer Bordin, who would be the only consistent members of the band. After going through several early vocalists, including a young Courtney Love, the band eventually decided on Chuck Mosley (a similar plethora of guitarists came and went before the more metallic-tinged Jim Martin joined the band in 1984).

Sadly, despite the minor hit with the catchy "We Care a Lot" and its epic football chorus, the band and Mosley had endured constant friction before Mosley was ousted from the band in favor of avant-**death metal** singer Mike Patton (from the band Mr. Bungle—Patton would continue with the Mr. Bungle project for the duration of the band). With a consistent lineup, Faith No More gelled with a bass-heavy sound, grounded by Martin's guitar hero soloing along with Patton's twisted and truly bizarre voice. In 1990 the band had a major hit with the epic song "Epic," which became a radio and MTV hit.

The record spawned several minor hits such as "Falling to Pieces" and a fairly faithful cover of Black Sabbath's "War Pigs," which gained the band a coveted slot on *Saturday Night Live*. The pressure of following up *The Real Thing* proved difficult, and the band responded with the *Angel Dust* album, a notoriously difficult album to listen to aside from the radio-friendly cover of the Commodores' "Easy," especially as Patton grew increasingly experimental in his vocal styling. At the same time, friction in the band led to the departure of guitarist Martin and several replacements that didn't really work out. After two more lackluster and less experimental releases, *King for a Day, Fool for a Lifetime*, and *Album of the Year*, the band called it quits at the end of 1998.

After the band's demise, Patton worked more on experimental music with Mr. Bungle, Tomohawk, and Fanotmas, among others. Roddy Bottum went on to form the peppier queer-friendly band Imperial Teen and Mike Bordin backed up Ozzy and played in place of Bill Ward during one of the Black Sabbath reunions. Although a reunion is unlikely, Patton has indicated that he would not rule it out. Faith No More demonstrates that metal can often be best when twisted in many directions and still retain its force and vitality. Although the band may not have enjoyed the comparison, they were also clearly a major influence on bands such as Korn and Limp Bizkit, who also tried to fuse rap/avant-garde vocals with metal tunes, but never to the extreme degree that Faith No More took the fusion. Avoid the newer groups. Faith No More, and Mike Patton's other groups, such as Fanotmas, are the real deal.

Discography: *We Care a Lot* (Mordam, 1985); *Introduce Yourself* (Slash/Rhino, 1987); *The Real Thing* (Slash, 1989); *Live at Brixton Academy* (Polygram, 1991); *Angel Dust* (Slash, 1992); *King for a Day, Fool for a Lifetime* (Slash/Reprise, 1995); *Album of the Year* (Slash/Reprise, 1997).

FARGO ROCK CITY. *Fargo Rock City: A Heavy Metal Odyssey in Rural North Dakota* (New York: Touchstone, 2001) is a book by rock critic Chuck Klosterman, who defends metal vigorously from its many detractors. To Klosterman, who grew up on a farm near Fargo, North Dakota, metal was a way for outsiders to feel as though they were part of a movement and that they were connected to people outside of their small-town life.

Klosterman later became a pop culture critic and has written numerous articles for *Spin* magazine among many others. He is also the author of four other books, *Sex, Drugs, and Cocoa Puffs: A Low Culture Manifesto; Killing Yourself to Live: 85% of a True Story; Chuck Klosterman IV: A Decade of Curious People and Dangerous Ideas;* and a novel not yet released. He remains one of heavy metal's deepest thinkers, which, as it may seem, is not a contradiction in terms, but indicates that there is depth to metal that skilled writers can analyze in detail and with great consideration conclude that metal, indeed, does rock.

FASHION AND METAL. While the idea of heavy metal and fashion may seem a bit of a contradiction in terms, for years the metal subculture has defined itself by various uses of clothing and other accessories to show either allegiance to metal in general or to a particular subgenre of metal. For many years fashion has evolved, but for young metal fans vintage concert T-shirts-as Seb Hunter puts it, "most importantly one with the tour dates on the back" (26)-demonstrate that one has been a fan for years before the current tour. Another school of thought also believes it is against the rules to wear a particular band's T-shirt to their own show.

During the eighties spandex jeans were popular, but gradually that hair metal look was succeeded by leather pants, black jeans, and leather jacket. While the red leather jacket look was acceptable for many in the pop and hair metal genres, eventually most fans adopted the Motorhead fan look as being more essentially masculine. Female fans could wear almost any combination of looks, as long as

Front row of an audience at a heavy metal rock concert shows long-haired, denim-clad fans. (© Redferns Music Picture Library/Alamy)

(at least during the eighties) teased hair, white or pink leather, and leg warmers were a part of the outfit. (There was also a brief tendency during the glam and hair metal phases for men to wear red leather jackets and leg warmers, but the less said about that the better.)

When denim jackets were worn, painted band album covers were popular, particularly during the eighties when Iron Maiden's *Number of the Beast* album cover was a frequent sight. For black and death metal fans, less and understated were better, and simply anything black, a band T-shirt, or black T-shirt was acceptable. Tattoos and piercings also became more popular during the nineties, and as bandanas became less and less popular (except for balding lead singers) band members were allowed to wear their hair simply down and sometimes parted in the middle, although fans of extreme bands were allowed to emulate their heroes and wear assorted studs, spikes, and skulls. Corpsepaint, discussed elsewhere in this book, was popular in the black metal scenes for quite some time as well.

The problem in identifying metal fashion is that because metal is an evolving subculture, the fashion tends to change from scene to scene and from subculture to subculture, and anyone wishing to join the metal underground should pay careful attention to how bands and fans dress before trying to do so themselves or else risk being labeled poseurs. Today, there is also a trend for retro looks, including mullets, vintage T-shirts bought at thrift shops, and dressing as an eighties hair metal band (or playing like one) in order to either emulate a particular moment in time or simply to mock its excess (see Satanicide).

While many outside the metal scene have long mocked metal bands for their dedication to fashion, all subcultures use fashion as signifiers of membership. In metal, different meanings are encoded in different metal costumes: Death metal fans usually dress fairly low key; black metal devotees, on the other hand, can be unusually outrageous in dress, with corpsepaint being very common at concerts, which would not be appropriate at a Motorhead, or even at a Mastodon, show.

FASTER PUSSYCAT (1987–PRESENT). Taime Downe (vocals), Greg Steele (guitar), Brent Muscat (guitar), Eric Stacy (bass), and Brett Bradshaw (drums).

Taking their moniker from the similarly sleazy but fun Russ Meyer film *Faster, Pussycat! Kill! Kill!*, this L.A. party band found some success, catching the last wave of the hair/pop metal scene in the late 1980s, before fading from the spotlight with the coming of grunge and alterative rock in the 1990s.

Fronted by vocalist Taime Downe, the band played a trashy glam metal, with a look borrowed from the New York Dolls and a sound not too distant from Poison. *Faster Pussycat* was released in 1987, the same year as Guns N' Roses debut, and Faster Pussycat shared with Guns N' Roses a more ragged and streetworn image than many of their contemporaries. Though the album wasn't all that successful, the band did build up a significant cult following that helped put their follow-up, *Wake Me When It's Over,* into gold status. Featuring the top forty hit "House of Pain," the album would be the commercial high point of their career. By the time of 1992's *Whipped*, the shift to alternative and grunge had decimated the band's potential audience, and they split shortly afterwards. After the turn of the new millennium, Downe had put together a new lineup to tour periodically with such former contemporaries as Cinderella and Poison. In 2006 Downe's new lineup released the suitably sleazily titled *The Power and the Gloryhole,* which added a more industrial element to their previous sound.

Discography: *Faster Pussycat* (Elektra, 1987); *Wake Me When It's Over* (Elektra, 1989); *Whipped* (Elektra, 1992); *The Power and the Gloryhole* (Full Effect, 2007); *Between the Valley of the Ultra Pussy* [compilation] (Deadline, 2001).

FATES WARNING (1982–PRESENT). John Arch (vocals, replaced by Ray Alder), Jim Matheos (guitar), Victor Arduini (guitar, replaced by Frank Aresti, others, Aresti again), Joe Dibiase (bass, replaced by Joey Vera), and Steve Zimmerman (drums, replaced by Mark Zonder, Mike Portnoy).

Fates Warning are a Progressive Metal band from Connecticut who are regarded by many critics as one of the major progressive bands of the eighties. The band has struggled to find consistency over the years, with numerous personnel changes leaving guitarist Jim Matheos as the only original member, along with longtime vocalist Ray Alder. *Awaken the Garden* is probably the best for new fans to try, although all of their work is highly recommended for fans of progressive metal.

Discography: *Night on Brocken* (Metal Blade, 1984); *The Spectre Within* (Metal Blade, 1985); *Awaken the Garden* (Metal Blade, 1986); *No Exit* (Metal Blade, 1988); *Perfect Symmetry* (Metal Blade, 1989); *Parallels* (Metal Blade, 1991); *Inside Out* (Metal Blade, 1994); *Pleasant Shade of Gray* (Metal Blade, 1997); *Still Life* [live] (Metal Blade, 1998); *Disconnected* (Metal Blade, 2000); *FWX* (Metal Blade, 2004).

FESTIVALS. There are hundreds of annual heavy metal festivals held all over the world. Perhaps due to the fact that heavy metal is somewhat marginalized by mainstream media, yet remains extremely popular with fans, festivals have

The front row of an audience at a heavy metal rock concert is a full-contact event.
(© Redferns Music Picture Library/Alamy)

emerged as a primary means for fans to experience and appreciate the music en masse. A notable example of such festivals was the 1969 legendary Woodstock Music and Arts Festival. Huge, open-air concert gatherings like Woodstock have long been one of the more visceral manifestations of heavy music communities.

Tens of thousands of music fans coming together in communion to experience the live performance of music at the thunderous volume levels that can only truly occur in a live concert setting has given rock festivals a particular appeal and unique place in popular music culture. Heavy metal, largely marginalized by much of mainstream media culture, and a musical genre that is so based on displays of power and spectacle, has thrived in festival settings, and there are now hundreds of them worldwide that cater to metal fans and bands.

Some of the most prominent of metal festivals are: Britain's Reading and Download (held at the former Monsters of Rock location of Castle Donnington) festivals, and Germany's Wacken Open Air festival, which hosts over 70,000 metalheads at a time, and Brazil's Rock in Rio festival, whose attendance regularly exceeds 200,000. Other major festivals include Bloodstock (UK), Gods of Metal (Italy), Metalmania (Poland), among hundreds of others. There is also Pryor, Oklahoma's Rocklahoma, which taps into the growing nostalgia for hair and pop metal bands from the eighties and has for several years now been a major stop for metal bands like Poison, Cinderella, and Ratt, on the summer touring circuit.

In addition to festivals hosted at specific locations, there have been a number of traveling metal roadshows that have been established in the last few years that operate on the model of the Lolapallooza tour initiated by Perry Farrell of Jane's Addiction. Perhaps the best known of these is Ozzy Osbourne's OzzFest, which traditionally features Ozzy as headliner or co-headliner and features a variety of other metal bands on the bill and also on smaller alternate stages. Other such traveling festivals include the Mayhem festival, Earthshaker Roadshock, Gigantour, and Family Values tours.

FILTER (1995–PRESENT). Richard Patrick (vocals, guitar, programming), various others.

On the heels of Nine Inch Nails' success in bringing the industrial sound to a more mainstream audience, Filter was formed by former NIN touring band member Richard Patrick, who hooked up with Brian Liesegang after NIN's first tour and began recording together to create an industrial-influenced brand of rock. They signed with Reprise Records and issued their debut, *Short Bus*, in 1995. The album was a hit, largely due to the success of the single "Hey Man, Nice Shot," which deftly combined industrial electronic textures with a moody alternative sound. While Patrick and Liesegang had largely completed the album on their own, they added musicians Eeno Lenardo (guitar), Frank Cavanaugh (bass), and Matt Walker (drums) to tour in support of the album.

After the tour Liesegang left because of creative differences with Patrick, who continued to helm the band, releasing *Title of Record* in 1999, which added to the band's success, going platinum on the strength of the hit/video "Take a Picture." *The Amalgamut* followed in 2002, after which Patrick put Filter on hold in order to front a new band called Army of Anyone with Robert and Dean Delillo, formerly of Stone Temple Pilots. Patrick returned in 2008 with a new Filter album, *Anthems for the Damned,* featuring collaborations with John 5 of Marilyn Manson, guitarist Wes Borland (Limp Bizkit), and drummer Josh Freese (A Perfect Circle, Nine Inch Nails, Guns N' Roses).

Discography: *Short Bus* (Reprise, 1995); *Title of Record* (Warner Bros., 1999); *The Amalgamut* (Warner Bros., 2002); *Anthems for the Damned* (Pulse, 2008); *Single Collection* (Wea International, 2000).

FIREHOUSE (1989–PRESENT). C. J. Snare (vocals), Michael Foster (drums), Bill Leverty (guitar), Perry Richardson (bass).

Firehouse found some success at the end of the pop-metal era, largely on the basis of solid, if clichéd, songwriting craft that produced melodic commercial hard rock. Lacking the streetwise image of some of their contemporaries, the band also had a safer, more mainstream appeal that a broader group of fans seemed to connect with.

Formed in 1989, the band won a contract with Epic Records after a showcase later that year. The band's self-titled first album, released in 1991, quickly went platinum on the strength of the singles "Don't Treat Me Bad" and "Love of a Lifetime," both of which well represented the band's ability to deliver solidly commercial, if somewhat corny, radiofare. The band rocked as solidly as many of their contemporaries but were the kind of metal band your mother could listen to. 1992 saw the release of *Hold Your Fire,* which went gold. In 1995, with popular tastes firmly established in alternative rock, Firehouse took a left turn into their softer more MOR-style leanings, delivering *Firehouse III,* which was a relative success given the musical climate of the time. The acoustic *Good Acoustics* album was released in 1996 and was a success, particularly in Asia, where the band would continue to build a strong following, even as their efforts in the states were not as rewarding. Signing with Japanese label Lightyear, the band released the album *Category 5* in 1999. The live album *Bring 'Em Out Live* followed in 2000. With the revival of interest (at least in live venues) for eighties bands, Firehouse has increasingly toured with their former contemporaries, most notably on the "Rock Never Stops" tour with Slaughter and Quiet Riot.

Discography: *Firehouse* (Epic, 1991); *Hold Your Fire* (Epic, 1992); *Firehouse III* (Epic, 1995); *Good Acoustics* (Sony, 1996); *Category 5* (Lightyear, 1999); *Bring 'Em out Live* (Spitfire, 2000); *O2* (Spitfire, 2000); *Prime Time* (Pony Canyon, 2004); *Here for You!* (Collectables, 1998); *Super Hits* (Sony, 2000); *Ultimate Collection* (Sony, 2003); *Firehouse/Hold Your Fire* (Acadia, 2007).

FLOTSAM & JETSAM (1985–PRESENT). Eric A. K. (vocals), Michael Gilbert (guitar), Edward Carlson (guitar), Troy Gregory (bass), and Kelly David-Smith (drums).

Perhaps best known as the band in which Metallica bassist Jason Newsted cut his teeth, Arizona's Flotsam & Jetsam first broke on the scene as an up-and-coming thrash metal band in 1986 with their debut Metal Blade album *Doomsday for the Deceiver*. Soon after its release, Newsted made his departure for Metallica, replacing the band's late bassist Cliff Burton, who had perished in a tour bus accident.

Replacing Newsted with new bassist Troy Gregory, the band released *No Place for Disgrace* on Elektra in 1988, but the album failed to get the band much attention beyond thrash metal circles. 1990 saw the band releasing *When the Storm Comes Down*, the first of three more major label releases (now on the MCA label), but neither it nor its successors would serve to break the band into the big leagues. Nonetheless, the band has continued to record, albeit on smaller labels, plying their brand of thrash for fans of the genre, most recently *Live in Phoenix* in 2006.

Discography: *Doomsday for the Deceiver* (Metal Blade, 1986); *No Place for Disgrace* (Elektra, 1988); *When the Storm Comes Down* (MCA, 1990); *Cuatro* (MCA, 1992); *Doomsday+Flotz* (Roadrunner, 1993); *Drift* (MCA, 1995); *High* (Metal Blade, 1997); *Unnatural Selection* (Metal Blade, 1999); *My God* (Metal Blade, 2001); *Dreams of Death* (Crash, 2005); *Live in Phoenix* (Magick, 2006); *High/Unnatural Selection* (Metal Blade, 2002). .

FOGHAT (1972–PRESENT). Classic lineup: Dave Peverett (lead vocals, guitar), Rod Price (lead and slide guitar), Roger Earl (drums), Craig McGreggor (bass).

While not a heavy metal band per se, Foghat's massive success in the 1970s with their heavy yet accessible brand of boogie rock made them one of the most popular hard rock bands of the seventies, and their classic live album *Foghat Live* was an important precursor to the development of arena rock.

Formed in 1972 in England by former Savoy Brown members Peverett, Earl, and Tony Stephens (bass), the band added guitarist Rod Price before moving to the States and releasing their debut album that same year. Featuring a rocking version of the Willie Dixon blues tune "I Just Want to Make Love to You," the album became a hit on FM radio and set the stage for further success. A string of seven hit records followed, all selling at least half a million copies each, with 1975's *Fool for the City* and 1977's *Foghat Live* (featuring the hit "Slow Ride") being stand-outs. With their infectious boogie energy and leader Dave Peverett setting an upbeat tone, the band always conveyed a positive, good-time vibe, and became one of the most popular touring attractions of the decade.

After Price left the band in 1981, the band's popularity gradually declined, with the band breaking up in the mid-eighties. After a few years, Earl started touring with a new lineup, and in 1993, the original members reunited for a series of albums and tours that lasted until Peverett's death from cancer in February of 2000. Rod Price died in 2005.

Earl currently leads a version of the group featuring vocalist/guitarist Charlie Huhn (formerly performing with Ted Nugent).

Discography: *Foghat* (Bearsville, 1972); *Foghat (Rock and Roll)* (Rhino, 1973); *Energized* (Bearsville, 1974); *Rock & Roll Outlaws* (Bearsville, 1974); *Fool for the City* (Bearsville, 1975); *Night Shift* (Bearsville, 1976); *Foghat Live* (Bearsville, 1977); *Stone Blue* (Bearsville, 1978); *Boogie Motel* (Bearsville, 1979); *Tight Shoes* (Bearsville, 1980); *Girls to Chat & Boys to Bounce* (Bearsville, 1981); *In the Mood for Something Rude* (Bearsville, 1982); *Zig-Zag Walk* (Bearsville, 1983); *The Return of the Boogie Men* (Atlantic, 1994); *Live* (EMI-Capitol Special Markets, 2000); *Family Joules* (Besh, 2003); *Drivin' Wheel* (Live 2005) (Metro City, 2007); *Live II* (Metro City/Foghat, 2007); *Before Foghat Days* (London, 1979); *The Best of Foghat, Vol. 2* (Rhino, 1992); *The Best of Foghat* (Rhino, 1992); *Slow Ride & Other Hits* (Rhino Flashback, 1997); *Road Cases* [live] (Plum, 1998); *King Biscuit Flower Hour* [live] (King Biscuit, 1999).

LITA FORD (1958–). Along with Joan Jett, Lita Ford was one of the two members of the teen punk/metal/exploitation all-girl band the Runaways from the late seventies and early eighties who went on to solo success. Ford's career peaked in the 1980s pop metal scene with a string of successful releases. Like, Jett, Ford's tough girl with a guitar image did much to open rock to the idea of women who could play their instruments as well as any man, even if Ford's own image often involved a certain amount of calculated cheesecake.

After the release of her first two light metal albums, 1983's *Out for Blood* and 1984's *Dancin' on the Edge*, which were moderately successful at best, Ford returned in 1988 with *Lita*. Given a slick sheen by producer/songwriter Mike Chapman, the album featured the hits "Kiss Me Deadly" and "Close My Eyes Forever," a ballad duet with Ozzy Osbourne which made the top ten. Unfortunately, her commercial success was short-lived, as her follow-ups, *Stiletto* (1990) and *Dangerous Curves* (1991), failed to replicate *Lita*'s success, and tastes turned toward alternative rock.

Discography: *Out for Blood* (Mercury, 1983); *Dancin' on the Edge* (Mercury, 1984); *Lita* (Dreamland, 1988); *Stiletto* (RCA, 1990); *Dangerous Curves* (RCA, 1991); *Black* (ZYX, 1995); *In Concert* [live] (Records, 2004); *The Best of Lita Ford* (Dreamland, 1992); *Platinum & Gold Collection* (RCA/BMG Heritage, 2004); *Greatest Hits Live!* (Cleopatra, 2006); *Best of Lita Ford: Kiss Me Deadly* (Collectables, 2006); *The Best of Lita Ford* (Synergie, 2006); *Kiss Me Deadly: Live* (Cleopatra, 2008).

FU MANCHU (1990–PRESENT). Glen Chivens (vocals, replaced by Scott Hill), Scott Hill (guitar), Scott Vatow (guitar, replaced by Eddie Glass, Bob Balch), Greg McCaughey (bass, replaced by Mark Abshire, Brad Davis), Ruben Romano (drums, replaced by Brant Bjork, Scott Reeder)

Fu Manchu (named either after the legendary super-villain or more likely the stoner mustache) not only have one of the best names in new metal but are also one of the most fascinating metal bands working today. Like many post-modern metal bands, they started their career as a hardcore punk band called Virulence, before gradually growing out their hair, discovering "weed" and irony, and becoming a stoner rock classic. Fu Manchu started out as a cross between a stoner rock band and the **Amboy Dukes** flights into the stratosphere. The first record, *No One Rides For Free*, was a stoner rock classic. Scott Hill, formerly the guitarist, had become the vocalist by then and had solidified the band's sound as they evolved from a straight-ahead revival band to one that once again featured elements of punk. The band's connection to stoner rock veterans Kyuss was cemented when former Kyuss drummer Brant Bjork joined the band in 2002. Today Fu Manchu, despite numerous personnel changes (Hill is the only long-term member), remain the perfect band for a soundtrack that re-imagines the eighties as an age where SST (Black Flag's record company) was as important a label as Metal Blade.

Discography: *No One Rides for Free* (Bong Load Records, 1994); *Daredevil* (Bong Load Records, 1995); *In Search of ...* (Mammoth Records, 1996); *The Action Is Go* (Mammoth Records, 1997); *Return to Earth 91–93* (Elastic, 1998); *Eatin' Dust* (Man's Ruin Records, 1999); *King of the Road* (Mammoth, 2000); *California Crossing* (Mammoth, 2001); *Go for It ... Live!* (SPV, 2003); *Start the Machine* (DRT Entertainment, 2004); *Out To Dry* [EP] (Liquor And Poker Music/Century Media Records, 2006); *We Must Obey* (Liquor And Poker Music/Century Media Records, 2007).

FUNERAL (1991–PRESENT). Tori Snyen (vocals, replaced by Sara Eick, Hanne Hukkelberg, Frode Forsmo), Anders Eek (guitar/drums), Christian Loos (guitar), Thomas Angell (guitar), Einar Frederikson (bass).

Funeral is a slow, sludgy, doom metal band in the style of Black Sabbath or Cathedral, only for much of their career, Funeral had a succession of female vocalists before finally settling on Frode Forsmo and solidifying their depressively gloomy doom metal sound. Bassist Frederikson committed suicide in 2003 and guitarist Loos died in his home in 2006.

Discography: *Tragedies/Tristesse* (Firebox, 2006); *From These Wounds* (Tatu, 2007).

G

GIRLSCHOOL (1977–88, 1992–PRESENT). Kim McAuliffe (vocals/guitar), Kelly Johnson (guitar, replaced by Cris Bonacci, Jackie Bodimead), Enid Williams (bass, replaced by Gil Weston, Traci Lamb), Denise Dufort (drums).

Girlschool were one of the key bands of the eighties that demonstrated that women could hold their own in the metal scene, which was unquestionably a boys' club at the time. The band started out in London in 1977 as Painted Lady, before settling on the far more suggestive Girlschool. After releasing their first single, "Take It All Away," they came to the attention of Motorhead and were subsequently signed to Motorhead's label and management company, and soon the band became the foremost female heavy metal band in the world. Additional hits followed, including the famous duet with Motorhead, the "Please Don't Touch" single, which was credited to "Headgirl." The band continued to tour and record, but the loss of key member bassist Williams signaled the end of the first gold period of Girlschool.

In the early nineties, the band essentially changed their name to the She Devils, a project with Toyah Wilcox that led to a period of inactivity for the band. They regrouped in the mid-nineties and the band toured and recorded sporadically, reinvigorated when Williams rejoined the band in 2000. Sadly, guitarist Kelly Johnson died of cancer in 2007, but the band continues to record and perform today with a lineup consisting of McAuliffe, Williams, Dufort, and new guitarist Jackie Chambers. Fans are advised to approach *Running Wild* with caution, as it was the only record made with a different lead singer, Jackie Bodimead. Girlschool continue to be the premier female metal band in metal's history.

Discography: *Demolition* (Bronze, 1980); *Hit & Run* (Stiff, 1981); *Screaming Blue Murder* (Bronze, 1982); *Play Dirty* (Bronze, 1983); *Running Wild* (Mercury, 1985); *Nightmare at Maple Cross* (GWR, 1986); *Race with the Devil* (Raw Power, 1986); *Take a Bite* (Enigma, 1988); *Girlschool* (Progressive, 1992); *From the Vaults* (Progressive, 1995); *Live* (Communiqué, 1995); *King Biscuit Flower Hour Presents in Concert* (King Biscuit, 1997); *Emergency* (Snapper, 1998); *Race with the Devil Live* (Receiver, 1998); *Believe* (Communiqué, 2004).

Girlschool proved that women could rock as hard as men, but they also were mocked for their gender. (Polygram/Photofest)

GOATSNAKE (1996–2001, 2004–PRESENT). Pete Stahl (vocals), Greg Anderson (guitar), Guy Pinhas (bass, replaced by Stuart Dahlquist, Scott Reeder), Greg Roberts (drums, replaced by JR).

Goatsnake are a doom metal band featuring Greg Anderson of Sunn O))) along with the rhythm section for the Obsessed and vocalist Pete Stahl, formerly of Washington, D.C., punk heroes Scream. The band started in 1996 after the demise of the Obsessed. Along with the charismatic Stahl, who had also been in more mainstream band Wool, they began a series of slow and brooding doom metal/stoner metal recordings not too far from Kyuss territory. The band eventually started shedding members of the Obsessed. Dahlquist, formerformerly of Anderson's bandmate in Burning Witch, joined before the band went on hiatus for several years, finally culminating in a reunion featuring Stahl and Anderson and a new rhythm section, for the underrated *Trampled Under the Hoof* EP on Anderson's Southern Lord records. It is unclear at this time if the band's reunion will continue, or if there will be any more recordings or a tour.

Discography: *IV* [7″] (Prosthetic Records, 1998); *Man of Light* [7″] (Warpburner Records, 1998); *Goatsnake Vol. 1* (Man's Ruin Records, 1999); *Flower of Disease* (Man's Ruin Records, 2000); *Goatsnake/Burning Witch Split* (Hydra Head Records, 2000); *Dog Days* (Southern Lord Records, 2000); *Trampled Under the Hoof* (Southern Lord Records, 2004).

GOBLIN COCK (2005–PRESENT). Lord Phallus, aka Rob Crow (vocals, guitar), Bane Ass-Pounder Dave Drusky (guitars), King Sith Sam Mura (bass), Braindeath Anthony Fusaro (drums), Loki Sinjuggleradam Ekrtoh (keyboards), Larben the Druid, aka Lara Benscher (backing vocals, guitar).

Goblin Cock is a doom metal band from San Francisco. If ever there were a band that took the metal equivalent of the double entendre to its obvious and ludicrous extreme, it would be Goblin Cock. The band actually plays a sort of wonderfully sludgy brand of early metal with tongue planted firmly in cheek. The aforementioned "Lord Phallus" is actually Rob Crow from Pinback using the Goblin Cock persona as a way of blowing off steam. According to one critic, Goblin Cock "pairs sludgy, Sabbath-inspired power chords with references to obscure sci-fi and Snuffleupagus. Comic-Con fans, take note" (*Sign On*). Perhaps they are only a joke, but for a joke band, they produced the best slow metal record of 2005, not a miniscule accomplishment.

Discography: *Bagged and Boarded* (Absolutely Kosher, 2005).

GOD DETHRONED (1991–94, 1997–PRESENT). Henri Sattler (vocals/guitar), Issac de Lahaye (guitar), Beef (bass, replaced by Henk Zinger), Roel (drums, replaced by Arien Van Weesenbeek).

God Dethroned are a Dutch band among the harshest of the extreme bands. The band was started by only constant member Henri Sattler in 1991, and only managed to record one album before breaking up in 1992. The band reunited in 1995 with a new lineup and continues to perform and tour to this day. The most recent album finds them solidly on course with songs such as "Typhoid Mary" and "Falling Down."

Discography: *Christhunt* (Shark, 1992); *The Grand Grimoire* (Metal Blade, 1998); *Bloody Blasphemy* (Metal Blade, 1999); *Christhunt* [reissue](Cold Blood Industries, 2000); *Ravenous* (Metal Blade, 2001); *Ancient Ones* (Import, 2001); *Into the Lungs of Hell* (Metal Blade, 2003); *The Lair of the White Worm* (Metal Blade, 2004); *The Toxic Touch* (Metal Blade, 2006).

GODFLESH (1988–2002). Justin Broadrick (vocals/guitar), J.C. Green (bass), Machines (drums, replaced by Bryan Mantia, Ted Parsons).

Godflesh were an English band that combined grindcore with industrial music and beats. They were influenced by unacknowledged key grindcore influence the Swans (as well as Enisterzende Neubaten). The band started in Birmingham, England, in 1988, and distinguished themselves from the other bands playing in the grindcore and death metal scenes by using a drum machine instead of a regular drummer, leading to a fast, clock-like industrial beat, reminiscent of vintage Ministry. The early releases are key slabs of industrial metal, but the Columbia years saw the band start to use actual humans on drums, leading to a loss of the factory-like mechanical beats that had been their staple. In 2001, Green quit the band, and although Paul Raven of Ministry was announced as a replacement, the band did not tour and soon had broken up for good. Along with Napalm Death (Broadrick was an early member), Godflesh are one of the key bands from the grindcore/death metal scene to set standards for other bands to follow. Broadrick now plays in the ambient electronic drone band Jesu.

Discography: *Godflesh* (UK Swordfish, 1988; UK Earache, 1990; Earache, 1995); *Streetcleaner* (UK Earache, 1989; Earache/Combat, 1990; Earache, 1999); *Slavestate* (Earache/Relativity, 1991, Earache, 1995); *Pure* (Earache/Relativity, 1992); *Merciless* [EP] (Earache/Columbia, 1994); *Selfless* (Earache/Columbia, 1994); *Songs of Love and Hate* (Earache, 1996); *Love and Hate in Dub* (Earache, 1997); *Us and Them* (Earache, 1999); *Hynms* (Koch International, 2001); *Messiah* (Relapse, 2003).

GODSMACK (1996–PRESENT). Sully Erna (vocals), Lee Richards (guitar, replaced by Tommy Rombola), Robbie Merrill (bass), Joey D'Arco (drums, replaced by Tommy Stewart, Shannon Larkin).

Godsmack are an American new metal band from Massachusetts who were popular during the late nineties. Like many new metal bands such as Limp Bizkit and Korn, the band played a confessional form of hard rock with metal tinges. The band also caused some mild controversy in the politically aware section of the metal contingent when two of the songs from their *Awake* album, "Sick of Life:" and "Awake," were used in U.S. Army recruiting commercials. For fans of Alice in Chains (who the band resembles musically) only, otherwise Godsmack are a well-selling footnote to the new metal craze (the album *Faceless* is aptly named). The band went on "hiatus" in 2007, and it is unclear if the hiatus will be permanent or not.

Discography: *Godsmack* (Universal/Republic, 1998); *Awake* (Universal/Republic, 2000); *Faceless* (Universal/Republic, 2003); *IV* (Universal/Republic, 2006); *Good Times, Bad Times ... Ten Years of Godsmack* (Universal/Republic, 2007).

GORGOROTH (1992–PRESENT). Hat (vocals, replaced by Gahl), Infernus (guitar), Tormentor (guitar), Samoth (bass, replaced by Infernus, Ares, King of Hell), Goat (drums, replaced by Satyricon, replaced by Frost, replaced by Grim, Frost, Sjt. Erichson, replaced by Kvitrafn).

Gorgoroth are a Norwegian black metal band whose lead singer, Gahl, is now in jail for attacking a man and attempting to ritually drink his blood as noted by Moynihan and Soderlind. Gorgoroth, who took their name from the classic fantasy series, *The Lord of the Rings,* played a little too close to fantasy at times in real life, as well. The band played a raucous type of black metal heavily influenced by Mayhem, although their sound was more modern with some progressive and industrial touches thrown in, especially on the later releases. The band also courted its share of controversy for their extreme anti-Christian views. The band was also mired in controversy in 2007, when founder and guitarist Infernus was either fired by Gahl and King of Hell, or fired them. After counter-lawsuits, both began new bands under the name Gorgoroth and have announced plans to tour under the name. Gorgoroth are one of the most extreme black metal bands in existence and their dedication to Satan has been unquestioned by many in the metal community. Drummer Grim died in 1998.

Discography: *Pentagram* (Malicious Records/Century Black/Season of Mist, 1994); *Antichrist* (Malicious Records/Century Black/Season of Mist, 1996); *Under the Sign of Hell* (Malicious Records/Century Black/Season of Mist, 1997); *Destroyer: Or How to Philosophize with the Hammer* (Nuclear Blast, 1998); *Incipit* (Nuclear Blast, 2000); *Twilight of the Idols: In Conspiracy with Satan* (Nuclear Blast, 2003); *Ad Majorem Sathanus Glorium* (Regain Records, 2006); *Quanots Possund Ad Satanitatum Trahunt* (Regain Records, 2009).

GREAT WHITE (1981–PRESENT). Jack Russell (vocals), Mark Kendall (guitar), Michael Lardie (keyboards/guitar), Tony Montana (bass), Audie Desbrow (drums).

Most active during the height of the pop metal boom in Los Angeles in the mid- and late-1980s, Great White were in fact much more old school, tapping into the blues-infused tradition of classic rock bands like Bad Company, Mott the Hoople, and Led Zeppelin. Still, they fit in with the other bands of the era because of their solid musicianship, songwriting, and frontman Jack Russell's distinct and powerful vocals, which were reminiscent of those of Robert Plant.

Having formed in the early 1980s by Russell and guitarist Mark Kendall, the band built up a following on the Los Angeles club circuit, playing their original blend of blues-based metal. Shrewdly managed by Alan Nivens (who would go on to guide the career of Guns N' Roses), the band released a series of independent recordings in 1983, an EP entitled *Out of the Night*, and the album *Shot in the Dark*. On the basis of their club following and local radio airplay, the band was able to sell some 20,000 copies of the recordings. Impressed with the band's sales, EMI signed the band, releasing their self-titled album in 1984. In 1987 the label re-released *Shot in the Dark*, and later that same year released the new *Once Bitten....* The latter album produced the hit single "Rock Me." By now, the band consisted of drummer Audie Desbrow, keyboardist-guitarist Michael Lardie, and bassist Tony Montana, in addition to Russell and Kendall.

In 1989, the band released *Once Bitten*'s follow-up, *Twice Shy*, which proved to be the band's breakthrough record. Featuring the hit single and video, a cover of Mott the Hoople's "Once Bitten, Twice Shy," it proved to be a massive success for the band. The band supported the album with extended tours with Ratt and Tesla, not returning to the studio until 1991's *Hooked*. The album was a modest success, selling half a million copies. When their subsequent album *Psycho City* sold even fewer copies, EMI dropped the band, only issuing a best of collection in 1993.

The years that followed found the band staying active but under more modest circumstances, releasing albums on smaller labels like Zoo, Imago, and Cleopatra.

The band reluctantly found themselves back in the national spotlight under tragic circumstances, when a pyrotechnical display in their show set the nightclub they were performing on fire in February 2003. One hundred people were killed in the blaze, including guitarist Ty Longley. The remaining band members were forced to deal with legal issues related to the pyrotechnics, and the band subsequently performed a series of benefits for the families of the victims.

By 2007, the original lineup had reunited for a series of 25th anniversary shows, and later that summer they released an album of new material entitled *Back to the Rhythm*.

Discography: *On Your Knees* (Enigma, 1982); *Great White* (EMI America, 1984); *Once Bitten ...* (Capitol, 1987); *Shot in the Dark* (Razor & Tie, 1987); *Recovery: Live!* (Enigma, 1988); *... Twice Shy* (Capitol, 1989); *Live in London* (Alex, 1990); *Desert Moon* (Capitol, 1991); *Hooked* (Capitol, 1991); *Psycho City* (Capitol, 1992); *Sail Away* (Zoo, 1994); *Stage* [live] (Volcano, 1996); *Let It Rock* (Imago, 1996); *Great Zeppelin: A Tribute to Led Zeppelin* (Deadline, 1999); *Can't Get There from Here* (Sony, 1999); *Gallery* (Axe Killer, 2001); *Recover* [live] (Cleopatra, 2002); *Thank You Goodnight* [live] (Knight, 2002); *Great White Salutes Led Zeppelin* (Legacy Entertainment, 2005); *Once Bitten, Twice Live* (Sidewinder Music, 2006); *Back to the Rhythm* (Shrapnel, 2007).

GRIM REAPER (1979–87). Steve Grimmett (vocals), Nick Bowcott (guitar), Dave Wanklin (bass), Mark Simon (drums).

Part of the New Wave of British heavy metal, Grim Reaper had some of the talent but not quite the presence to be true contenders. Still, they did manage to put out a few albums that satisfied metal fans of the eighties.

Coming together in 1979, the band placed a song on 1981's Heavy Metal Heroes compilation, and then went on to win a battle of the bands competition, claiming the prize of a chunk of studio time. That led to a three-song demo tape that in turn won them a contract with independent label Ebony Records. Their debut album, *See You In Hell* (1984) didn't set much of Europe on fire but did generate some interest stateside, reaching 73 on the album charts and selling a quarter of a million copies. The band's second album, 1985's *Fear No Evil*, fared less well, and their fortunes began to slide. A third album in 1987, *Rock You to Hell*, while initially charting, soon fell off the charts, never to be heard from again. The band soon went their separate ways.

Discography: *See You in Hell* (RCA, 1984); *Fear No Evil* (RCA, 1985); *Rock You to Hell* (RCA, 1987); *Best of Grim Reaper* (RCA, 1999).

GRINDCORE. One of the most extreme of the new metal genres to develop in the 1980s was the ultra fast and almost blurlike wave of noise that is grindcore. Pioneered by English metal stalwarts Napalm Death, grindcore takes the speed and ferocity of hardcore punk and thrash metal and then speeds it up ludicrously. Fed sometimes by a lightning-speed double bass drum attack, ridiculously fast snare "blast beats," and ultra sped-up guitar and vocals, grindcore took music beyond the parameters of hardcore punk and up to an entire new level of musical ferocity. The label was given to the new style of music from Napalm Death drummer and Swans fanatic, Mick Harris. According to Harris, "Grindcore came from 'grind,' which was the only word I could use to describe the Swans after buying their first record in '84 ... then with this new hardcore movement that started to bloom in '85, I thought 'grind' really fit because of the speed, so I started to call it grindcore" (Mudrian 2004, 35).

The main feature of early grindcore were the 64th notes that Harris played on the snare drum (which the drummer named "blast beats," along with the bass drum playing in quadruple time (many later drummers added a second bass drum or pedal to the bass drum to try and up the tempo on the bass as well as the snare). Drummer Steve Charlesworth of the underrated band Heresy also helped to up the ante on the beat by challenging Harris in "duels" to play faster and faster. Soon the style spread from the small town of Sparkhill in Birmingham to catch the attention of Digby Pearson of Earache records, who had released the Accused classic *The Return of Martha Splatterhead*. Digby released the first Napalm Death album *Scum* in 1987, which contained an accurate sticker announcing the debut of the "world's fastest band."

Other bands followed quickly, although most of the original bands soon moved on to death metal or black metal, and the original grindcore bands who were influenced more by Discharge and the crust punk scene soon dissolved into myriad different variations on the original theme, and even Napalm Death began to slow their sound down, although they later became faster again. Today most bands play some variation on the genre, such as the bands that use electronic drums for ultra sped-up beats (although ultra sped-up drum beats do not make someone part of the grindcore scene, artists such as the techno master Moby have played songs faster than any Napalm Death song, but their intention is not the same.) Bands such as Pig Destroyer, Nasum, and Soilent Green straddle the line between death metal and grindcore, and although the genre is not dead, it is unclear where one can go after already playing at lightning-fast speeds.

DAVE GROHL (1969–). While drummer/guitarist Dave Grohl may be best known for his stints in the grunge titans Nirvana or his widely successful rock band Foo Fighters, Grohl is also a veteran of the eighties D.C. punk scene and a major metal aficionado. Like many punks, Grohl was first attracted to modern metal by that classic gateway drug, Motorhead, and also quickly became a fan of many of the thrash and death metal bands that came of age in the late eighties.

In 2004 Grohl realized a longtime dream when he released the *Probot* record, a one-man project where Grohl played almost all of the instruments alongside guest vocalists such as Cronos from Venom, Lemmy, old D.C. friend Wino, and even King Diamond. While the record was not commercially successful, it was interesting to note the seriousness with which Grohl regarded the assignment, and many of the songs sound fresher than the recent work of some of the guest vocalists. Grohl has also worked as a guest drummer, most notably playing drums for the Queens of the Stone Age record *Songs for the Deaf* (2002).

Grohl is one of the most vocal champions of the old-school metal that many younger fans are rediscovering and illustrates the nexus between punk and metal in terms of music. Many fans found it easy to pass through the boundaries during the glory days of crossover punk and metal. At present it is unclear whether *Probot* was a one-off project or if Grohl will continue with his mainstream band Foo Fighters.

GRUNGE. Grunge is the term used by rock critics to describe the mid-1980s movement primarily located in the Pacific Northwest and epitomized by bands such as Nirvana, Mother Love Bone, Green River, Mudhoney, Soundgarden, Tad, Pearl Jam, and many others. Most of the pivotal bands from the grunge scene had played in bands on the punk scene before experimenting with longer song structures and more metallic riffs. To use two pivotal bands as touchstones, the movement can overall be described as being influenced by equal parts Black Flag and Black Sabbath in its blend of punk and early metal sensibilities

The movement was featured in a film, *Singles* (1992), which featured a soundtrack of numerous popular bands of the day. Even early on, many of the bands associated with the grunge scene and its attendant fashions (Converse All-Stars, plaid shirts usually tied around their waists, and old punk or metal T-shirts, along with long unruly hair) went to great lengths to disassociate themselves from the movement, and the music suffered as imitation bands such as Stone Temple Pilots and others moved in and became media darlings. The movement has no official set ending date, and bands such as Nickelback and Hinder can be seen as the descendents of grunge, but most assume the movement ended with the suicide of grunge icon Kurt Cobain of Nirvana, who shot himself in the head in 1994. Grunge can ultimately be looked at as an offshoot of both punk and metal. Bands such as Black Flag did a logical extension of the genre when they grew their hair long in the mid-eighties and pioneered a slowed-down version of punk, or a punk version of metal, depending on which aspect one likes to view it from. Either way, grunge was the death knell of numerous popular hair metal and glam bands and can now be seen as the sherbet course that cleansed the palate for the new wave of hard underground music.

GUITAR HERO. *Guitar Hero* is a video game where players can compete at various levels by emulating the guitar parts on various songs at different levels of difficulty. The plastic guitar that players are given does not actually require playing on the frets, but instead has several colored "keys" that the players push as they see the colors go by on a guitar neck as the song progresses. The easiest levels involve very little dexterity, but the upper levels demand a level of concentration, and hopefully a familiarity with the music being played. Ironically, many guitar players complain that the game is too difficult for real guitar players as it does not conform to guitar tablature, and many drummers or non-musicians often have an easier time playing the game. *Guitar Hero* is immensely popular and has sold at least 14 million copies and is one of the most popular video games ever created.

GUITARS. *See* Electric Guitars

GUNS N' ROSES (1985–PRESENT). Axl Rose (vocals), Slash (guitar, replaced by Robin Finck, Buckethead, Robert Finck, sometimes together in later years, now Finck), Izzy Stradlin (guitar, replaced by Gilby Clarke, Paul Tobias, Richard Fortus, Ron Thal), Duff McKagan (bass, replaced by Tommy Stinson), Steven Adler (drums, replaced by Matt Sorum, Josh Freese, Bryan Mantia, Frank Ferrer, Dizzy Reed (keyboards since 1990), and Chris Pittman (keyboards, programming, since 1998).

Guns N' Roses is one of the most famous, infamous, popular, and despised metal bands in metal's long and rich history. Despite their limited output and strained relationship with fans, the band is one of the key metal bands of any decade since the inception of metal. Led by the enigmatic Axl Rose (William Bruce Rose) the band started out as an amalgam of punk's anger mixed with a classic glam and a heavy edge, before descending into self-parody and ending up with Axl Rose as the only original member, struggling to release the album *Chinese Democracy* that he has been working on for over a decade.

The band was formed out of the ashes of legendary Los Angeles metal band Hollywood Rose in 1985, when members Axl Rose and Izzy Stradlin, along with L.A. Guns members Tracii Guns (guitar), Ole Beich (bass), and Rob Gardener on drums, formed a new band, a sort of Sunset Strip super-group. When Beich departed, Duff McKagan, formerly of punk band the Fartz, took over on bass, and following the departure of Tracii Guns to reform L.A. Guns, Slash was added on lead guitar. The classic lineup was completed with the addition of drummer Steven Adler in June of 1985. The band soon began playing the L.A. Sunset Strip where their high-energy live shows soon earned them a fanatical following, leading to the band's initial signing to Geffen Records and recording of the "live" *Live ?!@ Like*

Axl Rose of Guns N' Roses. (Photofest)

a Suicide, a four-song EP with audience applause added to create ambience. The band took their time in the studio to record their first album, because the band and record label smelled a winner, and also because the band was reportedly heavily reliant on drugs and alcohol at the time, as later confirmed by former guitarist Slash in his self-titled autobiography.

The band's acknowledged masterpiece is their first full-length album, *Appetite for Destruction*, a record that was apparently made in a fog of drugs, alcohol, and domestic drama. It is impossible to measure the importance of an album such as *Appetite for Destruction*. The singles it spawned, such as "Welcome to the Jungle," "Paradise City," and "Sweet Child O' Mine," were metal classics that brought the band a huge non-metal audience and in a way also sowed the seeds of the band's destruction. Their follow-up *Lies* EP was notable for its ballad "Patience" as well as the controversial song "One In a Million," in which Axl rails against "immigrants," "niggers," and "faggots" in what one hopes was a tongue-in-cheek manner. Still, the damage was done, and after talk of growing dissention in the GNR camp and the replacement of Steven Adler by former Cult drummer Matt Sorum, Axl announced his most grandiose project yet: a two-record project released individually, called *Use Your Illusion I &II*. Although fans faithfully lined up to buy the records when they came out at midnight, the band had clearly lost a sense of direction; while containing some good songs and even some classics, the records were bewildering and bloated, with none of the perks of the early GNR sound.

Besides the covers record, *The Spaghetti Incident*, things grew quiet in the GNR camp for quite some time. After leaving the band acrimoniously, Slash, Duff, and drummer Matt Sorum eventually formed the band Velvet Revolver with former Stone Temple Pilots frontman Scott Weiland and put out two successful records before Weiland left the band. Former guitarist Izzy Stradlin kept a low profile after kicking heroin and now lives a more sedate existence. Former drummer Steven Adler also kicked hard drugs (as also noted by Slash in his autobiography) and has indicated interest lately in a GNR reunion with all the original members. The band now features leader Axl Rose, with bassist and colonel Tommy Stinson (late of the punk/indie greats the Replacements) along with a floating cast of characters that have included Buckethead on guitar, as well as session drummer extraordinaire Josh Freeze.

After years of fervid speculation, Axl Rose finally delivered on *Chinese Democracy* (in November 2008). The CD was released exclusively in Best Buy stores in the United States and the album sold well, but nowhere near previous Guns N' Roses records. While the tanking market for CDs was blamed, and many critics argued over how groundbreaking an album could be after almost two decades of tweaking and re-recording, it may well be that many of the original fans have simply moved on, settled down, and are nowhere near as fanatical as they were during GNR's heyday. All in all *Chinese Democracy* may be an excellent record, but after 18 years since the release of the last original album by Guns N' Roses, many fans may also have asked, "Is that all there is?" But despite the album's possible shortcomings and its infamously delayed release, the band's influence on metal has been enormous. In retrospect, they defined the era of the late eighties and early nineties in rock and roll as well as any other band of that time.

Discography: *Appetite for Destruction* (Geffen, 1987); *G N'R Lies* (Geffen, 1988); *Use Your Illusion I* (Geffen, 1991); *Use Your Illusion II* (Geffen, 1991); *The Spaghetti Incident* (Geffen, 1993); *Collectors Box* (Chrome Dreams, 2006); *Chinese Democracy* (Geffen, 2008).

GWAR (1985-PRESENT). Oderus Urungos (vocals/guitar), numerous (guitar), too many (guitar), lots (bass), many more (drums).

GWAR is perhaps the most ridiculous band in metal history, but then again they may just be the logical conclusion to the silliness that has marked much of metal since its origins. The band members dress in bizarre and vulgar costumes that resemble a Las Vegas show on acid and spew forth fluids and goo onstage while staging mock executions and occasionally playing actual music. The band continues to be a stage draw and suggests that Gene Simmons of Kiss may be one of the smartest entrepreneurs in metal history, since many bands such as GWAR have realized that the music comes second to the spectacle. The Romans had a term for the free food and entertainment that kept the masses placated during times of political uncertainty: "Bread and Circuses."

Discography: *Hell-O* (Shimmy-Disc, 1988); *Scumdogs of the Universe* (Metal Blade, 1990); *The Road Behind EP* (Priority, 1992); *America Must Be Destroyed* (Metal Blade, 1993); *This Toilet Earth* (Metal Blade, 1994); *RagNaRok* (Metal Blade, 1995); *Carnival of Chaos* (Metal Blade, 1997); *We Kill Everything* (Metal Blade, 1999); *Violence Has Arrived* (Metal Blade, 2001); *War Party* (DRT Entertainment, 2004); *Beyond Hell* (DRT Entertainment, 2006).

H

HANOI ROCKS (1980–85, 2002–PRESENT). Mike Monroe, aka Matti Fager-holm (vocals, saxophone), Andy McCoy, aka Antti Hulkko (guitar), Nasty Suicide, aka Jan Stenfors (guitar, replaced by Conny Bloom), Sam Yaffa, aka Saki Takamati (bass, replaced by Andy Christell), Gyp Casino, aka Jesper Sporre (drums, replaced by Nicholas "Razzle" Dingley, replaced by Terry Chimes, Lacu, George Atlagic).

Hanoi Rocks were one of the great glam metal bands of the eighties, who played in a style closer to the New York Dolls than most of the eighties glam metal scene. The band, originally started in Finland of all places, cultivated an aura of sleaze and decadence, along with a catchy, hook-laden style of glam pop metal that should have caught on big, but tragically did not. Their first release, *Bangkok Shocks, Saigon Shakes, Hanoi Rocks*, is a gem-filled classic glam metal album, with catchy tracks including the ballad "Don't Never Leave Me Baby" and the crunchy punk-influenced "First Timer."

The record was a minor success and was impetus for the band to relocate to the United States, where they were a marginal but powerful presence in the glam scene in L.A. Most of the band members had previously been in punk bands in Finland, and the band's energy can be seen as a natural precursor to the more punk-influenced glam metal bands, such as Guns N' Roses a few years later. (Guns N' Roses would later acknowledge the debt, and Monroe sings the song "Ain't It Fun" on *The Spaghetti Incident* and plays harmonica on "Bad Obsession" on *Use Your Illusion I*.) The band released a stream of records that, although good, did not match the ferocity of the first record, with only *Back to the Mystery City* coming close.

One of the reasons most casual metal fans know the band is the notoriety of the demise of drummer Razzle (who had replaced the original drummer Gyp Casino) who was killed in a car accident with a drunken Vince Neil of Mötley Crüe behind the wheel, as detailed in Mötley Crüe's book, *The Dirt*. Although Razzle was killed and several people injured, Neil only paid a fine (and compensation to Dingley's family) and spent a mere month in jail. Razzle was replaced by former Clash drummer Terry Chimes, but the band had failed to make an impact and Monroe decided to end the band in late 1985. Suicide, Chimes, and McCoy found a new female lead singer and formed the short-lived Cherry Bombz. Sam Yaffa now plays in the reformed New York Dolls, an interesting example of life imitating art. Monroe Yaffa and briefly Nasty Suicide played in the punk band Demolition 23 in New York City for several years in the nineties, before that band imploded as well.

Despite their best efforts, the band is a footnote to most metal bands, which is a shame as their sound was miles above bands like Poison who aped the same poses to spectacular success. In 2002, Monroe and McCoy reformed the band with a new rhythm section and released a new record, *Twelve Shots on the Rocks*, before touring again as Hanoi Rocks. Despite their low profile, Hanoi Rocks are still a standard by which glam metal bands will be measured for years to come.

Discography: *Bangkok Shocks, Saigon Shakes, Hanoi Rocks* (Geffen, 1981); *Oriental Beat* (Geffen, 1982); *Self-Destruction Blues* (Geffen, 1982); *Back to the Mystery City* (Geffen, 1983); *Two Steps from the Move* (Epic, 1984); *All Those Wasted Years* (Geffen, 1985); *Rock and Roll Divorce* (Botolick, 1985); *Hanoi Rocks* (Castle, 1996); *A Day Late, a Dollar Short* (Victor Entertainment, 2003); *One Night Stand in Helsinki* (Japanese Victor Company, 2003); *Twelve Shots on the Rocks* (Major Leiden, 2003); *Another Hostile Takeover* (JVC Japan, 2005); *Fashion Street* (JVC Japan, 2007); *Street Poetry* (Demolition, 2007).

HARDCORE PUNK. Hardcore punk was a subdivision and logical successor to punk rock that evolved and was especially prevalent circa 1979–86, but still continues today in many forms and permutations. Early hardcore bands such as Middle Class (who probably had the first hardcore song, "Out of Vogue" in 1978), DOA (who may have been the first to use the term as the title of their 1981 record *Hardcore 81*), The Circle Jerks, Black Flag, TSOL, Minor Threat, Agnostic Front, and especially Bad Brains in the USA as well as English Dogs, Discharge, and others in the United Kingdom were all playing a style of music that reflected the younger, more suburban desire for a louder, more aggressive form of punk.

In the early nineties, the punk and metal scenes began to cross over as several hardcore punk bands such as DRI, Corrosion of Conformity, TSOL, and others began to play more metallic riffs. At the same time, many metal bands such as Metallica, Slayer, Anthrax, Venom, and others were being influenced by bands such as Black Flag, Minor Threat, and Bad Brains. At a certain point it was hard to distinguish between the speed/thrash metal genre and some more metallic hardcore bands. Many of the bands were influenced by Motorhead, a band where both early punks and metalheads found common ground and could be seen at the same shows.

Many punk hardcore bands had either broken up by 1986 (such as Black Flag, Minor Threat, and the Misfits), others such as TSOL had become full-fledged metal bands, and others such as Agnostic Front and the Exploited, Discharge, and English Dogs had begun to include numerous metal touches such as extended guitar solos and improved musicianship and production.

As many of the punk bands left the scene, many of the metal bands who had been influenced by the early hardcore bands (such as St. Vitus, Slayer, Metallica, and Venom) founded a new movement alternately called thrash or speed metal (depending on the fan base or the critics) and others made their way (such as Venom) into the new genre of black metal.

Today, numerous bands play in both styles, and the difference in musical style between a vegan straight-edge band such as Earth Crisis and a modern metal band is difficult to articulate unless lyrical content is taken as the indicator of a band's true genre. Numerous modern bands still pay tribute to the early hardcore punk bands, and both Slayer and Metallica released cover versions of early hardcore songs on tribute records, and many metal bands to this day wear T-shirts that represent the classic hardcore bands that many of them grew up on. Ultimately hardcore's lasting legacy to heavy metal was freeing it from the constraints of the established slow and mid-tempo musical styles that most metal bands played during the seventies and early eighties and allowing metal to be both slow as a dinosaur trudging its way across the tundra, and as fast as an explosion spreading quickly outwards in a fireball.

HATEBREED (1994–PRESENT). Jamey Jasta (vocals), Frank Novinec (guitar), Sean Martin (guitar), Chris Beattie (bass), Mat Byrne (drums).

Hatebreed are one of the most popular of the hard and heavy bands to come out of the new hardcore scene and have evolved into an amalgam of heavy metal, hardcore punk, and screamo. The band was started by Jasta in 1994 and was supposed be a straight-ahead hardcore punk band, but as the hardcore and metal scenes had merged to a certain degree in the late eighties, the band ended up playing a more metallic form of hardcore with longer solos and grunted vocals. The first two split 7-inch records are the most punk, and the band grew a keen metallic sheen by the late nineties. While many bands play in the style that Hatebreed helped to distill, they remain one of the best of the punk/metal hybrids to this day and high-profile slots, such as Hatebreed's headlining of the second stage at Ozzfest in 2007, indicate how accessible their sound was to both punk and metal fans. Sadly, former guitarist Lou Richards killed himself in 2006 at the age of 35.

Discography: *Split 7″ with Neglect* (Stillborn Records, 1995); *Split 7″ with Integrity* (Stillborn Records, 1995); *Under the Knife* (Smorgasbord Records, 1996); *Satisfaction is the Death of Desire* (Victory Records, 1997); *Perseverance* (Universal, 2002); *The Rise of Brutality* (Universal Records, 2003); *Supremacy* (Roadrunner Records, 2006).

HEADBANGING. Headbanging refers to the rocking back and forth motion of the head in time to the rhythm of the music when one is listening to heavy metal music. Audience members can often be seen, especially those at the edge of the stage, "banging" their heads in this manner. For the most part, "banging" is merely an expression, as the headbanger is usually merely moving his or her head to the music, and not literally banging his or her head against anything physical. However, it has been reported that the term first came into popular usage during Led Zeppelin's first tour of the U.S., when audience members were seen actually banging their heads *against* the stage! Lemmy Kilmister of Motorhead has also spoken about seeing one crazed fan repeatedly banging his head against the stage during a Motorhead performance, even as blood was flowing down his face! Overall, however, headbanging is usually just a marker of a listener getting lost in the music and moving to it.

HEAVEN AND HELL (2006–PRESENT). Ronnie James Dio (vocals), Tony Iommi (guitar), Geezer Butler (bass), Vinnie Appice (drums).

Pseudonym of a Black Sabbath lineup used by the Ronnie James Dio version of the band during their reunion tours in 2006 and 2007. By the late nineties the

Black Sabbath name had once again became a lucrative franchise and frequent tours with the original lineup of Iommi, Butler, Ward, and Osbourne had become a cash cow with new T-shirts being sold to enraptured fans that had never seen the original lineup play live. However, many older fans were also nostalgic for what was considered to be the second great Black Sabbath of the post-Ozzy band led by former Rainbow and Elf singer Ronnie James Dio (along with frequent drummer Vinnie Appice). When Iommi wished to take a break from touring with the original Black Sabbath, he proposed doing several tours with Dio, a move that was blocked by Osbourne's wife and manager, Sharon Osbourne, who insisted that the Ozzy-less band be clearly identified as not being the original Sabbath. The compromise solution was to call the band "Heaven and Hell" (named after one of the group's most popular albums) and the tour went on to fill huge venues in America and elsewhere. Perhaps it was the fact that the original Black Sabbath was no longer a novelty, or it might have been that Iommi and Butler appeared much more interested and lively than usual, but the Heaven and Hell tours inspired a level of fan interest almost unforeseen at the time. At this point the reunion has produced several new tracks but it is unclear if a new full-length album and future tours are in the works.

Discography: *Black Sabbath: The Dio Years* (Rhino, 2007).

HEAVY METAL KIDS (1973–78). Gary Holton (vocals), Mickey Waller (guitar), Ronnie Thomas (bass), Danny Peyronel (keyboards, replaced by John Sinclair), Keith Boyce (drums).

Heavy Metal Kids were an English metal band with punk leanings that were popular during the mid-seventies. The band was formed in London in 1973 and quickly established themselves as one of the most popular local bands playing in a glam, light metal, proto-punk style with little bits of pre-oi thrown in for good measure. Singer Gary Bolton was influenced by the stage antics of Iggy Pop and was one of the most physical and showman-esque of the metal bands of the time. A particular highlight of any Heavy Metal Kids show was the climax where Bolton blew up a dummy of himself onstage. Keyboard player John Sinclair later played with Ozzy Osbourne and Uriah Heep. The band's first keyboard player, Danny Peyronel, later joined UFO. After a semi-successful career as an actor, including roles in the films *Quadrophenia* and *Breaking Glass*, Holton dove into an abyss of substance abuse. Lead singer Holton died in October 1985 of a heroin overdose (Poulsen 2005, 171), which seemed to destroy the chance of any lucrative reunion tour, but the band got back together in 2002 with original members Boyce, Thomas, and keyboardist Peyronel on lead vocals, to some small acclaim. The Heavy Metal Kids were a major influence on punk, and a sadly overlooked band in terms of their influence on the glam and pop metal scene of the eighties.

Discography: *Heavy Metal Kids* (Atlantic, 1974); *Anvil Chorus* (Atlantic, 1975); *Kitsch* (Rak-Spak, 1977); *Hit the Right Button* (Import, 2003).

HEAVY METAL MUSIC. *See* Heavy Metal Music: An Introduction at the beginning of this encyclopedia.

HEAVY METAL PARKING LOT. The 1986 documentary *Heavy Metal Parking Lot* is a hilarious but realistic look at metal pre-show rituals as epitomized by the fans tailgating in a parking lot at a Judas Priest show. The various fans who are tailgating outside the show deliver their opinions on women, booze, metal, and other subjects, as the cameras rolls. The director also did several other films about parking lots after shows, including the drastically different *Neil Diamond Parking Lot*. The movie is an outrageous look at what pre-show metal rituals were like during the eighties and is proof that things have not changed significantly since then (at least as far as heavy metal parking lots are concerned).

HELLHAMMER 1982–84. Tom G. Warrior (vocals/guitar), Steve Warrior, aka Urs Sprenger (bass, replaced by Martin Eric Ain), Pete Stratton (drums, replaced by Bruce Day).

Hellhammer were an early version of the band that went on to become Celtic Frost. Although they did not last long or leave much of a recorded output, they are revered by many in the black metal scene for their innovation and are a major influence on both the black and death metal scenes. The band was started by Tom Warrior in 1982 in Zurich, Switzerland, and Urs Sprenger (Steve Warrior) as Hammerhead before changing their name to the more provocative Hellhammer and recording the *Triumph of Death* and *Satanic Rites* EEPs, which sound like a cross between Venom and what Celtic Frost would become a few years later. The four-song *Apocalyptic Raids* record was released in 2004 but only hinted at the possibilities of the band and what was to come in Celtic Frost. Ain and Warrior never performed under the name Helhammer again, although the band's influence on death and black metal is considerable. In 2008, Century Media finally released the authorized collection of the complete demos and compilation releases as *Demon Entrails*.

Discography: *Demon Entrails* (Century Media, 2008).

HELLOWEEN (1982–PRESENT). Classic lineup: Michael Kiske (lead vocals), Kai Hansen (vocals/guitar), Michael Weikath (guitar), Markus Grosskopf (bass), and Ingo Schwichtenberg (drums).

One of the most influential European heavy metal acts of the 1980s, Helloween combined the energy and speed of thrash metal with the harmonic structures of traditional metal bands like Judas Priest and Iron Maiden to create the template of what would come to be known as power metal. Though they never achieved worldwide success or U.S. stardom, the band remains a potent influence on the metal that followed them.

Starting out in 1982 as a four-piece out of Hamburg, Germany, the band initially consisted of guitarist/lead vocalist Kai Hansen, guitarist Michael Weikath, bassist Markus Grosskopf, and drummer Ingo Schwichtenberg. The band's first recording was a self-titled EP released in 1985, which was followed by the full-length album *Walls of Jericho* in 1986. The band's innovative mix of classic and thrash metal won them critical and fan appreciation in Europe and set the stage for their second full-length recording. Hansen, however, was not convinced that he had the vocal ability to carry the band to the heights that he envisioned for it, and the band sought a frontman to take over the vocals.

In 1987 vocalist Michael Kiske joined the band, and they entered the studio to complete their second album, *Keeper of the Seven Keys, Pt. 1*, released later that year. The album was a winner, and its unique combination of melodic songwriting and metal power made it an important contribution to the evolution of power metal. For his own part, Kiske fulfilled Hansen's hopes for the band, proving himself to be a fine vocalist in the tradition of belters like Rob Halford or Bruce Dickinson. The album was a hit in Europe where the band became stars and began to generate interest in the U.S. market as well, as the band went out to support it with an extensive tour.

Keeper of the Seven Keys, Pt. 2 came out in September 1988 and was another major hit for the band, despite a decline in the overall quality of the songwriting. A performance at the legendary Donnington Monsters of Rock Festival was a high point for the band around this time. Surprisingly, founding guitarist Hansen soon left the band, citing the fact that he felt he could no longer control the direction of the band once it had grown so big.

Nonetheless, the rest of the group continued, drafting ex-Rampage guitarist Roland Grapow into their ranks, and embarking on a successful U.K. tour. Around the same time, EMI records offered to take over the band's contract from their troubled label Noise Records. As a result, a legal dispute followed that effectively put a hold on the band's activities for close to two years.

Finally returning to work with a 1991 release with the strange title of *Pink Bubbles Go Ape,* the band didn't exactly put its best foot forward, as the album featured strange attempts at humor (the title track and another entitled "Heavy Metal Hamsters") and generally uneven songwriting quality. Not too surprisingly, the album was a failure commercially. The band's follow-up shared its fate, and shortly afterward both vocalist Kiske and drummer Schwichtenberg departed the band.

Despite the losses, and the loss of their EMI contract, the band regrouped, adding singer Andi Deris and drummer Uli Kusch, and recorded *Master of the Rings* in 1994, which proved an improvement over the band's previous two efforts.

When the band's former drummer Ingo Schwichtenberg, who had been suffering from mental health problems, took his own life, the shaken band dedicated their subsequent album, *The Time of the Oath,* to him in 1996. A fitting tribute to their friend, the album turned out to be the band's strongest showing in five years and went a long way toward repairing their reputation. A successful tour followed and produced a double-live release, *High Live,* which they put out later in 1996. The return to form seemed to take hold through 1998's *Better than Raw* and *Metal Jukebox* (an album of covers) in 1999, and 2000's *The Dark Ride.*

Longtime members Grapow and Kusch left in 2001 and were replaced by guitarist Sascha Gerstner and ex-U.D.O. drummer Stefan Schwarzmann.

Discography: *Helloween* (Banzai, 1985); *Walls of Jericho* (Noise, 1986); *Helloween/Mini LP* (Noise, 1987); *Keeper of the Seven Keys, Pt. 1* (RCA, 1987); *Keeper of the Seven Keys, Pt. 2* (RCA, 1988); *I Want Out: Live* (RCA, 1989); *Live in the U.K.* (EMI, 1989); *Pink Bubbles Go Ape* (Castle Music UK, 1991); *Chameleon* (European Import, 1994); *Master of the Rings* (Castle, 1994); *Mr. Ego* (Import, 1994); *The Time of the Oath* (Castle, 1996); *High Live* (Castle, 1996); *Better Than Raw* (Velvel, 1998); *Metal Jukebox* (Never/Sanctuary, 1999); *I Can* (Castle, 2000); *The Dark Ride* (Nuclear Blast, 2000); *Rabbit Don't Come Easy* (Nuclear Blast, 2003); *Keeper of the Seven Keys: The Legacy* (Steamhammer, 2005); *If I Could Fly* (Nuclear Blast, 2006); *Keeper of the Seven Keys: The Legacy World Tour 2005/ 2006* [live] (SPV, 2007); *Gambling with the Devil* (Steamhammer, 2007); *The Best, the Rest, the Rare* (Noise, 1991); *Pumpkin Box* (Victor, 1998); *Treasure Chest* (Metal-Is, 2002); *Treasure Chest* [Box] (Import, 2002); *Karaoke Remix* (Seoul, 2002); *Singles Box Set 1985– 1992* (Castle, 2006).

HIGH ON FIRE (1998–PRESENT). Matt Pike (guitar/vocals), George Rice (bass, replaced by Joe Preston, Jeff Matz), Des Kensel (drums).

High on Fire was formed by guitarist Matt Pike after the demise of his previous band, the stoner rock legend Sleep. In High on Fire, Pike wanted to move away from the intricate stoner rock of Sleep in a harder and faster direction. High on Fire is almost the total opposite of Sleep, with heavy, brutal drums anchoring Pike's massive (and brutally loud) riffage, ferocious drumming from Kensel, and Pike's lurid growl. Pike is also a keen guitar experimenter and in some songs such as "Khanrad's Wall" and "Turk" the band veers almost into Indian raga territory—just an example of Pike's prowess and willingness to experiment outside the parameters of modern metal. Bassist Rice left the band to be replaced by ex-Melvin (a key influence on Pike) Joe Preston temporarily, until Metz stepped in to fill out the bottom end. High on Fire are one of the best touring bands in metal, and the latest record, *Death is this Communion*, is a beautifully abrasive record. Although many fans yearn for a full-on Sleep reunion, High on Fire is testament to the fact that a band can be both brutal and beautiful at the same time.

Discography: *The Art of Self Defense* (Man's Ruin Records, 2000); *Surrounded by Thieves* (Relapse Records, 2002); *Blessed Black Wings* (Relapse Records, 2004); *Death Is This Communion* (Relapse Records, 2007).

HOLOCAUST (1977–PRESENT). Gary Lettice (vocals, replaced by John Mortimer), John Mortimer (vocals/guitar), Ed Dudley (guitar, replaced by John McCullim, Robin Begg (bass, replaced by Steve Cowen, Bryan Bartley), Nicky Arkless (drums, replaced by David Rosie, Ron Levine).

Holocaust is one of the longest lasting of the New Wave of British metal (NWOBM) that formed in the late seventies. The band, from Scotland, has been charting a heavy but sometimes-uneven course over almost thirty years, but still have an ardent following, despite numerous personnel changes that have left Mortimer as the last remaining member. *The Nightcomers* is considered by many to be their classic album, and they were a major influence on Metallica, who covered their song "The Small Hours" on *The $5.98 EP: Garage Days Revisited*. While Holocaust were not the most well-known band in the British New Wave of heavy metal, the first two records are particularly recommended.

Discography: *The Nightcomers* (Phoenix, 1981); *Live (Hot Curry and Wine)* (Phoenix, 1983); *No Man's Land* (Phoenix, 1984); *Hypnosis of Birds* (Taurus Moon, 1993); *Spirits Fly* (Feel the Power, 1996); *Covenant* (Neat, 1997); *No Escape* (Jack Move, 1998); *The Courage to Be* (Edgy, 2001); *Death or Glory* (Castle, 2003).

THE HORNS. The ubiquitous and universal hand gesture and symbol of heavy metal. The horns, also sometimes called the devil sign, are completed by extending the pinky and index finger up while holding the middle two fingers down with the thumb. While many have tried to take credit in the past for the symbol, the credit (or blame) most credibly goes to Ronnie James Dio (Dio, Elf, Rainbow, Black Sabbath, Heaven and Hell) who maintains that he learned it from his Italian grandmother and that it is a sign that would ward off the evil eye, although it also means vulgarities or curses depending on the culture.

I

IMMORTAL (1990–PRESENT). Abbath Doom Occulta (vocals/bass/guitar), Demona Doom Occulta (guitar, replaced by Abbath), Aeturnues Ares (bass-live, replaced by Iscariah), Armegadda (drums, replaced by Grim, Hellhammer, Horgh).

Immortal are a long-running Norwegian black metal band that were briefly associated with the cabal involving Varg Vikernes, but they quickly defined their own reputation as one of the best and darkest black metal bands. The band started out as more atmospheric, but they soon added more grindcore-style blast beats. The one constant member for the existence of Immortal is singer and multi-instrumentalist Abbath Doom Occulta, whose black vision has inspired the brutal soundscapes of albums such as *Sons of Northern Darkness* and the classic *Damned in Black*. Although the band has weathered several tragedies over the years (guitarist Demona Doom Occulta had to leave the band due to problems with tendonitis and ex-drummer Grim committed suicide in 1999), the band continues to record and perform and the latest album, *Blashrykh Kingdom*, is an excellent distillation of the band's trademark black and moody sound.

Discography: *Diabolical Full Moon Mysticism* (Osmose, 1992); *Pure Holocaust* (Osmose, 1993); *Blizzard Beasts* (Osmose, 1997); *At the Heart of Winter* (Osmose, 1999); *Damned in Black* (Osmose, 2000); *Sons of Northern Darkness* (Nuclear Blast, 2002); *Battles in the North* (The End, 2006); *Blashrykh Kingdom* (Conquer, 2008).

INCUBUS (1991–PRESENT). Brandon Boyd (vocals), Michael Einzinger (guitar), Gavin Koppell (DJ replaced by DJ Kilmore), Alex Katunich (bass, replaced by Ben Kenney), Jose Anotnio Pasillas (drums).

Incubus was one of the most popular bands of the nu metal movement, and although they were not musically similar to bands such as Korn and Limp Bizkit, they were inadvertently often lumped in with that crowd, despite the fact that their music was often far more melodic and interesting than most of the nu metal bands of that time. The band is also unusual for its use of a DJ. DJ Kilmore supplies the band with more of a balanced soundscape as well as expanding the group's musical palette. The band eventually sued Sony for improper accounting records (one of many bands trying to find out why record labels seemed to get the best of the economic situation). Out of the many nu metal bands, Incubus was one of the more interesting of the bands that added rap and noise to metal.

Discography: *Fungus Amongus* (Sony, 1995); *S.C.I.E.N.C.E.* (Immortal/Epic, 1997); *Make Yourself* (Sony, 1999); *Morning View* (Sony, 2001); *A Crow Left of the Murder ...* (Epic/Immortal, 2004); *Light Grenades* (Sony, 2006).

INFECTIOUS GROOVES (1991–2000). Mike Muir (vocals), Stephen Perkins (drums), Adam Siegel (guitars), Robert Trujillo (bass).

With a unique and innovative blend of metal and funk, Infectious Grooves, begun as a side project by Stephen Perkins of Jane's Addiction and Mike Muir of Suicidal Tendencies, shook up the rock community in the nineties with their musical hybrid, starting in 1991 with the album *The Plague That Makes Your Booty Move*.

Discography: *The Plague That Makes Your Booty Move* (Epic, 1991); *Sarsippius' Ark* (Epic, 1993); *Groove Family Cyco* (550 Music, 1994); *Mas Borracho* (Suicidal, 2000).

INSANE CLOWN POSSE (1988–PRESENT). Violent J (vocals), Shaggy 2 Dope (vocals).

ICP are a Detroit metal/rap crossover band with an extremely dedicated fan base known as the Juggalos. The two MCs are Violent J (Joseph Bruce) and Shaggy 2 Dope (Joseph Utsler) The group's lyrics are fairly misogynistic and sophomoric, but their stance of rebellion appeals tremendously to fans that see no real difference in the presumed hardness/heaviness of rap and metal. Although the band is often lumped in with the nu metal movement of the mid-nineties, in fact they have their roots in a Detroit group of MCs originally called Inner City Posse. The band has developed an elaborate mythology around themselves, releasing albums that supposedly contained secret messages and after a series of six "joker" cards were released would eventually trigger the apocalypse. (The band has also released records that are not supposed to be counted as part of the joker series.) Insane Clown Posse are an example of a rap/metal band with an ardent fan base, despite the relative crudeness of their lyrics and songs. They are also a precursor to much of the rap metal crossover scene that dominated the commercial metal scene in the early to mid-nineties.

Discography: *The Carnival of Carnage* (Psychopathic Records, 1992); *The Ringmaster* (Psychopathic Records, 1994); *Riddle Box* (Jive, 1995); *The Great Milenko* (Island Records, 1997); *The Amazing Keckel Brothers* (Island Records, 1999); *Bizzar* (Island Records, 2001); *The Wraith: Shangri-La* (Psychopathic Records, 2002); *The Wraith: Hell's Pit* (Psychopathic Records, 2004); *The Tempest* (Psychopathic Records, 2007).

IRON BUTTERFLY (1966–71). Doug Ingle (vocals/organ), Ron Bushy (drums), Erik Braun (guitar), Lee Dorman (bass).

With their heavy acid rock of the sixties, Iron Butterfly was one of the first bands to evolve a sound that presaged heavy metal, and their 17-minute opus,

"In-A-Gadda-Da-Vida" (a perversion of the phrase "in a garden of Eden") is often cited as one of the first heavy metal tracks (though its monotonous, psychedelic refrain may seem a bit old-fashioned to contemporary listeners).

Iron Butterfly was formed in 1966 after San Diegan Doug Ingle (vocals and organ) had moved to Los Angeles with drummer Ron Bushy and hooked up with bassist Jerry Penrod, vocalist Darryl DeLoach, and guitarist Danny Weis. After scoring a recording contract, the band released its first album, *Heavy*, in 1968. The band recorded a second album with guitarist Erik Braun and bassist Lee Dorman now joining Ingle and Bushy, *In-A-Gadda-Da-Vida* (1968), which contained the title track and became a hit, selling over four million copies. The album spent a year in the top ten, and an abridged single got as high as number 30. After a follow-up with 1969's *Ball*, which went gold, the band's fortunes declined and by 1971 they had broken up.

Discography: *Heavy* (Rhino, 1968); *In-A-Gadda-Da-Vida* (Atco, 1968); *Ball* (Collectors' Choice Music, 1969); *Iron Butterfly Live* (Rhino, 1970); *Metamorphosis* (Rhino, 1970); *Scorching Beauty* (Repertoire, 1975); *Sun and Steel* (Edsel, 1976); *Rare Flight* (Pair, 1991); *Light and Heavy: The Best of Iron Butterfly* (Rhino, 1993); *Greatest Hits* (Bellaphon, 1995); *Live* (Atlantic, 2005); *In-A-Gadda-Da-Vida* (Falcone Music, 2005); *The Best of Light and Heavy* (Rhino, 2007).

IRON MAIDEN (1976–PRESENT). Bruce Dickinson (vocals), Steve Harris (bass), Dave Murray (guitar), Adrian Smith (guitar), Nikko McBrain (drums), Janick Gers (guitar).

Arguably the most important and enduring heavy metal group to emerge during the New Wave of British heavy metal in the late seventies and early eighties, Iron Maiden have long specialized in a technically accomplished brand of riff-oriented yet melodic metal that capitalized on the members' highly polished playing skills and the considerable vocal power and stage dynamism of their singer Bruce Dickinson. With their fantasy-based lyrical imagery and creatively staged shows, they have managed to maintain and please a rabid fan base for over three decades, becoming along the way one of the most influential of heavy metal bands.

First put together by bassist Steve Harris in 1976, an evolving lineup of the band played around in the London clubs until stabilizing in 1978 to include Harris, guitarist Dave Murray, drummer Doug Sampson, and singer Paul Di'Anno. The band made its local reputation playing a harder and faster version of the classic melodic hard rock played by their influences such as Thin Lizzy, UFO, Wishbone Ash, and Deep Purple. In 1978, the group entered the studio, recording a three-song tape that came to be called *The Soundhouse Tapes*. In three weeks the band was able to sell five thousand copies, and the band began to get attention from the local rock press.

By 1979, the band had added a second guitarist in Dennis Stratton, and drummer Sampson had been replaced by Clive Burr. In December of the same year, the band had a record deal with EMI Records.

The band's first album, *Iron Maiden*, hit the UK album charts and reached the number 4 position with one week. The album contained the early classic Maiden tracks "Running Free," "Transylvania," and "Phantom of the Opera." The tunes, penned mostly by Harris, were indicative of the band's style: eschewing the mundane heavy metal themes of sex and booze, the band's lyrics were largely fantastical,

Iron Maiden were one of the key metal bands of the 1980s. (Epic/Photofest)

drawing inspiration from literature, science fiction, and history, all of which would contribute to the band's larger than life image and stage presentation.

The band followed up the album's release with a headlining tour of the UK, after which came supporting tours of Europe supporting Kiss and Judas Priest. In October 1980 guitarist Stratton was replaced by Adrian Smith.

Maiden's second album, *Killers*, built on the style of the first album although it added a heavier edge. The album also built on the lyrical imagery Harris had developed, with the track "Murders in the Rue Morgue" drawing inspiration from the short story of the same title by Edgar Allan Poe.

Unfortunately, *Killers* would be Di'Anno's last album with the band. Due to increasingly problematic drug and alcohol abuse, he was fired from the band at the end of 1981, and former Samson vocalist Bruce Dickinson soon took his place (Weber).

Dickinson made his recording debut with the band on 1982's *The Number of the Beast*, and any concerns about the band's ability to replace Di'Anno were dismissed. Dickinson's dynamic style and almost operatic range were clearly in evidence and fit particularly well with the band's dramatic style. The album gave the band their first UK number 1. While the album was a major hit in the U.S. as well, it also drew controversy over its title, which led a variety of fundamentalist

Christian groups to accuse the band of being Satanists. The band did what they could to deny the accusations and went on to perform an extensive world tour in support of the album.

In 1982, prior to the release of the band's fourth album, drummer Clive Burr was replaced by ex-Trust and Pat Travers drummer Nicko McBrain. Not unlike the addition of Dickinson, McBrain's joining gave the band another world-class performer whose abilities would only make the band stronger. In 1983, the band released *Piece of Mind,* which was another big hit. The band supported the album with two extensive tours.

Powerslave followed in 1984, and featured the songs "2 Minutes to Midnight," "Aces High," and "Rime of the Ancient Mariner," the last a 13-minute song based on Samuel Taylor Coleridge's poem of the same name. The band followed up the release with their biggest tour yet, with a stage show that now included the huge mechanical ghoul mascot dubbed "Eddie," who was based upon the ghoulish characters that were featured on a number of their album covers. Many of the shows from the tour were recorded for an upcoming live album, and after the tour, the band took a well-deserved six-month break.

Somewhere in Time released in 1986 featured some experimentation by the band. Most of the lyrics were related to time travel to some degree of another. More significantly, the band experimented with their sound by incorporating synthesized treatments and effects that complemented their traditional instrumentation of guitars, bass, and drums. Though a slight departure from their traditional sound it wasn't enough to alienate their fans, and the album performed well, especially thanks to the single "Wasted Years."

More lyrical adventures followed with *Seventh Son of a Seventh Son,* released in 1988. The album was based on the story of a mythical child possessing clairvoyant powers. Instrumentally, the album was the first to feature actual keyboards in addition to guitars. The album was a smash hit and gave the band its second number 1 in the UK.

As the band turned ten in 1990, they celebrated by releasing *The First Ten Years,* a collection of 10 CDs and 12-inch vinyl records.

In 1989, Adrian Smith released a solo album called *Silver and Gold* with his side project ASAP. Dickinson followed suit in 1990 with *Tattooed Millionaire,* featuring guitarist Janick Gers.

Adrian Smith left Maiden during sessions for the album *No Prayer for the Dying* and was replaced by Janick Gers. The album, released in 1990, marked a return to their more traditional sound and featured the number 1 hit single "Bring Your Daughter to the Slaughter," which was included on the soundtrack of the film *Nightmare on Elm Street 5: The Dream Child.*

Dickinson went on a short solo tour in 1991 before rejoining Maiden for 1992's *Fear of the Dark.* After the album's release, he announced that he was leaving the group although he stayed long enough to perform with the band on a farewell tour and to record two live albums. His final show with the band was on August 28, 1993, which was filmed and broadcast by the BBC and later released on video as *Raising Hell.*

After a long series of auditions, the band selected vocalist Blaze Bayley, formerly of the band Wolfsbane, as Dickinsons' replacement. He made his debut with the band on the album *The X Factor* in 1995. With Bayley's vocal style a departure from that of Dickinson's, reactions to the album were mixed. At the same time

Harris was experiencing the breakup of his marriage and critics speculated that this contributed to a difference in the album's sound as well. The band followed the album's release with an extended tour that took them through all of 1996, after which they released their first proper compilation of their hits.

The album *Virtual XI* was released in 1998 and was again a disappointment in the sales department and was the first Maiden album to miss the million sales mark.

1999 saw a return to form for the band as Bayley left and the group welcomed back both Dickinson and Smith (guitarist Gers remained as well). In celebration, the band embarked on a huge reunion tour dubbed "The Ed Hunter Tour," which referred to the band's recently released computer game *Ed Hunter*. After the tour the band began work on the album *Brave New World,* which was released in 2000. The album was followed by another world tour, which culminated in the band's appearance at the Rock in Rio festival. Their performance was recorded and released in 2002 as *Rock in Rio.*

The reinvigorated Maiden have kept busy in the new millennium, releasing both the hit collection *Edward the Great* and the studio album *Dance of Death* in 2003. Live DVDs *The Early Days, Part 1,* and *Raising Hell* were brought out in 2004. The two-disc collection *The Essential Iron Maiden* was released in 2005, which coincided with the band's co-headlining appearance with Black Sabbath on that year's Ozzfest tour. The live CD/DVD *Death on the Road* came out later in 2005, followed by the 2006 studio album *Matter of Life and Death.*

Discography: *Iron Maiden* (Capitol, 1980); *Killers* (Capitol, 1981); *The Number of the Beast* (Capitol, 1982); *Brain Damage Tour of Europe* [live] (Capitol, 1983); *Piece of Mind* (Capitol, 1983); *Powerslave* (Capitol, 1984); *Live After Death* (Capitol, 1985); *Somewhere in Time* (Capitol, 1986); *Seventh Son of a Seventh Son* (Capitol, 1988); *Stranger in a Strange Land* (EMI International, 1990); *No Prayer for the Dying* (Epic, 1990); *Running Free Run to the Hills* (EMI, 1990); *Fear of the Dark* (Epic, 1992); *A Real Live One* (Capitol, 1993); *A Real Dead One* (Capitol, 1993); *Live at Donington* (Virgin/EMI, 1994); *Virtual XI* (CMC International, 1998); *Brave New World* (Sony, 2000); *Rock in Rio* [live] (Columbia, 2002); *Dance of Death* (Columbia, 2003); *Death on the Road* [live] (Sony, 2005); *Maidenmania* (EMI, 1987); *Aces High* (EMI, 1988); *Somewhere Back in Time: The Best of 1980–89* (Sony, 2008).

ISIS. Aaron Turner (vocals, guitars), Randy Larson (guitars, replaced by Mike Gallagher), Jeff Caxide (bass), Aaron Harris (drums), Chris Mereshuk (keyboards/samples, replaced by Jay Randall, replaced by Cliff Meyer).

Isis are one of the new wave of innovative and groundbreaking metal bands that are revitalizing the current scene. The band was started in Boston in 1996 and pioneered a mixture of heavy dynamics and atmospheric riff-based, constantly evolving music that could almost be labeled post-metal. *The Red Sea* remains a high point in late-nineties metal.

Discography: *The Red Sea* (Second Nature, 1999); *SGNL>05* (Neurto, 2001); *Celestial* (Escape Artist, 2001); *Oceanic* (Ipecac, 2002); *Remixes* (Japanese Import, 2004); *Panopticon* (Ipecac, 2004); *Oceanic: Remixes/Reinterpretations* (Hydra Head, 2005); *Live, Vol. 2: Stockholm 3/19/03* (Troubleman Unlimited, 2005); *In the Fishtank, Vol. 14: Isis and Aereogramme* (In The Fishtank, 2006); *In the Absence of Truth* (Ipecac, 2006).

J

JACKYL (1991–PRESENT). Jesse James Dupree (vocals), Jeff Worley (guitar), Jimmy Stiff (guitar), Tom Bettini (bass), Chris Worley (drums).

Playing heavy rock in the early nineties, Georgia's Jackyl were automatically categorized by the industry as hair metal, but their roots were more in the boogie rock that informed much of Southern rock, and they were in many ways misunderstood by many potential fans. Nonetheless, enough rock fans got the message to support the band as they released a series of quality albums through the rest of the decade. Unfortunately, they are probably best remembered for their somewhat corny novelty hit "The Lumberjack" from their self-titled 1992 debut on Geffen Records, which featured a chain saw solo! After several successful tours, and 1994's follow-up, *Push Comes to Shove*, the hair metal label that they had been saddled with made it difficult to market the band, and the band's mainstream popularity waned significantly. After leaving Geffen and moving through a number of other labels, the band settled into a more modest and sporadic schedule of recording and touring, most recently releasing *Live at the Full Throttle Saloon* on Sanctuary Records in 2004.

Discography: *Jackyl* (Geffen, 1992); *Push Comes to Shove* (Geffen, 1994); *Night of the Living Dead* [live] (Mayhem, 1996); *Cut the Crap* (Sony, 1997); *Stayin' Alive* (Shimmering Tone, 1998); *Relentless* (Humidity, 2002); *Live at the Full Throttle Saloon* (Sanctuary, 2004); *Choice Cuts* (Geffen, 1998); *20th Century Masters—The Millennium Collection: The Best of Jackyl* (Interscope, 2003).

JETHRO TULL AND THE GRAMMYS (1989). Let it be stated up front that Jethro Tull is not, and never was, a heavy metal band (although some of their songs are heavy in style, they at best could be called a hard rock band who mostly play in a folkier manner.) It is unclear if before 1987 Tull ever regarded itself as a heavy metal band. However, when the Grammy awards decided to institute a new Grammy award for "Best Hard Rock/Heavy Metal" performance of the year in 1989, it went on to nominate Tull for the award, to the disgust of many in the metal community and to the presumed amusement of Jethro Tull. The band had demonstrated that the fogies in music industry who voted for the Grammy winners still had no real idea what heavy metal was, or what genre Jethro Tull played. Metallica, who had released *And Justice for All* that year, were the popular favorites, and when they finally did win the Grammy in 1992, drummer Lars Ulrich thanked Jethro Tull for "not putting out an album this year." In subsequent years the Grammys would try and concentrate more on bands that actually played in a harder style. Ironically, Black Sabbath guitarist Tony Iommi was briefly a member of Jethro Tull, playing live with them in the Rolling Stones Rock and Roll Circus, but not on any actual releases, so the mistake may have been an honest one after all.

JUDAS PRIEST (1973–PRESENT). Rob Halford (vocals), K.K. Downing (guitar), Glenn Tipton (guitar), Ian Hill (bass), Scott Travis (drums).

Rob Halford of Judas Priest was among the first to combine biker/gay fashion with metal. (Brian Rasic/Rex Features)

Arguably one of the most influential metal bands of all time, Judas Priest, along with Iron Maiden, were at the forefront of the New Wave of British heavy metal that emerged during the late seventies and early eighties. Featuring a formidable twin-guitar attack and the operatic vocals of leather-decked, motorcycle-riding frontman Rob Halford, the band took the gothic imagery of Black Sabbath and fused it with a faster and more energetic presentation, providing a classic template that many of the metal bands that came after them would follow, especially in the speed metal and death metal genres.

Judas Priest began in Birmingham, England, when bassist Ian Hill, guitarist K.K. Downing, vocalist Alan Atkins, and drummer John Ellis came together. Taking their name from a former band of Atkins' (the original inspiration having come from Bob Dylan's song "The Ballad of Frankie Lee and Judas Priest" from his *John Wesley Harding* album), the band began playing gigs under the name in 1971. In 1973, vocalist Atkins left the group. As it happened, bassist Hill was at the time dating a woman whose brother, Rob Halford, was a singer, and she suggested they check him out. Halford then joined the lineup and brought along drummer John Hinch, who replaced John Ellis, who had just left the band.

After more touring, including stints in Germany and the Netherlands, the band signed a contract with independent Gull records in 1974. Adding a second guitarist, Glenn Tipton, the band recorded their debut, *Rocka Rolla*, in 1974. The album failed to generate much interest.

After an appearance at the Reading Festival in 1975, Hinch left the band, to be replaced by Alan Moore on drums. Shortly thereafter, the band released *Sad Wings of Destiny*. The album, which the band had much more of a hand in production-wise than they did in their debut, established the band as a force to be reckoned with on the metal scene of the day. Featuring such cutting-edge tracks as "Victim of Changes," "The Ripper," "Tyrant," and "Genocide," the album represented an important step in the development of metal as a musical form and established the band as important innovators in the genre. The album was critical in helping to establish their fan base and remains a favorite of many fans to the present day and is generally considered one of the most influential metal albums ever released.

After signing an international deal with CBS Records, the band recorded *Sin After Sin*, which featured session drummer Simon Phillips, whose energy and technical skill gave the band's sound another shot in the arm. The album, released in 1977, contained the band's cover of Joan Baez's "Diamonds and Rust," and generated even more positive reviews and sold better than its predecessors. Adding drummer Les Binks to the lineup, the band set out for their first tour of the U.S.

Returning to England, the band released the 1978 album *Stained Class*, which further established them as a heavy metal force to be reckoned with. Featuring the tracks "Exciter," "Invader," and "Better by You, Better Than Me," the album saw the band refining its metal sound without diminishing any of its power, and the album would go on to be one of the most influential in the later development of speed metal. *Stained Class*, along with its successor *Hell Bent for Leather* (1979), were two of the key albums spearheading the New Wave of British heavy metal and Priest, who had by this time developed their leather-clad stage personas and had become hugely influential to a whole generation of metal bands that followed them.

Hell Bent for Leather, released in 1979 (under the title *Killing Machine* in the U.K.), featured the title track and "Delivering the Goods," and continued the band's domination of the metal scene. Next came a live album, recorded in Japan, called *Unleashed in the East*. Released in 1979, the album would become Priest's first million seller in the U.S. and marked their last recording with Binks. The drummer was replaced with Dave Holland, who had previously been a member of Trapeze.

Another classic album followed in 1980 with *British Steel*. The album featured two of the band's most enduring favorites as singles, "Breaking the Law" and the classic "Living After Midnight." The album charted in both the U.S. and U.K. and gave the band its second platinum album.

Point of Entry followed the next year and featured a somewhat more radio-friendly sound with the singles "Heading Out to the Highway," "Don't Go," and "Hot Rockin." The band also filmed two of the songs as videos for MTV. While not as successful with the critics, the album was another solid success for the band.

1982 would be a high point for the band. With the album *Screaming for Vengeance*, the band reached its height of popularity. On the basis of the singles (and videos) "You've Got Another Thing Comin'" and "Electric Eye," the album reached number 17 on the U.S. charts and sold over a million copies. The band supported the album with a sold-out worldwide tour.

While *Screaming's* follow-up, 1984's *Defenders of the Faith*, was similarly successful, metal tastes were changing, and as Priest had been moving in a slightly more pop and radio-friendly direction, the younger bands that they had so influenced—in particular bands like Metallica, Megadeth, and Slayer—had helped to give birth to speed metal and thrash metal and were shaping a new aesthetic in the genre.

Still, Priest continued to do well, earning another platinum seller with 1986's *Turbo*. Unfortunately, *Priest ... Live!*, released in 1987, failed even to earn gold status, and the writing seemed to be on the wall for the group.

After *Ram It Down* in 1988, drummer Holland left and was replaced by former Racer X drummer Scott Travis, a younger player whose drumming chops would go on to give the band much of the speed metal power that its younger rivals were exploiting. *Painkiller*, released in 1990, was the first album that would explore this potential.

During the summer of 1990, the band was the subject of a lawsuit brought by the families of two young men who had attempted suicide (one succeeded) by shooting themselves with a shotgun. The suit claimed that subliminal messages in the song "Better by You, Better Than Me" on the *Stained Class* album allegedly had influenced the victims' actions. It didn't seem to matter that the song itself was a cover of a Spooky Tooth song and was not written by Judas Priest. The suit was eventually dismissed, and the band exonerated, but it shook up the band, and was one of a number of accusations (others involved Ozzy Osbourne and Iron Maiden) directed at the heavy metal community and alleged the music's negative influence on young fans.

After the completion of the *Painkiller* tour in 1990, Halford left, forming his own thrash metal outfit, Fight. Without Halford, the band spent the better part of the next five years dormant. Then, in 1996, they announced the hiring of Tim Owens, a young American vocalist who was a huge Judas Priest fan and who had been the singer in the Priest tribute band British Steel. Giving Owens the more metal-friendly nickname "Ripper," the band recorded the *Jugulator*, which was released in 1997. Featuring a more contemporary sound with heavily detuned guitars, the album was actually a departure from the traditional Priest sound, although Owens showed off an impressive Halford-influenced vocal style. The album entered the charts at 82, but was generally given mixed reviews by fans and critics alike.

In a 1998 interview with MTV, the long-closeted Halford came out, speaking openly about his homosexuality. While the singer's sexuality had been something of an "open secret" and the band had been aware of it, there was a question of how metal fans would take the news. As it happened, Halford was happy to report, the response from the heavy metal community was in fact "tremendous," and has never seemed to be an issue adversely affecting the singer's career.

Meanwhile, Judas Priest issued another studio album with Owens, 2001's *Demolition*, as well as a pair of live albums.

In the summer of 2001, the film *Rock Star*, featuring Mark Wahlberg, was released that was based upon Owens' rags to riches experience with Priest. While the band had originally been connected with the project, they withdrew and the picture itself functioned far more as a parody of the band and the metal genre than as any sort of realistic representation of Owens' experience.

As if in answer to many a Priest fan's prayers, 2003 saw the announcement that Halford would be returning to the fold. The band marked the event with a European tour that coincided with the release of their *Metalogy* boxed set. They also co-headlined 2004's Ozzfest.

The first studio album of the reunited lineup was *Angel of Retribution*, released in March 2005. The album was a return to form for the band and was a commercial and critical success.

2008 saw the release of *Nostradamus*, an ambitious double length album based on the life of the seer.

Discography: *Rocka Rolla* (Repertoire, 1974); *Sad Wings of Destiny* (Koch International, 1976); *Sin After Sin* Columbia, 1977); *Stained Class* (Columbia, 1978); *Hell Bent for Leather* (Columbia, 1979); *Unleashed in the East* [live] (Columbia, 1979); *British Steel* (Columbia, 1980); *Point of Entry* (Columbia, 1981); *Screaming for Vengeance* (Columbia, 1982); *Defenders of the Faith* (Columbia, 1984); *Turbo* (Columbia, 1986); *Priest ... Live!* (Columbia, 1987); *Ram It Down* (Columbia, 1988); *Painkiller* (Columbia, 1990); *Jugulator* (CMC International, 1997); *Priest in the East* [live] (Import, 1998); *'98 Live Meltdown* (CMC International, 1998); *Dying to Meet You* (Sonotec, 2001); *Demolition* (Atlantic, 2001); *Never Satisfied* (Kiddinx, 2002); *Live in London* (Steamhammer/SPV, 2003); *Angel of Retribution* (Epic, 2005); *Nostradamus* (Epic, 2008); *The Best of Judas Priest* (Koch International, 2001); *Limited Collector's Box* (Columbia, 2002); *The Best of Judas Priest* (Sony, 2008).

JUGGALOS. This term is a nickname for fans of the Detroit rap/metal crossover band Insane Clown Posse, a long-running Detroit institution, who dress in twisted clown outfits and sing/rap largely misogynistic lyrics about sex and have their own version of conspiracy theories and mythology. Insane Clown Posses have a more active, rabid fan base then many in the metal subculture, possibly because of the extremely depressed socio-economic conditions in the Detroit metal scene and possibly because of the aggressive nature of their music, a clever mixture of rap and crunchy modern metal. Although the band itself is an interesting example of how metal bands have begun to mix disparate elements of various genres together, one of the most fascinating aspects of the band is their active fan base. The fans sometimes emulate the make-up and costumes of the band and also drink/spray Faygo soda, the favorite beverage of the band. The Juggalos are known for their extreme devotion to the band and can be seen as one of the last vestiges of legitimate sub-cultures in heavy metal. The Juggalos follow the band religiously and find meaning in the complex and often confusing mythology that the band has created around their records. It is also interesting to note that the Juggalos seem to be a particularly male phenomenon, and it raises questions as to how women can experience metal when so much of metal subculture is male dominated.

K

JEN KAJZER. A DJ on Sirius satellite radio's "Heavy Metal Attack/27." While there are many DJs who are metal experts, Eddie Trunk for example, Jen Kajzer is one of the few that actually is an expert in metalology, and consistently works on breaking new and innovative artists. Kajzer is one of the few DJs to make it a mission to publicize metal on a regular basis and is one of the key people exposing audiences to metal.

DIANE KAMIKAZE. Diane Kamikaze is one of the most influential and knowledgeable metal/punk DJs working in radio today. She is legendary for her knowledge of punk and extreme metal (particularly death metal) and any band that pushes the boundaries, as well as an engineer and sound mixer for various bands and a well-regarded tattoo artist. Her show, on the New Jersey/New York freeform radio station WFMU (one of the last and best freeform stations in the nation), plays a variety of black, death, thrash, and other kinds of metal on her weekly Thursday 4–6 P.M. show. She plays highlights of the past thirty years as well as new and upcoming bands, sprinkled in with classic punk tracks and vintage garage rock. Diane Kamikaze has been a fixture on WFMU since 1981. Since WFMU has long been a listener-supported station available on the Internet, the fan base of DJs such as Diane Kamikaze has expanded exponentially on a global basis, and whether she is playing a rare track by punk veterans such as the Stranglers, or something vintage from Celtic Frost, or from great contemporary bands such as Anaal Nathrakh or Mastodon (a particular favorite of Diane Kamikaze), she exhibits an extremely varied taste in metal and extreme music. Diane Kamikaze is an example of how a scholar and fan's perspective on extreme (or some might argue simply good) music can be successfully turned into a great radio program.

KAT (1986–PRESENT). Great Kat (vocals, guitar)

The Great Kat (Katherine Thomas) is a female metal guitar virtuoso, heavily influenced by classical music. A former violinist from Swindon in England, on entering the metal world, she reinvented herself as the blood-splattered Great Kat on an album whose title also serves as her informal motto, which refers to her attitude toward male fans as well as her ideas about audience involvement: *Worship Me or Die*. To some degree, the Great Kat demonstrates the extremes to which metal performers go to accentuate their virtuosity on various instruments. It also demonstrates that the *context* of how various songs are played is sometimes more important than merely the performance. The fascinating thing about the Great Kat is that her image seems to almost work against her actual talent on the guitar and violin and instead of being well respected she is sometimes mocked within the metal community for the ridiculous nature of her stage show. This can also be analyzed through the lens of mostly male metal fans rejecting a female guitar (and violin) player who is just as adept as any male player.

Discography: *Worship Me or Die* (Roadrunner, 1987); *Beethoven on Speed* (Roadrunner, 1990); *Wagner's War* (Thomas Public Relations, 2001).

KID ROCK (1990–PRESENT). (Various backing musicians)
   While not technically a metal act by the strictest definition of the term, Kid Rock (real name Robert James Ritchie, born 1971) has demonstrated that

Kid Rock performs in 2004. (NBC/Photofest)

American hard rock, country, metal, and other fans can be united under the banner of beer drinking and hell raising. Kid Rock is not a metal singer, but many often mistake him for one, or his efforts to maintain the "party all the time" image of early metal as being authentically metal. While Kid Rock may be more country rock or hard rock than heavy metal, his *intent* is to make popular music with metal leanings (actually as close to metal as classic Van Halen would be if the band lacked the virtuosity of Eddie Van Halen). Still, some of his songs lean in a metal direction; particularly if he is regarded as a part of the nu metal movement. Certainly some of his efforts rank closer to this genre than bands such as Limp Bizkit and Nickelback.

Discography: *Grit Sandwiches for Breakfast* (Jive, 1990); *The Polyfuze Method* (Continuum, 1993); *Early Mornin' Stoned Pimp* (Top Dog, 1996); *Devil without a Cause* (Lava, 1998); *Cocky* (Lava, 2001); *Kid Rock* (Atlantic, 2003); *Live Trucker* (Atlantic, 2006); *Rock n' Roll Jesus* (Atlantic, 2007).

KILLSWITCH ENGAGE (1999–PRESENT). Mike D'Antonio (bass), Howard Jones (vocals), Justin Foley (drums), Adam Dutkiewicz (guitar), Joel Stroetzel (guitar).

Along with Lamb of God, Killswitch Engage are at the forefront of the New Wave of heavy metal metalcore movement. From Westfield, Massachusetts, the band is comprised of bassist Mike D'Antonio, vocalist Howard Jones, drummer Justin Foley, and guitarists Adam Dutkiewicz and Joel Stroetzel.

Initially organized by D'Antonio in 1999, formerly of hardcore stalwarts Overcast, the band was originally conceived of as a part-time side project, but eventually grew along with the band's reputation. Originally a foursome, the band, comprising D'Antonio, Dutkiewicz (then on drums), Stroetzel, and vocalist Jesse Leach started gigging under the name Killswitch Engage, which was meant to signify a fresh new musical direction and a break with their collective musical pasts.

Signed to indie Ferret Records after impressive live shows, the band released *Killswitch Engage* in June 2000 and began to attract attention based on their unique take on metal, which included a more melodic approach combined with their heavy guitar and drum-based riffage that bristled with intensity.

Switching to the larger Roadrunner label, the band went into the studio and, with a larger recording budget, was able to spend more time crafting their sophomore album, the brutal *Alive or Just Breathing*. The album featured a fuller sonic palette and multiple guitar parts (mixed by British wunderkind producer Andy Sneap) and prompted the band to expand to a five-piece as drummer Dutkiewicz move to guitar and new drummer Tom Gomes joined the fold. *Alive* was released in May 2002, to positive reviews and a new round of touring.

Singer Leach, however, shortly thereafter decided to leave the band for personal reasons. After a series of auditions, vocalist Howard Jones of the hardcore band Blood Has Been Shed joined as Leach's replacement, and the band hit the road once more, with Jones' charismatic stage presence and formidable vocals taking the band to another level.

When drummer Tom Gomes exited the group a year later, Jones' former bandmate Justin Foley joined in time for the recording of the band's third album, *The End of Heartache*. Released in the spring of 2004, *Heartache* entered the charts at 21 and earned the band a Grammy nomination for Best Metal Performance. With their newfound notoriety, the band became ubiquitous on the concert trail and at metal festivals, performing at Ozzfest, the Warped Tour, and Britain's Leeds and Reading Festivals. Their live DVD *Set This World Ablaze* was released in 2005.

The band's fourth album, *As Daylight Dies* (produced—like its predecessors—by Dutkiewicz), was released in the fall of 2006, hitting as high as 32 on the Billboard charts. More touring followed, though Dutkiewicz was temporarily sidelined due to back problems and corrective surgery. By late summer he had recuperated and had joined the band back on tour.

Discography: *Killswitch Engage* (Ferret, 2000); *Alive or Just Breathing* (Roadrunner, 2002); *The End of Heartache* (Roadrunner, 2004); *As Daylight Dies* (Roadrunner, 2006).

KING DIAMOND (1985–PRESENT). King Diamond (vocals), Andy Laroque (guitar), Michael Denner (guitar, replaced by Mike Moon, Pete Blakk, Mike Wead, Herb Simonson, Glenn Drover, now Floyd Konstantin), Timmi Hansen (bass, replaced by Hal Patino, Sharlee d'Angelo, Chris Estes, Dave Harbour, now Hal Patino), Mikkey Dee (drums, replaced by Chris Whitemier, Snowy Shaw, Daren Anthony, Jean Luke Herbert, now Matt Thomas).

King Diamond is the solo project of Mecyful Fate frontman King Diamond, the band he started after the breakup of Mercyful Fate in 1985 but which continued on after Diamond reunited with the band in 1993 until the band went on hiatus after numerous personnel changes in 1999. Diamond's music uses his operatic vocals to great effect and continues the satanic and occult-influenced work of Mercyful Fate, and to the uninitiated, the bands do sound similar (especially as King Diamond was formed with Denner and Hansen of Mercyful Fate). However, there is more consistency and less commerciality in King Diamond, and from the *Abigail* album to the present the band has shown a remarkable consistency. Although like in Mercyful Fate members come and go (guitarist Laroque is the only original member left), King Diamond are a worthy successor to the legacy of Mercyful Fate and one of the darkest but most musically adept bands in the black metal genre. Diamond also had some notoriety in the mainstream press when Gene Simmons of Kiss tried to sue Diamond because of the similarities between the face paint of the two, which demonstrates not only the pettiness of Simmons (the bands do not sound alike at all, and the make-up was actually quite dissimilar) but the "Mercyful" nature of King Diamond, who chose to change his make-up rather than killing Simmons with a curse. King Diamond is one of the longest running and most influential of all the mainstream black metal bands and is a good introduction for fans that like their metal occult tinged, but more radio friendly and technically adept. And how can one not love an artist that titled one of his records, *Give Me Your Soul ... Please*?

Discography: *Fatal Portrait* (Roadrunner, 1986); *Abigail* (Roadrunner, 1987); *Them* (Roadrunner, 1988); *Conspiracy* (Roadrunner, 1989); *Family Ghost* (Roadrunner, 1990); *The Eye* (Roadrunner, 1990); *In Concert 1987: Abigail Live* (Roadrunner, 1991); *The Spider's lullabye* (Metal Blade, 1995); *The Graveyard* (Metal Blade, 1996); *Voodoo* (Metal Blade, 1998); *House of God* (Metal Blade, 2000); *Abigail II: The Revenge* (Metal Blade, 2002); *The Puppet Master* (Metal Blade, 2003); *Deadly Lullabyes: Live* (Metal Blade, 2004); *Give Me Your Soul ... Please?* (Metal Blade, 2007).

KING'S X (1988–PRESENT). Doug Pinnick (bass/lead vocals), Ty Tabor (guitar/vocals), Jerry Gaskill (drums/vocals).

Perhaps *the* most criminally overlooked and underappreciated (though widely respected in critical and musical circles) rock band in the past twenty years, King's X have had a long and productive, if under-heralded, career. Playing finely crafted rock that has evolved into more of a metal style, from its hard rock origins, the band has long blended heavy yet uniquely melodic guitar-based rock with rich, Beatlesque three-part harmonies, in songs that often feature lyrics that come from a spiritual perspective. A powerhouse live act, the band's power trio format has done nothing to limit its live sound, with all three members singing harmony, and the band being renowned for their live performances.

Bassist/lead vocalist Doug Pinnick and drummer/vocalist Jerry Gaskill first came together when the two played in the Christian rock group Petra in the late seventies. Hooking up with guitarist/vocalist Ty Tabor, the three played on the Missouri bar scene in a cover band, the Edge, before changing their name to Sneak Preview, and working on all original material, releasing an independent, self-titled album in 1983.

Relocating to Houston, Texas, the band caught the attention of ZZ Top video producer Sam Taylor, who took the band under his wing, helping them to get a contract with Megaforce Records and suggesting the name change to King's X.

Releasing their debut album, *Out of the Silent Planet*, in 1988, the band received critical praise, but the album seemed too diverse for immediate mainstream acceptance. *Gretchen Goes to Nebraska*, released the next year, was more successful, with the song "Over My Head" receiving some MTV airplay. The album also helped to build the band's reputation among fellow musicians, as well as critics, a reputation that the band has continued to enjoy ever since.

In 1990, the band released *Faith Hope Love* whose single "It's Love" received heavy airplay on MTV, and the band went out on tours with both AC/DC and Living Colour. After their followup *King's X* in 1992, the band and manager Taylor parted ways.

With the release of *Dogman*, produced by uber-producer Brendan O'Brien in 1994, the band adopted a heavier sound, featuring detuned guitars. The sound worked well for the band and in many ways complemented their previous approach; while the album has a metal tinge, it also fit in well with the grunge sound that, was then at its peak. Featuring such standout tracks as "Flies and Blue Skies," "Complain," and the title track, the album did relatively well, cracking the top 100. However, Atlantic was disappointed with sales, and when the band's followup *Ear Candy* did no better, the band left the label.

Returning to smaller labels (beginning with Metal Blade in 1998), the band has since continued to release standout material and tour regularly. Most recently, the band has collaborated with famed producer Michael Wagener on a pair of releases, 2005's *Ogre Tones*, which was a return to form for the band, and *XV* in 2008.

Discography: *Out of the Silent Planet* (Megaforce, 1988); *Gretchen Goes to Nebraska* (Megaforce, 1989); *Faith Hope Love* (Megaforce, 1990); *King's X* (Atlantic, 1992); *Dogman* (Atlantic, 1994); *Ear Candy* (Atlantic, 1996); *Tape Head* (Metal Blade, 1998); *Please Come Home ... Mr. Bulbous* (Metal Blade, 2000); *Manic Moonlight* (Metal Blade, 2001); *Black Like Sunday* (Metal Blade, 2003); *Live All Over the Place* (Metal Blade, 2004); *Ogre Tones* (Inside Out Music, 2005); *Go Tell Somebody* (Avalon, 2008); *XV* (Inside/Out, 2008); *Best of King's X* (Atlantic, 1997).

KISS (1973–PRESENT). Classic lineup: Paul Stanley (lead vocals/guitar), Gene Simmons (bass/vocals), Ace Frehley (guitar), Peter Criss (drums).

One of the most commercially successful rock bands of all time, Kiss were pioneers in developing and exploiting the theatrical potential of heavy metal while simultaneously making it a safe form of mainstream entertainment, creating cartoon-like characters out of the band members and crafting simple and hook-filled party anthems that they delivered in the midst of concerts that were as much visual spectacles as musical performances, featuring costumes, makeup, fog machines, elaborate light shows, smoking guitars, blood spitting, and fire breathing. Their hook-filled tunes and command of the stage created the template for the arena rock of the seventies and eighties and inspired a whole generation of bands that would follow them.

Emerging from New York City in the early seventies, Kiss took their cue from the early glam image and theatricality of Alice Cooper and the New York Dolls, and combined it with a straightforward hard rock style. The band first came together when Gene Simmons (bass, vocals) and Paul Stanley (lead vocals, rhythm guitar) responded to drummer Peter Criss's classified ad in *Rolling Stone,* and then placed one for a guitarist in the *Village Voice,* to which lead guitarist Ace Frehley responded. After working up a unique act involving face make-up and costumes, and a band logo featuring lightning bolts for the "s" in their name (Frehley's idea), the band held their first concert in New York. The concert generated serious interest in the band's entertaining proposition, and manager Bill Aucoin, who caught the show, offered to manage the band immediately afterward. Within two weeks, he had the band a record deal with impresario Neil Bogart's Casablanca Records.

KISS was one of the most popular heavy metal bands of the 1970s. (Courtesy Photofest)

Gene Simmons spun gold out of Kiss merchandise. (Courtesy Photofest)

The band's eponymous debut wasn't a blockbuster, but it did make it as high as 87 on the charts. The band hit the road hard, beginning to develop their fan base through heavy touring. It was a formula that was standard at the time, and Kiss followed it to the letter, releasing two more albums, *Hotter Than Hell* (1974) and *Dressed to Kill* (1975), in the next three years. By 1975, the band's constant touring had helped them to build a large and enthusiastic fan base. This set the stage for their major breakthrough in the fall of 1975 with the release of the live album *Alive!* Hitting number 12 on the album charts, the album made the band's name a household word, and the album was the must-have album of the year. With the single "Rock 'n' Roll All Nite," the band had it first radio hit, and Kiss were a mass phenomenon for the first time.

Their next album, *Destroyer*, was an ambitious undertaking and was heavily produced by producer Bob Ezrin. Where their previous albums had been very straightforward affairs, *Destroyer* was a much slicker-sounding album. At the same time, the band's songwriting was as solid as ever. The album featured the ballad "Beth" (sung by drummer Criss), which became their first top ten single, while the tune "Detroit Rock City," one of their best rockers, also gained significant airplay. As a result, the album became the band's first million seller. Kiss mania was in full swing, and in a foreshadowing of the band's commercial bent, Kiss took full advantage of the marketing potential their position and image offered. There were

Kiss dolls, comic books featuring the band, even a made-for-TV movie starring the band called "Kiss Meets the Phantom of the Park." By the end of the year the band's fan club—The Kiss Army—had over 10,000 members.

In the 1978 the band hit on the idea of simultaneous solo albums that still featured the band's logo. All four made the top 50, with Simmons at 22 the most popular. *Dynasty*, released in 1979, was another platinum seller, featuring the hit single "I Was Made for Loving You," which although alienating some fans because of its disco beat, was a radio smash. The album, however, would be the band's last with its original lineup, as Criss would leave in 1980.

Session drummer Anton Fig (later of Letterman Late Show band fame) would sit in on 1980's *Kiss Unmasked*, with Eric Carr joining the band in time for a world tour later that same year.

The band saw a decline in their fortunes with *Unmasked* selling less than a million copies. *Music from "The Elder"* in 1981 didn't even go gold. Frehley would leave later that year, forming a solo group, Frehley's Comet.

Creatures of the Night, featuring new guitarist Vinnie Vincent, sold somewhat better, making it to 45 on the charts. In 1983 the band took off their make-up and transitioned into a more mainstream rock image. The gambit seemed to work with the 1983 album *Lick It Up* going platinum and the title track becoming a radio hit. With Vincent leaving to form the Vinnie Vincent Invasion (remember them?), the band hired guitarist Mark St. John in time for *Animalize* in 1984, which was similarly successful. When St. John had to leave the band after developing Rieter's syndrome, guitarist Brue Kulick took his place.

There followed a string of successful albums, and then in 1990 drummer Eric Carr became ill with cancer, succumbing to the disease the following year at the age of 41.

Replacing Carr with drummer Eric Singer, the band released 1992's *Revenge*, which became a top ten hit. It was followed by the band's third live album, *Alive III* in 1993.

In 1996, sensing the time was ripe for a bit of nostalgia, Simmons and Stanley welcomed back Frehley and Criss for a reunion tour featuring the band in its full make-up. The tour was a huge success and moneymaker for the band and went all over the world treating fans to their first look at the vintage Kiss look in over fourteen years. In 1998 the reunited lineup released *Pyscho Circus*, which turned out to be a critical and commercial disappointment for the band. Nonetheless, the subsequent tour was another success. The following year the band announced a farewell tour, but before the tour hit its Japanese and Australian legs, Criss left the group over a salary dispute. In a move that proved controversial to some fans, Simmons and Stanley merely hired former drummer Eric Singer and had him don Criss's trademark make-up and costume and resumed the tour. (Criss, however, had no recourse since Simmons and Stanley have ownership of the designs.) Since the band's so-called farewell tour they have continued to tour and perform, albeit more sporadically, replacing Frehley with former Black 'n' Blue guitarist Tommy Thayer donning Frehley's makeup and costume.

Discography: *Kiss* (Casablanca, 1974); *Hotter Than Hell* (Casablanca, 1974); *Dressed to Kill* (Casablanca, 1975); *Alive!* (Casablanca, 1975); *Destroyer* (Casablanca, 1976); *Rock and Roll Over* (Casablanca, 1976); *Love Gun* (Casablanca, 1977); *Alive II* (Casablanca, 1977); *Ace Frehley* (Casablanca, 1978); *Gene Simmons* (Casablanca, 1978); *Paul Stanley*

(Casablanca, 1978); *Peter Criss* (Casablanca, 1978); *Dynasty* (Casablanca, 1979); *Unmasked* (Casablanca, 1980); *Music from "The Elder"* (Universal/Polygram, 1981); *Creatures of the Night* (Casablanca, 1982); *Lick It Up* (Mercury, 1983); *Animalize* (Mercury, 1984); *Asylum* (Mercury, 1985); *Crazy Nights* (Mercury, 1987); *Hot in the Shade* (Mercury, 1989); *Revenge* (Mercury, 1992); *Alive III* (Mercury, 1993); *MTV Unplugged* [live] (Mercury, 1996); *Carnival of Souls: The Final Sessions* (Mercury, 1997); *Psycho Circus* (Mercury, 1998); *Kiss Symphony: Alive IV* (Polygram, 2003); *Kiss Symphony: The Single Disc* (Sanctuary, 2003); *Greatest Kiss* (Mercury, 2007); *First Kiss, Last Licks* [Box] (Polygram, 2008).

KITTIE (1997–PRESENT). Morgan Lander (vocals, guitar), Fallon Bowman (guitar, replaced by Lisa Marx, replaced by Tara McLeod), Tanya Candler (bass, replaced by Talena Atfield, replaced by Jennifer Arroyo, replaced by Trish Doan), Mercedes Lander (drums).

Kittie were one of the new all-female metal bands of the late nineties who played as aggressively as any band, metal sexism aside. The band was started in high school by Mercedes Lander and Bowman and played covers until being signed by Artemis. The band's recorded output started strong with the *Spit* record in 2000, a fine alternative to the nu metal excesses that were dominating the airwaves at the time. However, constant lineup changes led to the Lander sisters being the only constants in the band. Kittie still tour today, playing a brutal and aggressive form of metal.

Discography: *Spit* (Artemis, 2000); *Oracle* (Artemis, 2001); *Until the End* (Artemis, 2004); *Funeral for Yesterday* (Merovingian, 2007).

KIX (1981–95). Steve Whiteman (vocals), Donnie Purnell (bass), Ronnie "10/10" Younkins (guitar), Brian "Damage" Forsythe (guitar), Jimmy Chalfant (drums).

Hailing from Baltimore, Maryland, Kix's music combined a catchy AC/DC-influenced and somewhat Stonesy-sounding brand of rock with hooks, and a great live stage show. Releasing a string of great albums in the mid- to late eighties, they nonetheless were unable to get the recognition they deserved, though they left us with a number of classic discs.

After earning a reputation as a great live act on the club circuit in their native Baltimore, Kix, featuring vocalist Steve Whiteman, bassist and main songwriter Donnie Purnell, guitarists Ronnie "10/10" Younkins and Brian "Damage" Forsythe, and drummer Jimmy Chalfant, inked a deal with Atlantic Records and released their self-titled debut in 1981. The album featured a number of fun, infectious rockers, like "Yeah, Yeah, Yeah," "The Kid," and "Atomic Bombs," but wasn't particularly successful. It did help the band to build its fan base, especially as they began to tour heavily behind the album. 1983's follow-up *Cool Kids* was slightly more commercial, featuring the single "Body Talk."

The band's creative high point came with 1985's *Midnight Dynamite*. Produced by Ratt producer Beau Hill, the album presents Kix in their best (and most accurate) light, with their strongest set of songs and performances. With songs like the single "Cold Shower," as well as "Sex" and "Bang Bang (Balls of Fire)," the band put its best foot forward, producing an album that remains a classic. The album was more successful than its predecessors but still not the breakthrough that the band and its label had hoped that it would be. Nonetheless, it helped to set the stage for their next album, *Blow My Fuse*, which would provide that break-through. Produced by famed producer Tom Werman (Cheap Trick, Mötley Crüe) and released in 1988, the album was similar to *Midnight Dynamite*, although perhaps not quite as strong, despite being somewhat more commercial. The ballad "Don't Close Your Eyes" provided the band its first and only hit and helped the album to enter the charts. Videos for the song and others gave the band newfound visibility, while they also found themselves opening on tours for Aerosmith and AC/DC.

With the success of *Blow My Fuse*, the band realized that its financial affairs were in bad shape because of the debt they had incurred with their label. As a result, they saw little recompense from their "successful" album. Although they would follow it up with the excellent *Hot Wire* in 1991, a move to Atlantic subsidiary East/West and a shift in musical trends toward alternative rock served to hinder the band's commercial progress, and they sold a mere 200,000 copies of the album. After the release of the 1993 live album *Kix Live*, the band's relationship with Atlantic was finished. The band would go on to release one more album on the smaller CMC label (1995's *Show Business*) before calling it a day, with the members going on to pursue separate projects, although they have periodically reunited for one-off gigs and small tours in recent years (minus bassist Purnell).

Discography: *Kix* (Atlantic, 1981); *Cool Kids* (Atlantic, 1983); *Midnite Dynamite* (Atlantic, 1985); *Blow My Fuse* (Atlantic, 1988); *Hot Wire* (Atlantic, 1991); *Kix Live* (Atlantic, 1993); *Show Business* (CMC International, 1995); *Live* (Wounded Bird, 2005); *The Essentials* (Warner Strategic, 2002); *Metal Hits* (Rhino Flashback, 2003).

KORN (1993–PRESENT). Jonathon Davis (vocals), James "Munky" Shaffer (guitar), Brian "Head" Welch (guitar), Reginald "Fieldy" Arvizu (bass), David Silveria (drums).

Korn are one of the most popular and respected of the nu metal wave of the early to mid-nineties, and one of the few bands from that time period that continue to produce listenable music to the present day. The band was founded in Bakersfield, California, in 1993, and their first album, *Korn*, established them as different from the usually more macho metal bands that formed around the same time. Lead singer Jonathan Davis writes lyrics that celebrate the loner and the misfit, providing the soundtrack and outlet for the dispossessed nerds of metal. While bands such as Limp Bizkit were singing empty anthems to misplaced anger, Korn was tying to articulate the anguish that the meekest members of the metal community go through and tried to articulate their rage, not against a nameless machine but at the very real oppressive teachers, parents, and school bullies. Surprisingly, the band, who tour and record infrequently, seem to be as popular today as they were in their nineties heyday, although drummer Silveria and guitarist Brian "Head" Welch both left the band in 2006. Welch apparently left to proselytize as a newly born again Christian. Korn remains one of the more emotional and honest bands of the new metal scene, and this is probably why they survive as a band to this day.

Discography: *Korn* (Immortal/Epic, 1994); *Life Is Peachy* (Immortal/Epic, 1996); *Follow the Leader* (Immortal/Epic, 1998); *Issues* (Immortal/Epic, 1999); *Live & Rare* (Immortal/Epic, 2006).

KREATOR (1982–PRESENT). Mille Petrozza (vocals/guitar), Wulf (guitar, replaced by Jorg Trezbiatowski, replaced by Frank Gosdzik, replaced by Christian Geisler, replaced by Tommy Vettereli), Rob Fioretti (bass, replaced by Andreas Herz, replaced by Sammy Yli-Sirnio), Ventor, aka Jurgen Reil (drums, replaced by Joe Cangelosi, now back in band).

Kreator was a particularly evil band from Germany who helped inspire both the thrash and death metal scenes. Their earliest work is fairly undistinguished from most of the other punk-influenced thrash bands of the time, but by the time of the *Pleasure to Kill* record, the band was relying less on power and speed and more on songwriting, particularly in songs such as "Death Is Your Savior" and "The Pestilence." These tracks show the band growing as musicians and also writing longer, more technically complex songs. After years of using touring second guitarists, the band added lead guitarist Frank Gosdzik for the *Coma of Souls* record, which was not as highly regarded by fans as the last Kreator classics.

Renewal was a challenge from the band to the black and death metal bands that had started in Kreator's wake to watch their backs, as Kreator's twin leads and hyper rhythm section were up to the competition from bands who were trying to take a genre that Kreator had helped lay the ground for to new and daring levels. After that, Kreator was silent for a few years, before coming back in the late nineties with a more ambient, atmospheric death metal style, one that marked a fallow point in the band's history (Remember Metallica in the nineties?) in which they largely abandoned what they did best. However, recent albums have been stronger and Kreator, for their spotty albums, remain one of thrash metal's classic bands and an influence on the black and death metal scenes.

Discography: *Endless Pain* (Noise, 1985); *Pleasure to Kill* (Noise, 1986); *Terrible Certainty* (Noise, 1988); *Extreme Aggression* (Epic, 1989); *Coma of Souls* (Epic, 1990); *Renewal* (Futurist, 1992); *Cause for Conflict* (Noise, 1995); *Outcast* (Fad, 1995); *Endorama* (Import, 1999); *Violent Revolution* (Steamhammer/Spv, 2001); *Live Kreation* (Steamhammer/Spv, 2003); *Enemy of God* (Steamhammer/Spv, 2005).

KROKUS (1976–PRESENT). Marc Storace (vocals), Fernando von Arb (guitar), Tommy Kiefer (guitar), Chris von Rohr (bass), Freddy Steady (drums)

With an obvious AC/DC influence, Swiss rockers Krokus enjoyed a good deal of popularity in the early eighties with their platinum album *Headhunter* (featuring the single "Long Stick Goes Boom") and tours with such heavyweights as Def Leppard, Motorhead, Rush, and AC/DC. While their popularity in the U.S. faded significantly after that time, they have continued to record and tour in Europe, remaining quite popular in their native Switzerland.

Discography: *Krokus* (Mercury, 1976); *To You All* (Schnoutz, 1977); *Painkiller* (Mercury, 1978); *Pay It in Metal* (Philips, 1978); *Metal Rendez-Vous* (Arista, 1980); *Hardware* (Ariola, 1981); *One Vice at a Time* (Arista, 1982); *Headhunter* (Arista, 1983); *The Blitz* (Arista, 1984); *Change of Address* (Arista, 1985); *Alive & Screamin'* (Arista, 1986); *Heart Attack* (MCA, 1987); *Stampede* (Krokus, 1991); *To Rock or Not To Be* (Phonag, 1995); *Round 13* (Angel Air, 2000); *Rock the Block* (WEA International, 2003); *Hellraiser* (AFM, 2006); *The Dirty Dozen* (BMG, 1993); *Best of Krokus* (Cas, 2000); *Headhunter Blitz* (BMG, 2002); *Long Stick Goes Boom: The Anthology* (Castle, 2003); *Fire and Gasoline: Live!* (Reality, 2004).

KYUSS (1989–95). John Garcia (vocals), Josh Homme (guitar), Chris Cockrell (guitar), Nick Oliveri (guitar, later switched to bass and later left band), Josh Cockrell (bass, replaced by Nick Oliveri, Scott Reeder), Brant Bjork (drums, replaced by Alfred Hernandez).

Kyuss were a classic stoner metal band featuring a young Josh Homme, who later went on to form the Queens of the Stone Age with early Kyuss guitarist/bassist Nick Oliveri. The band started as Katzenjammer in the late eighties and evolved into Sons of Kyuss in 1989, releasing their first album under that name. In 1991 they shortened the name to Kyuss and started a tradition of playing free parties in the desert, a practice that Homme keeps to this day. The band was much beloved by many in the metal underground who grooved to their psychedelic slow version of metal. After the demise of Kyuss, Homme and Hernandez recruited Oliveri for the Queens of the Stone Age project and Brant Bjork started a solo career and played with Fu Manchu. Although Kyuss has long denied any plans of a reunion, their influence of the stoner metal scene of today is considerable. Their desert parties are continued by Homme, who tries to keep the tradition alive with his "Desert Sessions" records, where members make up songs on various illicit substances in the desert and record them with an air of spontaneity and spliff fumes reminiscent of Kyuss.

Discography: *Sons of Kyuss* (Black Highway, 1990); *Wretch* (Dali Records, 1991); *Blues for the Red Sun* (Dali, 1992); *Welcome to Sky Valley* (Elektra, 1994); *... And the Circus Leaves Town* (Elektra, 1995).

L

LAMB OF GOD (1988–PRESENT). Randy Blythe (vocals), Mark Morton (guitar), Willie Adler (guitar), John Campbell (bass), Chris Adler (drums).

Often referred to as the cutting edge of the New Wave of American metal, Lamb of God play a tightly crafted, riff-based style of metal. Originating as Burn the Priest, they changed their name to Lamb of God after realizing the booking limitations of their previous name in and around their native Richmond, Virginia. Founding members guitarist Mark Morton, drummer Chris Adler, and bassist John Campbell were joined by vocalist Randy Blythe and guitarist Abe Spear shortly before the release of Burn the Priest's debut on Legion records in 1998. Spear was then replaced by Chris Adler's brother Will in time for the first release by the newly dubbed Lamb of God, *New American Gospel* on Prosthetic Records in 2000. The band toured relentlessly behind the album, building up their fan base.

The band's touring began to pay off when *As the Palaces Burn* was released in 2003 and garnered the band a great deal of critical praise from *Rolling Stone* to metal mags *Metal Hammer* and *Revolver*. The band also signed a new deal with major Epic records, who released their fourth album, *Ashes of the Wake*, in 2004. This album reached number 27 on the Billboard album charts, cementing the band's reputation as one of the leading acts on the U.S. metal scene.

In 2006 the band released *Sacrament*, which debuted at number 8 and earned them a Grammy nomination for the song "Redneck."

Discography: *New American Gospel* (Metal Blade, 2000); *As the Palaces Burn* (Prosthetic, 2003); *Ashes of the Wake* (Epic, 2004); *Killadelphia* [live](Epic, 2005); *Burn the Priest* (Epic, 2005); *Sacrament* (Epic, 2006).

L'AMOURS. L'Amours was a famous rock club in Brooklyn, New York (there was also a L'Amours in Queens for a time), that hosted numerous metal bands during its heyday in the eighties and nineties. The club was located on 63d street in Brooklyn, but another L'Amours is located on Staten Island of all places, where bands such as Raven still find an enthusiastic audience on their reunion tours. L'Amours was for many years the main east coast location for metal bands on tour to stop by, not unlike the many clubs that dominated the Sunset Strip scene during the eighties and early nineties.

LEATHER. Although it was not present to much of an extent on the early metal scene, where denim and typical rock star outfits of open shirts and an almost Victorian look prevailed, black leather (along with different variants such as pink, blue, and red) has become a staple of the heavy metal scene and was especially prevalent in the early eighties. While black leather jackets had been traditionally worn by veterans of the armed forces, particularly the air force, the vogue of black leather in the general popular culture grew in the late 1940s, when returning GIs formed motorcycle groups (such as the embryonic Hell's Angels). Leather soon began to be associated with youth culture and rebellion by the early fifties. In the 1953 film *The Wild Bunch*, Marlon Brando helped codify the association between leather and rebellion with his portrayal of a sneering motorcycle gang member, who, when asked what he was rebelling against, asked "What ya got?". The

Rob Halford of Judas Priest (© Pictorial Press Ltd/Alamy)

Judas Priest in full leather regalia. (Photofest)

movement was further helped along by the now-classic movie *Rebel Without a Cause,* where the popularity of the young and doomed James Dean further cemented black and brown leather as signifier of subversion and youth culture. Also in the 1950s, there was a growing leather underground in the gay community, evolving slowly from gay biker gangs where leathermen, extremely macho gay men, would wear leather to demonstrate their sexual status. In addition, the early New York Dolls and many early members of the New York and London punk scenes, such as the Ramones in their uniform of beat-up leather jackets also con-tributed greatly to the rise of leather as a band uniform. These disparate trends all contributed to the rise of leather in the metal scene.

In gay culture, one of the key popularizers of leather in metal was the band Judas Priest and in particular their lead singer, Rob Halford, who would often roar on stage in full leather regalia, including bondage-type straps and hat on a Harley motorcycle. The fact that Halford was gay (although fairly nonchalant about his sexual orientation early on) was a major factor in leather being more accepted in the metal community as a natural way of looking tough and masculine. Halford had come from the gay leather subculture, and his arresting look was soon adopted by many in the metal scene, although few took the look to the extreme that Halford would.

In terms of color, as the glam influence on metal became popular in the so-called "hair metal" scene in L.A. and other cities, the look began to expand, and brightly colored and sometimes almost effeminate-looking uses of leather arose, with bands wearing red and pink and blue leather jackets and pants, along with copious amounts of make-up and hairspray.

From the eighties to the present the metal scene has adopted for the most part a much less glam rock look, and the basic uniform of leather pants and jacket (and occasionally vest) has been de rigueur among the harder bands with members of the black and death metal scenes wearing leather jackets and black outfits almost as a standard uniform. Despite the many permutations in how leather is worn and what it signifies (there is still a vibrant subculture in the gay, transgender, and lesbian communities who wear leather on a regular basis), it is clear that Halford's look and the influence of punk and motorcycle culture were a major turning point in making metal fashion look even harder and more menacing. What was originally associated with rebellious youth culture in the early fifties more or less still connotes the same meaning to this very day. As Judas Priest put it best, many metal bands and fans are still "Hell Bent for Leather," whatever that means.

LED ZEPPELIN (1968–80). Robert Plant (vocals), Jimmy Page (guitar), John Paul Jones (bass/keyboards), John Bonham (drums).

Led Zeppelin was for all intents and purposes the ultimate heavy metal band. Although the band was far more eclectic in its approach than any of its peers, utilizing everything from blues to Celtic folk to Moroccan music and mythology in its sonic stew, it also provided the most enduring template for bands that would follow. With Jimmy Page's charismatic flights of the fretboard, Robert Plant's high-pitched vocals, and Bonzo's (John Bonham's) drums of thunder, the band provided the text that others would follow, even if they could only try. Misunderstood by the critics of their day who largely disliked them, the band rarely gave interviews,

Singer Robert Plant of Led Zeppelin: the epitome of a metal frontman. (© Lewton Cole / Alamy)

and in a day before MTV, this gave them a power of mystique that their mystical lyrics and powerful sound only enhanced.

The band first came together when former session guitarist Jimmy Page's tenure in the final version of the Yardbirds was coming to a close. In order to fulfill a number of scheduled concert dates after singer Keith Relf and James McCarty had left the band, Page and bassist Chris Dreja set about finding a singer and drummer. After approaching vocalist Terry Reid, who couldn't join the group, Page checked out vocalist Robert Plant, whom Reid had recommended. Liking what he heard, Page enlisted Plant, who in turn suggested his former bandmate from the Band of Joy, John Bonham on drums. Ironically, it took some convincing to secure Bonham, who had been offered more money to play in a number of local groups. Seeing the potential that the new group offered, however, Bonham took the gig. Before the obligatory Yardbirds gigs could be filled, Chris Dreja left the band, and Page recruited his session buddy John Paul Jones—with whom he had recently recorded Donavan's "Hurdy Gurdy Man"—on bass.

After playing the Yardbirds dates under the moniker "The New Yardbirds," the band rechristened itself Led Zeppelin, purportedly after a few derogatory comments from the Who's John Entwistle, who had allegedly declaimed that the new group would likely go over like a "lead zeppelin." Misspelling "lead" to ensure its proper pronunciation, the new band was born. The band's manager, Peter Grant, soon secured the group a recording contract with Atlantic Records, and the band set to work recording their eponymous debut. *Led Zeppelin*, released in 1969, was a product of its time, featuring as it did a variety of blues covers and blues-influenced originals. But like the Jeff Beck Group of the day (the band's closest competitor), Led Zeppelin cranked up the volume and intensity, their melding of the blues form and rock power giving birth to a prototypical version of heavy metal that had no real precedent. And unlike Beck's group, Robert Plant's high and emotional vocals and Bonham's heavy yet virtuosic work on the drums set the group apart yet again. At the same time, the track "Black Mountain Side" was an indicator of the acoustic elements that would balance the band's heavier nature throughout their career.

Grant's plan for the band involved heavy American touring, and the band spent two months on the road in the U.S. before the album was even released. As a result, word of mouth about the band's powerhouse live shows set the stage for the album's positive reception, and it quickly made its way into the top ten.

The band continued to tour heavily throughout 1969, recording their second album piecemeal along the way. Despite such a recording process, *Led Zeppelin II*, produced by Page, is among the most consistent and powerful albums in the band's catalog. Dubbed the "brown bomber" by fans due to its brown cover and heavy content, the album built upon the promise of the debut and saw the band refining its approach at the same time.

Rockers like "Whole Lotta Love" and "Heartbreaker" saw the band flexing its muscles, while numbers like "What Is and What Should Never Be" and "Thank You" showed an evolution of the band's softer side and revealed a growing engagement with the Celtic folk tradition. The two sides of the band provided a synergistic yin-yang dynamic that added to their depth and served to make their heaviest moments all the more powerful. While this fact may have been lost on the critics, it certainly wasn't lost on the fans who came to the band's concerts in ever-increasing numbers. They also helped to make the album a smash hit, spending seven weeks as the top-selling album in the U.S. after its release.

Robert Plant and Jimmy Page redefined what it meant to be a rock star. (Ian Dickson/ Rex Features)

The band again toured heavily to support the album, and in October 1970 released *Led Zeppelin III*. The album was another success, and somewhat surprisingly emphasized the band's folk side, featuring such tracks as "Tangerine" and the traditional folk tune "The Gallow's Pole." After touring for *Led Zeppelin III*, the band took a short break and decamped to Headley Grange, a former poor house in Headley, East Hampshire, England, that had become a popular location for British bands to rehearse and record in.

Using the Rolling Stones' mobile recording unit, the band, along with engineer Andy Johns, set about recording what would become the band's masterpiece. Released in November 1971, the officially untitled album—often referred to as the "Zoso" album or, more commonly, *Led Zeppelin IV*—was the band's biggest hit to date. Featuring the classics "Rock and Roll," "Black Dog," and "When the Levee Breaks" (which had the legendary drum sound that was facilitated by Johns's inspired recording of Bonham's drums in Headley Grange's foyer), the album also featured the band's most popular song, "Stairway to Heaven." While the song may be among the most overplayed on FM radio, it nonetheless remains one of *the* signature songs of the band's career (with the only competition perhaps coming from "Kasmir" or "Whole Lotta Love"). It ably melded both the light and dark sides of the band as it built from its acoustic beginning to its thundering climax, with the band's heavy guitars and drums erupting as Plant howls out the final chorus of the song, before dropping back down into the song's end.

Led Zeppelin IV was a certifiable smash and cemented the band's musical reputation and commercial position. "Stairway to Heaven" became a huge radio hit, despite the fact that the band refused to edit the song for a single release.

John Bonham of Led Zeppelin appears in *The Song Remains the Same* (1976), one of the key metal movies. (Warner Bros./Photofest)

And while the album never made it to number 1 on the charts, it became their best-selling album by selling over 16 million copies over the next two decades.

The band continued touring, but focused now on larger venues like Madison Square Garden and the LA Forum. Their next album, *Houses of the Holy*, continued their musical experimentation, even as they remained consistently in delivering heavy tracks. The single "Dyer Maker" incorporated a reggae feel, while "The Crunge" added funk elements to the band's palette. Released in the spring of 1973, *Houses of the Holy* was another solid hit for the band, and they embarked on an extensive tour in support of it. Throughout the tour the band broke attendance records, most of which had been previously set by the Beatles, another testament to the juggernaut that the band had become. The '73 tour concluded with a series of shows at Madison Square Garden, which were filmed by the band, and later seen as the concert footage in the film *The Song Remains the Same*, which was released in 1976.

Taking a well-deserved break after the 1973 tour, the band laid low, doing little other than establishing their own record imprint, Swan Song Records, which would release all of their subsequent albums, as well as those by such artists as Bad Company, Dave Edmunds, Monarch, and the Pretty Things.

1975 saw the release of *Physical Grafitti*, a double album of new material. Although the band launched a major tour in support of the album, it was suspended after Plant was injured in a serious automobile accident while vacationing briefly in Greece.

Led Zeppelin's luck seemed to change somewhat with the arrival of 1976. That year saw the release of a new studio album, *Presence*, which although it quickly went to number 1 on the album charts, was fairly panned by critics. More significantly, though, while the band was on tour in 1977, Robert Plant's son Karac died as a result of a stomach infection. With Plant devastated, the tour was immediately cancelled, and Plant spent most of the next two years in seclusion, leading to speculation that the band might be finished.

In the summer of 1978, the band went back into the studio, working on their next album. Before its release, they went on a short tour of Europe that culminated in two concerts at Knebworth that would be the last the four would ever play together in England.

In Through the Out Door was finally released in September 1979 and went straight to the top of both the American and English charts, entering at number 1. In May the band completed a European tour, and in September were preparing for a major tour of America, rehearsing at Jimmy Page's house. On the 25th of September, after a day of reported binge drinking, John Henry Bonham was found dead in his bed, having choked on his own vomit. In December 1980, citing the impossibility of continuing without him, the remaining members announced that they would disband.

In the following years, Page, Plant, and Jones all engaged in various solo endeavors. Plant established a solid solo career, releasing a variety of adventurous and sometimes popular albums. Page released two albums with the Firm, featuring Bad Company and Free vocalist Paul Rodgers, and later released an album with David Coverdale. Jones released a solo album, *Zooma,* in 1999, and spent time producing and arranging. In 1985, Page, Plant, and Jones reunited briefly to play at Live Aid. Nine years later Page and Plant reunited as "Page and Plant," recording a segment of *MTV Unplugged,* released as "No Quarter," and followed it up with a studio album, *Walking Into Clarksdale,* produced by Steve Albini.

In December 2007, Led Zeppelin reunited for a concert in memory of Atlantic Records founder Amhet Ertegun, with John Bonham's son Jason filling in for his dad. The concert showed that the band members still had a lot of fire in their bellies and fueled speculation that they might embark on a full-scale tour, a possibility that the band have entertained but not as of yet committed to.

Discography: *Led Zeppelin* (Atlantic, 1969); *Led Zeppelin II* (Atlantic, 1969); *Led Zeppelin III* (Atlantic, 1970); *Led Zeppelin IV* (Atlantic, 1971); *Houses of the Holy* (Atlantic, 1973); *Physical Graffiti* (Swan Song, 1975); *Presence* (Swan Song, 1976); *The Song Remains the Same* [live] (Swan Song, 1976); *In Through the Out Door* (Swan Song, 1979); *Coda* (Swan Song, 1982); *How the West Was Won* [live] (Atlantic, 2003); *Led Zeppelin* [Box Set] (Swan Song, 1990); *Led Zeppelin Remasters* [Bonus Disc] (Swan Song, 1990); *Led Zeppelin Remasters* (Swan Song, 1992); *Led Zeppelin* [Box Set 2] (Swan Song, 1993); *Complete Studio Recordings* (Swan Song, 1993); *BBC Sessions* [live] (Atlantic, 1997); *Early Days: The Best of Led Zeppelin, Vol. 1* (Atlantic, 1999); *Latter Days: The Best of Led Zeppelin, Vol. 2* (Atlantic, 2000); *Complete Studio Sessions* (WEA/Warner, 2002); *Box Set, Vol. 1* (Classic Compact Disc, 2003); *Mothership* (Rhino, 2007).

LENG TCH'E (2001–PRESENT). Isaac Roelaert (vocals, replaced by Boris Cornelissen, replaced by Serge Kasongo), Glen Herman (guitars, replaced by Nir "The Goat" Doliner, replaced by Geert Devenster), Nicholas (guitars, replaced by Frank Rizzo, replaced by Jan "Spleenventer" Hallaert), Kevin (bass, replaced by Nicholas, replaced by Frank Rizzo, replaced by Johan Anotnissen, replaced by Nicolas Malfeyt), Sven De Caluwé (drums, replaced by Tony Van den Eynde).

Leng Tch'e is a classical sounding grindcore band from Ghent in Belgium (a relatively peaceful city, all things considered) on Relapse Records. Although Leng Tch'e are a relatively new band as far as the grindcore/death metal scene goes, they manage a credible approximation of a modern sped-up sound that still destroys just like the band's name. This Chinese term, which means "death by a thousand cuts," is based on an ancient and particularly painful form of torture in which the victim is cut again and again until he dies slowly and horribly. However, Leng Tch'e is much faster than this horrific torture and much better. If one should die slowly and horribly, at least one should die with a brutal and evocative soundtrack of Leng Tch'e in the background. Although the band has gone through numerous personnel changes, it is well worth checking out, and the most wonderfully torturous record is *The Process of Elimination*, followed by the most recent *Marasmus* album in 2007.

Discography: *Death By a Thousand Cuts* (Spew Records, 2002); *Man Made Predator* (Willowtip, 2003); *The Process of Elimination* (Relapse Records, 2005); *A Musical Propaganda for Sociologic Warfare* [split with Warscars] (Bones Brigade, 2006); *Marasmus* (Relapse Records, 2007).

LEZ ZEPPELIN (2004–PRESENT). Sarah Mclellen (vocals), Steph Paynes (guitar), Lisa Brigatino (bass), Helen Destroy (drums).

One of the more engaging and talented of the tribute circuit acts is this (allegedly) all, lesbian tribute to Led Zeppelin. While tribute bands are a common occurrence in the heavy metal scene—there are almost a countless number of cover bands, including "official" cover bands that accurately reproduce the sounds and image of many bands—Lez Zeppelin is one of the more popular of the recent cover bands, partly because of their all female and possibly lesbian lineup, but also because the band can actually recreate the sounds of Led Zeppelin. This also indicated the misogyny inherent in much of the metal culture, as many male bands who cover Zeppelin are assumed to be musically competent, as opposed to a female cover band, who are often seen as a gimmick. Although Lez Zeppelin does have a definable image, they are still much better and more musically adept than many bands who play the covers circuit and are possibly one of the better heavy metal bands currently touring, despite the fact that they are a cover band and have yet to release an album.

LIMP BIZKIT (1994–PRESENT). Fred Durst (vocals), Wes Borland (guitar), Sam Rivers (bass), DJ Lethal (DJ), John Toto (drums).

Limp Bizkit are a nu metal band from Florida who became one of the most popular bands in the world during the nu metal craze of the late nineties. While there were many worthwhile bands that tried to mix rap's kinetic vocal style with metal's power, Limp Bizkit quickly became the epitome to many metalheads of what was wrong with current metal. Led by the anti-charismatic Fred Durst, Bizkit took metal's frat boy tendency to gleeful extremes, saved occasionally by the interesting and innovative guitarist Wes Borland along with former House of Pain DJ, DJ Lethal.

The band hit its heyday in the late nineties, including memorable appearances on MTV's spring break special in 1999 and a controversial appearance at the 1999 Woodstock festival, where the band were blamed, whether or not correctly, for inciting the riots that marred the festival. As the nineties became the twenty-first century, the band became less relevant, particularly after the departure of guitarist Borland. The band soldiered on, largely because of Durst's role as a vice-president at Interscope Records. But their fame diminished as the years went on, and even the return of Borland for *The Unquestionable Truth Part 1* record didn't seem to save them from the inevitable. Although LB had some fairly interesting songs, they ultimately will be regarded as a footnote to metal, despite their brief but astounding popularity.

Discography: *Three Dolla Bill Y'all* (Interscope, 1997); *Significant Other* (Interscope, 1999); *Chocolate Starfish and the Hot Dog Flavored Water* (Interscope, 2000); *New Old Songs* (Interscope, 2001); *Results May Vary* (Flip/Interscope, 2003); *The Unquestionable Truth Part 1* (Geffen, 2005).

LIVING COLOUR (1984–95; 2001–PRESENT). Corey Glover (vocals), Vernon Reid (guitar), Muzz Skillings (bass, replaced by Doug Wimbish), Will Calhoun (drums).

Living Colour is a hard rock/metal/punk hybrid band led by guitar hero Vernon Reid, along with lead singer Corey Glover, bassist Muzz Skillings and drummer Will Calhoun, who mostly came from jazz backgrounds but also wanted to prove that an all-African-American group could rock as hard as any white group. This went up against the prejudices of many in the metal community, who regarded black musicians as alien to the hard rock and metal scene. The band started out gigging largely in New York and in particular at CBGB's, where they were "discovered" by Mick Jagger, who championed them and helped set up a record deal. It was a worthy attempt at education, and the band's first album is full of guitar pyrotechnics such as the riveting hit single "Cult of Personality" and the Talking Heads cover "Memories Can't Wait."

Although Living Colour was an excellent band, they were unfortunately trying to prove a point that had been made with no uncertainty several years before by a band that proved to be the best American punk/hardcore band, the incomparable Bad Brains, who in their prime put any ridiculous prejudices to rest with a stake through the heart of bigots and ignorant idiots back in the early eighties. Another thing stacked up against them in the metal scene is that they were more comfortable doing hard rock with a jazz tinge, a direction that various members of the band would continue in. After their first breakup in 1995, the band reunited for sporadic tours and shows starting in 2001, while guitarist Vernon Reid played out in a variety of jazz groups. They lacked also the cohesive brilliance that many other metal bands possessed, although their main innovation, Reid's jazz sqwank, was an appealing addition to the played-out metal guitar bag of tricks. Fans who like Living Colour's discourse on race and overall hardness are urged to check out Bad Brains, a band who broke the color barrier in punk and set new standards for musicianship and power in both punk and metal years before Living Colour.

Discography: *Vivid* (Epic, 1988); *Time's Up* (Epic, 1990); *Stain* (Epic, 1993); *Colledeoscope* (Sanctuary, 2003); *Live at CBGB's 12/19/1989* (Sony, 2005); *What's Your Favorite Color: Remixes B-sides and Rarities* (Sony, 2005).

LORD OF THE RINGS. Popular series of fantasy books (published in 1954–55 by English author J. R. R. Tolkien) that has influenced many metal bands, particularly

Led Zeppelin singer Robert Plant. While Tolkien wrote his masterpiece long before the advent of heavy metal, its themes of ancient magic races such as elves, dwarfs, and hobbits fighting alongside wizards and rangers against the ancient evil of Sauron proved to be instantly appealing not just to the hippie movement, but also to the embryonic metal scene of the sixties. They saw in Tolkien's worlds a template connecting not just the myths and legends that so many metal fans felt an affinity with, but equally compelling visions of both good and evil (it seems clear that many in the metal community found both Sauron, and his predecessor Morgoth, as compelling as the Valar and the elves. While fantasy in general has always been rich fodder for metal songs (see Dio in particular), *Lord of the Rings* provides a ready-made mythology that allowed metal heads to live out their fantasies. Some bands were directly inspired by these novels, such as Cirith Ungol, Led Zeppelin, Gorgoroth, and sadly, because of their crimes, Count Grisnakh and his black metal band Burzum.

LORDS OF CHAOS. *Lords of Chaos* (Feral House 1998) is a book by Michael Moynihan, an American journalist, and Didrik Soderlind from Norway that looks at the Norwegian black metal scene of the nineties. It is perhaps one of the most authentic and informative nonacademic looks at a specific metal scene, but it also is problematic for several reasons. The books covers the rise and eventual fall of the black metal scene from its inception to the years in the mid-nineties in Norway where various black metal groups and activists were responsible for several deaths and for the destruction via arson of several priceless historical churches in Norway and Sweden.

The book was controversial because it viewed the scene from a journalistic perspective, one that was impartial to the point of questionability and gave equal time to both sides of the story, including convicted murderer Varg Vikernes (aka Count Grisnakh), who was part of the black metal underground and the convicted killer of Euronymous. Also, primary author Moynihan has connections to white power movements and Aryan supremacy groups himself and has stated on his website and in interviews that he has pagan ties and a fairly radical philosophy by most objective standards, although Moynihan denies that he is a Nazi. However, the book is a fascinating look at a metal subculture and was one of the first books to take an in-depth look at the extremes to which a subculture can go.

MACHINE HEAD (1992–PRESENT). Robert Flynn (guitar), Phil Demmel (guitar), Adam Duce (bass), Dave McClain (drums).

More popular in Europe than in their native U.S., the speed metal four-piece Machine Head combine a flair for thrash and progressive in a unique blend that has long earned them a solid reputation among metal fans and a significant following in Europe.

Formed in 1992, the band, consisting of guitarists Robert Flynn and Phil Demmel, bassist Adam Duce, and drummer Chris Kontos, Machine Head signed with Roadrunner Records, after self-recording a demo, releasing the scorching 1994 debut *Burn My Eyes*. The well showcased the band's uniquely brutal brand of metal and established them as an up-and-coming thrash band to reckon with, selling over half a million copies and earning them a rabid European following. The band went on tour to support the album, staying out the better part of two years. The band's follow-up, *More Things Change*, released in 1997, only bolstered their growing reputation and saw them introducing speed and progressive metal elements into the mix. 1999's *Burning Red* produced the band's first successful single, "From This Day." Subsequently the band has released 2001's *Supercharger*, 2003's *Through the Ashes of Empires* and the live *Hellalive*, *Elegies* in 2005, and *Blackening* in 2007.

Discography: *Burn My Eyes* (Roadrunner, 1994); *The More Things Change* (Roadrunner, 1997); *Burning Red* (Roadrunner, 1999); *Year of the Dragon: Japan Tour Diary* (Roadrunner International, 2000); *Supercharger* (RoadRunner, 2001); *Through the Ashes of Empires* (Roadrunner International, 2003); *Hellalive* (Roadrunner, 2003); *The Blackening* (Roadrunner, 2007).

YNGWIE MALMSTEEN (1963–). One of the most important and technically advanced guitarists of the past two decades, Yngwie J. Malmsteen's (pronounced "ing-vay") phenomenal technique on the guitar—involving lightning-fast scale runs and sweeping arpeggios borrowed from classical violin—raised the bar on state-of-the-art rock guitar playing and led to the phenomenon of "shredding," the playing of impossibly fast scale and arpeggio lead playing, and also ignited the subgenre of neoclassical metal.

After becoming interested in music in his native Sweden after seeing a television program about Jimi Hendrix, a young Yngwie (born Lars Johann Yngwie Lannerback) took up the guitar and was soon exposed to classical music as well through his sister. Obsessive about practicing, he began to develop his extraordinary technique by practicing hours and hours a day, often till his fingers bled. Inspired by guitarists like Hendrix and Deep Purple's Ritchie Blackmore in particular, as well as by the classical composers Bach, Beethoven, Mozart, and particularly the violinist/composer Niccolo Paganini, whose charismatic image and instrumental style would provide a model for his own performance style, Yngwie began early to develop his own brand of music fusing rock and classical.

After spending some years playing in bands in Sweden and not achieving the success or recognition he felt he deserved, Yngwie sent out demo tapes to a variety of record labels. In response, Mike Varney of Shrapnel Records—whose label has long served as a showcase for exceptional rock guitarists—brokered an invitation for Malmsteen to join the L.A. metal band Steeler, led by vocalist Ron Keel. Moving to the states in 1981, Malmsteen recorded an album with the band but was dissatisfied with their mainstream style. Soon enough he was tapped to join former Rainbow singer Graham Bonnett's new group Alcatrazz that was very much in the tradition of Rainbow. Recording both a studio and live album with the band (1983's *No Parole from Rock 'n' Roll* and 1984's *Live Sentence*), Yngwie was finally given an opportunity to show what he was capable of instrumentally and compositionally, with tracks like "Jet to Jet" showcasing both his phenomenal technique and neoclassical writing style.

While the Alcatrazz albums weren't particularly successful, they proved an apt launching pad for the young guitarist, and he quickly began to build a reputation among guitar aficionados. Leaving the band, he quickly went solo, releasing the seminal instrumental album *Rising Force* on the Polydor label in 1984. The album went on to make the young guitarist's reputation and was a watershed moment for the development of rock guitar, showcasing as it did Yngwie's technique and style even more effectively than had the Alcatrazz albums. Yngwie went on to win numerous readers' polls in guitar magazines, and the album itself rose to number 60 on the Billboard charts and was nominated for a Grammy for Best Rock Instrumental Performance.

Yngwie went on to record two more albums in the same vein, 1985's *Marching Out* and 1986's *Trilogy*, which were similarly successful and confirmed his reputation. After a series of personal setbacks and tragedies, including a severe automobile accident and the death of his mother, he reemerged in 1988 with *Odyssey*, a more commercial album that included the single "Heaven Tonight," which helped it to crack into the top forty. Following the release of *Eclipse* in 1990, which failed commercially due to lack of record company support, Yngwie left the Polygram label and has recorded for smaller independent labels ever since, remaining prolific.

While his commercial appeal has diminished since the nineties, he continues to tour and record regularly, supported by a strong following, particularly in Europe and Japan. His latest release was *Instru-Mental* in 2007.

Discography: *Rising Force* (Polydor, 1984); *Marching Out* (Polydor, 1985); *Trilogy* (Polydor, 1986); *Odyssey* (Polydor, 1988); *Live in Leningrad: Trial by Fire* (Polydor, 1989); *Eclipse* (Polydor, 1990); *Fire & Ice* (Elektra, 1992); *The Seventh Sign* (Spitfire, 1994); *I Can't Wait* (Pony Canyon, 1994); *Power and Glory* (Pony Canyon, 1994); *Magnum Opus* (Import, 1995); *Inspiration* (Foundation, 1996); *Facing the Animal* (Polygram, 1998); *Concerto Suite for Electric Guitar and Orchestra in E Flat Minor Op. 1* (Import, 1998); *Live in Brazil 1998* (Import, 1998); *Alchemy* (Pony Canyon, 1999); *Young Person's Guide to the Classics, Vol. 1* (Pony Canyon, 2000); *Young Person's Guide to the Classics, Vol. 2* (Pony Canyon, 2000); *Double Live* (Spitfire, 2000); *War to End All Wars* (Pony Canyon, 2000); *Concerto Suite with the New Japan Philharmonic* (Pioneer, 2002); *Concerto Suite Live with Japan Philharmonic* (Pony Canyon); *Trial by Fire: Live in Leningrad* (Universal, 2002); *Birth of the Sun* (Cargo, 2002); *Attack!!* (Import, 2002); *The Genesis* (Pony Canyon, 2002); *Unleash the Fury* (Spitfire, 2005); *Live* (Dream Catcher, 2005); *Instru-Mental* (Spitfire, 2007); *Concerto Suite for Electric Guitar and Orchestra* (Dream Catcher Classic, 2007); *The Collection3* (Polygram, 1992); *The Best of Yngwie Malmsteen Live* (Import, 1998); *Anthology 1994–1999* (Pony Canyon, 2000); *Best of Yngwie Malmsteen: 1990–1999* (Dream Catcher, 2000); *Archives* (Pony Canyon, 2001); *Magnum Opus/I Can't Wait* (Pony Canyon, 2003); *Instrumental Best* (Import, 2004); *20th Century Masters—The Millennium Collection: The Best of Yngwie Malmsteen* (Polydor, 2005); *Yngwie Malmsteen Collection* (Universal, 2006); *Complete Box: Polydor Years* (Universal, 2006).

MANOWAR (1980–PRESENT). Eric Adams (vocals), Joey DeMaio (bass), Karl Logan (guitars/keyboards), Scott Columbus (drums).

Manowar's career seems to be largely guided by the question comedian Bill Murray once asked on a game show spoof on *Saturday Night Live:* "Quién es mas macho?" With little doubt, in the pantheon of macho heavy metal bands, Manowar is the most macho, no small achievement given the macho context of heavy metal in general. And the band have long based much of their career doing their level best to live up to the heroic standards that have been set by heavy metal lyrics of their own and others' songs, writing songs with a large degree of swords and sorcerers imagery and wearing leather outfits that go well beyond the typical.

Formed in the early eighties by former Dictators guitarist Ross the Boss Friedman and Joey DeMaio, the pair quickly added vocalist Eric Adams and drummer Donnie Hamzik and set about conquering the world with their primal brand of heavy metal. Beginning with their first release, 1982's *Battle Hymns*, each album has featured aggressive metal songs with themes of aggression, death, and metal itself, with songs such as "Blood of My Enemies," "Kill With Power," "All Men Play on 10," and "Sign of the Hammer." While they failed to be taken seriously by the press or the music industry at large, Manowar have gradually been able to attract a cult following (especially in Europe), which has allowed them to continue recording and touring up to the present.

Discography: *Battle Hymns* (Liberty, 1982); *Into Glory Rid* (Music For Nations, 1983); *Hail to England* (Music For Nations, 1984); *Sign of the Hammer* (Grand Slamm, 1985); *Fighting the World* (Atco, 1987); *Kings of Metal* (Atlantic, 1988); *The Triumph of Steel* (Atlantic, 1992); *Louder Than Hell* (Geffen, 1996); *Secrets of Steel* (MCA International, 1998); *Hell on Stage Live* (Metal Blade, 1999); *Hell on Wheels Live* (Metal Blade, 1999); *Fire and Funk* (Flipnflava, 2001); *Skillz Dat Killz: The First Dimension* (Flipnflava, 2001); *Warriors of the World* (Metal Blade, 2002); *The Sons of Odin* (Inside/Out, 2006); *Gods of War* (SPV, 2007); *Gods of War: Live* (SPV, 2007); *The Very Best* (Mayhem, 1998); *The Kingdom of Steel: The Very Best of Manowar* (MCA, 1999).

Marilyn Manson (MTV Networks/Photofest)

MARILYN MANSON (1989–PRESENT). Marilyn Manson, aka Brian Warner (vocals), Daisy Berkowitz (guitar, replaced by various others), Twiggy Ramirez (bass), Chris Vrenna (drums), Madonna Wayne Gacy (keyboards till 2007).

Marilyn Manson is not particularly a metal artist, although he was nominated for a metal Grammy in 2004, but many, especially those who wish to point out the excessive nature of rock lyrics and lifestyle, have often lumped Manson in the category. In essence, Manson is as metal as Alice Cooper and owes his career to a point to both Cooper and industrial rocker Trent Reznor, who was Manson's former mentor. Manson has gone through several phases, and even went "glam" for several records but is still more of a reemergence of the kind of shock rock that Alice Cooper and Kiss pioneered several decades before. It's not particularly original, but it does scare the parents, and that must be the point.

Discography: *Portrait of an American Family* (Nothing Interscope, 1994); *Antichrist Superstar* (Nothing Interscope, 1996); *Mechanical Animals* (Nothing Interscope, 1998); *Holy Wood: In the Shadow of the Valley of Death* (Nothing Interscope, 2000); *The Golden Age of Grotesque* (Nothing Interscope, 2003); *Eat Me Drink Me* (Nothing Interscope, 2007).

MASTERS OF REALITY (1987–PRESENT). Classic lineup: Chris Goss (vocals and guitar), Tim Harrington (lead guitar), Vinnie Ludovico (drums), and Googe (bass).

Named after the classic Black Sabbath album, Masters of Reality played a unique brand of hard rock influenced by Cream and Led Zeppelin, which also featured Beatlesque influences and unusual lyrical content. Led by vocalist/guitarist (and now producer) Chris Goss, the band has only released a handful of albums, yet they have been quite influential, especially to such latter-day bands as Queens of the Stone Age.

Beginning as a quartet in the late eighties, the first iteration of the band featured leader Chris Goss on vocals and guitar, Tim Harrington on lead guitar, Vinnie Ludovico on drums, and Googe on bass.

Their first self-titled album was released in 1988. Produced by Rick Rubin, the album featured such tracks as "Candy Girl" (which received some airplay), as well as "John Brown," "Doraldina's Prophecies," and "Kill the King." The songs begin with straightforward, Zep- or Cream-type riffs but bloom into something else as Goss's inspiration often takes the tunes into Beatlesque or even King Crimson (minus the instrumental displays) type of prog rock. And Goss's clear and sweet voice (not unlike that of Cream's Jack Bruce) keeps even the heaviest of the band's songs from sounding overly heavy.

After the album, Goss disbanded the group for a while, then relocated to L.A. with Googe, and recruited ex-Cream drummer Ginger Baker, for the excellent *Sunrise on the Sufferbus*. Featuring a somewhat lighter sound, the album was another creative success for the band with songs like "She Got Me" and "Ants in the Kitchen" (containing the memorable line, "stuck in Indiana with a bug in my banana") transcending their blues-based forms. Baker's playing is perfect, and his spoken word performance on T.U.S.A. (a treatise on "the inability of Yanks to brew a decent cup of tea" is hilarious). The album, like the first, was moderately successful, yet the band's (read Goss's) penchant for following the beat of their own drummer (figuratively speaking, of course) meant that the band never fit into the prevailing rock trends of the time, instead becoming a favorite of fellow musicians and creating more of a cult following.

Goss eventually moved out to the Joshua Tree area of the California desert, working more and more as a producer, with such groups as Kyuss, and later Queens of the Stone Age, as well as others, and becoming a central player in the development of the "desert rock" scene. He has continued to sporadically release albums under the Masters of Reality name and occasionally tours with a changing lineup of musicians.

Discography: *Masters of Reality* (Delicious Vinyl, 1988); *Blue Garden* (Def American, 1990); *Sunrise on the Sufferbus* (Chrysalis, 1993); *How High the Moon: Live at the Viper Room* (Delicious Vinyl, 1997); *Welcome to the Western Lodge* (Spitfire, 1999); *Deep in the Hole* (Brownhouse, 2001); *Reality Show* (Cargo, 2002); *Flak 'n' Flight* [live] (Import, 2003); *Give Us Barabbas* (Brownhouse, 2004).

MASTODON (1999–PRESENT). Troy Sanders (vocals/bass), Brent Hinds (vocals/guitar), Bill Kelliher (bass), Brann Dailor (drums), Eric Saner (lead vocals on demo).

Mastadon is one the most powerful and influential metal crossover bands of the past decade and one of the bands credited with the resurgence of American metal. The band redefines the idea of "heavy" music, even while working on extremely complex math rock riffs in combination with idea-driven lyrics. This included a concept record about Moby Dick in their classic *Leviathan* release, which set new standards for post-hardcore influenced metal vocals and multi-layered guitar parts. In an interview in *Rolling Stone* magazine, bassist and singer Troy Sanders explained that they chose the name of the band based on the fact that "the mastadon was this lumbering Beast. It creates the idea of the Music we want to create: Just a Powerhouse" (O'Donnell 2008, 40).

The band got its wish, at times lumbering and at times ferocious, often within the same song, Mastadon simply reeks of power. Mastodon came out of the influential noise metal band Today is the Day, which featured Dailor and Kelliher as the rhythm section. Mastodon soon became the heaviest band and one of the most musically intricate bands in metal's history, fusing post-hardcore with math-like precision over lumbering metal riffs. As powerful as metal should be and seldom has been.

Discography: *Lifesblood* (Relapse, 2001); *Remission* (Relapse, 2001); *Leviathan* (Relapse, 2004); *Call of the Mastadon* (Relapse, 2006); *Blood Mountain* (Warner Brothers, 2006).

MAYHEM (1985–PRESENT). Messiah (vocals, replaced by Dead, then Attila Csihar, Maniac, then Attila Csihar), Euronymous (guitar/vocals, replaced by Blasphemer), Nerobutcher (bass, replaced by Varg Vikernes, then Nerobutcher), Manheim (drums, later Maniac, then Hellhammer).

Mayhem are a notorious black metal band from Norway who are better known for the controversy and death that has surrounded the band rather than for their music. The band originally started in 1985 as a trio with a lineup of Euronymous (Oyestein Aarseth) on vocals and guitar, Nerobutcher on bass, and Manheim (Sven Kristiansen) on drums, before hiring full-time vocalist Messiah (Erik Norheim) and lead vocalist Dead, who committed suicide in 1991. Depressed by the death of Dead, Nerobutcher briefly left the band and was replaced by Varg Vikernes, aka Count Grisnackh (a name taken from the name of an Orc in Tolkien's *Lord of the Rings* trilogy), who was the creator of the ominous black metal project Burzum, along with new vocalist Atilla Csihar. This lineup resumed recording the *De Mysteriis Dom Sathanas* record. However, in an even more disturbing series of events, Mayhem made themselves the focus of the metal world's attention when, on August 13, 1993, Varg Vikernes traveled seven hours from Bergen to Oslo, to Euronymous's apartment, where he killed the guitarist. Although Vikernes claimed it was self-defense, he was convicted of murder, and under Norway's progressive penal system, was only sentenced to twenty-one years in prison as well as for the burning of three irreplaceable Stave churches in Norway. In prison, he soon became a white supremacist and recorded music for his Burzum project. In 2003 Vikernes escaped while on a prison furlough and was discovered in a stolen car with numerous weapons, after which he was sentenced to an additional thirteen months in prison, where he continues to write and espouse his nihilistic, propagan/proaryan pride philosophy (Moynihan and Soderlind 1998, 122).

With Mayhem in ruins, Hellhammer decided to reform the band with new guitarist Blasphemer Rune Erickson, along with Nerobutcher on bass and old drummer Maniac on vocals. After a few successful tours and the *Chimera* album being acclaimed by some black metal fans and denounced by others for being insufficient evil, the band returned to form and continued their notorious tours where the band performed with pigs' heads on stakes as macabre stage props. After a fight with Blasphemer, Maniac was kicked out of Mayhem, and Attila Csihar resumed lead vocal duties, leading Mayhem in a more experimental direction, with longer, more atmospheric songs.

The band continues to produce music and tour to this day with drummer Hellhammer and bassist Nerobutcher as the only long-lasting members of the band, and as of summer 2008, guitarist Blasphemer has left the band, leaving it without a guitarist. While most fans pay attention to Mayhem as a black metal train wreck, there is dark and horrible beauty to the band's music; if one can put aside the horrific lifestyles of many members of Mayhem, their music is experimental and in some ways more accessible than some other black metal bands.

Discography: *Pure Fucking Armageddon* (Unknown, 1986); *De Mysteriis Dom Sathanus* (Century Media, 1995); *Live in Leipzig* (Century Media, 1997); *Wolf's Alit Abyss* (Misanthropy, 1998); *Mediolanum Capta Est* (Avant Garde, 1999); *Grand Declaration of War* (Season of Mist, 2000); *US Legions* (Renegade, 2001); *Freezing Moon Carnage/Jihad* (Supernal Music, 2003); *Legions of War* (Seasons of Mist America, 2003); *Chimera* (Season of Mist, 2004); *European Legions* (Season of Mist, 2005); *Buried Alive* (US Metal, 2005); *Ordo Ad Chao* (Seasons of Mist, 2007).

MEGADETH (1983–PRESENT). Dave Mustaine (vocals, guitar), Matt Kisselstein (bass, replaced by David Ellefson), Lee Rausch (drums, replaced by Gar Samuelson, Chuck Behler, Nick Menza, Jimmy Degrasso, Vinnie Colaiuta, Shawn Drover).

Magadeth is one of the longest lasting of the speed/thrash metal bands of the early eighties, and although lead singer/guitarist Dave Mustaine has grown in talent, the essential Megadeth formula has not. They started in 1983, after Mustaine's acrimonious and bitter departure from a prerecorded Metallica (disputes over songwriting credits continued for years after Mustaine left the band). Mustaine wished to build a band as hard and fast as Metallica and in Megadeth he found his true calling. The first record, *Killing Is My Business ... And My Business Is Good,* was a thrash classic, showing that Mustaine had not slowed down a bit by the lack of his partners in Metallica, and with bassist Dave Ellefson, he had a reliable new band for the inevitable conquest of America.

The next two records, *Peace Sells ...* and *So Far, So Good ...,* gave new definition to what could almost be called "melodic thrash" with Mustaine's gritty vocals and guitar pyrotechnics anchoring the band's signature sound. (They also proved that a band could use the ellipses successfully, at least for several records.) However, as the nineties commenced, a sense of sameness began to creep into the music, and by *Cryptic Writings*, it seemed as though Mustaine was only going through the motions. Mustaine apparently had enough as well, and from 2002–04 the band was dormant until he decided to revive it with yet another slew of new members.

A key problem with Megadeth was consistency, and the band has gone through a bewildering array of personnel changes, with only bassist Ellefson lasting more than a few years (Ellefson was in the band for almost twenty years, 1983–2002), and culminating in the band's break-up for two years from 2002–04. Today the band consists of Mustaine and three members who have only been in the band for a few years, and Ellefson has sued Mustaine over the ownership of the name Megadeth.

Mustaine revived Megadeth in 2004 for *The System Has Failed* and was back angrier than ever, but for different reasons than in the past. Apparently Mustaine has surprisingly become a born-again Christian and will no longer play some earlier songs live because of their lyrical content (Mustaine will apparently no longer cover the Sex Pistols' "Anarchy in the UK" for the opening line about being the anti-Christ.) Mustaine has also evolved into a fairly conservative political commentator. In an interview with The *American Spectator,* Mustaine has railed against the United Nations (the source of the last Megadeth studio record *United Abominations*) for including nations like Syria on the UN Security Council and has written pro-Israel and explicitly Christian songs.

Mustaine is one of the most intriguing and frustrating men in heavy metal. He is without doubt a true innovator and one of the most successful guitarists and vocalists in metal history, but his inability to get through most interviews and his abrupt shifts in opinion make him almost unreadable. Perhaps that's okay and fans should concentrate more on the music than on the man himself.

Discography: *Killing Is My Business ... and Business Is Good!* (Combat, 1985); *Peace Sells ... But Who's Buying?* (Combat/Capitol, 1986); *So Far, So Good ... So What!* (Capitol, 1988); *Rust in Peace* (Combat/Capitol, 1990); *Countdown to Extinction* (Combat/Capitol, 1992); *Youthanasia* (Capitol, 1994); *Hidden Treasures* (Capitol, 1995); *Cryptic Writings* (Capitol, 1997); *Risk* (Capitol, 1999); *Capitol Punishment: The Megadeth Years* (Capitol, 2000); *The World Needs a Hero* (Sanctuary, 2001); *Rude Awakening Live* (Sanctuary, 2002); *The System Has Failed* (Sanctuary, 2004); *United Abominations* (Roadrunner, 2007); *That One Night: Live in Buenos Aires* (Image Entertainment, 2007).

MELVINS (1986–PRESENT). Buzz "King Buzzo" Osbourne (vocals/guitar), Matt Lukin (bass, replaced by Lori Black, Mark Deutrom, Kevin Rutmanis), Dale Crover (drums).

The Melvins are also the definition of early metal as epitomized by Sabbath, slooooooooooow and sludgy riffs and a drum beat that almost allows one to go out for a cup of coffee before the next beat finally crashes down on the snare. A Washington state band, the Melvins, a particular influence on Kurt Cobain, have been relentlessly pursuing sludge perfection for over twenty years and over the course of more than twenty records, not to mention solo records and collaborations with like-minded souls such as Fanotmas and Jello Biafra.

The band also notoriously released three "solo" EPs from all three members at the same time with album covers that were a mock-up of the famous Kiss solo records. The band also once featured Lori Black, the daughter of former child star Shirley Temple, on bass for several years. Although usually lumped in with the alternative or the "grunge" scene, the Melvins have been truer to the original musical intent of metal than the countless number of better-known hair bands that once dominated the landscape in the days of yore.

Discography: *Melvins* [EP] (C/Z, 1986); *Gluey Porch Treatments* (Alchemy, 1986; Ipecac, 2000); *Ozma* (Boner, 1989); *Eggnog* [EP] (Boner, 1991); *10 Songs* (C/Z, 1991); *Your Choice Live Series, Vol. 12* (Ger. Your Choice, 1991); *Bullhead* (Boner, 1991); *Melvins* (Boner/Tupelo, 1992); *Houdini* (Atlantic, 1993); *Stoner Witch* (Atlantic, 1994); *Live* (X-mas, 1996); *Stag* (Mammoth/Atlantic, 1996); *Honky* (Amphetamine Reptile, 1997); *Singles 1–12* (Amphetamine Reptile, 1997); *Alive at the Fucker Club* (Amphetamine Reptile, 1998); *The Maggot* (Ipecac, 1999); *The Bootlicker* (Ipecac, 1999); *The Crybaby* (Ipecac, 2000); *Melvins at Slim's on 8-Track 6.17.99* [8-track] (Life Is Abuse, 2000); *The Trilogy on Vinyl* (Ipecac, 2000); *Hostile Ambient Takeover 7' Singles* (Ipecac, 2000); *Electroretard* (Man's Ruin, 2001); *Colossus of Destiny* (Ipecac, 2001); *Hostile Ambient Takeover (H.A.T.)* (Ipecac, 2002); *26 Songs* (Ipecac, 2003); *Melvinmania: The Best of the Atlantic Years 1993–1996* (Atlantic, 2003); *Pigs of the Roman Empire* (Ipecac, 2004); *Mangled Demos from 1983* (Ipecac, 2005); Snivlem: *Prick* (Amphetamine Reptile, 1994); Fanotmas Melvins Big Band: *Fanotmas Melvins Big Band* (Ipecac, 2002); King Buzzo: *King Buzzo* [EP] (Boner/Tupelo,

1992); Dale Crover: *Dale Crover* [EP] (Boner/Tupelo, 1992); Joe Preston: *Joe Preston* [EP] (Boner/Tupelo, 1992).

MERCYFUL FATE (1980–85, 1994–99, POSSIBLY PRESENT). King Diamond (vocals), Michael Denner (guitar, replaced by Mike Wead), Hank Shermann (guitar), Timi "Grabber" Hansen (bass, replaced by Charlee D'Angelo), Kim Ruzz (drums, many others, now Bjarne Holm).

Mercyful Fate are a long-running black metal band with explicitly satanic lyrics, and the original band of long-running solo artist, the fancifully face-painted King Diamond (Kim Peterson). The band was known for the dark lyrics, frequent references to Satan, and overall dark mood as if they were doing the soundtrack to a particularly bleak horror film where the monster wins in the end. Filled with songs about witches and the return of the dead from the spirit world (particularly on the *Melissa* songs), Mercyful Fate were also remarkable for the amazing range of vocalist King Diamond, who could go from a guttural growl to a shrieking operatic falsetto within the space of a single note.

The band was one of the most successful precursors to black metal and their first two records were major influences on the bands that followed in the black and death metal scenes. However, the band suffered with conflicts between King Diamond and guitarist Shermann about the potential commerciality of the music, and after the tour for the second record the band called it quits, with Diamond decamping for his own bands along with guitarist Denner and bassist Hansen. After a long hiatus, the band got back together for the *In the Shadows* record, which showed the band picking up where it had left off. The following records were of varying equality, as Diamond balanced a solo career with his involvement with the band and various members left.

There has been little new music from Fate in the last decade, and if *9* was their swan song, it appears that they went out with an album as interesting and frightening as anything they had done since *Don't Break the Oath*. Former drummer Mikey Dee now drums for Motorhead, and King Diamond remains one of the respected and satanic elders of the black and death metal movements.

Discography: *Melissa* (Megaforce, 1983); *Don't Break the Oath* (Megaforce, 1984); *In the Shadows* (Roadrunner, 1993); *Time* (Metal Blade, 1994); *Into the Unknown* (Metal Blade, 1996); *Dead Again* (Metal Blade, 1998); *9* (Metal Blade, 1999).

MESHUGGAH (1987–PRESENT). Jens Kidmand (vocals), Marten Hagstrom (guitar), Fredrik Thorendahl (guitar), Dick Lovgran (bass), Tomas Haake (drums).

Meshuggah are an amazingly complex and intriguingly dark Swedish band formed in 1987 that constantly challenges the established parameters of metal. The band is comprised of vocalist Jens Kidmand, who mostly sings in English, along with bassist Dick Lovgran, and drummer Tomas Haake. The intricacy of Meshuggah's music and its quick and abrupt changes in timing and key have led many critics to label them as a more of a "math" metal band for their sheer intricacy. Meshuggah has evolved gradually since its start in the late eighties, and each album shows advancements that eschew all the usual metal clichés for new and innovative ways of combining the traditions of black and death metal's eeriness with a sheer wall of guitar sound that also includes the virtuosity of key metal players like Joe Sotriani, along with experimental new music. *Obzen,* with its elaborate twists, may be one of the most fascinating metal albums of the past decade. Highly recommended for fans of more extreme music who seek more complexity on the fringe of metal.

Discography: *Contradiction Collapse / None* (Nuclear Blast, 1991); *Destroy Erase Improve* (Nuclear Blast, 1995); *Chaosphere* (Nucelar Blast, 1998); *Nothing* (Nuclear Blast, 2002); *Catch Thirty-Three* (Nuclear Blast, 2005); *Self Caged* (Nuclear Blast, 2006); *Obzen* (Nuclear Blast, 2008).

METAL. *See* Heavy Metal Music: An Introduction.

METAL BLADE (1981–PRESENT). Metal Blade is an influential, early heavy metal record label from the eighties founded by Brian Sclagle. They are known for releases by Cryptic Slaughter, GWAR, King Diamond, Anvil, Dirty Rotten Imbeciles (DRI), Mercyful Fate, and Slayer, among many others. Ironically, for a long time the label's best-selling artist were the Goo Goo Dolls, a once-punk band now gone mainstream pop, who released several good records on the label. Today Metal Blade continues as a nationwide label and the current roster includes bands such as Amon Amarth, As I Lay Dying, Bolt Thrower, Cannibal Corpse, God Dethroned, and Vader. It has been one of the most consistent metal labels and gave exposure to numerous bands who could not get a record deal at the time, especially in the eighties. Today the label has many harsh and extreme bands, including some that blur the line between metal and hardcore punk such as Shai Hulud.

METAL CHURCH (1981–PRESENT). Mike Murphy (vocals, replaced by David Wayne, Mike Howe), Kurdt Vanderhoof (guitar), Craig Wells (guitar, replaced by John Marshall, Rick Van Zandt), Duke Erickson (bass), Kirk Arrington (drums, replaced by Jeff Plate).

Metal Church were a thrash metal band from the early eighties who somehow flew below the radar of many in the metal community, despite their classic records such as *The Dark,* which was a huge-selling thrash metal landmark. The first vocalist, Murphy, was less strident than many thrash singers and more indebted to classic metal than many in the thrash scene at the time. Subsequent vocalists saw the band turn in a harder direction, but just as Metal Church was hitting their stride again, they fell prey to the rise of grunge and the punk revival and were largely inactive from the early nineties till 1999, when they reformed with a new lineup with Wayne singing again, although he soon left the band. Sadly former singer Wayne passed away in 2005, but the band soldiers on to this day, spreading the gospel of Metal Church to true believers far and wide.

Discography: *Metal Church* (Elektra, 1985); *The Dark* (Elektra, 1987); *Blessing in Disguise* (Elektra, 1989); *Human Factor* (Epic, 1991); *Hanging in the Blance* (Blackheart, 1993); *Masterpeace* (Nuclear Blast, 1999); *Live* (Nuclear Blast, 2000); *The Weight of the World* (Steamhammer/Spv, 2004); *A Light in the Dark* (SPV, 2006).

"METAL UP YOUR ASS." A metal slogan of the mid-eighties that originated with the band Metallica, who wanted to call one of their records "metal up your ass" instead of the much more appropriate *Kill 'Em All*. Eventually the term, along with the picture of a sword coming out of a toilet, became a popular T-shirt sold in many metal shops in the mid- to late eighties. The slogan was probably not meant to be homophobic, but is certainly one of the least subtle images in the marketing of heavy metal and the thought of accidentally sitting on a sword when simply wanting a bathroom break must have been an interesting dilemma for metal fans.

METALHEADS. A common term (like headbangers) for especially enthusiastic fans of heavy metal. The metalhead moniker is often bestowed on those fans (by themselves or by others) who not only listen to the music as much as possible but also label themselves as metal fans by wearing typical metal clothing such as denim or leather jackets, often festooned with embroidered patches featuring the names or insignias of metal groups.

METALLICA (1981–PRESENT). James Hetfield (vocals/guitar), Kirk Hammet (guitar), Cliff Burton (bass, died in 1986, replaced by Jason Newsted, later Robert Trujillo), Lars Ulrich (drums).

Metallica are one of the longest lasting and most successful of the so-called thrash or speed metal bands of the early eighties, and, despite personnel problems and intragroup infighting (as documented in the poignant and frequently hilarious documentary *Some Kind of Monster*), Metallica maintain their position as one of the most popular and influential American heavy metal bands of all time. Early on the band worked with guitarist Dave Mustaine and bassist Ron McGovney, but personnel conflicts between Mustaine and the rest of the band led to his departure, along with McGovney prior to the recording of *Kill 'Em All*, although several of Mustaine's co-compositions remain on the record, including the classics "Metal Militia," "The Four Horsemen," "Jump in the Fire," and "Phantom Lord." The first record was a landmark of its time, a brutal mix of thrilling guitar pyrotechnics and riffs that change several times within a song, essentially making even the longer numbers ("the Four Horsemen" clocks in at 7:08, and no songs are shorter than four minutes) seem as though each song has several movements reminiscent of classical music, but with a heavy sensibility and speed that comes from Metallica's love of hardcore punk rock. In particular, the song "Seek and Destroy" with its title reminiscent of the Stooges classic "Search and Destroy" is one of the songs more reminiscent of a punk band, or at least a punk sensibility as channeled through heavy metal.

If the first record was a bold statement of musical purpose, the next record, *Ride the Lightning*, expanded on the ground broken on the first record and saw Metallica fully gelling as a band and saw new members Hammet and Burton fully establishing themselves as equal partners in constructing Metallica's sound. Although the record still had two songs at least co-written by Mustaine ("Ride the Lighting" and "Call of Ktulu," two of the more powerful songs on the record), the non-Mustaine songs demonstrate Metallica refining the raw thrash of the first record into a tight and intricate machine, backed by the precise rhythm section of Burton and Ulrich. In particular, "Fade to Black" and "Creeping Death" were instant metal classics, and the band soon saw its popularity grow from the metal underground to the mainstream.

Metallica: A band that combined punk's velocity with metal's fury. (Elektra/Photofest)

With the next record, the all-time classic metal album *Master of Puppets*, Metallica moved into the big leagues. The monumental epic title track and "Damage Incorporated" and "Welcome Home (Sanitarium)" gave Metallica a new audience beyond the realm of the underground. The album went Top 40 in America, leading to an upsurge in new fans from the punk and traditional metal communities. Some older metalheads, who had trouble with thrash's speed and raw power, could now see that the music was played by true jazz-like virtuosos of metal and began to give Metallica their due.

At the height of their success, tragedy struck Metallica as bassist Burton, who had been sleeping in Hetfield's bunk on a tour of Sweden, was killed instantly when he was thrown outside of the tour bus and the bus landed on top of him. This stopped Metallica in its tracks and after much careful deliberation, the band regrouped and, with the permission of the Burton family, auditioned for new bassists, finally settling on Jason Newsted, who had previously played in Flotsam and Jetsam. The band reunited for the ... *And Justice for All* record, which finally cracked the top ten for the band in 1988, and led to a hit video with "One." The band were even nominated for a Grammy award but inexplicably lost out to Jethro Tull, much to the bemusement of the rock establishment. However, something seemed to be missing. Whether is was the absence of Burton or the relative newness of Newsted, the band seemed to lack direction, and the songs, long even for Metallica standards, meandered without any real sense of menace of cohesion. While the album was Metallica's most successful to date, it proved to be a crossroads for the band: would they return to their roots or try and break out commercially?

The next album answered the question decisively. Metallica, after years of existing on the fringes of the music industry, respectable underground, and extreme music fan base, finally crossed over with the *Black* album in 1991. They finally achieved mainstream success with the hit singles (and videos) for "Nothing Else Matters," "The Unforgiven," "Wherever I May Roam," and "Enter Sandman" (which later became a staple intro song for New York Yankees reliever Mariano Rivera).

Many of the fans who had been disappointed by the band's mainstream direction on the ... *And Justice for All* records were doubly disappointed by what they saw as Metallica pandering to commercial radio. However, many other fans, unaware of Metallica's history, were won over by the hardest music they had ever heard on mainstream radio. Bob Rock's keen production made the band sound much fuller and had a much more pronounced rythym section than on previous releases and the record almost begged for commercial radio play. Whether Metallica had sold out or not, they had finally succeeded in breaking heavy metal, undiluted by hair-metal pop hooks, onto the commercial airwaves; the question was, what would, or could, Metallica do next?

As it turns out, the remainder of Metallica's career since then has been a collection of small steps forward and backward and frequent entrenchments. It was as though once Metallica had reached the top, they had no idea what to do next. If going through the metal motions of *Load* was a disappointment to most fans (although as usual by this time, it sold well), then *Reload* was the sound of a band floundering for purpose, clearly unsure of what direction to go in next. What happened next was chaos, with Newsted leaving the band for personal reasons in 2001, followed by Hetfield's lengthy stay in a rehab clinic and then at home with his family in an effort to stay sober (Weiderhorn 2002). The sessions for *St. Anger* were documented in the hilarious but poignant documentary *Some Kind of Monster*, the Spinal Tap of heavy metal documentaries.

Metallica's influence on modern metal is incalculable. The band was one of the first bands to take the speed and urgency of hardcore punk bands like the Misfits and early Black Flag and to combine them with metal's virtuosity and crunch. Metallica's well-known personnel problems eventually became so widely known that the group decided to make a documentary film about their time preparing for their new record and working with "performance coach" Phil Towle, who was grossly overpaid to work out their group dynamics. The film, instead of demonstrating how much Metallica worked, actually showcased them as a completely dysfunctional group who relied too heavily on the advice of "Coach" Towle, who increasingly began to resemble the famous discredited psychiatrist Eugene Landy (who for a long time handled the affairs of Brian Wilson of the Beach Boys).

In the end, despite their personnel troubles, Metallica will always be known for the power and thrash magnificence of their first three records, which set a standard that thousands of other bands have yet to live up to even today. So many bands use Metallica as a template that it cannot be denied that they are one of the top five or so metal bands in terms of influence. It is hoped that the band can regain their former momentum, but it seems as though the band will need to learn from their mistakes and set the bar higher for their next record.

Discography: *Kill 'Em All* (Megaforce, 1983; Elektra, 1987); *Ride the Lightning* (Megaforce, 1984; Megaforce/Elektra, 1984); *Whiplash* [EP] (Megaforce, 1985); *Master of Puppets* (Elektra, 1986); *The $5.98 E.P. Garage Days Re-Revisited* [EP] (Elektra, 1987); ... *And Justice for All* (Elektra, 1988); *The Good, the Bad and the Live* (UK Vertigo, 1990); *Metallica* (Elektra, 1991); *Live Shit: Binge & Purge* (Elektra, 1993); *Load* (Elektra, 1996);

Reload (Elektra, 1997); *Garage Inc.* (Elektra, 1998); *S&M* (Elektra, 1999); *St. Anger* (Elektra, 2003); *Metallica Collectors Box* (Elektra, 2006).

MISFITS (1977–83, 1996–PRESENT). Glenn Danzig (vocals replaced in reunion by Michael Graves, then Jerry Only), Frank Licata, aka "Franche Coma" (guitar), Jerry "Only" Caiafa (bass, now lead vocals as well), James "Mr. Jim" Catania (drums, later Arthur Googy, then Robo, then Dr. Chud, then Marky Ramone, now Robo), Doyle "Wolfgang Von Frankenstein" Caiafa (guitar, replaced by Dez Cadena).

The Misfits were one of the key punk and hardcore bands of the late seventies and early eighties, and their influence on metal is considerable. The band was one of the few punk bands influenced by the occult, B-grade zombie films, cheesy monster films, and their nostalgia for late-night double features that led them to become the poster boys for combining Halloween with everyday life. The band pioneered the blood-drenched look, the classic devilock haircut (hair grown extremely long in the front and slicked into a spike, almost a flattened-down, extremely long Mohawk), and dark and chilling lyrics about death, murder, and horror.

To a certain extent it was a joke, at least for most of the band, but for lead singer Glenn Danzig, it was either dead serious or a great career move to keep the shtick going in his subsequent bands, the goth/punk Samhain, and the opera-meets-Elvis version of metal/whatever he founded with the much more popular Danzig. But even before Danzig left to form his later projects, the Misfits were certainly a template not only for the thrash/speed metal crossover scene (along with dark bands like the Swans) but also for the burgeoning death and black metal scenes. (It can be argued that the Misfits touch equally on both subjects at length in their songs and can therefore be considered a major influence based on lyrical content alone, much less their music, which was also a template.) But it was within the thrash community that the Misfits would receive the most recognition. Numerous metal bands, notably Metallica, were huge fans of the Misfits. The black metal bands that followed in their wake who were not borrowing directly from Venom or Black Sabbath surely owe the Misfits a debt of gratitude, as do thrash metal and grindcore band's who were clearly influenced by the bands last great record with Danzig, the ultra-fast *Earth A.D.*, one of the most brutal musical and lyrical records ever put down on vinyl.

Although the band's classic period was relatively short, their legacy was long lasting on the metal scene. The next Danzig band, Samhain, was also a key influence on the black metal scene, with their lyrics dedicated to paganism and the occult and the raw darkness associated with the band. Danzig's later band, Danzig, was more blues-based metal with occult leaning who sounded more like Elvis fronting Venom. Today Glenn Danzig still tours with a new version of Danzig, while the Misfits name and lucrative merchandising rights are held, by original member Jerry Only who valiantly still keeps the band going to this day. A reunion with Danzig has been rumored for years, but at this date there is no indication that it will happen any time soon, although during the last several years Danzig has included a short Misfits set in many of his longer headlining shows.

Discography: *Bullet* [EP] (Plan 9, 1978); *Beware* [EP] (Cherry Red, 1979); *Evilive* [EP] (Plan 9, 1982); *Walk among Us* (Ruby, 1982, 1988); *Earth A.D./Wolfsblood* (Plan 9,

1983); *Earth A.D./Die Die My Darling* [tape] (Plan 9, 1984); *Legacy of Brutality* (Plan 9/Caroline, 1985); *Misfits* (Plan 9/Caroline, 1986); *Misfits* (Plan 9, 1986); *Evilive* (Plan 9/Caroline, 1987); *Static Age* (Caroline, 1995); *Collection II* (Caroline, 1995); *Box Set* (Caroline, 1996); *American Psycho* (Geffen, 1997); *Famous Monsters* (Roadrunner, 1999); *Cuts from the Crypt* (Roadrunner, 2001); *12 Hits from Hell* (Caroline, 2001); Undead: *Nine Toes Later* EP (Stiff, 1982); *Never Say Die!* (Ger. Rebel, 1986); *Act Your Rage* (Post Mortem, 1989); *Live Slayer* (Skyclad, 1991); *Dawn of the Undead* (Shagpile/Post Mortem, 1991; Shock/Post Mortem, 1997); *Evening of Desire* EP (Overground, 1992); *Til Death!* (Underworld/Post Mortem, 1998); Samhain: *Intium* (Plan 9, 1984; Plan 9/Caroline, 1986); *Unholy Passion* EP (Plan 9, 1985; Plan 9/Caroline, 1986); *November-Coming-Fire* (Plan 9/Caroline, 1986); *Final Descent* (Plan 9/Caroline, 1990); *Box Set* (E-Magine, 2000); *Samhain Live, 85–86* (E-Magine, 2002); Kryst the Conqueror: *Deliver Us from Evil* EP (Cyclopean, 1989).

M.O.D. (METHOD OF DESTRUCTION) (1987–96, 2003–PRESENT). Billy Milano (vocals), Scott "the Rod" Sargeant (guitar), Dawson Clawson (bass), Derek "Lennon" Lopez (drums).

M.O.D. are a thrash metal band that was formed after the demise of the short-lived supergroup Stormtroopers of Death (S.O.D.). The band's lead singer and only constant (they have gone through far too many lineup changes to mention here) is the former S.O.D. singer Milano, who interrupted the band several times for short-lived S.O.D. reunions. The sound was overall thrash with a more standard metallic edge than the S.O.D. stuff, and for completists the first two records are the best. Although M.O.D. had never strayed that far from their formula, erring only toward more of a punk sound in some songs and more thrash metal or speed metal in others.

After several years of inactivity, Milano assembled a new version of the band in 2003 for a new record and is still recording under the Method of Destruction moniker after twenty years. Milano remains politically incorrect and a stern advocate of a musical style from the early eighties.

Discography: *USA for MOD* (Megaforce, 1987); *Surfin' MOD* (Megaforce, 1988); *Gross Misconduct* (Megaforce, 1989); *Rhythm of Fear* (Megaforce, 1992); *Devolution* (Music for Nations, 1994); *Loved by Thousands, Hated by Millions* (Megaforce, 1995); *Dictated Aggression* (Music for Nations, 1996); *The Rebel You Love to Hate* (Nuclear Blast Records, 2003); *Red, White & Screwed* (Index Entertainment, 2007).

MONSTER MAGNET (1992–PRESENT). Dave Wyndorf (vocals, guitar), Tim Cronin (vocals), John McBain (guitar), Joe Callandra (bass), Jon Kleiman (drums).

Monster Magnet are one of the leaders of the "stoner" and space rock retro rock scene. Led by vocalist/guitarist Dave Wyndorf, the band struggled for success during the grunge era when their music was not in fashion until their 1998 breakthrough, *Powertrip*, which featured the single "Space Lord," which was also a popular video on MTV. After losing their record contract due to problems related to their follow-up *God Says No*, the band later signed with the German SPV label issuing *Monolithic Baby!* in 2004 and *4-Way Diablo* in 2007.

Discography: *Spine of God* (Caroline, 1992); *Superjudge* (A&M, 1993); *Tab ... 25* (Caroline, 1993); *Dopes to Infinity* (A&M, 1995); *Powertrip* (A&M, 1998); *God Says No* (A&M, 2001); *Monolithic Baby!* (SPV, 2004); *4-Way Diablo* (SPV/Steamhammer, 2007);

Greatest Hits (Universal/A&M, 2003); *20th Century Masters—Millennium Collection* (A&M, 2007).

MONTROSE (1973–77; 2002–PRESENT). Ronnie Montrose (guitar), Sammy Hagar (vocals), Bill Church (bass), Denny Carmassi (drums).

Perhaps one of the most criminally overlooked American bands of the seventies, Montrose was nonetheless also one of the most influential when it came to informing how American hard rock and bands would adapt the heavy blues-based rock of Led Zeppelin to the U.S. scene. Formed in 1973 by guitarist Ronnie Montrose, who had just left the Edgar Winter Group, the band also featured drummer Denny Carmassi, bassist Bill Church, and newcomer Sammy Hagar on vocals. Their first album, *Montrose*, released in 1973, was (and remains) a bona fide hard rock classic. Produced by Ted Templeton, who would go on to produce Van Halen, the album presented a distinctly American take on Zeppelin's primal stomp—eliminating the acoustic and Celtic forays yet retaining the heavy blues-based riffs and spinning them into an even more refined, power-chord-driven roar. Combining Montrose's clever and precise guitar riffs with Carmassi's John Bonham-influenced drumming, and arguably the best singing of Hagar's career, the album is a masterpiece of American hard rock. Songs like "Bad Motor Scooter," "Space Station #5," and especially the Zep-like stomp "Rock Candy" took mystery and sophistication out of the lyrics, and distilled the remaining musical content into a powerhouse of rock performance. By the time the band went out on tour, bassist Church had left, to be replaced by Alan Fitzgerald, a future member of Night Ranger.

For their second outing, *Paper Money*, the band attempted to branch out more musically, yet the power of their debut was largely lacking, and vocalist Hagar soon left to embark on his subsequently successful solo career.

Nonetheless, Ronnie Montrose soldiered on, replacing Hagar with vocalist Bob James, and adding keyboardist Jim Alcivar. Although James was a talented vocalist, Hagar's shoes were big ones to fill, and Ronnie Montrose had lost the magic of his songwriting foil, and the album ultimately failed to stir much interest in what was left of its fan base.

1976's *Jump on It,* with its inimitable cover design of a woman's crotch, was something of a last-ditch effort to recapture the magic of the band's debut. However, despite a rocking title track and excellent production from famed Aerosmith producer Jack Douglas, the album was not the commercial success that the band had hoped for, and the group disbanded after touring for the album.

Ronnie Montrose would go on to form a new band, Gamma, and to release a solo album (*Open Fire*). In 1987 he released the album *Mean* under the Montrose name, with a group featuring future Foreigner vocalist Johnny Edwards, drummer James Kottak, and bassist Glenn Letsch.

2002 saw the assembly of yet another lineup featuring vocalist Keith St. John, bassist Chuck Wright, and drummer Pat Torpey who toured in support of the Rhino greatest hits package that had been released.

Discography: *Montrose* (Warner Bros., 1973); *Paper Money* (Warner Bros., 1974); *Warner Brothers Presents … Montrose* (Warner Bros., 1975); *Jump on It* (Warner Bros., 1976); *Open Fire* (Warner Bros., 1978); *Mean* (Enigma, 1987); *The Very Best of Montrose* (Rhino, 2000).

MOONSORROW (1995–PRESENT). Henri Sorvali (vocals/guitar/keyboards), Mitja Harvilahti (guitar), Ville Sorvali (vocals/bass), Marko Tarvonen (drums).

Moonsorrow are an inventive Finnish heavy metal band who play in the Viking metal subgenre. Their last record, *Viides Luku: Havitetty,* was an epic with just two long songs each about half an hour. Henry Sorvali (also of the Finnish band Finntroll), along with his cousin Ville Sorvali, formed the band in 1995, as a duo, before recruiting others members to fill out their sound and expand on their vision. The band engages in a wide array of styles, from your typical black and death metal flourishes to Tolkien-inspired flights of Dungeons and Dragons fantasy lyrics. The band has been one of the most consistent Finnish bands to produce engaging music, with a prog tendency as well as elements of traditional Finnish music and lyrics of epic quests and deities.

Discography: *Sudden Uni* (Plasmatic, 2000); *Of Strenth and Honor* (Spinefarm, 2002); *Kivenkantaja* (Import, 2003); *Chapter V: Ravaged* (Spinefarm, 2007); *Viides Luku: Havitetty* (Unruly Sounds, 2007).

MORBID ANGEL (1984–PRESENT). Dallas Ward (vocals/bass, replaced by David Vincent, Steve Tucker, Jared Anderson), Trey Azagthoth (guitar), Sterling Scarborough (guitar, replaced by Richard Brunelle, replaced by Erik Rutan, himself, Thor Ander Myhern), Mike Browning (drums, replaced by Wayne Hartsell, Pete Sandoval).

Morbid Angel are one of the most innovative and longest-lasting death metal bands from the American scene, known for their dark lyrics and uncompromisingly aggressive music. The band started in the infernal heat of Florida in 1984 by Trey Azagthoth (George Emmanuel), who was inspired by some of the most extreme sounds in punk and grindcore, and helped, along with the band Death, to found the most extreme of the early death metal bands to develop the core of true underground extreme music in American heavy metal.

The band was started in Florida in the early eighties by H. P. Lovecraft fan Emmanuel, along with original drummer and vocalist Mike Browning and bassist Dallas Ward, singing songs inspired by the fictional Necronomicon and after recording some singles and a first album, Azagthoth decided that the band was not gelling and dissolved it, reforming with a new lineup of David Vincent on bass and vocals, and new drummer Wayne Hartsell, for the new version of Morbid Angel 2.0. At this point the band began to write even more extreme music, and their onstage shows soon began to respect the band's commitment to their music, with Azagothoth and Brunell opening up their veins on stage and spewing blood over the stage and sometimes the audience, as noted by Mudrian. The band at that point discovered the growing grindcore scene and soon was incorporating blast beats into their music.

When Hartsell was not working out as the drummer, the band recruited noted metal drummer Pete Sandoval to form the nucleus of what would be called the "classic" Morbid Angel lineup. After the more successful *Blessed Are the Sick* record, Brunell departed and the band continued for a while as a three piece, before signing to major label subsidary Giant for the next few records. This was a less-than-perfect fit, because Earache knew how to market bands to the death and black metal scenes but Giant did not. After a few lackluster albums, Vincent departed to be replaced by Steve Tucker from Ceremony, but the magic was gone and the band began to record less and less although they continued to tour with regularity. But something was missing.

Morbid Angel can also be considered a death metal supergroup of sorts, as drummer Sandoval also played in the equally extreme death metal band Death among many others. Today the band continues under the leadership of Azagthoth, along with Sadoval, and Vincent, who rejoined the band in 2004, marking the reunion of most of the classic Morbid Angel lineup. Although Morbid Angel was a band who sang songs about horrific deities and netherworlds, particularly the Sumerian gods, they were most often lumped in with the death metal scene in the late eighties and early nineties. Certainly their lyrics could also mark them as part of the black metal scene. Either way, Morbid Angel, along with Death, are two of the most influential of the early death metal bands and they continue to be among the most popular extreme bands in the world.

Discography: *Merciless Death* (Metalstorm, 1988); *Altars of Madness* (Earache, 1989); *Abominations of Desolation* (Earache, 1991); *Blessed Are the Sick* (Combat, 1991); *Covenant* (Giant, 1993); *Domination* (Giant, 1995); *Entangled in Chaos: Live* (Earache, 1997); *Formulas Fatal to the Flesh* (Earache, 1998); *Gateways to Annihilation* (Earache, 2000); *Heretic* (Earache, 2003).

MOSHING. Moshing is an activity much like slam dancing and pit diving that originated in the punk scene but was adopted by the thrash and crossover metal scenes in the eighties and continues today, especially in the hard-edge black and death metal subgenres. Key early bands that popularized the mosh were Anthrax, who wrote one of the odes to moshing, "Caught in a Mosh," and also Stormtroopers of Death, led by Billy Milano, who helped popularize moshing in their song "Milano Mosh." The practice consists of members of the audience coming together in a large area on the concert floor in front of the stage, usually called "the pit," and ritualistically bouncing off each other in a manner reminiscent of punk slamming, only occasionally more violent.

Rituals vary from scene to scene and band to band, and some bands openly encourage a large and active pit while others try and discourage the practice for insurance and safety issues. The ritualistic act of stage diving often accompanies the moshing, where a fan lucky enough to get up on stage with their favorite band can try and jump quickly back into the audience or try and go for a victory lap onstage until bouncers throw them off again or much worse, they are brought backstage and ejected from the club. For fans, moshing also serves as a form of release, a way of getting rid of aggression, or as a form of catharsis. As William Tsitsos has noted, there is a distinct difference between traditional slam dancing in the early punk scene and the moshing that dominates today, in that "... moshers' explanations for their dancing tend to focus more on the venting of individual aggression" (Tsitsos 2006, 125).

Moshing is mostly a masculine activity, at last in heavy metal where the pits seem to be more aggressive and less inviting to women, who frequently find themselves groped or even attacked by newcomers who do not understand the respectful attitude that is inherent in a successful pit. To this day, for better of worse, the pit continues to be a place to be entered at one's own risk, and moshing is still prevalent, depending on the scene and the tolerance of the band and the promoters.

MÖTLEY CRÜE (1981–PRESENT). Vince Neil (1981–1992, 1997–present; lead vocals, replaced by John Corabai), Nikki Sixx (bass), Mick Mars (guitar), Tommy Lee (1981–99, 2004–present; drums, replaced by Randy Castillo, Samantha Maloney).

Mötley Crüe are one of the most influential and popular metal bands of the eighties and nineties (if not in the history of American heavy metal), who also may be as well known for their off-the-road escapades with drugs, alcohol, flirtations with the law, reality shows, public feuds, and X-rated appearances. The band started in 1981 when the rhythm section of Nikki Sixx and Tommy Lee decided to form their own band, eventually settling on guitarist Mick Mars and vocalist Vince Neil. The band quickly became a favorite, playing relentlessly in Los Angeles, and self-released their first record, which soon sold an astounding (for that time) 20,000 copies, getting the band a record deal with Elektra, and making them one of the first metal bands to make the leap to the majors so quickly.

By the time the band had released the *Too Fast for Love* album, they had begun to solidify their sound that borrowed from classic metal, glam rock pop, and a little punk thrown in as well. When the album *Shout at the Devil* was released, the Crüe formula was finally in place. Hook-laden choruses plus dynamic guitars bottomed out with the steady rythym section of Sixx and Lee. The band had also developed a signature stage appearance that, although it would influence many up-and-coming metal bands, was also strikingly original in its use of leather, spiked metal-style hair, and face paint. The killer hooks of songs like "Shout at the Devil" and "Looks that Kill" with their anathematic choruses were also extremely radio- (and MTV-) friendly, with enough crunchy guitar to satisfy most metal purists.

The next album, *Theatre of Pain* in 1985, found the band retrenching (years later Crüe would identify that record as particularly weak considering the power of the previous two records), particularly in a cover of the Brownsville Station classic "Smoking in the Boys' Room" that played to the Crüe's macho audience but also helped to pioneer what was fast becoming a staple of the metal scene: the power ballad. In the mid-eighties many bands began to realize that they were selling records to a predominantly male audience who enjoyed the macho swagger of

Mötley Crüe: Kings of L.A. metal decadence. (Gunter W. Kienitz/Rex Features)

the band. But to the Crüe and many other bands this also raised a dilemma, both how to expand the audience base beyond metal fans and how to attract a female demographic. The answer was the power ballad, and Crüe's "Home Sweet Home" was the kind of "lift your lighter in the air" soft ballad designed to appeal to both sexes, and presumably, to lure more girls to go backstage after the show.

Girls, Girls, Girls, which came next, was a retrenchment of sorts with even fewer good ideas but demonstrated the Crüe's mastery of the metal video in the self-titled offering that featured strippers cavorting on poles. The formula seemed to be wearing thin, and the band's nonstop touring was starting to put pressure on not only the interband relationships but also on their songwriting chops. Although the next record contained classics by Crüe standards, such as the title song, the magic was running out. Many of the group's members were more than dabbling in illicit substances. In 1987 Sixx nearly overdosed on heroin, leading to a cancellation of a lucrative European tour and he continued to do drugs for many more years, starting the day after his overdose (Sixx 2007). In 1992 interband tensions finally reached the boiling point, and vocalist Neil was sacked in favor of John Corabi, a choice that infuriated many fans, especially after hearing the lackluster follow-up album, 1994's *Mötley Crüe.* The band seemed to be floundering in a musical landscape where the simplicity of grunge fashion and its Black Sabbath meets Black Flag riffs made the Crüe seem outdated and maybe even sad. Almost inevitably, Neil was reinstated in 1997. By 1999, Lee had left the band to form his own group, the rather forgettable Methods of Mayhem. He was replaced first by Ozzy Osbourne drummer Randy Castillo and then perhaps inexplicably by Hole drummer Samantha Maloney.

The band found time to write a group autobiography, *The Dirt,* in 2001, including input from all four original members, but Lee still refused to rejoin for a reunion tour. Following the death of Castillo in 2002, the band went through various media-related sniping against each other, although they eventually reunited as a full group in 2005 for a tour. Currently Mötley Crüe are touring with all the original members, although how long the band will last as a group is still up in the air at this point.

To many born past their heyday, the band is better known for reality show appearances and books than for their music. Drummer Tommy Lee is notorious for his escapades outside the band. He was famously married to ex-*Baywatch* star Pamela Lee Anderson from 1995–98 and was the star of a "leaked" sex tape that showed the two cavorting in various positions. Lee also starred in a short-lived reality show, where he went back to college, took classes, and joined the college marching band.

Lead singer Vince Neil has also had his share of notoriety outside the band. In December 1984 he was involved in a drunken automobile accident that killed Razzle (aka Nicholas Dingley), the drummer of Finnish glam rockers Hanoi Rocks, and seriously injured the two passengers in the other car. Neil served 30 days in jail, paid an undisclosed financial settlement to the families of the passengers involved and made numerous public safety announcements about drinking and driving. Neil was also the star of reality shows, including the D-list celebrity *Surreal Life* and another on VH1 called *Remaking Vince Neil,* where he underwent a career makeover that involved a strict physical fitness regimen as well as plastic surgery to make him look younger, all captured on television. Mick Mars has kept a relatively low profile aside from his health concerns, including a reported bout with substance abuse and a degenerative bone disease that led to a hip replacement in 2004 as mentioned in *The Dirt.* Bassist Nikki Sixx penned a surprisingly well-written and shocking autobiography called *The Heroin Diaries* (Pocket Books 2007) in which he detailed his years on the road, sexual exploits, and struggles with years of drug addiction. The Crüe's legacy is unmistakable; they are one of the most successful bands in metal history. In spite of their numerous break-ups and reformations, the band continues to be a draw on the metal circuit and will go down in metal history as one of the bands that helped break a new poppier style of metal mixed with hard rock to an enthusiastic audience on MTV.

Discography: *Too Fast for Love* (Mötley/Beyond, 1981); *Shout at the Devil* (Mötley/Beyond, 1983); *Theatre of Pain* (Mötley/Beyond, 1985); *Girls, Girls, Girls* (Mötley/Beyond, 1987); *Dr. Feelgood* (Mötley/Beyond, 1989); *Mötley Crüe* (Mötley/Beyond, 1994); *Generation Swine* (Mötley/Beyond, 1997); *Live: Entertainment or Death* (Beyond, 1999); *New Tattoo* (Mötley/Beyond, 2000); *Carnival of Sins: Live, Vols. 1-2* (Eleven Seven Music, 2007).

MOTORHEAD (1975–PRESENT). Classic lineup: Lemmy Kilmister (vocals/bass), "Fast" Eddie Clarke (guitar, replaced by Brian Robertson, Phil Campbell), Wurzel (guitar, 1984–95), Phil "Philthy Animal" Taylor (drums, replaced by Peter Gill, then Taylor, then Mikkey Dee).

Motorhead are a key part of both punk and heavy metal history, as epitomized in songs such as "Ace of Spades." Led by the charismatic gravelly voiced and wart-sporting (he has often joked about removing and selling his wart on eBay) lead singer and bassist Lemmy Kilmister, Motorhead have been on the vanguard of hard and heavy music for over thirty years. The band was originally started by Lemmy, an ex-Jimi Hendrix roadie and member of psychedelic pioneers Hawkwind. Lemmy originally recorded the song "Motorhead" that gave the band its name. This term is derived from an American expression for a "speed freak," a drug Lemmy was particularly fond of, and was written by Lemmy in one of his few songwriting contributions to the band. The song later became a favorite of Motorhead fans across the globe.

The original lineup consisted of Larry Wallis on guitar and drummer Lucas Fox, who recorded their debut album with Dave Edmunds (!) but both the lineup and the producer didn't click. Soon Edmunds was out and followed soon after that by Fox (the debut album was not released until 1979 as the *On Parole* record), who was replaced by fan favorite Phil "Philthy Animal" Taylor, and although Fast Eddie Clarke was originally brought in to augment the band's sound, eventually Wallis left the band and the classic, and most crucial, lineup finally consisted of Lemmy on bass and lead vocals (singing upward to his trademark elevated mic stand) along with drummer Phil "Philthy Animal" Taylor and guitarist "Fast" Eddie Clarke.

The band scored a quick and puzzling chart hit with a rough-edged cover of the garage rock warhorse "Louie Louie," which propelled them up the charts and led to a bizarre appearance on the top of the charts. The band signed to Bronze records (home of Uriah Heep) in 1979 and released the classic *Overkill* record that year. The trio sound like a five piece thanks to Fast Eddie's innovative guitar work and Lemmy's distorted bass. Motorhead was quickly becoming a favorite of people who enjoyed harder music, and early punks as well as metalheads flocked to Motorhead shows. This may have been partially due to the distinct look of the band, who all dressed in black leather like the Ramones or a more butch Judas Priest. Some said they looked more like a biker gang than a rock and roll band (not too far from the truth). The *Ace of Spades* album was their masterpiece, and the title single, with its hardcore beat and lyrics about being "born to lose" made Lemmy an iconic figure. The song's theme was akin to what many rock and roll

Motorhead, a key crossover band between punk and metal (REX USA)

fans felt: that they were fated to bad luck and to forever be dealt the "dead man's hand" (aces over eights in poker is known as the dead mans' hand, because it was what legendary gunfighter Wild Bill Hickok was holding when he was shot in the back of the head). *Ace of Spades* increased Motorhead's popularity exponentially and massive touring soon followed, and the band's formidable back line eventually helped them garner the title "the loudest band in the world" by the *Guinness Book of World Records*. Motorhead at that time also helped mentor the all-female metal group Girlschool and collaborated on the "Please Don't Touch" single and the double entendre–filled "Headgirl." The original lineup was starting to show cracks, and in 1982 Clarke left the band to start his own project, Fastway, and was replaced by Brian Robertson of Thin Lizzy fame. This would be the start of a revolving door of guitarists and eventually drummers for Motorhead. Robertson left and was replaced by two guitarists, Philip Campbell and Wurzel, and Taylor left as well, replaced by Peter Gill for the classic "Killed By Death" single, leaving Lemmy as the sole creative voice in the band.

Although the *Orgasmatron* record that followed was a strong effort, the band had lost momentum, and much of the late eighties' material is forgettable, except for the "comeback" record *1916*, where Taylor briefly rejoined the band, only to be replaced by Mikkey Dee, formerly of satanic metal band Mercyful Fate. Wurzel left acrimoniously in 1995, the year in which Motorhead celebrated both their twentieth anniversary and Lemmy's fiftieth birthday, complete with a Motorhead "tribute" band called "The Lemmys" (actually Metallica) playing Motorhead classics.

Today Motorhead continues on their way, perhaps one of the most beloved metal bands on all sides of the aisle. Their catalog of songs, including "Overkill," "Eat the Rich," "Jailbait," and the classic ode to the men who load the Econoline vans, "We Are the Road Crew," made Motorhead one of the highest-drawing acts in metal to this day. Motorhead always acknowledged their debt to the Ramones, and on the World War I-themed *1916* album, they wrote a song called "R.A.M.O.N.E.S.," which the Ramones themselves would later cover. Lemmy also contributed vocals to the Dave Grohl Probot side project in 2004.

As of 2008, Motorhead was very active and participating in the historic Monsters of Metal tour along with Testamant, Judas Priest, and Heaven and Hell. Motorhead, a band that predated the Sex Pistols, is one of the most lasting and ferocious influences on both the punk and metal scenes, and their influence on speed metal, thrash, and hardcore punk alone would have been enough to make them legendary had they stopped recording twenty-five years ago. They continue on, an unstoppable juggernaut, the true Orgasmatron of rock and roll.

Discography: *Motörhead* (UK Chiswick, 1977; UK Big Beat, 1978; Roadracer Revisited, 1990); *Overkill* (UK Bronze, 1979; Profile, 1988); *Bomber* (UK Bronze, 1979; Profile, 1988); *On Parole* (UK Liberty, 1979; UK Fame, 1982; EMI America, 1987); *Motörhead* [EP] (UK Big Beat, 1980); *The Golden Years* [EP] (UK Bronze, 1980); *Ace of Spades* (Mercury, 1980; Profile, 1988); *No Sleep 'Til Hammersmith* (Mercury, 1981; Profile, 1988); *Iron Fist* (Mercury, 1982; Roadracer Revisited, 1990); *Stand by Your Man* [EP] (UK Bronze, 1982); *What's Words Worth?* (UK Big Beat, 1983); *Another Perfect Day* (Mercury, 1983); *No Remorse* (Bronze, 1984; Roadracer Revisited, 1990); *Anthology* (UK Raw Power, 1985); *Born to Lose* (UK Dojo, 1985); *Orgasmatron* (GWR/Profile, 1986); *Rock 'n' Roll* (GWR/Profile, 1987); *Another Perfect Day/Overkill* (UK Castle Comm., 1988); *No Sleep at All* (GWR/Enigma, 1988); *Blitzkrieg on Birmingham '77* (UK Receiver, 1989); *Dirty Love* (UK Receiver, 1989); *The Best of & the Rest of Motörhead Live* (UK Action Replay, 1990); *Welcome to the Bear Trap* (UK Castle Comm., 1990); *Bomber/Ace of Spades* (UK Castle Comm., 1990); *Lock Up Your Daughters* (UK Receiver, 1990); *The Birthday Party* (GWR/Enigma, 1990); *From the Vaults* (UK Sequel, 1990); *1916* (WTG, 1991); *Meltdown* (UK Castle Comm., 1991); *March or Die* (Sony, 1992); *Sacrifice* (CMC, 1995); *Overnight Sensation* (CMC, 1996); *Stone Dead Forever* (Receiver, 1997); *Snake Bite Love* (CMC, 1998); *Everything Louder than Everyone Else* (CMC, 1999); *We Are Motorhead* (CMC, 2000); *Hammered* (Metal-Is/Sanctuary, 2002); *Motorhead with Girlschool St. Valentine's Day Massacre* [EP] (UK Bronze, 1980).

MR. BIG (1988–2002). Eric Martin (vocals), Paul Gilbert (guitar, replaced by Richie Kotzen), Billy Sheehan (bass), Pat Torpey (drums).

Mr. Big were one of the most popular metal supergroups made up of virtuoso musicians. The band started in 1988, when bassist Billy Sheehan had grown tired of playing with perpetual man-child David Lee Roth and went off in search of another group of musicians. He soon found them in ace guitarist Paul Gilbert, lately of Racer X, and the more obscure but equally talented Eric Martin on vocals, and Pat Torpey on drums. The first record was a warm-up for the popular second record, which scored hit singles and videos with the relatively soft, but still well-played, singles "To Be With You" and "Just Take My Heart."

Sadly, after *Bump Ahead* failed to chart, the band was derailed by grunge, as most metal bands had been around the same time. Luckily, as many other metal bands of the time also found out, there was a lucrative Japanese market, and the band toured there and the Far East for most of the next decade as one could infer from the number of live releases from Japan. Gilbert left to work on his own projects after the release of *Static* and was replaced by early Poison axe-man Richie Kotzen for a few more years, but the band eventually called it quits in 2002. Mr. Big are best known for the virtuoso combination of Sheehan and Gilbert, one of the great bass and guitar combos in metal history. More proof that the Japanese market is more interested in sheer shredding than the American market.

Discography: *Mr. Big* (Atlantic, 1989); *Lean into It* (Atlantic, 1991); *Bump Ahead* (Atlantic, 1993); *Japandemonium* [live] (Atlantic, 1994); *Raw Like Sushi* [live] (Import, 1994); *Raw Like Sushi 2* [live] (Import, 1994); *Big, Bigger, Biggest! The Best of Mr. Big* (Atlantic, 1996); *Hey Man* (Atlantic, 1996); *Live at Budokan* (WEA, 1997); *Live at the Hard Rock Cafe* (WEA, 1998); *Static* (WEA, 1999); *Get Over It* (Atlantic, 2000); *Deep Cuts: The Best of the Ballads* (WEA/Atlantic, 2000); *Deep Cuts: The Very Best of Mister Big* (WEA International, 2000); *Actual Size* (Atlantic, 2001); *In Japan* [live] (East West Japan, 2002).

MUDVAYNE (1996–PRESENT). Kud (vocals), Gurrg (guitar), Ryknow (bass), sPaG (drums).

Mudvayne was formed in 1996 by Kud (Chad Grey), Gurrg (Greg Tribbett), and sPaG (Mathew McDonough), eventually joined by bassist Ryknow (Ryan Martinie). The band is best known for their outlandish make-up and sense of style, appearing in matching outrageous costumes that fall somewhere between GWAR and Spinal Tap meets Devo in a food fight. The music is utterly forgettable nu metal with touches of electronica. Why bands like this continue to sell millions while Motorhead has to struggle is a mystery to metal.

Discography: *L.D. 50* (Sony, 2000); *The Beginning of All Things To End* (Sony, 2001); *The End of All Things to Come* (Epic, 2002); *Lost and Found* (Epic, 2005); *Shades of Gray* (Epic Japan, 2007); *By the People, for the People* (SMJI, 2007).

MUSHROOM HEAD (1993–PRESENT). Jason Popson, aka J. Mann (vocals, replaced by Waylon Reavis), Jeffrey Hatrix, aka Jeff Nothing (vocals), Richie Moore, aka "Dinner" (guitars, replaced by Dave Felton, aka Gravy), John Sekula, aka JJ Righteous (guitars, replaced by Marco Vukcevich, aka Bronson), Tom Schmitz, aka Shmtoz (keyboards), Joe Kilcoyne, aka Mr. Murdernickel (bass, replaced by Jack Kilcoyne, aka Pig Benis) Steve Felton, aka Skinny (drums and founder), Joe Lenkey, aka DJ Virus (turntables and samples, replaced by Rick Thomas, aka DJ Stitch).

Mushroom Head are a nu/alternative metal band from Cleveland, Ohio, with touches of industrial, hip-hop techno, punk, and other genres thrown into the mix, creating an engaging, but much more interesting on paper than on record, sound. The band was also known for wearing black masks, somewhat akin to the kinds that bands like Slipknot wore, although slightly more like gas masks. The band continues to tour today, expanding the sounds that are accepted as part of metal.

Discography: *Superbuick* (Shroomco, 1996); *M3* (Shroomco, 1999); *XX* (Eclipse, 2001); *Mushroomhead* (Mushroomhead, 2003); *XIII* (Universal, 2003); *Savior Sorrow* (Megaforce, 2006).

N

NAPALM DEATH (1982–PRESENT). Lee Dorian (vocals, replaced by Mark Greenway), Mick Harris (drums, replaced by Danny Herrera), Jim Whitley (bass, replaced by Shane Embury), Justin Broadrick (guitars, replaced by Mitch Harris), Bill Steer (guitar, replaced by Jesse Pintado, no longer in band).

There may have been bands that played as loud and aggressively as Napalm Death, but it would be hard to find one as completely brutal as this band. Napalm Death are an English group who established the metal subgenre known as grindcore. Original drummer Mick Harris patented the ultra-fast "blast beat" that is the hallmark of the grindcore style, in which the drums speed up faster than a hardcore beat and the guitars and bass become blurs of noise, accompanied by vocals that are either incomprehensible or simply also blurs of sound.

The first Napalm Death record was actually recorded in parts by the original lineup (for most of their career Napalm Death has contained no original members), featuring original bassist Whitley and guitarist Broadrick with only drummer supreme Mick Harris appearing on both sides of the landmark *Scum* album, which literally shook metal by its feet and raised the ante for extreme music. The band was heavily influenced by noise merchants the Swans, as well as classic English hardcore band Discharge, who were among the most extreme hardcore acts of the time.

When Mick Harris left Napalm Death, the band inevitably had to do a lateral move and slow down (as obviously they could not have gotten any faster) and bassist Shane Embury essentially took control of the band, where he has remained the one constant since joining in the early eighties. Influential British DJ John Peel was an early fan of the band and championed them early on, playing extremely fast songs such as "You Suffer" (0:1.5) on his radio show over and over again and eventually having the band in to play on one of his *Peel Sessions*.

When vocalist Lee Dorian grew frustrated with the relentless touring schedule, he exited to play in a band that in many ways is Napalm Death's polar opposite, the ultra slow Cathedral. Soon after, Harris was out of the band, leaving Napalm

Napalm Death, live in Sofia, Bulgaria, 2007. (Pictorial Press Ltd/Alamy)

Death with no original and only one long-lasting member. Napalm Death continued to tour with new lineups, experimented with slowing down at some points,
but never lost sight of being the most extreme band in the world. To this date Napalm Death is still regarded as one of the most extreme bands in musical history
and a benchmark for what musicians could achieve. They pretty much invented a
new genre almost all by themselves and raised the stakes for extreme musicians all
over the world.

Discography: *Scum* (Earache, 1986); *From Enslavement to Obliteration* (Earache, 1988);
The Peel Sessions [EP] (UK Strange Fruit, 1989); *Napalm Death* [EP] (UK Rise Above,
1989); *Mentally Murdered* [EP] (UK Earache, 1989); *Harmony Corruption* (Earache/Com-
bat, 1990); *Live Corruption* (UK Earache, 1990); *Suffer the Children* [EP] (UK Earache,
1990); *The Peel Sessions* (Strange Fruit/Dutch East India Trading, 1991); *Mass Appeal Madness* [EP] (Earache/Relativity, 1991); *Death by Manipulation* (Earache/Relativity, 1991);
Utopia Banished (Earache/Relativity, 1992; Earache, 1996); *The World Keeps Turning* [EP]
(Earache, 1992); *Nazi Punks Fuck Off* [EP7] (Earache, 1993); *Fear, Emptiness, Despair*
(Earache/Columbia, 1994); *Greed Killing* [EP] (Earache, 1995); *Diatribes* (Earache, 1996);

Bassist Shane Embury, of Napalm Death, one of the most brutal bands in the world. (© Pete Jenkins/Alamy)

Inside the Torn Apart (Earache, 1997); *Bootlegged in Japan* (Earache, 1998); *The Complete Radio One Sessions* (BBC/Fuel 2000/Var? Sarabande, 2000); *Leaders Not Followers* [EP] (Relapse, 2000); *Enemy of the Music Business* (Spitfire, 2001).

NASHVILLE PUSSY (1996–PRESENT). Blaine Cartwright (vocals/guitar), Ruyter Suys (guitar), Corey Parks (bass, replaced by Karen Cuda), Jeremy Thompson (drums).

Nashville Pussy is a Grammy-nominated band who ape both the best elements of Southern rock and Motorhead, along with a powerful stance on female sexual gratification. (The cover of their best record, *Let Them Eat Pussy*, shows two fans of the band pleasuring the female guitarist and bass player). The band is also known for its memorable stage antics, for example, former bassist Corey Parks blowing fire on stage. The first record is the best introduction to the band, and while Nashville Pussy is not for everyone, they are one of the most aggressive southern-tinged metal bands and well worth seeking out.

Discography: *Let Them Eat Pussy* (The Enclave, 1998); *High as Hell* (TVT, 2000); *Say Something Nasty* (Artemis, 2002); *Nashville Pussy* (Artemis, 2002); *Get Some* (Spitfire, 2005).

NEUROSIS (1985–PRESENT). Scott Kelly (vocals/guitar), Dave Edwardson (bass), Steve Von Till (vocals/guitar), Jason Roeder (drums), Noah Landie (keyboards, replaced by Simon McIlroy).

One of the few hardcore punk bands to successfully transition to heavy metal, Neurosis was a hardcore band (their first record was released on Jello Biafra's *Alternative Tentacles* record label, and they also released music on classic pop/punk label *Lookout*) before they gradually transformed themselves into a much more atmospheric and almost tribal-sounding metal band, that wisely chose not to follow the glam metal examples of other bands such as TSOL, who made the transition much less successfully. Sometimes the keyboards-based Neurosis could even be mistaken for an art rock band, if the music was not so incredibly dark.

Neurosis has helped to redefine the punk/metal nexus. While most of their music is recommended, *A Sun That Never Sets* and *Enemy of the Sun* are the band's most consistent. They are also a key influence on many modern metal bands that experiment with dynamics such as the Swedish band Cult of Luna.

Discography: *Pain of Mind* (Alternative Tentacles, 1988); *The Word as Law* (Lookout, 1990); *Souls at Zero* (Virus, 1992); *Enemy of the Sun* (Alternative Tentacles, 1994); *Through Silver in Blood* (Relapse, 1996); *Times of Grace* (Relapse, 1999); *A Sun that Never Sets* (Relapse, 2001); *Live in Lyons* (Howling Bull, 2002); *Live in Stockholm* (Neurto, 2003); *Neurosis and Jarboe* (Neurto, 2003); *The Eye of Every Storm* (Neurto, 2004); *Given to the Rising* (Neurto, 2007).

NEW YORK DOLLS (1971–77, 2004–PRESENT). David Johansen (vocals), John Gezale, aka Johnny Thunders (guitar), Rick Rivets (guitar, replaced by Syl Sylvain), Arthur "Killer" Kane (bass), Billy Murcia (drums, replaced after death by Jerry Nolan).

New York Dolls were among the fathers of the punk and glam movements and their blues-based style and glitter/drag image went a long way to inspiring numerous bands musically, and in particular, the L.A. Sunset Strip scene. It would be difficult to imagine the look of a band like Poison, or Cinderella, or the sound of a band like Guns N' Roses without the New York Dolls. The Dolls were founded in 1971, and by the early seventies the band had established their reputation as innovators largely by their residencies at the (now demolished) Mercer Arts Center in New York City.

The band was led by the charismatic David Johansen (who would later find commercial success as the ubiquitous Buster Poindexter in the eighties), along with guitarists Johnny Thunders and Syl Sylvain, bass player Arthur "Killer" Kane, and drummer Billy Murcia. Murcia died in 1972 and was replaced by new drummer Jerry Nolan. The band put out two classic records, the eponymous self-titled album, followed by the grittier but more sixties girl-group influenced *Too Much Too Soon*, which seemed to epitomize the band's way of life.

After an unsuccessful tour with McLaren managing the band, things got worse and the band splinted down the middle, with Nolan and Thunders taking off to from the more straightforward punk Heartbreakers in 1976. For a while Sylvain and Johansen tried to keep the band going by themselves, but eventually Johansen spun off into a solo career, aided for a while by Sylvain, while Kane went into a downward spiral that lasted for several years. After a short and influential career with the Heartbreakers, Thunders went solo and released brilliant material sporadically throughout the years.

Many have said (e.g., McNeil and McCain 1996) that Thunders became a junkie after the Dolls broke up, with Nolan not far behind. Thunders was also allegedly largely responsible for introducing heroin to the English punk scene and eventually succumbed to a drug overdose under mysterious circumstances in New Orleans in 1991. Nolan died of meningitis in 1992, partly brought on by years of drug abuse. This would have marked the end of most bands but the Dolls' story was not over yet. A chance for a reunion curated by uber-Dolls fan Morrissey (who had once been the head of the English branch of the New York Dolls fan club) led to a reunion gig at the Meltdown festival in 2004 featuring Kane, Johanson, and Sylvain who played a rapturous set of Dolls classics for a sold-out crowd.

The reemergence of the Dolls following their performance with original bassist Arthur "Killer" Kane at Meltdown marked a new chapter for the band, although tragically Kane did not live to see it, as he succumbed to leukemia shortly after the festival. The two remaining Dolls continued the tour in his memory with new guitarist Steve Conte, bassist Sam Yaffa (formerly of Hanoi Rocks), drummer Brian Delaney, and keyboardist Brian Koonin. Their new record, the first in over thirty years, proved to be just as exciting and even more complex than the early Dolls' records, a rare instance of a band with more deceased members than living members can still be a force to reckon with. The Dolls were a huge influence on metal and glam metal in particular, and Johnny Thunders's junkie-fueled guitar hero persona (partially based on Keith Richards) was a very obvious influence on the L.A. metal scene of the eighties, and on Slash and Izzy from Guns N' Roses, among many others.

Discography: *New York Dolls* (Mercury, 1973); *Too Much Too Soon* (Mercury, 1974; Mercury/Hip-O Select; 2005); *New York Dolls* (Mercury, 1977); *Lipstick Killers: The Mercer Street Sessions 1972* (tape, Roir, 1981; CD, Roir/Important, 1990; Roir, 2000); *Red Patent Leather* (Fr. Fan Club, 1984); *Best of the New York Dolls* (UK Mercury, 1985); *Night of the Living Dolls* (Mercury, 1986); *Personality Crisis* [EP] (UK Kamera, 1986); *Morrissey Presents the Return of the New York Dolls Live from Royal Festival Hall, 2004* (Attack/Sanctuary, 2004); *One Day It Will Please Us to Remember Even This* (Roadrunner, 2006); *David & Sylvain: Tokyo Dolls Live!* (Fr. Fan Club, 1986); *The Original Pistols/New York Dolls: After the Storm* (UK Receiver, 1985).

NICKELBACK (1996–PRESENT). Chad Kroeger (vocals/guitar), Ryan Peake (guitar), Mike Kroeger (bass), Ryan Vikedal (drums).

While not a heavy metal band, per se, Canada's Nickelback are one of the most successful post-grunge heavy rock bands, drawing upon grunge and metal traditions in the formulation of their highly successful commercial brand of heavy rock. With their origins as a cover band, Nickelback are a self-made success story, having independently managed themselves and released their initial albums before being "discovered" by Roadrunner Records in 1998.

The band's first recordings, *Hesher* (an EP) and the full-length *Curb* in 1996, and *The State* in 2000 were released independently. With the single "Leader of

Men" receiving airplay in their native Canada, they began to tour heavily and to build a solid fan base. Signed to Roadrunner in the U.S. and EMI in Canada, *The State* was re-released and became the band's first gold record.

The band's next album, *Silver Side Up*, went to number 1 in both Canada and the U.S. on the strength of the single "How You Remind Me," making the band stars in both countries. Nickelback replicated its success in 2003 with *The Long Road,* which would go platinum five times over. 2005 saw the release of another hit, *All the Right Reasons*, on which Vikedal was replaced by ex-3 Doors Down drummer Daniel Adair.

Discography: *Curb* (Roadrunner, 1996); *The State* (Roadrunner, 2000); *Silver Side Up* (RoadRunner, 2001); *The Long Road* (Roadrunner, 2003); *All the Right Reasons* (Roadrunner, 2005); *Three Sided Coin* (Roadrunner International, 2002); *Silver Side Up/Live at Home* (Roadrunner, 2005).

NIGHT RANGER (1982–PRESENT). Jack Blades (vocals/bass), Brad Gillis (guitar), Jeff Watson (guitar), Kelly Keagy (drums/vocals), Alan Fitzgerald (keyboards).

With their breakout hit "Don't Tell Me You Love Me" from their debut *Dawn Patrol* hitting the airwaves in 1982, Night Ranger quickly became one of the most popular rock bands of the era. The band combined the twin guitar attacks of ex-Ozzy Osbourne guitarist Brad Gillis and Jeff Watson—both of whom were masters of their instruments—with well-crafted, radio-ready songs. Night Ranger enjoyed a string of hit albums and singles throughout the decade. The band also featured lead vocalist/bassist Jack Blades, and drummer/lead vocalist Kelly Keagy, as well as former Montrose keyboardist Alan Fitzgerald.

The band's commercial success peaked with their second album, *Midnight Madness,* which went platinum, featuring the hit singles "(You Can Still) Rock in America" and the ballad "Sister Christian." After enjoying success with two subsequent albums, the band called it quits after their fifth, 1988's *Man in Motion,* failed to go gold. Blades subsequently formed the supergroup Damn Yankees with ex-Styx guitarist Tommy Shaw and Ted Nugent. Night Ranger saw most of its members reuniting in the late 2000s for occasional touring and released a new studio album, *Hole in the Sun* in 2007.

Discography: *Dawn Patrol* (Camel, 1982); *Midnight Madness* (Camel, 1983); *7 Wishes* (Camel, 1985); *Big Life* (MCA, 1987); *Man in Motion* (Camel, 1988); *Live in Japan* (MCA, 1990); *I Did It for Love* (Camel, 1991); *Neverland* (Sony, 1997); *Seven* (CMC International, 1998); *Hole in the Sun* (Frontiers, 2007); *Rock in Japan 1997* [live] (Universal, 2008); *20th Century Masters—The Millennium Collection: The Best of Night Ranger* (MCA, 2000); *Greatest Hits* (Universal, 2007); *Box* (Universal, 2007).

NILE (1993–PRESENT). Karl Sanders (vocals/guitar), Dallas Toter-Wade (guitar), Chief Spires (bass, replaced by John Vesano, Chris Lollis), Pete Hammoura (drums, replaced by Tony Laureano, George Collias).

Nile are an unusual band by black metal standards, incorporating not only the mythology of the Norse gods or of Satanism but also the mythology of ancient Egypt. Like many other bands in the black metal genre, they also mention early twentieth-century horror writer H. P. Lovecraft and his creation the Necronomicon as a starting point. The first record, *Among the Catacombs of Nephren-Ka*, is as fresh an America black metal record as any in the nineties. Nile soon established themselves as different by their hard but intricate approach to the genre, incorporating Middle Eastern influences and sometimes authentic Egyptian instruments on some of their songs. This eclectic mix gave Nile the sound of a metal update of the classics sixties experimental world music/rock groups Kaleidoscope.

Karl Sanders is the undisputed leader, who created the band's elaborate mythology. After the departure of longtime members Spires and Hammoura in 2001, the band was reconfigured. Sanders may be a mad genius, but he's among the most technically adept working in American black metal and also one of the most interesting in terms of world—view and mythology. All of the first four records are highly praised by critics and newcomers should start with the early material.

Discography: *Among the Catacombs of Nephren-Ka* (Relapse, 1998); *Black Seeds of Vengeance* (Relapse, 2000); *In the Beginning* (Relapse, 2000); *In Their Darkened Shrines* (Relapse, 2002); *In the Beginning* (Hearthammer, 2003); *Annihilation of the Wicked* (Relapse, 2005); *Treasures From the Catacombs* (Relapse, 2007); *Ithphalliac* (Nuclear Blast, 2007); *Legacy of the Catacombs* (WEA/Relapse, 2007).

NORWEGIAN BLACK METAL. One of the most infamous examples of black metal transgressing the boundaries that most normal metal scenes were afraid to cross was the Norwegian black metal scene of the late eighties to mid-nineties. The scene was inspired by the early founders of black metal such as Venom, Slayer, and King Diamond and strongly emulated both the fast and uncompromising pseudo-hardcore style of these performers and their lyrical bent that emphasized Satanism and the occult. Some Norwegian bands were also known for crossing over into the nationalistic, fascist, and white power scenes as well, and numerous church burnings and several deaths have been attributed to members of the Norwegian black metal scene during its heyday.

The most prominent band of these was Mayhem, which included vocalist Dead (who killed himself and was later replaced by Attila Csihar), guitarist Euronymous, occasional bassist Count Grishnakh (originally Kristian Vikernes, later Varg Vikernes), and drummer Hellhammer, who today remains the only longstanding member of the band. As detailed in the entry on Mayhem, Vikernes was convicted of killing Euronymous and is currently serving a twenty-one-year sentence in a Norwegian prison.

Much of the early scene and the controversy around the band Mayhem was chronicled both in back issues of *Kerrang* magazine and in the book *Lords of Chaos* by Michael Moynihan and Didrik Soderlind. The book itself is also controversial, because (as indicated on his website) Moynihan has connections to neofascist and white power groups.

TED NUGENT (1948–PRESENT; PERFORMING 1967–PRESENT). Ted Nugent is a quintessentially American guitar hero, one part gunslinger, one part carnival barker, always courting controversy and enjoying turning up his nose at convention (including having eschewed drugs and alcohol), even if he has in recent years gotten more attention for his politically conservative views. After starting his career with the psychedelic outfit the Amboy Dukes, Nugent hit the road as a solo act in 1975 where he found his greatest fame and fortune. Nugent signed a deal with Columbia and released his first solo album later that same year.

Featuring a crack band of Derek St. Holmes on second guitar and vocals, Rob Grange on bass, and Cliff Davies on drums, the album was successful, largely due to the over-the-top stage show put on by the Nuge and company, which often featured Nugent jumping down off of the top of his amp stacks and wildly wielding his huge hollow-body Gibson guitar (usually associated with jazz players) and performing guitar duels with guesting guitarists.

Two more studio albums helped establish his position as a preeminent rock star of the seventies, 1976's *Free for All* and 1977's *Cat Scratch Fever,* which featured the title track hit single and the cut "Wang Dang Sweet Poontang." The album established Nugent as a household name, and the band was a regular feature at concerts, festivals, and late-night rock shows like *The Midnight Special,* with the Nuge often going into "battle" wearing little more than a buckskin loincloth and swinging from a rope onto the stage to start his concerts.

Double Live Gonzo in 1978 capped Nugent's golden era, though, as his tight-fisted leadership style began to grow old with band members and they began jumping ship, with the greatest loss being co-vocalist/guitarist St. Holmes, who would go on to briefly front the Whitford/St. Holmes band with Aerosmith guitarist Brad Whitford. As a result many of Nugent's albums through the next decade were a mixed bag and lacked the verve of his earlier work.

Nugent joined with ex-Night Ranger bassist/vocalist Jack Blades and ex-Styx singer/guitarist Tommy Shaw to play lead guitar for the super group Damn Yankees in 1990. Their first self-titled album was a hit due to the single "High Enough," and was followed by *Don't Tread* in 1992, after which the band split up.

With something of a return to form with *Spirit of the Wild* in 1995, Nugent resumed his solo career, touring and releasing albums somewhat more sporadically, along with issued hits collections and archival material. He also became a right-wing radio host, extending his outspoken entertaining persona to the realm of politics. In addition, Nugent has built on his lifelong love of hunting and the outdoors, running a hunting supply store, releasing outdoor instruction videos, and serving on the board of the NRA. In 2001 he published his autobiography, *God, Guns, and Rock n' Roll.*

Discography: *Ted Nugent* (Epic, 1975); *Free-for-All* (Epic, 1976); *Cat Scratch Fever* (Epic, 1977); *Double Live Gonzo!* (Epic, 1978); *Weekend Warriors* (Epic, 1978); *State of Shock* (Epic, 1979); *Scream Dream* (Epic, 1980); *Intensities in 10 Cities* [live] (Epic, 1981); *Nugent* (Atlantic, 1982); *Penetrator* (Atlantic, 1984); *Little Miss Dangerous* (Atlantic, 1986); *If You Can't Lick 'Em ... Lick 'Em* (Atlantic, 1988); *Spirit of the Wild* (Atlantic, 1995); *Live at Hammersmith '79* (Sony, 1997); *Full Bluntal Nugity* [live] (Spitfire, 2001); *Craveman* (Spitfire, 2002); *Love Grenade* (Eagle/Red, 2007); *Out of Control* (Epic/Legacy, 1993); *On the Edge* (Synergie, 1996); *Over the Top* (Thunderbolt, 1996); *Ted Nugent's Greatest* (Platinum Disc, 2003); *Original Album Classics* (Sony/BMG, 2008).

O

OM (2003–PRESENT). Al Cisneros (bass/vocals), Chris Hakius (drums, replaced by Emil Amos).

Om is an avant-garde noise/drone/art metal band formed by former members of legendary stoner rock band Sleep. After Sleep's *Jerusalem* album (considered by many critics to be a classic of the genre), guitarist Matt Pike departed to form the brutally heavy High On Fire while his former bandmates Al Cisneros and Chris Hakius formed the more experimental Om. If the music of Sleep, where a single song could riff on for the entire length of a record, could be seen as lethargic majesty, Om takes the music in a slightly more, but also slightly less accessible, direction. The music drones, not unlike Tibetan chanting, in ways that dull the listener into almost a trance state, at which point the beauty of the music emerges. In 2008 Hakius left the band and was replaced by new drummer Emil Amos.

Discography: *Variations on a Theme* (Holy Mountain, 2005); *Conference of the Birds* (Holy Mountain, 2006); *Pilgrimage* (Southern Lord, 2007).

ORGY (1998–PRESENT). Jay Gordon (vocals), Amir Derakh (guitar/synthesizer), Ryan Shuck (guitar), Paige Haley (bass), Bobby Hewitt (drums).

An industrial metal group from L.A., Orgy play a particularly melodic brand of electronic-laden metal. Featuring L.A.-mainstay ex-Rough Cutt guitarist/synthesist/producer Amir Derakh, along with vocalist Jay Gordon, guitarist Ryan Shuck, bassist Paige Haley, and drummer Bobby Hewitt, the band adopted a glam/electronica image in the late nineties, releasing their debut, *Candyass*, on Korn's Elementree label (a subsidiary of Reprise) in 1998. Fueled by a cover of New Order's *Blue Monday*, the album was moderately successful, and their second album, *Vapor Transmission*, hit number 16 on the album charts. *Punk Statik Paranoia* followed in 2004, after which the band took a break with members pursuing a variety of outside projects.

Discography: *Candyass* (Elementree/Reprise, 1998); *Vapor Transmission* (Warner Bros., 2000); *Punk Statik Paranoia* (Punk Statik, 2004).

OZZY OSBOURNE (1948–). Having achieved worldwide success with Black Sabbath, Ozzy Osbourne (born John Michael Osbourne) has gone on to be as successful if not more so as a solo artist. Initially partnering with guitarist Randy Rhoads for the hugely successful Blizzard of Ozz band, Ozzy's name went on to become a household word, going on, like Kiss, to make heavy metal safe for mass consumption and becoming an MTV reality show star in *The Osbournes*, even as he battled the demons of his own substance abuse and occasional protests from religious groups.

After leaving Black Sabbath in 1979, Ozzy assembled his first solo band, Blizzard of Ozz, with the aid of his wife and manager Sharon, featuring ex-Rainbow bassist Bob Daisley, ex-Uriah Heep drummer Lee Kerslake, and L.A. hot-shot guitarist Randy Rhoads. Releasing their first album, *Blizzard of Ozz* in 1980, the album was a hit and showcased Ozzy in a new light, still heavy metal but now with the writing of Daisley and Rhoads, a much more melodic yet gothic style. Rhoads' contributions were particularly significant, and the guitarist soon became a star in his own right. This was due to his classically influenced melodic soloing style that sounded somewhat similar to Eddie Van Halen's tapping technique but was original in its own right. For his own part, Ozzy's vocals were in a much more melodic vein than they'd been in Sabbath. The album spawned two hit singles, "Crazy Train" and "Mr. Crowley," and made the charts in both the U.S. and UK.

A second album, *Diary of a Madman*, followed in 1981 (both albums had actually been recorded during the same sessions) and was a similar success, featuring the singles "Flying High Again" and "Over the Mountains." Shortly before the album's release, Daisley and Kerslake were replaced by ex-Pat Travers drummer Tommy Aldridge and Rhoads' former Quiet Riot bandmate bassist Rudy Sarzo whose pictures and credits appeared on the album even though they didn't play on it. (After Ozzy lost a 1986 court case brought by Daisley and Kerslake over writing and performance credit and royalties for the first two albums, the two musicians' performances were replaced with those of his then-current band members bassist Robert Trujillo and drummer Mike Bordin on the 2002 reissues of the two albums.)

Shortly after *Diary*'s release, the first of several controversies involving the singer erupted when Ozzy bit the head off of a bat during a concert in January of 1982. What sounded like a sick publicity stunt was actually much more mundane: a fan had thrown the bat onto the stage, and Ozzy, assuming it was fake, decided to have some fun with the crowd and bite its head off. He was as surprised as anyone when it turned out to be real, and the concert was brought to a halt as he was rushed to the hospital for rabies shots.

More tragically, the first era of Ozzy's solo career was shortly thereafter brought to a close when Rhoads, going for a joyride in a small plane, was killed along with other passengers when the plane's wing clipped the band's tour bus and crashed. With Ozzy and the rest of the band in mourning, the tour was temporarily suspended. A week later, the band resumed the tour with ex-Gillan guitarist Bernie Torme holding down Rhoads' position, even as Ozzy was in a deep depression over the loss of his friend and collaborator. Torme himself lasted for less than a month before leaving the band, and future Night Ranger guitarist Brad Gillis took his place, recording the live album of Sabbath material *Speak of the Devil* in 1982.

Signing a new contract with Epic Records, Ozzy released 1984's *Bark at the Moon*, which featured new guitarist Jake E. Lee, formerly of Ratt. While not the innovator that Rhoads had been, Lee was nonetheless a charismatic player with a style of his own. 1986's *Ultimate Sin* wasn't as strong an album and received a number of negative reviews, but it still sold well and continued Ozzy's winning streak.

1986 was also the year of another controversy, this time involving a court case which alleged that the song "Suicide Solution" encouraged suicide, even though Ozzy and co-writer Daisley claimed the song was about alcohol abuse. The case was eventually dismissed (Sadler).

The following year saw the release of *Tribute*, a live album from 1981 that featured Randy Rhoads and was dedicated to his memory. Lee left the band later that year, and Ozzy found his most durable collaborator in young guitarist Zakk Wylde with whom he would work off and on for the next twenty years. Wylde made his debut with the Ozzy on 1988's *No Rest for the Wicked*, which would be one of Ozzy's strongest records to date, featuring the track "Miracle Man" that took aim at the hypocrisy of televangelists.

No More Tears followed in 1991, and Ozzy claimed he would retire after the tour. Following the tour the double live *Live & Loud* was released.

After a break of two years, Ozzy came out of retirement with *Ozzmosis*, which went on to triple-platinum status within a year of its release. The album's tour proved to be one of the singer's most lucrative, and he started the package tour Ozzfest, which featured many other, mostly younger metal bands. 1997's Ozzfest featured a Black Sabbath reunion, Pantera, and Marilyn Manson and was the second-most successful tour of the year. Ozzy reunited with Black Sabbath for the next year's live *Reunion* album, following it up with another tour, and headlining the next Ozzfest.

Another solo album, *Down to Earth*, followed in 2001 and was supported with an extensive tour with Rob Zombie. More significantly, Ozzy and his family became TV stars when the MTV reality/sitcom *The Osbournes* began airing, and the gothic heavy metal "Satanist" was recast as the wacky yet lovable husband and father. The show became the biggest success the network had ever had and made Ozzy's name a household word. A collection of cover songs appeared as *Under Cover* in 2005, with a new studio album *Black Rain* released in 2007.

Discography: *Blizzard of Ozz* (Jet, 1980); *Diary of a Madman* (Jet, 1981); *Speak of the Devil* (Jet, 1982); *Bark at the Moon* (Epic, 1983); *The Ultimate Sin* (Epic, 1986); *Tribute* [live] (Epic, 1987); *No Rest for the Wicked* (Epic, 1989); *Just Say Ozzy* [live] (Epic, 1990); *No More Tears* (Epic, 1991); *Live & Loud* (Epic, 1993); *Ozzmosis* (Epic, 1995); *Down to Earth* (Sony, 2001); *Live at Budokan* (Epic, 2002); *Under Cover* (Sony, 2005); *Black Rain* (Epic, 2007); *The Ozzman Cometh: Greatest Hits* (Epic, 2002); *Bible of Ozz* (Sony, 2004); *Prince of Darkness* (Epic, 2005).

OVERDOSE (1985–PRESENT). Pedro Alberto "Bozó" Amorim (vocals), Claudio David (lead guitar), Jairo Guedz (rhythm guitar), Gustavo Monsanto (bass), André Marcio (drums).

Overdose has long been one of the top thrash metal bands in Brazil, although their albums were for many years unavailable outside of the country. The band, who are outspoken advocates for social justice within Brazil, have a unique take on thrash metal, which includes the use of percussion and tribal rhythms of their native country.

Discography: *Tight Action* (Bonebreaker, 1985); *Progress of Decadence* (Futurist, 1994); *Scars* (Fierce, 1996); *Circus of Death* (Pavement, 1999).

OVERKILL (1984–PRESENT). Classic lineup: Bobby "Blitz" Ellsworth (vocals), Bobby Gustafson (guitar), D. D. Verni (bass), Sid Falck, (drums).

One of the longest-running thrash metal bands from New York City, the four members of Overkill—vocalist Bobby "Blitz" Ellsworth, guitarist Bobby Gustafson, bassist D. D. Verni, and drummer Sid Falck—first came together in 1984. They quickly earned a deal with Atlantic's Megaforce subsidiary on the basis of their pounding yet precise version of thrash metal and have subsequently gained a loyal underground following, although they have never achieved larger commercial success. Their albums on the Megaforce label were moderate successes, with their 1991 album *Horrorscope* perhaps the strongest and most interesting of their releases. Moving to the smaller CMC International label in 1995, the band has continued to record and tour with a changing lineup.

Discography: *Feel the Fire* (Megaforce, 1985); *Taking Over* (Megaforce, 1987); *Under the Influence* (Megaforce, 1988); *The Years of Decay* (Megaforce, 1989); *Horrorscope* (Megaforce, 1991); *I Hear Black* (Atlantic, 1993); *W.F.O.* (Atlantic, 1994); *Wrecking Your Neck* [live] (CMC International, 1995); *The Killing Kind* (CMC, 1996); *Fuck You and Then Some* [live] (Megaforce, 1996); *From the Underground and Below* (CMC International, 1997); *Necroshine* (CMC International, 1999); *Coverkill* (International, 1999); *Bloodletting* (METAL-IS, 2000); *Wrecking Everything: Live* (Spitfire, 2002); *Hello from the Gutter* (Import, 2002); *Kill Box 13* (Spitfire, 2003); *Unholy* (Snapper, 2004); *Relix IV* (Spitfire, 2005); *Devil by the Tail* (Membran/Ambitions, 2005); *Immortalis* (Bodog, 2007); *Greatest Hits Live* (CMC, 1995); *10 Years of Wrecking Your Neck—Live* (Edel, 1995); *Then & Now* (Sanctuary, 2002).

P

PARIAH (1990–95, 2000–PRESENT). Dave Derrick (vocals), Kyle Ellison (guitar), Jared Tuten (guitar), Sims Ellison (bass,), Shandon Sahm (drums).

Pariah are a San Antonio-based metal band who had some popularity during the nineties with a fairly traditional form of lite metal that was reminiscent of the hair-metal craze of the mid- to late eighties. The band never really clicked and broke up after the first album, but a later version of the group reformed in the late nineties to record *Standing at the Crossroads* and *Youths of Age*. Sadly, original bassist Sims Ellison committed suicide in 1995. The band reformed in 2000.

Discography: *To Kill a Mockingbird* (Geffen, 1993); *Standing at the Crossroads* (Pariah, 2000); *Youths of Age* (Poshboy, 2004).

JOHN PEEL (1939–2004). John Peel was an influential British DJ and tastemaker, self-nicknamed "the most boring man in Britain." Although John Peel is probably best known for championing many punk bands early in their careers, Peel had an unusually broad taste in music and was also one of the key inspirations for the popularity of the grindcore and death metal subgenres. He played numerous tracks from the most extreme bands on his program (including memorably playing Napalm Death's "You Suffer" over and over again on his radio show in amazement at the power and brevity of the song). Peel also recorded numerous live sessions on his program, later released as *The Peel Sessions*. Bands featured on this release included Napalm Death and Bolt Thrower. Sadly, Peel died of an undiagnosed heart condition in 2004. To many, Peel was the example of what a good radio DJ should be: eclectic, honest, opinionated, and ever ready to expose the world to new music regardless of genre. It is unfortunate that there are few DJs today who play and champion the breadth of music that Peel did during his years on BBC radio.

PENTAGRAM. A pentagram is a geometric figure in the form of a five-pointed star, with every alternating point connected by a solid line segment in the interior, but the perimeter points themselves left unconnected by line segments (in contrast to a pentagon, which takes the opposite form), although most often, arcs connect the perimeter points, leading to a circled star, probably the figure's most familiar form.

Frequently used symbolically in various branches of Western occult traditions, the pentagram has also frequently been appropriated (most often inappropriately) as a symbol in heavy metal. In the Western Hermetic tradition, the upright (one point upward) pentagram represents, among other symbolic meanings, Mankind (cf. Leonardo da Vinci's famous "Universal Man" drawing), as well as the four classical Greek "elements" of air, water, fire, and earth, crowned with spirit, while its inversion (two points up) indicates the material dominating the spiritual and has also been used to represent Baphomet, the purported androgynous goat-headed god of the Knights Templar.

More recently, the pentagram has become most associated with contemporary Wiccans, who use the upright form as a symbol of their neopagan, nature-oriented religion, and LaVeyan Satanists, who use the inverted from as a symbol of theirs, which is actually not a religion, but a philosophy which denies the existence of any deity, and uses Satan as a symbol of rebellion against societal norms.

With notable exceptions such as Jimmy Page, Ronnie James Dio, King Diamond, Marilyn Manson, and various Scandinavian groups, few heavy metal acts have any actual experience with or real connection to the occult in any of its forms; most simply use the symbol of the pentagram to associate themselves with a pseudo-mystical cachet that has generated record sales since the early days of Black Sabbath.

PIERCINGS. Copious body piercings have become de rigueur on the heavy metal scene, but the early scene was actually quite conservative in terms of body modification, and while the early glam bands sometimes one earring. It was not until the punk metal crossover of the mid-eighties that body modification along with tattoos became more a part of the day-to-day metal scene, to the point where many members of the more aggressive metal bands are pierced not simply in the ears, but also lip, chin, and nose rings are extremely common. Piercing would have seemed extremely out of place during the glory years of Led Zeppelin or Black Sabbath (as would overt tattoos, although Ozzy himself was a notable exception), but soon the style caught on and numerous bands in the most extreme bands in metal seem hell-bent on proving their dedication to body modification via piercings.

PIG DESTROYER (1997–PRESENT). J. R. Hayes (vocals), Scott Hull (guitar), Blake Harrison (noise), Brian Harvey (drums).

Pig Destroyer are one of the most acclaimed death metal/grindcore bands still touring to this day. The band started in 1997 in Washington, D.C., and soon began to attract the attention of fans of extreme noise and death metal with their morbid but often uncomfortably funny lyrics (Sample lyric: "Your rib cage is open like a great white's jaws"). Despite the horror movie context of most of the songs, the music is just as powerful as any traditional death metal or grindcore, and Pig Destroyer remain today one of the most powerful bands still touring.

Discography: *Explosions in Ward 6* (Reservoir, 1999); *38 counts of Battery* (Relapse, 2001); *Prowler in the Yard* (Relapse, 2001); *Pig Destroyer/Gnob* [split CD] (Robotic Empire, 2002); *Terrifier* (Relapse, 2004); *Phantom Limb* (Relapse, 2007).

THE PIT. One of the many overlapping terms between punk and metal (particularly thrash and speed metal) is the pit, or the space reserved for moshing in front of the band. The pit can be seen as a ritualized way for (mostly) young men to express their aggression during a concert. The pit is somewhat dangerous, especially for newcomers who do not understand its complex but very real etiquette, and it is advised that members of the audience know what they are getting into before they jump into the pit.

POISON (1986–PRESENT). Brett Michaels (lead vocals), C. C. Deville (guitar), Bobby Dall (bass), Rikki Rocket (drums).

Not unlike Kiss, one of their influences, Poison, is a quintessentially American band, who, with a modicum of talent and huge amount of determination rose to the top of the rock heap in the 1980s with a series of solid albums of hook-filled, feel-good rock tunes.

Poison formed in Los Angeles in 1984 when Michaels, Rocket, and Dall, (all recently relocated from Harrisburg, PA) joined forces with former Brooklynite Deville, whose hook-oriented songwriting and flamboyant sense of style meshed well with the band's own sensibilities. After honing their live show on Hollywood's Sunset Strip, the band soon gained the attention of Enigma Records who released their debut, *Look What the Cat Dragged In* in 1986. Poison's live act and melodic tunes translated well to the medium of music video and MTV helped to make the band stars of the era. The debut sold over two million copies with help from videos for the hit singles "I Want Action," "I Won't Forget You," and the band's breakout hit, "Talk Dirty to Me."

Open Up and Say … Ahh! (1988), with "Every Rose Has Its Thorn," "Fallen Angel," and the band's calling card, "Nothin' But a Good Time," took the band to superstardom, with radio airplay and MTV videos giving the band its second platinum disk. Another hit, *Flesh and Blood* followed in 1990. Unfortunately, growing tensions between Deville and the rest of the band were growing, and after the live *Swallow This Live*, he was fired.

After an album with guitarist Richie Kotzen in 1993, and further activity with Blues Saraceno, Deville returned in 1999, and an episode of VH1's *Behind the Music* began comeback efforts with a reunion tour. With a studio album in 2002, a twenty-year anniversary hits collection and tour with Cinderella in 2006, the band showed the nostalgic potential of eighties acts, and have managed to maintain much of their renewed vitality.

Discography: *Look What the Cat Dragged In* (Enigma, 1986); *Open Up and Say…Ahh!* (Capitol, 1988); *Flesh & Blood* (Capitol, 1990); *Swallow This Live* (Capitol, 1991); *Native Tongue* (Capitol, 1993); *Poison's Greatest Hits* (Capitol, 1996); *Crack a Smile… And More!* (Capitol, 2000); *Power to the People* (Cyanide Music, 2000); *Hollyweird* (Cyanide Music, 2002); *Best of Ballads and Blues* (Capitol, 2003); *The Best of Poison: 20 Years of Rock* (Capitol, 2006); *Poison'd!* (Capitol, 2007); *Seven Days Live* (Armoury, 2008).

POISON THE WELL (1998–PRESENT). Aryeh Lehrer (vocals, replaced by Jeff Moreira), Ryan Primack (guitar), Derek Miller (guitar, replaced by Jason Boyer), Mike Gordillo (bass, replaced by Benjamin Brown), Chris Hornbrook (drums).

Poison the Well are a metalcore band, or a metal band with hardcore punk roots, from Florida. The original members were guitarist Primack and vocalist Lehrer. The band has gone through numerous personnel changes but has finally settled on a fairly stable lineup. Their music has evolved from closer to a modern hardcore band to one that is as aggressive as classic thrash metal, with metallic touches.

Discography: *The Opposite of December* (Trustkill, 1999); *Tear from the Red* (Trustkill, 2002); *Distance Makes the Heart Grow Fonder* (Undecided, 2002); *You Come Before You* (Atlantic, 2003); *Versions* (Ferret, 2007).

POSSESSED (1983–87). Jeff Becerra (vocals/bass), Mike Torrao (guitar), Brian Montana (guitar, replaced by Larry LaLonde), Mike Sus (drums).

Possessed were an American death metal/punk band that claimed to have been the first ones to have coined the term *death metal* or at least to have used it in a song, "Death Metal" on their classic *Seven Churches* record. The band started in 1983, and their musical evolution was marked by the tragic suicide of original lead singer Barry Fisk before the band had recorded any material. However, replacement vocalist and bassist Jeff Becerra was a more-than-adequate replacement and soon the band was gigging and eventually signed to Combat Records. The first Possessed release, *Seven Churches,* is a death metal landmark, with pounding drums, growled vocals, and dark tuned-down guitars all at thrash speed, but with darker, more evil lyrics than most bands (outside of Death) were playing at the time. LaLonde later went on to play with Primus for many years. Sadly, vocalist Becerra was shot during a botched robbery and confined to a wheelchair, most likely ending any hopes of a Possessed reunion, although the possibility was raised by Becerra in 2007 and a version of Possessed was touring in 2008. The influence of Possessed on the death metal movement and the extreme metal that came into vogue in the eighties continues to this day.

Discography: *Seven Churches* (Relativity, 1985); *Beyond the Gates* (Combat, 1986); *Lyrical* (Holy South, 2003); *Agony in Paradise: Live* (Agonia, 2004); *Exploration* (Rise Above Relics, 2006); *Cat's Life* (Daemonic, 2007).

POWER MAD (1984–90, 2007–PRESENT). Joel Dubay (vocals/guitar), Todd Haug (guitar), Jeff Litke (bass), Adrian Liberty (drums, replaced by John Macluso, now Dodd Lowder).

Power Mad were an obscure but worthy speed metal band from Minnesota, mostly active in the late eighties, best known for the inclusion of their amazing song "Slaughterhouse" in the classic David Lynch film *Wild at Heart* (1990). The band put out two EPs and two records in their prime, before taking over a decade off and returning in 2007 with new drummer Lowder and a MySpace page, which has their albums available as MP3s. While not the most famous speed metal band in their time, their two records are well worth finding either via eBay or the website.

Discography: *Absolute Power* (Reprise, 1989); *The Madness Begins* (Reprise, 1990).

POWERMAN 5000 (1991–PRESENT). Spider One, aka Michael Cummings (vocals), M.33, aka Mike Tempesta (guitar, replaced by Terry Corso, replaced by

Dave Pino), Adam 12, aka Adam Williams (guitar, replaced by Johnny Rock, aka Johnny Heatley, replaced by Evan Rodaniche), Dorian 27, aka Dorian Heartsong (bass, replaced by Siggy Sjursen), Al 3, aka Al Pahanish (drums, replaced by AD7, aka Adrian Ost).

Powerman 5000 were a nu metal band led by Michael Cummings, aka Spider One, who is Rob Zombie's younger brother. The band started in Boston as a hybrid band using electronic sounds, somewhat reminiscent of the experimentation of later White Zombie. They turned to a lighter punk phase in later years. Although never in the big leagues, Powerman 5000 plays a respectable analogy to Triple A metal, opening for Metallica and Korn and playing at Ozzfest. In perhaps a nod to glam metal pioneers, the band also developed a science fiction themed look and names for most of the band, which underwent numerous personnel changes, leaving Spider One as the sole remaining original member.

Discography: *The Blood Splat Rating System* (Conscience, 1995); *Mega Kung Fu Radio* (Dreamworks, 1997); *True Force* (Curve of the Earth, 1997); *Tonight the Stars Revolt* (Dreamworks, 1999); *Anyone for Doomsday?* (Dreamworks, 2001); *Transform* (Dreamworks, 2003); *Destroy What You Enjoy* (DRT, 2006).

PROBOT (2004). Various performers, including King Diamond, Lemmy, Tom Warrior, Mike Dean (vocals), Dave Grohl (guitar/bass/drums).

Probot was a metal tribute record by David Grohl (Nirvana, Foo Fighters), who assembled an all-star cast of metal singers to work with him on a project where the singers added lyrics and vocals and Grohl provided the riffs and instrumentation. Guests included Lemmy Kilmister from Motorhead, Cronos from Venom, Wino from the Obsessed and St. Vitus, Tom Warrior from Celtic Frost, and many others. The one-off (so far) project gave a fresh chance for some of the cream of the thrash, death, and black metal scenes to showcase their pipes for a new generation who looked to icons like Grohl as tastemakers. The Probot project also demonstrates that the punk/metal crossover exposed many a young punk to some of the more extreme forms of heavy metal and that there were many similarities between the two genres.

Discography: *Probot* (Southern Lord, 2004).

PRONG (1985–96). Tommy Victor (vocals/guitar), Mike Kirkland (bass, replaced by Troy Gregory, Paul Raven), Ted Parsons (drums).

Prong were a punk metal band from New York City led by former CBGB's sound man Tommy Victor, who looked no farther than the door of where he worked to recruit doorman Mike Kirkland on bass, and eventually former Swans drummer Ted Parsons, to create a mathematically proficient form of New York thrashlike metal akin to bands such as early Helmet. The band toured relentlessly, and despite several good albums, never seemed to make it. Eventually Victor joined Danzig's band for several years after the demise of Prong. *Beg to Differ* is the most riff-laden of their records.

Discography: *Primitive Origins* (Sound League, 1987); *Force Fed* (In-Effect, 1988); *Beg to Differ* (Epic, 1990); *Prove You Wrong* (Epic, 1991); *Cleansing* (Epic, 1994); *Rude Awakening* (Epic, 1996); *100% Live* (Locomotive, 2002); *Scorpio Rising* (Locomotive, 2003); *Power of the Damager* (13th Planet, 2007).

Q

QUEENS OF THE STONE AGE (1998–PRESENT). Josh Homme (guitar/vocals), Troy van Leeuwen (guitar/keyboards), Joey Castillo (drums), various others.

Without a doubt one of the most innovative hard rock bands at work in the new millennium, Queens of the Stone Age rose from the ashes of stoner rock pioneers Kyuss. After Kyuss's breakup, Homme left the California desert for Seattle, where he played with a variety of bands, most notably Screaming Trees as touring guitarist.

Beginning work on new material, Homme enlisted drummer Alfredo Hernandez for the recordings that would be released as the first Queens of the Stone Age album. Shortly after its release in 1998 on the independent Loose Groove label, Nick Oliveri and Catching joined the band for touring.

Led by guitarist/vocalist Josh Homme, the band originally consisted of fellow Kyuss veterans, bassist Nick Oliveri and drummer Alfredo Hernandez, as well as new guy Dave Catching on guitars and keys. After the first album, the band toured heavily. Even so, the creatively restless Homme found time to begin releasing the first volumes of "The Desert Sessions," recordings that chronicle the collaborative songwriting and recording that he instigated at the Rancho de la Luna recording studio in the Joshua Tree, California, desert, which have proven to be inspiration and proving ground for a number of QOTSA tunes.

In mid-2000, the Queens released their playfully titled sophomore album *R*. More touring ensued, including a stint with Ozzfest, after which Hernandez left the group. The band began to build more of a reputation with fans and the press. At the massive Rock in Rio festival Oliveri got busted for performing in the nude. But the Queen's best publicity stunt was yet to come, when they asked Foo Fighters guitarist/vocalist (and ex-Nirvana drummer) Dave Grohl to drum on their next album. To the surprise of many, Grohl enthusiastically agreed. The subsequent album, *Songs for the Deaf*, was their critical and artistic breakthrough. Released in the summer of 2002, and featuring such songs as "Go with the Flow" and "First It Giveth," the album demonstrated not only a confident mastery of songwriting craft but also a willingness to take sonic chances in the recording process, producing an album that fit into the hard rock tradition without attempting to replicate it. Grohl's willingness to put Foo Fighters on temporary hiatus and tour with the band was both a testimony to the band's importance and gave them great press. The ensuing tour also saw the joining of former A Perfect Circle guitarist/keyboardist Troy Van Leeuwen, who would prove to be a worthy creative foil to Homme.

In keeping with Homme's restless variation and penchant for collaboration, yet another permutation of the band was in place for *Deaf*'s follow-up, *Lullabies to Paralyze*, in 2005. In addition to Homme, Van Leeuwan, and Lanegan, the album featured the contributions of new drummer Joey Castillo and bassist/guitarist Alain Johannes from the band Eleven, as well as guest spots from ZZ Top guitarist Billy Gibbons and Homme's longtime collaborator guitarist/vocalist/producer Chris Goss from Masters of Reality.

The DVD/CD *Over the Years and Through the Woods* was also released in 2005, featuring live recordings and footage from the Lullabies tour, as well as older footage from the band. *Era Vulgaris* was released in 2007.

Discography: *Queens of the Stone Age* (Loose Groove, 1998); *R* (Interscope, 2000); *Songs for the Deaf* (Ipecac, 2002); *Lullabies to Paralyze* (Interscope, 2005); *Over the Years and Through the Woods* [live] (Interscope, 2005); *Era Vulgaris* (Interscope, 2007).

QUEENSRŸCHE (1983–PRESENT). Classic lineup: Geoff Tate (vocals), Chris DeGarmo (guitar), Michael Wilton (guitar), Eddie Jackson (bass), Scott Rockenfield (drums).

Unlike the many pop metal bands that served as their contemporaries, Seattle's Queensrÿche drew their inspiration more from progressive European metal bands and art rock groups like Pink Floyd and Queen, developing their own unique sound during the 1980s. Hitting their stride with the albums *Operation: Mindcrime* and its follow-up, *Empire,* the band dwindled in popularity with the coming of grunge in the nineties, although an enthusiastic cult fan base has supported them to the present.

Getting their start in the Seattle suburb of Bellevue in 1981, the band focused on their original music, rehearsing and writing for two years before releasing a four-song tape. Record store owners Kim and Diana Harris, impressed by their material, offered to manage the band. In 1983 the band released the EP *Queen of the Reich* independently and sold 20,000 copies. EMI signed the band and released a full-length version of the album, which peaked at number 81 on the charts.

After tours with such bands as Metallica and Bon Jovi and releasing the moderately successful albums *The Warning* and *Rage for Order,* in 1984 and 1986, respectively, the band had its breakthrough with *Operation: Mindcrime* in 1988, which brought the band's progressive influences to the fore. The album went platinum within a year. Their next record, 1990's *Empire,* was even more successful, going double platinum and reaching the number 7 spot on the charts, helped along by the hit ballad "Silent Lucidity."

The live *Operation: LIVEcrime* followed in 1991, with *Promised Land* arriving three years later, in 1994, debuting at number 3, despite the emergence of grunge. *Hear in the New Frontier* (1997) found the band pruning its sound of its progressive elements for a more basic approach that seemed to alienate some fans and reviewers. The album performed poorly and soon after guitarist DeGarmo left the band, with guitarist Kelly Gray taking his position. A greatest hits package followed in 2000.

The double live *Live Evolution* CD and DVD were released in 2001, with a new studio effort, *Tribe,* coming in 2003. *Operation: Mindcrime II* came in 2006. Another best of collection appeared in 2007, along with *Take Cover.*

Discography: *The Warning* (EMI America, 1984); *Rage for Order* (EMI America, 1986); *Operation: Mindcrime* (EMI America, 1988); *Empire* (EMI America, 1990); *Operation: LIVEcrime* (EMI America, 1991); *Promised Land* (EMI America, 1994); *Hear in the Now Frontier* (EMI America, 1997); *Q2K* (Atlantic, 1999); *Live Evolution* (Sanctuary, 2001); *Tribe* (Sanctuary, 2003); *The Art of Live* (Sanctuary, 2004); *Operation: Mindcrime II* (2006); *Mindcrime at the Moore* [live] (Rhino, 2007); *Take Cover* (Rhino, 2007); *Greatest Hits* (Virgin, 2000); *Revolution Calling* (EMI, 2003); *Sign of the Times: The Best of Queensrÿche* (Capitol, 2007).

QUIET RIOT (1977–2007). Kevin DuBrow (vocals), Carlos Cavazo (guitar), Rudy Sarzo (bass), Frankie Banali (drums).

Quiet Riot enjoyed a huge burst of success in the early eighties, with a chart-topping album, but their overnight success, which was a long time in coming, would fade sooner than they might have expected. The band had its roots in the late-seventies club scene and was the band that Ozzy Osbourne guitarist Randy Rhoads cut his teeth with. The band released a pair of records with Columbia Records in Japan before losing Rhoads, and later Sarzo, to Ozzy's band. By 1982, vocalist Kevin DuBrow had reformed the band with guitarist Carlos Cavazo and bassist Chuck Wright and had begun work on an album for independent Pasha Records. Soon enough, however, Sarzo had quit Ozzy and taken Wright's place, bringing along Frankie Banali on drums to finish the sessions for the album *Metal Health,* released in 1983. On the strength of the album's title track and its cover of the Slade song "Cum on Feel the Noize," the album shot to the top of the album charts and sold over five million copies.

With pressure from their record company to capitalize on their good fortune, Quiet Riot were forced to record a follow-up before they were truly ready and the record company's strategy backfired when the 1984 album *Condition Critical* failed to duplicate the previous album's performance. Even another Slade cover ("Mama Weer All Crazee Now") couldn't help, and the band saw their winning streak come to an abrupt halt.

A number of comeback releases between 1986 and 1995 failed to generate any significant interest. Dubrow nonetheless kept a version of the band on the road, releasing occasional albums until his death from a cocaine overdose in 2007 at the age of 52.

Discography: *Quiet Riot* [1977] (CBS, 1977); *Quiet Riot II* (CBS, 1978); *Metal Health* (Pasha, 1983); *Condition Critical* (Pasha, 1984); *QR III* (Pasha, 1986); *Quiet Riot* [1988] (Pasha, 1988); *Terrified* (Moonstone, 1993); *Down to the Bone* (Kamikaze, 1995); *Alive and Well* (Deadline, 1999); *Guilty Pleasures* (Bodyguard, 2001); *The Randy Rhoads Years* (Rhino, 1993); *The Greatest Hits* (Epic/Pasha, 1996); *Live and Rare, Vol. 1* (Cleopatra, 2005); *Metal Health: The Best of Quiet Riot* (Golden Core, 2008).

R

RACER X (1985–88, 1999–PRESENT). Jeff Martin (vocals, replaced by John Corabi), Paul Gilbert (guitar, replaced by Chris Arvin), Bruce Bouillet (guitar), John Alderete (bass), Harry G Schoesser (drums, replaced by Scott Travis, replaced by Walt Woodward III).

Racer X were a progressive metal band composed of virtuoso musicians, especially Paul Gilbert, the original guitar player who was known as one of the key shredders in metal during the eighties. Gilbert left after the 1988 album to join the supergroup Mr. Big with bassist Billy Sheehan and was replaced by Chris Arvin, who, although good, could not match Gilbert's guitar wizardry. The first three records are essential listening for aspiring shredders. Gilbert revived Racer X in 1999, and the band has played sporadically since then, alternating with Gilbert's solo career, which is decidedly not metal, but Beatle-esque pop.

Discography: *Street Lethal* (Shrapnel, 1986); *Second Heat* (Shrapnel, 1987); *Live Extreme, Vol. 1* (Shrapnel, 1988); *Live Extreme, Vol. 2* (Shrapnel, 1992); *Technical Difficulties* (Shrapnel, 2000); *Adventure of Racer X-Men* (Universal, 2001); *Live at the Whiskey: Snowball of Doom* (Universal, 2001); *Superheroes* (Shrapnel, 2001); *Snowball of Doom* [live] (Shrapnel, 2002); *Getting Heavier* (Shrapnel, 2003); *Official Bootleg: Snowball of Doom, Vol. 2* (Rock Empire, 2003).

RAGE AGAINST THE MACHINE (1991–2000, 2007–PRESENT). Zack de la Rocha (vocals), Tom Morello (guitar), Tim Commerford (bass), Brad Wilk (drums).

Despite the limited amount of time that Rage Against the Machine was around during their limited life span, the band was enormously influential and their combination of hip-hop sound effects (all created by Tom Morello's guitar, along with the maniac screeching and rapping of frontman Zack De La Rocha) created a new sound that made the heavy styling of bands such as Limp Bizkit look as punchless as an Air Supply record. However, it was never clear how the band could "rage" against a machine while signed to a major label, and despite plenty of leftist talk (support of Mumia, the Zapatistas), it seemed that after a while, the band spent more time fighting themselves than they did the machine. Although their two "proper" records had some great singles on them—"Killing in the Name of" and "Bulls on Parade" are two sonically stunning songs—they couldn't seem to keep to a regular recording session, and in their original incarnation came out with only two proper albums, plus a live record and a record of covers. The band went on hiatus in 2000 and Morello, Commerford, and Wilk formed Audioslave with Chris Cornell from Soundgarden. When that band petered out, Rage got back together in 2007 but has yet to release new material.

Discography: *Rage Against the Machine* (Epic, 1992); *Evil Empire* (Epic, 1996); *The Battle of Los Angeles* (Epic, 1999); *Renegades* (Epic, 2000); *Live at the Grand Olympic Auditorium* (Epic, 2003).

RAGING SLAB (1983–PRESENT). Greg Strzempka (guitar/vocals), Elyse Steinman (slide guitar), Mats Rydström (bass), Niklas Matsson (drums).

Raging Slab are one of the best Southern rock boogie bands to come out of New York City. Slab, who have been described as a combination of Lynyrd Skynyrd and Metallica, have long put out some of the best rock of its kind since their debut in 1987 with *Assmaster*. Although the band has probably never been taken as seriously as they might by potential fans outside of New York City, they have continued to record and tour with their postmodern version of rootsy yet ballsy seventies-flavored rock, hitting a creative and commercial peak with the 1993 album *Dynamite Monster Boogie Concert*, whose title pretty much says it all. Cuts like "Anywhere But Here" and "Take a Hold" showcased the band's classic yet innovative songwriting and performing style, sounding like a thoroughly retro yet modern group. The album remains the band's high point, as legal complications following their departure kept them from recording until 2000. They have since begun to record and tour again, though somewhat sporadically.

Discography: *Assmaster* (Buy Our, 1987); *True Death* (Restless, 1989); *Raging Slab* (RCA, 1989); *Slabbage* (Restless, 1993); *Dynamite Monster Boogie Concert* (Warner Bros., 1993); *Sing Monkey Sing* (Warner Bros., 1996); *The Dealer* (Tee Pee, 2001); *Pronounced Eat Shit* (Tee Pee, 2002); *Slabbage/True Death* (Restless, 1991).

RAINBOW (1975–84). Classic lineup: Ritchie Blackmore (guitar), Ronnie James Dio (vocals), Jimmy Bain (bass), Cozy Powell (drums), Tony Carey (keyboards).

Formed in 1975 by former Deep Purple guitarist Ritchie Blackmore, Rainbow was a vehicle that let him explore his musical ideas outside of the democratic confines of his former band. Along with main collaborator vocalist Ronnie James Dio from the band Elf—whose penchant for medieval and mythical imagery seemed to match his own—Blackmore developed Rainbow into a successful rock group whose reputation and success were only overshadowed by his former group.

The first Rainbow album featured the entire Elf lineup minus guitarist David Feinstein (who would go on to front the heavy metal power trio The Rods). Quickly a hit in Europe, the album featured the classic "Man on the Silver Mountain," and established the band's—and Dio's—reputation. Dio was a fundamentally different kind of vocalist than Deep Purple's Ian Gillan or David Coverdale,

Rainbow was in their prime during the 1970s. (Photofest)

with an extended range and an operatic style, albeit with the edge required by heavy rock.

Revamping the lineup for 1976, Rainbow's *Rising* album fulfilled Dio and Blackmore's potential and found both at the peak of their powers, with Blackmore's neoclassical innovations and Dio's fantasy lyrics complementing each other. The band supported the album with a world tour, during which the live *On Stage,* released in 1977, was recorded.

By 1978, tensions and musical difference between Dio and Blackmore led to Dio's leaving the band to replace Ozzy Osbourne in Black Sabbath.

Pursuing a more mainstream approach on 1979's *Down to Earth,* Rainbow now featured the leather-lunged Graham Bonnet, but despite two hit singles, the album performed poorly and Bonnet was sacked after a single gig at the Donnington festival.

The next version of Rainbow was even more mainstream and featured American vocalist Joe Lynn Turner. Thanks to the single "I Surrender," the 1981 album *Difficult to Cure* was a success, even charting in the U.S., where Rainbow had been trying to make progress. Blackmore's bid for U.S. acceptance, however, contributed to generally weaker albums, and two more albums failed to generate much excitement, and when a Deep Purple reunion was in the offing in 1984, Blackmore pulled the plug on the band, later founding the medieval folk group Blackmore's Night after ending his run with Purple.

Discography: *Ritchie Blackmore's Rainbow* (Polydor, 1975); *Rising* (Polydor, 1976); *On Stage* (Polydor, 1977); *Long Live Rock 'n' Roll* (Polydor, 1978); *Down to Earth* (Polydor, 1979); *Difficult to Cure* (Polydor, 1981); *Straight Between the Eyes* (Mercury, 1982); *Bent Out of Shape* (Mercury, 1983); *Live in Munich 1977* (Eagle, 2006); *Rainbow Rising/Ritchie*

Blackmore's Rainbow (Polydor, 1980); *The Best of Rainbow* (Polydor, 1981); *Final Vinyl* [live] (Mercury, 1986); *Live Between the Eyes* (Pony Canyon, 1996); *All Night Long: An Introduction* (Polydor, 2002); *Catch the Rainbow: The Anthology* (Polydor, 2003); *Rainbow Box* (Universal, 2007).

RAMMSTEIN (1993–PRESENT). Till Linderman (vocals), Paul Landers (guitar), Richard Kruspe (guitar), Christian Lorenz (keyboards), Ollie Reidel (bass/drums).

Rammstein are a German industrial/metal band that plays a brutal fascistic form of metallic industrial opera. The band is best known in the United States for their radio hit "Du Hast" (You Hate) on the *Sehnsucht* album. They combined European techno and dance beats with crunchy guitar and brutal lyrics in German that reflected themes of alienation, disgust, and anger. The band was also noted for amazing stage shows with bondage gear, elaborate head gear, and band members being set on fire.

Discography: *Herzeleid* (ILS International, 1996); *Sehnsucht* (Motor Music, 1998); *Live Aus Berlin* (Slash, 2000); *Mutter* (Universal, 2001) *Reise*; *Resise* (Republic, 2004); *Rosenrto* (Universal, 2005).

RATT (1983–PRESENT). Steven Pearcy (lead vocals), Warren DeMartini (lead guitar), Robin Crosby (guitar), Juan Croucier (bass), Bobby Blotzer (drums).

One of the most successful bands of the eighties pop metal era, and in fact the poster children for the genre, Ratt had a knack for melding pop hooks, sexy grinding rhythms, and face-melting guitarwork. Their good looks and MTV videos helped them to ride a series of albums to the top of the charts from the late eighties to the early nineties when grunge put an end to the party.

Featuring lead vocalist Steven Pearcy, lead guitarist Warren DeMartini, guitarist Robin Crosby, bassist Juan Croucier, and drummer Bobby Blotzer, the L.A.-based Ratt released an independent self-titled album and attracted the attention of Atlantic Records, who released *Out of the Cellar* in 1984. *Cellar* was a huge hit, reaching triple platinum on the strength of the single "Round and Round." Subsequent albums, *Invasion of Your Privacy* (1985), *Dancin' Undercover* (1986), *Reach for the Sky* (1988), and *Detonator* (1990), also were chart hits, and the band were rulers of the roost on MTV and on the concert trail.

With Pearcy leaving to form the band Arcade in 1992, and music styles changing, the band was dormant for much of the nineties. The band reunited for 1997's *Collage* and 1999's *Ratt*, both albums selling modestly.

With Pearcy leaving again in 2000, the band continued with former Love/Hate vocalist Jizzy Pearl as frontman. In 2002, guitarist Robin Crosby died after suffering from AIDS (which he only disclosed in 2001) for several years.

In recent years Pearcy, DeMartini, and Blotzer have toured in a new version of Ratt and have spoken of plans to reenter the studio to work on a new album.

Discography: *Out of the Cellar* (Atlantic, 1984); *Invasion of Your Privacy* (Atlantic, 1985); *Dancin' Undercover* (Atlantic, 1986); *Reach for the Sky* (Atlantic, 1988); *Detonator* (Atlantic, 1990); *Collage* (D-Rock, 1997); *Ratt* (Portrait, 1999); *Ratt & Roll 8191* (WEA, 1991; Portrait, 1999); *The Essentials* (Warner Strategic, 2002); *Metal Hits* (Rhino Flashback, 2003); *Rarities* (Deadline, 2007); *Tell the World: The Very Best of Ratt* (Atlantic/Rhino, 2007).

RAVEN (1975–PRESENT). Mark Gallagher (vocals/guitar), John Gallagher (bass), Rob "Wacko" Hunter (drums, replaced by Joey Hassewander).

Raven were one of the more energetic of the thrash metal bands of the eighties and one of the few to graduate out of the New Wave of British heavy metal. Raven were also immensely popular with fans earlier on for their heavy mixtures of thrash styling with progressive playing. Raven were also best known for the football-helmet-masked antics of drummer Wacko, who departed the band after the *Life's a Bitch* record to become an audio engineer. The band played to smaller crowds and did not record at all from 1988 until their comeback in 1995, which saw a return to the more classic Raven sound. Raven are one of the great lost bands of the eighties, and although they still tour to this day, their peak was in the mid-eighties and their first two albums are still thrash metal classics. Bring back Wacko!

Discography: *Rock Until You Drop* (Roadrunner, 1981); *Wiped Out* (Roadrunner, 1982); *All for One* (Neat, 1983); *Live at the Inferno* (Discovery, 1984); *Stay Hard* (Atlantic, 1985); *Mad* (Megaforce, 1985); *The Pack Is Back* (Atlantic, 1986); *Life's a Bitch* (Atlantic, 1987); *Nothing Exceeds like Excess* (Relativity, 1988); *Glow* (Fresh Fruit, 1995); *Destroy All Monsters: Live in Japan* (SPV, 1996); *Everything Louder* (WEA, 1997); *One for All* (Metal Blade, 2000); *All Systems Go* (Sanctuary, 2002); *Architect of Fear* (Steamhammer UK, 2003).

RIOT (1973–PRESENT). Guy Speranza (vocals, replaced by Rhett Forrester), Mark Reale (guitar), L.A. Kouvaris (guitar, replaced by Rick Ventura, others), Jimmy Iommi (bass, replaced by Kip Lemming, others), Peter Bitelli (drums, replaced by Sandy Slavin, others).

Riot are a U.S. heavy metal band founded in Brooklyn, N.Y., in 1973. Although they never attained an arena-headlining level of success, they were enormously influential in the development of eighties metal (especially the NWOBHM), and the band carries on under the leadership of guitarist Mark Reale, the sole remaining original member, to this day.

Signed by New York producer Steve Loeb, Riot released their debut album, *Rock City*, in 1977, with the lineup consisting of Reale and L.A. Kouvaris on guitar, vocalist Guy Speranza, bassist Jimmy Iommi, and drummer Peter Bitelli. After touring as an opening act for AC/DC and Molly Hatchet, they entered the studio to record their second album, 1979's *Narita*, with guitar virtuoso Rick Ventura replacing Kouvaris, adding a much heavier edge to the band's sound and greatly enhancing their songwriting ability. After the album's release, the band revamped the rhythm section, replacing Iommi and Bitelli with Kip Lemming on bass and powerhouse drummer Sandy Slavin, then toured the UK with Sammy Hagar, whose record label, Capitol, the band had signed with to distribute *Narita*, only to have Capitol unceremoniously drop them following the tour. The band's management (Billy Arnell and Ezra Cook, as well as producer Loeb) responded with a blitz campaign of advertising and airplay on U.S. FM-radio stations, which led to enough attention and publicity for the band that embarrassed Capitol Records executives reversed their decision and picked up Riot's option for a follow-up album.

Subsequently, Riot recorded their second album for Capitol, *Fire Down Under*. Amazingly, Capitol not only refused to release it, deeming its heavier, faster sound as "commercially unacceptable," but in a reversal of their previous position, now refused to let the band out of their contract to sign with another label. Outraged fans protested around the world, including a gathering of thousands at a rally in London outside the offices of Capitol's parent company, EMI (which was given major news coverage in the U.S. on the newly born MTV network), and other bands began to refuse to deal with EMI unless the album was released, or Riot were released from their contract. Eventually, Capitol relented and released the band from their contract, and *Fire Down Under* finally came out on Elektra Records in 1981, making the Billboard Top 100 chart in the U.S., and selling well worldwide.

Featuring the band's anthem, "Swords and Tequila," and regarded by many fans as their definitive studio album, it ranks as their best-selling record to date, and laid the groundwork for much of eighties metal, with Speranza's vocal pyrotechnics and Ventura and Reale's dual lead guitar assault leading the way over Lemming and Slavin's propulsive bass and drums, convincingly demonstrating the short-sightedness of Capitol executives. An opening slot on Rush's "Moving Pictures" U.S. tour followed.

Unfortunately, on the brink of stardom, the lineup did not remain stable, and further record label troubles lay ahead. Charismatic frontman Guy Speranza, uncomfortable with the "rock and roll lifestyle" on the road, left the band to raise his family and was replaced by Rhett Forrester, with whom the band recorded *Restless Breed* in 1982, and toured with the Scorpions and Whitesnake, after which the band and Elektra Records parted ways. A live album (*Riot Live*), recorded in 1980 and 1981 in the UK, featuring the *Fire Down Under* lineup performing material from *Rock City* and *Narita*, was released in Europe in 1983, and ranks as one of the definitive live albums of its era. *Born in America* followed in 1984, on the Quality Records label, as well as a tour with Kiss and Vandenberg, after which the band dissolved.

Rhett Forrester was shot to death during a robbery in Atlanta in 1994; Guy Speranza died of pancreatic cancer in November 2003. Rick Ventura, Kip Lemming, and Sandy Slavin continued their musical careers, including playing together in the band Adrenalin. Guitarist Mark Reale re-established Riot with new members in 1988, and leads the band to date as the sole remaining member from their glory days. Since then, they have released several albums featuring a variety of lineups on a variety of labels, to little commercial interest in the U.S., although they retain a following elsewhere, especially in Japan.

Discography: *Rock City* (Fire Sign, 1977); *Narita* (Capitol, 1979); *Fire Down Under* (Elektra, 1981); *Restless Breed* (Elektra, 1982); *Riot Live* (European release only, 1983, U.S. CD release by Metal Blade, 1993); *Born In America* (Quality, 1984); *Thundersteel* (CBS, 1988); *The Privilege of Power* (CBS, 1990); *Riot Live In Japan* (CBS, 1992); *Night Breaker* (CBS, 1994); *The Brethren Of The Long House* (Metal Blade, 1996); *Inishmore* (Metal Blade, 1998); *Shine On* (Metal Blade, 1998); *Angel Eyes* (4-song EP) (Metal Blade, 1998); *Sons of Society* (Metal Blade, 1999); *Through the Storm* (2002); *Army of One* (LongHouse, 2006).

ROADRUNNER RECORDS (1980–PRESENT). Roadrunner Records was founded in the Netherlands in 1980 and soon found success with early releases by King Diamond and Sepultura. Although the label is not a mandatory place to graze on new material, Roadrunner Records was one of the premier heavy metal labels during its heyday in the 1980s and today, now a subsidiary of Warner

Brothers, the label hosts acts such as Dream Theater, Opeth, Cradle of Filth, The Cult, Machine Head, Slipknot and Obituary. While the label started as an indie in the Netherlands, created by Cees Wessels, it is not a large label and a force to reckon with in the metal and outsider music community.

THE RODS (1981–94). David "Rock" Feinstein (guitar, lead vocals), Garry Bordonaro (bass, vocals), Carl Canedy (drums, vocals).

While they never attained significant commercial success, New York's The Rods were stalwart keepers of the metal faith, playing a streetwise version of hard rocking metal that eschewed some of the more flashy trappings of their peers for a down and dirty image (think heavy metal Ramones: blue jeans and leather jackets) and performance style that focused on no-nonsense delivery of high-energy hard-rock-derived metal in a blazing power trio format.

Featuring Ronnie James Dio's cousin David "Rock" Feinstein (who had played with Dio in the regionally successful pre-Rainbow group Elf), bassist Garry Bordonaro, and powerhouse drummer (and producer) Carl Canedy. Releasing their first self-titled album in 1981, the group gained a reputation as a powerful live act, their power trio format bringing out the best in the three members. They delivered a series of consistent albums throughout the '80s that showcased their straightforward metal style, before calling it a day in the early '90s, with Canedy pursuing a career as a producer. The band reformed briefly in 2004 for a performance at Germany's Wacken Open Air Festival.

Discography: *The Rods* (Arista, 1981); *Wild Dogs* (Arista, 1982); *In the Raw* (Shrapnel, 1983); *The Rods Live* (Music For Nations, 1983); *Let Them Eat Metal* (Music For Nations, 1984).

THE RUNAWAYS (1975–1978). Michael "Micki" Steele (vocals/bass, replaced on vocals by Cherie Currie, and on bass by Jackie Fox), Joan Jett (guitar), Lita Ford (guitar), Sandy West (drums).

The Runaways were one of the key female rock bands. Although they played a variety of styles, including proto-punk and glam, they were primarily a metal band. This was in spite of the efforts of Los Angeles music mogul Kim Fowley, who brought the band together in much the same way that Lou Pearlman put together boy bands in the eighties and nineties. The difference was that the Runaways, particularly Jett and Ford, had real talent. The Runaways were recruited by Fowley in 1975, and as a result of Fowley's repulsive behavior toward the young girls in his care, went through several lineup changes (as documented in McNeil and McCain 1996). Members included future stars Jett and Ford on guitar, Cherie Currie on vocals, Sandy West on drums and vocals, and Micki Steele on bass and vocals (who later went on to a lengthy career with the pop band the Bangles and who was subsequently replaced by Jackie Fox on bass and later by Peggy Foster and Laurie McAllister).

Fowley, best known as a songwriter and manager, most famous for his novelty single "They're Coming to Take Me Away Ha Ha" as Napoleon XIV, marketed the Runaways as a girl group playing macho balls-to-the-wall rock and roll. For a while the group caught on, particularly in Los Angeles and overseas, where rock-starved Europeans appreciated the band's metallic crunch and energy more than the lethargic American audiences did. Realizing that he didn't have a female perspective, nor any real sensitivity to write songs for the group, Fowley recruited Kari Krome to write songs for the band that they would find more palatable to sing. After lengthy tours, and years of verbal abuse by Fowley, Jackie Fox left the band, along with Cherie Currie. This left Jett as the de facto lead singer, before the band eventually broke down altogether and dissolved.

Jett went on to the most successful solo career of anyone in the band with hits such as "I Love Rock and Roll" and a cover of "Crimson and Clover." Lita Ford established herself as a top-selling metal act for a while, best known for her hit single "Kiss Me Deadly" and her duet with Ozzy on "Close My Eyes Forever." Various members of the band went on to solo careers of limited success. Sadly in 2006, former drummer Sandy West died of cancer. The Runaways were a huge influence on almost all hard-rocking female groups, such as Vixen who came later. Jett and Ford established that women could have successful solo careers in hard rock and heavy metal.

Discography: *The Runaways* (Mercury, 1976; Cherry Red, 2003); *Queens of Noise* (Mercury, 1977; Cherry Red, 2003); *Live in Japan* (Mercury, 1977; Cherry Red, 2004); *Waitin' for the Night* (Mercury, 1977; Cherry Red, 2004); *And Now ... the Runaways* (Cherry Red, 1979; Cherry Red, 1999); *Flaming Schoolgirls* (Cherry Red, 1980; Cherry Red, 2004); *Little Lost Girls* (Rhino, 1981; Rhino, 1990); *The Best of the Runaways* (Mercury, 1982; Mercury/Universal, 2005); *I Love Playing with Fire* (Laker/Cherry Red, 1982); *Born to Be Bad* (Marilyn Records, 1991).

RUNNING WILD (1984–PRESENT). Rolf Kasparak (vocals/guitar), Peter Jordan (guitar), Peter Pichl (bass), Matthias "Metalmachine" Liebetruth (drums).

Originally from Hamburg, Germany, the speed metal group Running Wild has had a long, if moderately successful, career. Releasing their first album, *Gates of Purgatory,* in 1984, the band successfully adopted a heavy metal pirate image on release of their third album, *Under Jolly Roger,* in 1987. The band has stayed active to the present day with a variety of lineups under the leadership of longtime guitarist/vocalist Rolf Kasparak.

Discography: *Gates of Purgatory* (Noise, 1984); *Branded and Exiled* (Noise, 1985); *Under Jolly Roger* (Noise, 1987); *Port Royal* (Noise, 1988); *Ready for Boarding* [live] (Noise, 1988); *Death or Glory* (Noise, 1989); *Blazon Stone* (Noise, 1991); *Pile of Skulls* (Noise, 1992); *Black Hand Inn* (Noise, 1994); *Masquerade* (Noise, 1995); *The Rivalry* (Ariola, 1998); *Victory* (Pavement, 2000); *The Brotherhood* (BMG/Gun, 2002); *Live* (GUN, 2002); *Rogues en Vogue* (Gun, 2005); *Legendary Tales* (Drakkar, 2006); *The Brotherhood: Live* (Drakkar, 2006).

RUSH (1974–PRESENT). Alex Lifeson (guitar), Geddy Lee (bass/lead vocals), Neil Peart (drums, replaced John Rutsey in 1974).

Starting off as a howling Led Zeppelin-influenced blues-based hard rock group, Canadian power trio Rush would go on to evolve into one of the most influential progressive-leaning rock groups, especially to progressive metal groups, and in constantly pushing their own limits have demonstrated the outer limits of the three-piece format. While they have rarely topped the charts, their instrumentally demanding music, with philosophical lyrics by Peart, have won them a large and loyal following, and one of the most enduring careers in rock.

Formed in 1968 in Toronto, Ontario, the band featured bassist and lead vocalist Geddy Lee (originally Gary Lee Weinrib), guitarist Alex Lifeson (originally Alexander Zivojinovich), and drummer John Rutsey. The band originally was heavily influenced by the bluesrock of the day, as played by Cream and Led Zeppelin. After playing the Toronto club scene, the band released a single of Buddy Holly's "Not Fade Away" backed with their first original "You Can't Fight It" in 1973. In 1974, Rush released their debut self-titled album on their own Moon records. *Rush* featured the band playing blues-based hard rock. Tunes like "Working Man" and "In the Mood" were clearly Led Zeppelin-influenced with Lee's high-pitched vocals emulating Robert Plant, and Lifeson's crunching guitars giving Jimmy Page's a run for their money. Although the album only did well locally, "Working Man" eventually became a favorite with a DJ in Cleveland, Ohio, and began to catch on, gaining the attention of Mercury Records, who rereleased the album in the States. Shortly afterward, Rutsey, who suffered from diabetes, decided to leave the band due to concerns about his ability to tour with his disease. Drummer Neil Peart was chosen as his replacement after a series of auditions.

Rutsey had been the band's primary lyricist, and Peart took on that role with the band as well, bringing to bear his highly intelligent and well-read sensibility as well as an interest in science fiction and fantasy that would make its way into the band's songs. The band's first album with the new lineup was *Fly by Night* (1975), which began to introduce a progressive rock influence into Rush's sound, in particular on the cut "By-Tor and the Snow Dog." *Caress of Steel* later that year did as well, and saw the band delve into more storytelling lyrics. In 1976 the band released the concept album *2112*, which dealt with a futuristic dystopian society, and was influenced by the writings of Ayn Rand. The album featured much more of their progressive rock influences, including much longer tracks and much more instrumental complexity from the band. *2112* was their breakthrough release and was highly popular with fans and earned the band their first gold record. It was also largely unappreciated by the critics.

The tour for *2112* culminated in a three-night stand at Toronto's Massey Hall, which was recorded for the band's live album *All the World's a Stage*, released later in 1976. The album marked the end of an era and heralded a new one to come for the band. Feeling that they had taken their sound as far as they could, they considered adding a fourth member, but ultimately decided to expand their repertoire as a three-piece. Consequently, Lee added synthesizers to his duties, and both he and Lifeson began to master bass pedals which allowed them to play bass while otherwise playing synths or guitars. They also incorporated double-neck guitars, with Lifeson exploiting the possibilities of the 12-string and classical guitar, as well as utilizing the unique sounds of the chorus pedal, an effect that had just recently been invented. For his part, Peart expanded his drum kit, incorporating a wider array of percussion instruments into his sound.

The first album to feature the band's expanded Palette was 1977's *A Farewell to Kings*, which was the band's most progressive rock-sounding album to date, and which featured the band's classic track "Closer to the Heart." The track showcased the band's new sound, starting with quiet acoustic guitar work and gradually building in layers as the band built up the song. The album was a success, and consolidated the band's reputation as a creatively ambitious outfit whose playing and songwriting were constantly growing.

Hemispheres, in 1978, continued the band's evolution, and was the band's most realized album yet, featuring the classic tracks "The Trees" and the instrumental "La Villa Strangiato." The band's next effort, 1980's *Permanent Waves*, became their next breakthrough album and saw them taking their mature sound into shorter, more concise compositions, which led to the band's first hit single in "The Spirit of Radio," which deftly blended their sophisticated sound and lyrics with the harder rock of their past. 1981's *Moving Pictures* was even more successful, with the band scoring two radio hits, "Tom Sawyer" and "Limelight." *Moving Pictures* began a series of successful albums for the band that would also involve a number of hit singles as well, and the band continued to grow their fan base on the basis of their tight live performances, which rivaled the precision of their studio recordings.

While Rush's sound got somewhat slicker through the late eighties, as on *Hold Your Fire* (1987) and *Presto* (1989), by the time of 1991's *Roll the Bones*, the band had returned to a heavier, more guitar-oriented approach, and both it and its follow-up, *Counterparts* (1993), had made the top of the U.S. album charts.

Toward the end of the nineties, the band, and Peart in particular, suffered a series of tragedies, first with the death of Peart's daughter Selena in an automobile accident in 1997, and then the passing of his wife, Jacqueline, from cancer in 1998. The band would be on hiatus for five years as Peart dealt with his losses. Peart would go on to travel on his motorcycle as part of his mourning, covering more than 55,000 miles as he crossed North America, later chronicling his experience in the book *Ghost Rider: Travels on the Healing Road* (ECW Press, 2002).

In 2002, Peart returned to the band as they released *Vapor Trails*, their 17th album together. 2004 saw the band celebrate their 30th anniversary with a tour. And in 2007 they released *Snakes and Arrows*, which was produced by Foo Fighters producer Nick Raskulinecz. *Snakes & Arrows Live* followed in 2008.

Discography: *Rush* (Mercury, 1974); *Fly by Night* (Mercury, 1975); *Caress of Steel* (Mercury, 1975); *2112* (Mercury, 1976); *All the World's a Stage* [live] (Mercury, 1976); *A Farewell to Kings* (Mercury, 1977); *Hemispheres* (Mercury, 1978); *Permanent Waves* (Mercury, 1980); *Moving Pictures* (Mercury, 1981); *Exit ... Stage Left* [live] (Mercury, 1981); *Signals* (Mercury, 1982); *Grace Under Pressure* (Mercury, 1984); *Power Windows* (Mercury, 1985); *Hold Your Fire* (Mercury, 1987); *A Show of Hands* [live] (Mercury, 1989); *Presto* (Atlantic, 1989); *Roll the Bones* (Atlantic, 1991); *Counterparts* (Atlantic, 1993); *Test for Echo* (Atlantic, 1996); *Vapor Trails* (Anthem/Atlantic, 2002); *Rush in Rio* [live] (Anthem/Atlantic, 2003); *Snakes & Arrows* (Atlantic, 2007); *Snakes & Arrows Live* (Atlantic/WEA, 2008); *Archives* (Mercury, 1978); *Rush Through Time* (Mercury, 1980); *Chronicles* (Mercury, 1990); *Retrospective, Vol. 1 (1974–1980)* (Mercury, 1997); *Retrospective, Vol. 2 (1981–1987)* (Mercury, 1997); *Different Stages: Live* (Atlantic/Anthem, 1998); *The Spirit of Radio: Greatest Hits 1974–1987* (Universal, 2003).

S

SACRED REICH (1986–99). Phil Rind (vocals/bass), Wiley Arnett (guitar), Jason Rainey (guitar), Dave McClain (drums, then Greg Hall).

Sacred Reich was a thrash metal band with punk leanings that played primarily during the mid-eighties and released the classic *Surf Nicaragua* record among others, before calling it quits in 1999. Much like the Crumbsuckers, DRI, and Corrosion of Conformity, Sacred Reich helped pioneer the punk/metal crossover style that helped metal evolve and grow even harder and were one of the more politically active of the crossover bands, as epitomized on the anti-Republican *Surf Nicaragua* record. The band reunited for several shows in 2007, but it is unclear if the tour will continue or will lead to any new music.

Discography: *Ignorance* (Hollywood, 1987); *Surf Nicaragua* (Hollywood, 1988); *American Way* (Hollywood, 1990); *A Question* (Hollywood, 1991); *Independent* (Hollywood, 1991); *Heal* (Metal Blade, 1996); *Still Ignorant Live* (Metal Blade, 1997).

SAIGON KICK (1988–97). Matt Kramer (vocals), Jason Bieler (guitar/vocals), Tom Defile (bass), Phil Varone (drums).

Initially a hard rock outfit out of Miami, Saigon Kick was formed in 1988 by lead vocalist Matt Kramer, guitarist Jason Bieler, bassist Tom Defile, and drummer Phil Varone. The band signed with Atlantic subsidiary Third Stone Records in 1990 after gigging around the southeast and released their self-titled first album that same year. A breakthrough of sorts occurred in 1992 with the hit single "Love Is on the Way," off of their second album, *The Lizard*. When vocalist Kramer and bassist Defile left shortly afterward, the band welcomed Chris McLernon on bass, and guitarist Bieler took over lead vocals for the band. The subsequent release, *Water* in 1993, was a commercial disappointment, and the band was dropped by their label. By 1997 the band had officially called it quits.

Discography: *Saigon Kick* (Third Stone, 1990); *The Lizard* (Third Stone, 1992); *Water* (Atlantic, 1993); *Devil in the Details* (CMC International, 1995); *Moments from the Fringe* (Ranch Life, 1998); *Bastards* (Pony Canyon, 1999).

SAMSON (1977–2002). Paul Samson (guitar), Bruce Dickinson (vocals), Barry Graham, aka "Thunderstick" (drums), Chris Aylmer (bass).

Best known as the band that Bruce Dickinson was in immediately before joining Iron Maiden, Samson was one of the initial bands of the New Wave of heavy metal, putting out a string of solid albums from 1979 through the 1980s.

Formed in 1977 by guitarist Paul Samson, the best-known lineup contained vocalist Dickinson (then going by the handle "Bruce Bruce"), bassist Chris Aylmer, and their drummer Barry Graham, who went by the name "Thunderstick," and who played up his wild-man image to such an extent that he appeared onstage wearing a leather S&M-style mask and performing inside of a metal cage. Releasing their first album, *Survivors*, in 1979 (with Samson singing lead as well as playing guitar), the band hit their peak when Dickinson joined the band and they released two albums, 1980's *Head On* and 1981's *Samson*, with him before he left to join Iron Maiden. The band would continue to record and tour sporadically, until Paul Samson's death from cancer on August 9, 2002.

Discography: *Survivors* (Sanctuary, 1979); *Head On* (Repertoire, 1980); *Samson* (Gem, 1981); *Shock Tactics* (Grand Slamm, 1981); *Before the Storm* (Polydor, 1982); *Don't Get Mad Get Even* (Polydor, 1984); *Last Rites* (Thunderbolt, 1984); *Head Tactics* (Capitol, 1986); *Refugee* (Maze/Kraze, 1990); *Live at Reading '81* (Grand Slamm, 1991); *1993* (Thunderbolt, 1996); *Thank You & Goodnight* [live] (Magnum America, 1996); *Joint Forces* (Magnum America, 1996); *Test of Time* (Delta, 1999); *Live in London 2000* (Zoom Club/Windsor, 2001); *Tomorrow and Yesterday* (Angel Air, 2006); *N.W.O.B.H.M. Rarities, Vol. 2* (Cherry Red, 1996); *Riding with the Angels: The Anthology* (Castle, 2002); *BBC Sessions* (High Voltage, 2005).

SARCÓFAGO. Antichrist (vocals), Fabio Jhasko (guitar), Zeber (guitar), Gerald Minelli (bass), Eduardo (drums, later Joker, then Lucio Olliver).

Sarcófago (translated into English as sarcophagus) were a Brazilian black metal band that primarily played during the late eighties and early nineties. At a time when many Brazilian bands were becoming more political in response to the military junta that ruled the country at the time, Sarcófago went in a darker and more ominous direction, combining punk and black metal. Their sound owed as much to later hardcore as well as black metal, despite their dark and anti-Christian imagery. The band was led by guitarist and vocalist Antichrist (Wagner Lamounier), who had been acrimoniously booted from an earlier version of Sepultura. Sarcófago were relentless in their pursuit of the evilest-sounding music, succeeding particularly well on the brutal *The Laws of Scourge* album in 1991. Sadly, Sarcófago never did get as big as Sepultura, or even Soulfly, possibly due to the relative inaccessibility of their music and the band's refusal to make their lyrical content any less blasphemous. The band sputtered out at the end of the nineties, and it is unclear if there will be any new music from Sarcófago. The band proved that black metal was not bound by geography, but could pop up across the world, not just in the colder climates, but everywhere were kids looked for the darkest of musical extremes.

Discography: *Rotting* (Maze/Kraze, 1989); *The Laws of Scourge* (Cogumelo, 1991); *I.N.R.I.* (Pavement, 1999); *Hate* (Cogumelo, 2005).

SATAN (1979–87). Trevor Robinson (vocals, replaced by Ian Swift, Lou Taylor, then Michael Jackson), Steve Ramsey (guitar), Russ Tippins (guitar), Graeme English (bass), Andey Reed (drums, replaced by Sean Taylor).

Satan were a British New Wave of heavy metal band, who eventually evolved into the band Pariah and also had connections to the classic NWOHM band, not to be confused with the object of worship for many in the black metal scene. The band had a hard time keeping a consistent vocalist; at one of the most confusing twists in the Spinal Tap-esque world of metal, the band changed its name to Blind Fury, the band formerly led by then-current Satan vocalist Lou Taylor, for the *Out of Reach* record, after which the band changed its name back to Satan and dismissed vocalist Taylor. After several records, the band essentially changed its name to the more commercial-sounding Pariah and released *The Kindred*, a classic thrash album, before dissolving after their second record. Although the original Satan lineup has been rumored to be reforming for various festivals, at this date the band remains dormant, and a legend in the British New Wave of heavy metal scene.

Discography: *Court in the Act* (Metal Blade, 1983); *Suspended Sentence*, (Steamhammer, 1987); *Live in the Act* (Metal Nation, 2004); *Blind Fury Out of Reach* (Roadrunner, 1985).

SATANICIDE (1999–PRESENT). Devlin Mayhem (vocals), Aleister Cradley (guitar), Vargas Von Goaten (bass), Sloth Vader (drums).

Satanicide are a mock heavy metal band who play with all of the fervor and energy one would expect from a New Jersey metal band circa the mid-eighties, which is exactly the sound and attitude that Satanicide mock so well. The band is adept at mixing and parodying different styles of metal, from hair metal to power ballads, including a rambunctious metal take on Celine Dion's "My Heart Will Go On," the theme from the movie *Titanic*, to the occult leaning of metal in songs such as "Twenty Sided Die," which directly riffs on the popular game Dungeons and Dragons. The band is led by the falsetto screeching of lead singer Devlin Mayhem, who aptly parodies the quintessential rock and roll frontman shtick (shirt open to the waist, leading sing-along with the audience) aided and abetted by guitarist Aleister Cradley, who channels the decadence and sexual ambiguity of classic glam; bassist Vargas von Goaten, a parody send-up of the black and death metal adherents of Norway, and drummer Sloth Vader, who channels Tommy Lee to perfection. The most fascinating thing about Satanicide is not only that they channel a Jersey bar band so well, but that they also do it while playing engaging and hard music, with lyrics that predictably leave nothing to the imagination (a typical example, the chorus of the song "Heather" indicates that Mayhem wants to "get into your leather") Their CD is well worth finding, and if one is nostalgic for long bass solos, lyrics straight from the mind of a thirteen-year-old dungeon master with sex on his mind, or at least an excellent parody of a now-gone genre, then Satanicide is a must buy.

Discography: *Satanicide: Heather* (Enabler Records, 2003).

SATANIC ROCK. Satanic Rock is a slang term sometimes used by critics of rock and heavy metal who critique the music for its supposed or, in the case of black metal, deliberate use of lyrical themes related to Satan and devil worship. While bands that actually feature such themes in their music generally embrace the term *black metal*, the term *Satanic rock* has generally functioned as a label that has been hastily affixed to a variety of rock acts whose actions, appearance, or lyrics were deemed evil or "Satanic" by their often Christian critics. Often such claims of Satanism stemmed from a misunderstanding of black metal's obsession with Satanic imagery in lyrics, or from more mainstream bands' playful uses of such imagery in lyrics or visual design.

The term started to be used in the seventies when rumors abounded that the band Kiss's name actually was short for "Knights in Satan's Service," a claim which was never substantiated (and an odd claim at that as others might say that the only god that Kiss actually worship is money). Critics argue that the term itself both trivializes the many bands that have an interest in Satanism as a moral and political philosophy and over-emphasizes the many cartoonish uses of Satanic imagery and lyrics in metal songs. Despite the alarmism of groups such as the PMRC and other critics, there has never been a direct connection made between Satanic metal and antisocial behavior, and all of the brouhaha seems to have been much ado about nothing.

JOE SATRIANI (1956–). Among the key metal guitar heroes and virtuosos who usually shun playing with egotistical frontmen, Satriani is a rare example of a guitar innovator of the eighties and nineties who still maintains his relevance to the present day. Satriani started as a sideman, playing with Mick Jagger and Deep Purple before starting off on his own, and quickly became a solo artist, specializing in dynamic and fluid solos that are more artistic than merely musical wanking. Most of his followers would point to the *Surfing with the Alien* album as the most essential of all his works, but others are fond of his work with G3 along with guitarists Steve Vai and a rotating third guitarist. Satriani is a guitarist's guitarist and many believe that there is no point in trying to explain how he sounds in print, suggesting that those interested go and listen to his records.

Discography: *Not of This Earth* (Food For Thought, 1986); *Surfing with the Alien* (Food For Thought, 1987); *Dreaming 11* [EP] (Food For Thought, 1988); *Flying in a Blue Dream* (Food For Thought, 1989); *The Extremist* (Epic, 1992); *Time Machine* (Epic, 1993); *Joe Satriani* [EP] (Epic, 1995); *G3 Live in Concert* [with Steve Vai and Eric Johnson] (Epic, 1997); *Crystal Planet* (Epic, 1998); *Engines of Creation* (Epic, 2000); *Live in San Francisco* (Epic, 2001); *Strange Beautiful Music* (Epic, 2002); *G3 Live: Rocking the Free World* (Epic, 2004); *Is There Love in Space?* (Epic, 2004); *G3: Live in Tokyo* (Epic, 2005); *One Big Rush—The Genius of Joe Satriani* (CMG, 2005); *Super Colossal* (Epic, 2006); *And Satriani Live!* (Red Ink, 2006); *Professor Satchafunkilus and the Musterion of Rock* (Epic/Red, 2008).

SAVATAGE (1983–PRESENT). Jon Oliva (vocals, piano), Criss Oliva (guitar), Steve "Doc" Wacholz (drums), Keith Collins (bass).

Savatage was formed by brothers Jon and Criss Oliva, vocals and guitar, respectively, in Florida, in the late seventies (when they were called Avatar). Along with drummer Steve "Doc" Wacholz and bassist Keith Collins, the band initially played a classic style of metal akin to Judas Priest or Iron Maiden. Eventually, however, they moved to include symphonic elements into their sound as a result of Jon's viewing of the musical *Phantom of the Opera*, and through working with producer Paul O'Neil, who encouraged the development. The 1989 album, *Gutter Ballet*, was the first to feature the band's new style, which was at times operatic (as on the title track) as well as symphonic, incorporating piano and featuring tightly arranged guitar parts that functioned with the dynamism of classical strings. The band next tried their hand at a rock opera, *Streets*, in 1991. A critical and artistic success, the album coincided with the emergence of grunge and had a hard time finding an audience, though a core of hardcore fans continued to grow and support the band.

Tragedy struck in 1993 when Criss Oliva was hit and killed by a drunk driver. The band carried on in time, initially hiring Alex Skolnick, originally of Testament. Further lineup changes occurred through the nineties, but when Jon and producer O'Neil found surprising success with their side project, the Trans-Siberian Orchestra, Savatage was placed on indefinite hiatus.

Discography: *Sirens* (Combat, 1983); *Dungeons Are Calling* (Combat, 1985); *Power of the Night* (Atlantic, 1985); *Fight for the Rock* (Atlantic, 1986); *Hall of the Mountain King* (Victor, 1987); *Gutter Ballet* (Atlantic, 1989); *Streets: A Rock Opera* (Atlantic, 1991); *Edge of Thorns* (Atlantic, 1993); *Handful of Rain* (Atlantic, 1994); *Dead Winter Dead* (Atlantic, 1995); *The Wake of Magellan* (Atlantic, 1998); *Final Bell* (Nuclear Blast, 1999); *Japan Live '94* (SPV, 2000); *Ghost in the Ruins* (Import, 2000); *Poets & Madmen* (Nuclear Blast, 2001); *From the Gutter to the Stage: Best of Savatage* (Import, 2000).

SCATTERBRAIN. Tommy Christ (vocals) Glen Cumming (guitar), Paul Neider (guitar), Guy Brogna (bass), Mike Boyko (drums).

Scatterbrain were a goofy metal act featuring ex-members of the punk/metal band Ludichrist. The band incorporated funk and rapping into their music and had a minor hit with the song "Don't Call me Dude." The band played mostly jokey but complex punk-tinged metal and their slick-yet-vibrant production, as well as the clever musical in-jokes of "Down with the Ship (Slight Return)," made the first record a pleasure. The next two records were more of the same to a smaller audience, and the band went on hiatus in 1994.

Discography: *Here Comes Trouble* (Combat, 1990); *Scamboogery* (Elektra, 1991); *Mundus Intelectualis* (Pavement, 1994).

SCORPIONS (1972–PRESENT). Classic lineup: Klaus Meine (vocals), Rudolph Schenker (guitar), Matthias Jabs (lead guitar), Francis Buchholz (bass), Herman Rarebell (drums, replaced by James Kottak).

With a history that goes back to the early seventies, the Scorpions are best known for breaking into worldwide success in the 1980s with their song "Rock You Like a Hurricane," which led to a string of classic hard rock hits for the band. Along the way, they launched the careers of Uli Jon Roth and Michael Schenker and became Germany's most successful rock band. While not as evident in their mainstream hits, their album track lyrics are often uniquely flavored with an offbeat, sometimes bizarre sense of humor. And in vocalist Klause Meine the Scorpions have perhaps the best and most unique of all hard rock vocalists, whose extended vocal range and distinct tone combine with his tongue-and-cheek delivery to make him a virtuoso of the microphone.

After the band's first album, *Lonesome Crow*, was released in 1972, lead guitarist Michael Schenker was drafted into the British band UFO, and Uli Jon Roth joined the band, leading them into a harder rock direction. (It should be noted here that Roth's fluid, melodic, virtuosic lead style is without a doubt a missing link between more old-school players like Ritchie Blackmore and Eric Clapton and the newer school of faster players like Eddie Van Halen and Yngwie Malmsteen who emerged in the later seventies and eighties, and was most certainly heard by, if not acknowledged by, these later players.) This version of the band released a string of albums for RCA—*Fly to the Rainbow* (1974), *In Trance* (1975), *Virgin Killer* (1976), and *Taken by Force* (1977)—over the course of which the Scorpions honed a precise and high-energy style, that while not particularly commercial was melodic and unique. Finding a ready audience in Japan as well as in Europe, the band released the live *Tokyo Tapes* in 1978, after which Roth left to pursue other musical interests, forming the band Electric Sun, which incorporated Hendrix influences.

As Michael Schenker had recently left UFO, the band welcomed him back and began recording the classic *Lovedrive* album that would move them into a somewhat more commercial direction. Released on their new label Mercury, the album featured the title track and the classic "Loving You Sunday Morning." While there were no singles that charted, the album did begin to attract American fans who found the band's new approach to be both heavier and more melodically interesting than that found on the band's previous albums. Unfortunately, the album was actually banned for a period due to its risqué artwork depicting a glamorous couple in the back of a limousine, the man removing a wad of bubble gum from the woman's breast.

After touring with the group in the U.S., Michael Schenker once again left the band, and guitarist Mattias Jabs, with whom the band had been working before Schenker's return, joined the band to replace him. With Jabs on board, the band's classic lineup of Jabs, Klaus Meine (vocals), Rudolph Schenker (guitar), Francis Buchholz (bass), and Herman Rarebell (drums) was in place.

Animal Magnetism, released in 1980, fared better in the States, going gold, and the band supported it with a world tour. After a delay during which singer Klaus Meine underwent surgery for problems with his vocal cords, the band returned with the 1982 album *Blackout*, which would prove to be their commercial breakthrough. Featuring the single "There's No One Like You," the album was a worldwide smash, going platinum in the U.S. *Love at First Sting* in 1984 was an even bigger hit for the band, which with the help of the single and video "Rock You Like a Hurricane" sold two million copies in the U.S.

With a combination of well-crafted rockers and power ballads, the band continued a string of successful releases through 1990's "Crazy World," after which the band lost much of its momentum. Due in part to a style that had become somewhat tired in its commercial orientation and to the fact that musical styles were changing, the band's successes became much more modest.

With a few lineup changes in the rhythm section, the band continues to tour and record, most recently releasing *Unbreakable* in 2004.

Discography: *Lonesome Crow* (Rhino, 1972); *Fly to the Rainbow* (RCA, 1974); *In Trance* (RCA, 1975); *Virgin Killer* (RCA, 1976); *Taken by Force* (RCA, 1978); *Tokyo Tapes* (RCA, 1978); *Lovedrive* (Mercury, 1979); *Animal Magnetism* (Mercury, 1980); *Rock Galaxy* (RCA, 1980); *Blackout* (Mercury, 1982); *Love at First Sting* (Mercury, 1984); *World Wide Live* (Mercury, 1985); *Savage Amusement* (Mercury, 1988); *Crazy World* (Mercury, 1990); *Face the Heat* (Mercury, 1993); *Deadly Sins* (EMI, 1995); *Pure Instinct* (Atlantic, 1996); *Eye II Eye* (Wea International, 1999); *Moment of Glory* (EMI, 2000); *Acoustica* [live] (Wea International, 2001); *Unbreakable* (BMG International, 2004); *Humanity Hour, Vol. 1* (Sony BMG, 2007); *The Hot & Slow: The Best Ballads* (RCA, 1991); *Hot & Heavy* (RCA, 1993); *20th Century Masters—The Millennium Collection: The Best of Scorpions* (Mercury, 2001); *Platinum Collection* [Box Set] (EMI, 2006); *No. 1's* (EMI, 2006); *Best of Scorpions: Green Series* (Universal Int'l, 2008).

SEPULTURA (1984–PRESENT). Wagner Lamounier (vocals, replaced by Max Cavalera), Max Cavalera (guitar), Jairo Guides (guitar, replaced by Andreas Kisser), Paolo Jr. (bass), Igor Cavalera (drums).

When metal historians talk about the "big four" thrash metal bands (Anthrax, Slayer, Metallica, and Megadeth), some change it to the "big five" including the Brazilian band Sepultura as well. Formed in Brazil in 1984, an early lineup contained vocalist Wagner Lamounier, who later went on to front black metal titans Sarcófago. When Lamounier left, Cavalera took up vocals as well as guitar and Sepultura was born. The first album was the classic *Morbid Visions*, which established them as one of the foremost thrash bands on any continent, as well as an early band in the death metal vein. With the releases of *Beneath the Remains* and *Arise*, Sepultura gained a considerable American following, perhaps culminating in the classic *Roots* album, which saw them mixing thrash and death metal with traditional Brazilian instruments. However, following the record, Max Cavalera reportedly quit the band after an argument over management (his wife had been managing the band). Cavalera later went on to from the more commercially oriented band Soulfly, and Sepultura continued with new singer Derrick Green, but the magic wasn't there, and sales dropped. With Soulfly and Sepultura still both touring, a reunion may be unlikely, but Igor Cavalera has joined Soulfly on stage for some Sepultura songs in recent years, so a full-scale reunion of the "classic" Sepultura lineup may be possible at some point.

Discography: *Morbid Visions* (Roadrunner, 1986); *Schizophrenia* (Roadrunner, 1987); *Beneath the Remains* (Roadrunner, 1989); *Arise* (Roadrunner, 1991); *Chaos A.D.* (Roadrunner, 1993); *Roots* (Roadrunner, 1996); *Against* (Roadrunner, 1998); *Nation* (Roadrunner, 2001); *Under a Pale Gray Sky* [live] (Roadrunner, 2002); *Revolusongs* (Japanese Import, 2003); *Roorback* (Steamhammer, 2003); *Live in Sao Paulo* (Steamhammer, 2005); *Dante XXI* (Steamhammer, 2006); *No Coracao dos Deuses* (Mascto, 2006).

SHOCK ROCK. Shock rock is a term applied to members of the metal scene, although it was also used in punk rock, to refer to bands that seemed less about musical talent than about simply raising eyebrows with outrageous behavior and tactics that are designed to upset the parents of the youth of America. Early on the term was applied to performers such as Alice Cooper, who pioneered the image and sound that many would identify with metal as the years went on. Cooper (although the band was originally called Alice Cooper, eventually lead singer Vincent Furnier took the name for his own stage name) staged mock executions, threw live chickens into the audience, and played with a large snake while singing about "loving the dead" and "welcome to my nightmare."

The idea of shock rock was perhaps deflated a little when Alice Cooper appeared on *The Muppet Show* in 1978, performing his hits "Welcome to My Nightmare" and "School's Out," all the while trying to buy the souls of the Muppets! (Although many acknowledged that it was a funny episode.)

Perhaps the term was best epitomized in the early eighties by the punk/metal band the Plasmatics—a group whose look and early music was decidedly influenced by punk, but by the early eighties had moved into a far more pedestrian metal sound. The Plasmatics, led by Wendy O. Williams, were more famous for such stunts as blowing up a car on stage, destroying a television set with a sledgehammer, or even blowing up a bus in a video as it went off a cliff, nearly taking lead singer Williams with it.

While many bands do deliberately work on shock during their stage shows—as an example, the band GWAR warns patrons who are sitting in the first few rows of their concert that they may be sprayed with various bodily fluids—the idea that a stage show can be shocking to the jaded metal audience seems almost passé. Even the animal corpses and real and fake blood that various death and black metal bands have used as stage props have been so done to death (so to speak) that they have lost any shock value and only seem shocking to the audience outside metal aficionados.

In some ways this may be a typical act of a subculture who do not want to cross over to mainstream success to make the music seem unmarketable, as the failure of various record labels to "break" death and black metal bands in the nineties probably demonstrated. Either way, the act of shocking the audience in metal is still a way to make metal seem less palatable for the wary, and therefore maintain its position as outsider music.

SHOTGUN MESSIAH (1988–93). Zinny J. San (vocals), Harry K. Cody (guitar), Tim Skold (bass), and Stixx Galore (drums).

One of the most talented bands to come out of Sweden in the eighties, Shotgun Messiah took their shot in the days of hair metal and couldn't quite get the break that they deserved.

Originally from Sweden, the band began as glam rockers King Pin, releasing the album *Welcome to Bob City*. The album was a success, and the band, consisting of vocalist Zinny J. San, guitarist Harry K. Cody, bassist Tim Skold, and drummer Stixx Galore, uprooted to L.A. to try their luck in the big leagues. Changing their name to Shotgun Messiah, the band put out an updated version of their debut, as *Shotgun Messiah* on Relativity Records in 1989. Featuring generally well-crafted, original-sounding pop metal, very tightly played, the album also served as a showcase for Cody's highly developed virtuosic guitar chops, which were as finely honed as any of his peers and served the music exceedingly well. The album also included an early rap-metal track, "Shout It Out," whose vocal delivery was reminiscent of the Beastie Boys.

With the album failing to make much impression in the U.S., Zin soon left the band, and the group soon reorganized around Skold as lead singer, with Bobby Lycon taking over bass duties. When 1991's *Second Coming* failed to generate much interest, Skold and Cody took the band into industrial metal, releasing *Violent New*

Breed in 1993. The album was a strong effort, but when it too failed commercially, the band officially called it a day. Skold continued to persevere in the industrial realm, however, releasing a solo album in 1996 before going on to work with industrial mainstays KMFDM and MDFMK, and later, Marilyn Manson.

Discography: *Shotgun Messiah* (Combat, 1989); *Second Coming* (Combat, 1991); *Violent New Breed* (Relativity, 1993); *I Want More* (Combat, 1993).

SIR LORD BALTIMORE (1970–73, 2006–PRESENT). Louis Dambra (guitar), Gary Justin (bass), John Garner (drums/vocals).

Sir Lord Baltimore were and are now a Brooklyn-based power trio and well-known as an early version of metal in the late sixties and early seventies. Louis Dambra on guitar and Gary Justin on bass saw an ad in *The Village Voice* looking for "heavy band to record album." The story is that the band was named after a minor character in the film *Butch Cassidy and the Sundance Kid*, which first started playing in theaters in 1970. Their first album was *Kingdome Come*, which helped establish the American heavy metal sound. Sir Lord Baltimore are also famous for being one of the earliest bands to be called "metal" by then-rock critic "Metal" Mike Saunders (later of the punk band Angry Samoans), who referred to the band as heavy metal in a review. Many others claim to have also coined the term (see the introduction for more theories on the origin of the term).

The band at its best was a stripped-down power trio who played a hard boogie-based bluesrock with unusual, almost jazz-like dexterity. The first two records are highly recommended. But the band never had much success and went on an indefinite hiatus that lasted thirty years, due to a lack of critical acclaim. In 2006 Sir Lord Baltimore returned with a new record featuring Dambra on guitar and John Garner on drums and vocals with session bassists Tony Franklin and Sam Powell. The new record is a good indication that although Dambra is now a pastor at a Christian church in Los Angeles working with the homeless, Sir Lord Baltimore had not lost its punch. The band was also praised for Garner's work on the drums in which he tried to make them a featured instrument in the band, and tried to emulate the sound of a guitar.

Discography: *Kingdom Come* (PolyGram, 1970); *Sir Lord Baltimore S/T* (PolyGram, 1971); *Sir Lord Baltimore III: Raw* (2006).

SKID ROW (1989–PRESENT). Sebastian Bach (vocals, replaced by Sean McCabe, Johnny Solinger), Dave "the Snake" Sabo (guitar), Scotti Hill (guitar), Rachel Bolan (bass), Rob Affuso (drums).

One of the more ubiquitous of the glam metal bans of the late eighties, Skid Row was as well known for singer Sebastian Bach's in-your-face presence (he once foolishly wore a T-shirt that said "AIDS Kills Fags Dead" during an interview) as for their catchy pop metal. The band started strong with their first album, *Skid Row*, which contained the popular singles "18 and Life" and "Youth Gone Wild," which quickly established them as one of the top hair/glam/pop metal bands.

They followed up with the equally successful and somewhat harder record *Slave to the Grind*, which debuted at number 1 and would have seemed to cement the band's position as one of the kings of the metal world, but things were not to work out that way. A quantum shift in music took place the next year when the grunge revolution made most metal bands seem redundant and insignificant. Skid Row plowed on with determination, and, although they still sold records, by the time of the *Subhuman Race* album the formula had worn thin and soon Bach was ousted from the band, which soldiered on without him. Bach eventually did the reality show circuit on VH1 and also played some roles on Broadway, where his theatrical voice no doubt came in handy.

Discography: *Skid Row* (Atlantic, 1989); *Slave to the Grind* (Atlantic, 1991); *Subhuman Race* (Atlantic, 1995); *Thick Skin* (Blind Man Sound, 2003); *Revolutions Per Minute* (SPV, 2006).

SLAUGHTER (1988–PRESENT). Mark Slaughter (vocals), Dana Strum (bass), Tim Kelly (guitar, 1988–98), Blas Elias (drums), Jeff Blando (guitar, 1999–present).

Slaughter got their start in 1988 with a lineup of former Vinnie Vincent Invasion vocalist Mark Slaughter, bassist/talent scout Dana Strum (Strum was responsible for introducing Ozzy Osbourne to both Randy Rhoads and Jake E. Lee), guitarist Tim Kelly, and drummer Blas Elias. Hitting the pop metal wave with their 1990 debut *Stick It to Ya*, the album was a hit thanks to the Kiss-like anthemic rocker "Up All Night (Sleep All Day)" and the power ballad "Fly to the Angels." The album would go on to sell more than two million copies.

1992's *The Wild Life* was a similar, if somewhat more modest, success, after which the turn to alternative music had pretty much put an end to the pop metal phenomenon. Subsequently, the band signed with the smaller CMC International label, and put out a handful of other releases through the rest of the nineties.

In February 1998, guitarist Tim Kelly was tragically killed in an automobile accident. His final work would appear on 1999's *Eternal Live*. Guitarist Jeff Blando joined the band that year for the studio album *Back to Reality*. The band has been fairly quiet since then, although they have recently begun to tour occasionally, most notably on the Rock Never Stops tour, which features other hard rock bands from the eighties.

Discography: *Stick It Live* (Chrysalis, 1990); *Stick It to Ya* (Chrysalis, 1990); *The Wild Life* (Chrysalis, 1992); *Fear No Evil* (CMC International, 1995); *Revolution* (CMC International, 1997); *Eternal Live* (CMC International, 1998); *Back to Reality* (CMC International, 1999); *Surrender or Die* (Utopian Vision, 2000); *Mass Slaughter: The Best of Slaughter* (Capitol, 1995); *The Best of Slaughter* (Capitol, 2006).

SLAYER (1981–PRESENT). Tom Araya (vocals/bass), Kerry King (guitar), Jeff Hanneman (guitar), Dave Lombardo (drums, replaced by Paul Bostaph, John Dette, Lombardo again).

Slayer are one of the key bands of the thrash metal scene and have been considered by some critics to be categorized in either the black or death metal scenes as well. Slayer are certainly one of the more ferocious and dark bands of the eighties and their music's obsession with death, darkness, the satanic, and evil made them both a lightning rod for controversy and one of the most popular metal bands of the last three decades.

Kerry King of Slayer shreds onstage at Ozzfest in 2002. (Brian Rasic/Rex Features)

The band started in the early eighties and quickly established themselves as one of the most macabre metal bands around with their first two records, *Show No Mercy* and the even darker *Haunting the Chapel*, in which they established new standards for American crossover metal with punk influences and an obsession with the occult. The third record, *Hell Awaits*, was among the most brutal albums recorded at that time, and the band's recording of "Necrophiliac," about sex with the dead, was a bloody proto-death metal song (arguably, Slayer could be classified as both death and black metal).

The original classic Slayer lineup of guitarist Kerry King, bassist and singer Tom Araya, guitarist Jeff Hanneman, and drummer Dave Lombardo were among the fastest and most punk-influenced of all the thrash metal titans. Their records were alternately brutal and uncompromising, especially *Haunting the Chapel* and *Reign in Blood*, which may contain the most brutal songs in metal history. Chuck Klosterman, the rock critic and metal expert, recalls watching a Slayer show when the band played "Reign in Blood" and a member of the crowd inexplicably punched someone next to him, overcome by the sheer brutality of the music.

Slayer slowed down slightly in *South of Heaven*, which was a worthy successor to the first few records, and soon saw mainstream success with the next few albums. Slayer also paid tribute to the punk bands that had inspired their early sound on the *Undisputed Attitude* album in 1996.

With the record industry declining in sales overall during the past decade, Slayer decided to ally themselves with the enemy (no, not Christianity) in 2006, when they announced a partnership with popular mall-punk and light-metal store Hot Topic. With the release of their *Christ Illusion* album in 2006, Slayer allowed the store to sell copies of the record, which landed on number 5 on the Billboard charts, largely due to Hot Topic's promotional pull and the band's in-store appearances in various malls.

Despite having to work harder to get the younger kids into the raw mayhem that is Slayer, the band also remained constantly on the road, introducing new, younger fans into some of the hardest and heaviest music possible.

Discography: *Show No Mercy* (Metal Blade, 1983); *Haunting the Chapel* (Metal Blade, 1984); *Hell Awaits* (Metal Blade, 1985); *Live Undead* (Metal Blade, 1985); *Reign in Blood* (Def Jam, 1986); *South of Heaven* (Def Jam, 1988); *Seasons in the Abyss* (Def American, 1990); *Live: Decade of Aggression* (Def American, 1991); *Divine Intervention* (American, 1994); *Undisputed Attitude* (American, 1996); *Diabolus in Musica* (American/Columbia, 1998); *God Hates Us All* (American, 2001); *Christ Illusion* (American, 2006).

SLEEP (1990–98). Justin Marler (guitar), Matt Pike (guitar), Al Cisneros (bass), Chris Hakius (drums).

Sleep were one of the quintessentially sludgy riff rock bands, often labeled under the stoner rock label. They pioneered a new sound for metal, bringing it back to its roots in Sabbath-era sludge with a passing nod to the Melvins and St. Vitus. The band started out as a quartet, but original guitarist Marler eventually left to become a monk, and the band continued as a three piece for the rest of their career.

The band signed to London Records with great expectations, but then delivered the promised record, *Dopesmoker*, as an hourlong complex epic about, well, smoking dope. The record company refused to release it, and the band reconfigured it as *Jerusalem*, where, as on *Dopesmoker*, the band played just one track, the title song (time 52:00), which seemed to seethe and move almost as though it were a metal symphony, albeit one that was entirely about pot. London once again refused to release the album and the band fell apart. A version of *Jerusalem* was eventually released by Music Cartel in 1999, and the eventual full version was released posthumously on the Tee Pee record label in 2003.

After the breakup of Sleep, guitarist Matt Pike went on to put together High on Fire, while bassist and drummer Chris Hakius and Al Cisneros went on to the much more disturbing Om. Marler and Hakius also formed the more accessible the Sabians side project.

Discography: *Volume One* (Very Small, 1991); *Volume Two* (Off the Disk, 1992); *Sleep's Holy Mountain* (Earache, 1993); *Jerusalem* (Music Cartel, 1999); *Dopesmoker* (Tee Pee, 2003).

SLIPKNOT (1995–PRESENT). Corey Taylor (vocals), Mick Thomson (guitar), James Root (guitar), Paul Grey (bass), Joey Jordison (drums), Sid Wilson (DJ), Craig Jones (sampler), Shawn Crahan (percussion), Chris Fehn (percussion).

Slipknot are an American heavy metal band from Des Moines, Iowa, who had roots in grindcore but also were lumped into the nu metal scene of the mid-nineties. The band's gimmick was that no members were identified by name on stage and wore grotesque masks while playing live (and possibly in the studio, who knows?). This gave the band a sense of mystery. Their first album was probably the best as it harkened back more to their grindcore and death metal influences. Subsequent records start to veer into nu metal territory and are not nearly as adventurous as the early material.

Discography: *Mate Feed Kill, Repeat* (Ismist, 1996); *Slipknot* (Roadrunner, 1999); *Iowa* (Roadrunner, 2001); *Vol. 3: The Subliminal Verses* (Roadrunner, 2004); *9.0* [live] (Roadrunner, 2005); *Collector's Box* (Chrome Dreams, 2006).

SMOKEWAGON (2000–PRESENT). Kevin Omen (vocals/guitar), Pat Fondiller (bass), Jesse James (drums).

Smokewagon are a country metal band from Brooklyn, New York, who play a doom and gloom old-fashioned sludge meets Johnny Cash country. The band's first record, the self-titled *Smokewagon*, combined metal bombast with the best dirge rock of bands like Sleep and the Melvins, but the country tinges made the album stand out in a field already crowded with innovative new metal bands. The second record took things to a new level as drummer extraordinaire Jesse James, along with bassist Pat Fondiller, provided a sturdy bottom for lead singer/guitarist Kevin Omen's shrieks of despair. At times gloomy as all hell, Smokewagon proves that the anguished wails of underground country and the best of doom and stoner metal make a potent match. Bassist Fondiller also plays with Michael Gira (ex-Swans) in his Angels of Light project.

Discography: *Smokewagon* (Smokewagon, 2002); *Deuce* (Smokewagon, 2006).

ANDY SNEAP (1969–). One of the most important contemporary heavy metal record producers and mix engineers currently working, Andy Sneap got his start as a guitarist for British thrash metal band Sabbat in 1986 before moving into producing. Sneap is the owner of Backstage studios in the English countryside of Derbyshire outside of London. He has produced or mixed albums for Arch Enemy, Benediction, Exodus, Machine Head, Megadeth, Cradle of Filth, Killswitch Engage, Kreator, Opeth, and Testament, among others.

S.O.D. (1985, 1992, 1997–2002, 2007). Billy Milano (vocals), Scott Ian (guitar), Dan Lilker (bass), Charlie Benante (drums).

S.O.D., or Storm Troopers of Death, were a joke super group featuring Scott Ian on guitar and Charlie Benante on drums from Anthrax, as well as Dan Lilker on bass from Nuclear Assault and former Anthrax roadie Billy Milano on vocals. The group's typical song was often short and to the point (as in the "Ballad of Ronnie James Dio" and the "Ballad of Jimi Hendrix"), both of which clock in at well under a minute. S.O.D. proved to be surprisingly successful among both metal and punk fans, both of whom could find common ground in the band's relentless but jokey thrash attack.

The band recorded one album to some success, a follow-up live record, and a less successful follow-up in the late nineties. Milano continued in that vein with several records in his follow-up band M.O.D. that took the Storm Troopers of Death formula to its inevitable and ridiculous extreme. The *Live in Budokan* album, which *was* live but not recorded in Budokan, was a good showcase of the band's material, including a cover of Nirvana's "Territorial Pissings" that seemed more natural in S.O.D.'s hands than it did when Nirvana played it.

Discography: *Speak English or Die* (Megaforce, 1985); *Live at Budokan* (Megaforce, 1992); *Bigger than the Devil* (Nuclear Blast, 1999).

SODOM (1982–PRESENT). Angel Ripper (vocals/bass), Aggressor (guitar/vocals, replaced by Grave Violator, Destructor, then Blackfire, others, Bernemann), Witchhunter (drums/vocals, replaced by Atomic Steif, others, now Bobby Schottkowski).

Sodom are a German thrash band that heavily influenced the German black metal scene and are among the hardest-hitting bands in that genre. The band started in 1982 with original guitarist Aggressor, who left before recording the first album, the thrash classic *Obsessed by Cruelty*. Sodom could not maintain a stable lineup, going through constant guitar players, and finally even original drummer Witchfinder left the band, leaving Angel Ripper in complete control. Unfortunately, Destructor died in a motorcycle accident in 1995.

Discography: *Obsessed by Cruelty* (Steamhammer, 1986); *Persecution Mania* (Roadracer, 1987); *Agent Orange* (Roadracer, 1989); *Tapping the Vein* (Century Media, 1992); *Live at Zeche Bochum* (Steamhammer, 1994); *Masquerade in Blood* (SPV, 1995); *Till Death Do Us Unite* (Gun, 1997); *Better Off Dead* (SPV, 1997); *Get What You Deserve* (SPV, 1998); *In the Sign of Evil* (SPV, 1998); *Opening the Vein* (SPV, 1999); *Mortal Way of Live* (Roadrunner, 1999); *Code Red* (Pavement, 1999); *Marooned* [live] (Steamhammer, 2000); *M-16* (Steamhammer/SPV, 2001); *One Night in Bancock Live* (Steamhammer/SPV, 2003); *In the Sign of Evil* (Vinyl Maniacs, 2005); *Sodom* (Steamhammer/SPV, 2006); *Final Sign of Evil* (King Japan, 2006).

SOILENT GREEN (1988–PRESENT). Glenn Rambo (vocals, replaced by Ben Falgoust), Brian Patton (guitar), Donovan Punch (guitar, replaced by Ben Stout, Tony White, Gregg Harney, now vacant), Marcel (bass, replaced by Scott Williams, Scott Crochet), Tommy Buckley (drums).

Soilent Green is a sludgy grindcore band that is almost as famous for the tragedies that have surrounded them as their exceptional music. The band started in 1988 in a suburb of New Orleans and quickly established themselves as one of the finest and fastest grindcore bands in the United States. Although the band started in the eighties, they did not get to record their brutal attack on record until 1995, after changing vocalists. The band likes to joke that a black cloud hangs over them, and there may be something to what they say. In 2001 a significant van accident severely hurt Patton and Williams, and the band was barely back on the road before yet another van crash occurred in the spring of 2002, which injured Falgoust so badly that he was unable to walk for several months. In 2003 bassist

Scott Williams was killed by his roommate, and in 2005 former vocalist Glenn Rambo was killed in Hurricane Katrina. The band's tragedies inspired the concept record *Inevitable Collapse* about tragedy and the nature of life and resistance.

Discography: *Pussysould* (Dwell Records, 1995); *A String of Lies* (Relapse Records, 1998); *Sewn Mouth Secrets* (Relapse Records, 1998); *A Deleted Symphony for the Beaten Down* (Relapse Records, 2001); *Confrontation* (Relapse Records, 2005); *Inevitable Collapse in the Presence of Conviction* (Metal Blade Records, 2008).

SOULFLY (1996–PRESENT). Max Cavalera (vocals/guitar), Jackson Banderia (guitar, replaced by Mark Rizzo), Marcello Rapp (bass, replaced by Bobby Burns), Roy Mayorga (drums, replaced by Joe Nunez).

When Max Cavalera left Sepultura in 1996, it looked like both the end of his career and of the band he had founded. While Sepultura found considerable success without Cavalera, Cavalera also found new success and new purpose with his new band, Soulfly. In terms of a comparison with Sepultura, Soulfly is more of a combination of nu metal, extreme heavy thrash, reggae, gypsy music, and world music. The first record saw Soulfly take stumbling first steps, but by the time of the *Dark Ages* record, Cavalera was challenging Sepultura as the true master of dark thrash, although constant personnel changes have made it difficult for the band to have a cohesive lineup. For thrash fans, Soulfly is an essential addition to the thrash canon and a worthy successor to Cavalera's work in Sepultura. After making up with his brother Igor, Cavalera has also begun recording new material as a side project with his brother, called Cavalera Conspiracy.

Discography: *Soulfly* (Roadrunner, 1998); *Primitive* (Roadrunner, 2000); *III* (Roadrunner, 2002); *Prophecy* (Roadrunner, 2004); *Dark Ages* (Roadrunner, 2005); *Maximum Soulfly/ Sepultura* [split] (United States dist., 2006).

SOUNDGARDEN (1984–97). Chris Cornell (vocals), Kim Thayil (guitar), Hiro Yamamoto (bass, replaced by Ben Shepherd), Scott Sundquist (drums, replaced by Matt Cameron).

Soundgarden were a heavy/metal grunge band from Seattle and one of the most successful bands to emerge from the explosion of grunge in the early nineties. The band started out by pairing the two "black" bands together, adding elements of both Black Sabbath and Black Flag to a sound that became increasingly commercialized as time went on. Their success was largely due to both guitarist Kim Thayil's chops and the classic metal screeching voice of singer Chris Cornell. The band started out small, signed originally to Sub Pop, before Nirvana turned Sub Pop into a brand name for grunge. On that label they released two gloriously sludgy EPs, *Screaming Love* and *FOPP*, before they moved to indie legend SST records, run by ex-Black Flag guitarist Greg Ginn, for whom they recorded *Ultramega OK*, which was enough to gain the notice of major label A&M. In 1990, Cornell and Matt Cameron joined up in what could retrospectively be billed as a supergroup in the Temple of the Dog project. Temple of the Dog was a tribute to the late Andrew Wood, former singer of Mother Love Bone who had died of a heroin overdose in 1990. Cornell, a friend and former roommate of Wood's, decided to do a tribute record featuring members of Wood's band, as well as relative unknown Eddie Vedder. The result was a hit single in "Hunger Strike," which mixed Vedder's baritone with Cornell's wails of grief, an unlikely single that helped further the career of Soundgarden and effectively launch Pearl Jam.

The next album on A&M, *Badmotorfinger*, was an alternative metal classic, which demonstrated Soundgarden's growing skills at songwriting, particularly in "Rusty Cage" (which was later covered to great effect by Johnny Cash) and the almost hit "Outshined." This album, one of the last to have a truly "heavy" sound, made Soundgarden one of the brighter lights of the alternative scene. The next record, *Superunknown*, was a major hit for the band, particularly from the singles "Black Hole Sun" and "Spoonman" (perhaps the only hit single to feature a spoon solo), along with could-have-been-hits such as the Buzzcocks-esque "Kickstand" and the lonely "Fell on Black Days." However, it felt as though the band was playing more for a presumed radio (and MTV) audience, instead of trying to make any musical progress.

Their last album, *Down on the Upside*, sounds like the last gasp of a band who had run out of steam (although, thankfully, there were no more spoon solos), and it proved to be Soundgarden's last, as they broke up the next year. Since the band's demise Cornell made several interesting solo records and joined the remains of Rage Against the Machine for several forgettable records as Audioslave, before that band broke up in 2007 when the other three members left to rejoin the re-formed Rage Against the Machine. Drummer Cameron later joined grunge icon Pearl Jam, whom he had previously backed up as a member of Temple of the Dog. Soundgarden demonstrated both the positive and negative connotations of fusing punk and sludge metal, mostly because they had the songwriting chops. Their back catalog is well worth finding, except for the largely forgettable last record.

Discography: *Screaming Life* [EP] (Sub Pop, 1987); *FOPP* [EP] (Sub Pop, 1988); *Ultramega OK* (SST, 1988); *Louder than Love* (A&M, 1990); *Badmotorfinger* (A&M, 1991); *Superunkown* (A&M, 1994); *Down on the Upside* (A&M, 1996).

SOUTHERN LORD RECORDS (1998–PRESENT). Southern Lord Records is one of the most innovative and experimental modern metal labels, releasing bands such as Sunn O))), Boris, Orthodox, Oren Amabachi, a reunited Earth, and others who are not strictly metal by the standard definition of the genre, but who are breaking new ground in a genre that might eventually have to be labeled postmetal. Southern Lord was founded in the late nineties by Stephen O'Malley and Greg Anderson of the band Sunn O))) in order to have an outlet for new bands that did not sound like orthodox heavy metal bands, but instead used different kinds of tuning, long droning songs, and feedback as much for atmosphere as to indicate a heavy song.

To date the two most popular bands on the label are Boris and Sunn O))), who collaborated on the acclaimed *Altar* album in 2006. The label has also issued rereleases from influential bands such as Burning Witch and St. Vitus. This is especially impressive as the name of the label is a rather silly joking reference both to Slayer's *South Side of Heaven* record, and, of course, the Devil. Satanic references aside, the label is one of the most important new metal record labels in years. Fans of hard and heavy music would be well advised to seek out releases by many of their bands to expand their musical palette.

SPEED METAL. Speed metal, sometimes used along with thrash metal, is a term used to define a group of bands mostly from the mid-eighties, who were influenced by the speed of hardcore punk and decided to pick up the tempo away from metal's traditional dinosaur-like crawl as epitomized by bands like Black Sabbath, or boogie rock shuffle of many of the seventies bands to make it as musically powerful as the best hardcore punk. In particular, the speed metal bands of the eighties took their cue from punk bands such as Black Flag (who slowed down in their later years as if in a tribute to classic heavy metal) and bands such as the Misfits, Minor Threat, DI, and Bad Brains. Many bands in this subgenre were also clearly influenced by the English hardcore band Discharge, who pioneered the classic D-Core sound in England that influenced many metal bands and also helped establish the crossover scene in the punk community.

This type of metal can be defined by bands such as Anthrax, Metallica, Slayer, Megadeth, and others (although many of these band also fit into other subgenres of metal, and many fans and even band members of various bands would argue furiously about how they are grouped or what their sound should be defined as, especially by critics). The speed metal era was invigorating for both the punk and metal communities, and although it is not mentioned in every book on metal, much credit has to be given to Motorhead, who pioneered the punk/metal fusion as far back as 1977.

At the same time that numerous metal bands were speeding up, many punk bands were adding metal-style solos and growing their hair out, essentially removing many of the differences that had separated punk and metal for years. The term *speed metal* has not been especially used by rock critics or fans over the last decade or so, and it is accepted in the post-grindcore era that many bands can rapidly speed up to techno speeds without being called sellouts or having their metal credentials checked at the door.

SPEEDCORE. Speedcore is another name for a metal subgenre that mixed heavy metal's virtuosity with the speed and aggression of hardcore punk. The term was not used as much as terms such as "crossover" and "thrash" metal. The term *speedcore* demonstrates the efforts by many in the metal community and of rock critics and scholars to try and contextualize and understand the different subgenres that metal split off into during the eighties. The term is not widely used to this day and has fallen out of favor as a term by both critics and metal fans.

SPIKES. Spikes, usually worn on leather wristbands or on the back of leather jackets, are originally from the punk and gay leather scenes, and bands such as Judas Priest helped introduce them to heavy metal in the 1970s. By the mid-eighties the look had spread to many hair metal bands and to harder, more serious bands such as Manowar, who wore huge spikes and cultivated a medieval image. Thor, the heavy metal icon, also wore large fake spikes, possibly inspiring later bands like GWAR who essentially made fun of the idea. The most ridiculous use of spikes was notably in the band W.A.S.P., where sawblades were used as spikes, although bands such as GWAR and Thor also used large fake spikes to project an image of fantasy or silliness.

Most modern metal bands no longer wear spikes, but some throwback bands do either out of a sense of nostalgia or in tribute to classic metal bands of yore. For many bands and for many fans, spikes were also a way to demonstrate the impulse toward exaggerated masculinity in the metal community, much as they had functioned in the punk, biker, and leather scenes years earlier. In terms of moshing, spikes also added another layer of menace for those not protected from impact by large leather jackets.

SPINAL TAP. David St. Hubbins, played by Michael McKean (vocals/guitar), Nigel Tufnel, played by Christopher Guest (guitar), Derek Smalls, played by Harry Shearer (bass), Mick Shrimpton, played by R. J. Parnell (drums, usually Mick Shrimpton, or his brother Rick, many other previous drummers died in accidents, including bizarre gardening accidents, so too many to mention here), Viv Savage, played by David Kaff (keyboards).

Spinal Tap may or may not be the best metal band of all time, featuring lead singer and guitarist David St. Hubbins, guitarist Nigel Tufnel, bassist Derek Smalls, in later years keyboardist Viv Savage, and a variety of drummers who usually died in bizarre gardening accidents or by choking on someone else's vomit. The band started as the Thamesmen, before becoming the Originals and then the New Originals, when they found that another band already had that name.

After leaving their garage rock and psychedelic phases, Spinal Tap began to tour more regularly and as their sound became more metallic, they began to adapt a more tolerant misogyny as epitomized in songs such as "Big Bottom," "Tonight I'm Gonna Rock You, Tonight," in which lyrics such as "you're too young and I'm too well hung" epitomized exactly what the band wanted to do with the ladies backstage. Spinal Tap were also maligned unfairly by critics, who hailed their concept album *Shark Sandwich* as "shit sandwich." Although Spinal Tap failed to chart in later years, they did help expand the metal lexicon with their grandiose stage sets, including in one notable instance clear plastic pods, one of which failed to open, trapping bassist Derek Smalls inside. In a notably metal moment, the band designed a giant Stonehenge prop to come down, but because the designer mistook inches for feet, the Stonehenge set was in danger of being crushed by a dwarf.

Although the band went through its sets of ups and downs, they remained popular in Japan, where they were last seen doing a successful comeback tour to rapturous fans. The band was largely forgotten by many Americans (who also failed to remember the Rutles, the legendary band who were a "legend that would last a lunchtime"), but most metal fans know them from the documentary that acclaimed filmmaker Rob Reiner did about them in 1984 called *This is Spinal Tap*. There is an urban legend circulating in the metal community that the documentary is actually a "mockumentary" due to the extreme silliness of the events chronicled in the film, but when comparing it to the film *The Decline of Western Civilization, Part II: The Metal Years* or a Dio or W.A.S.P. stage set, it is clear that *This Is Spinal Tap* is just a well-shot documentary about a typical British metal band.

Sadly, few of Spinal Tap's records are in print, but the two compilations listed below are well worth investing in for serious students of metalology. (Note for gullible readers: *This Is Spinal Tap* was actually a "mockumentary" directed by Rob Reiner and created by McKean, Guest, and Shearer)

Christopher Guest (as Nigel Tufnel) in the hit 1984 movie *This Is Spinal Tap*.
(Embassy Pictures/Photofest)

Discography: *This is Spinal Tap* (Polydor 1984, 2000); *Break Like the Wind* (MCA, 1992). There were many other Spinal Tap albums, such as *Shark Sandwich*, which are naturally long out of print due to the incompetence of record label owners and the bad taste of various jealous A&R men, but are well worth seeking out at yard sales or at Salvation Army stores.)

SPREAD EAGLE (1989–94). Ray West (vocals), Paul DiBartolo (guitar), Rob De Luca (bass), Tommi Gallo (drums).

Featuring a down and dirty streetwise image that was akin to an east coast version of Guns N' Roses, New York City's Spread Eagle should have had a chance to rival that band in some of its popularity, but coming late in the game they never quite had the chance to show what they were capable of. Releasing their stellar self-titled debut in 1990, the band stood out with a gritty image and sound. Fronted by vocalist Ray West, whose snarling vocals were a match for Axel's wail, they also possessed a sleeper guitar hero in Paul DiBartolo, whose casual, devil-may-care demeanor belied a highly developed technique. Standout tracks like "Broken City" and "Switchblade Serenade" were at once gritty and slyly complex in their compositional sophistication, down and dirty songs that musically went beyond the street punk veneer they hid behind. After receiving some initial attention, the album lagged in sales, and the follow-up *Open to the Public* released in 1993 stiffed due to lack of promotion and the rising popularity of alternative rock.

The band (minus original guitarist DiBartolo) has recently reunited, and their original debut was rereleased in 2006 and is well worth seeking out.

Discography: *Spread Eagle* (MCA, 1990); *Open to the Public* (MCA, 1993).

STATIC X (1994–PRESENT). Wayne Static (vocals/guitar programming), Koichi Fukuda (guitar/programming, replaced for several years by Tripp Eisen before returning to band), Tony Campos (bass), Ken Jay (drums, now Nick Oshiro).

Static X is a fast and heavy band with grindcore and industrial aspects thrown in for good measure. Led by the cleverly coiffed leader/singer/guitarist Wayne Static, who plays a new breed of metal, one that is unceasingly brutal, but in strange ways danceable as well. The band was started by Static. The first record is perhaps the most brutal, and also the most "sellable" metal record ever made, with numerous tracks licensed to video games (a promotional tactic the band uses to this day). Fukuda left for several years, and was replaced by Tripp Eisen, who in a particularly embarrassing incident was dismissed due to a scandal involving statutory rape of two underaged girls (Harris, 2005). Fukuda returned and reinvigorated the band, leading to *Cannibal*, one of the most brutal industrial albums ever made. While Static X may have used video games to sell their songs, they are almost literally the embodiment of the video game aesthetic and a key influence on bands who use computers and samples in order to reach new and brutal depths for heavy metal.

Discography: *Wisconsin Death Trip* (Warner Bros., 1999); *Machine* (Warner Bros., 2001); *Shadow Zone* (Warner Bros., 2003); *Beneath ... Between ... Beyond* (Warner Bros., 2004); *Start a War* (Warner Bros., 2005); *Cannibal* (Warner Bros., 2007).

STEVE STEVENS (1959–). While a guitarist of many talents, including progressive rock and flamenco, Steve Stevens is without a doubt best known as Billy Idol's stage and studio foil, where, armed with a Les Paul and a glam rock image borrowed from equal parts Johnny Thunders and Siouxsie Sioux, he has infused the best of the veteran punk rocker's material with a hard rock edge that helped the two crossover into mainstream success in the 1980s and has continued to drive their career into the new millennium.

Beginning guitar at the age of seven, the Brooklyn-bred Stevens quickly became a progressive rock aficionado of bands like Yes, ELP, and King Crimson. After playing on the Manhattan club scene for a number of years, Stevens met up with ex-Generation X singer Billy Idol, who had moved to New York to start a solo career. Marrying Stevens' hard rock edge and Idol's sneering punk stance to an often dance-music beat, the two soon found themselves with a formidable and marketable hybrid style that was complemented by the pair's striking visual image of Idol's neo-Elvis blond spikes and Stevens' black mane and painted fingernails. Debuting their act just as MTV was beginning, the pair experienced massive success with the albums *Billy Idol* (1982) and *Rebel Yell* (1983), with heavy airplay on radio and MTV.

Stevens also collaborated with other artists during the mid-eighties, including Michael Jackson, Robert Palmer, and the Thompson Twins. In 1986 Stevens won a Grammy Award for Best Pop Instrumental Performance for his work with keyboardist Harold Faltermeyer on "Top Gun Anthem," which appeared on the hit soundtrack to the popular Tom Cruise movie *Top Gun*.

After Idol's disappointing *Whiplash Smile* (which used drum machines instead of drummer Thommy Price, whose unique sound and groove had powered previous Idol releases), Stevens left to pursue his own more rocking muse. Signed to Chrysalis Records, he released *Atomic Playboys* with vocalist Perry McCarty and drummer Price in 1989. Stevens' trademark sonic and visual style was in evidence, although the album went in a more hard rock direction, stripped as it was of punk and dance influences. Even so, it also showcased Stevens' growing competence on flamenco and jazz styles. Although Stevens toured for the album, the futuristic glam image that accompanied the album (and found Stevens decked out in head-to-toe black vinyl) didn't quite fit in with the hair metal of the day and failed to find much of an audience beyond guitar enthusiasts.

After the turn of the decade, Stevens hooked up with former Hanoi Rocks vocalist Michael Monroe to form the group Jerusalem Slim, which unfortunately never released any material even though the pairing seemed inspired. 1993 saw Stevens collaborating with ex-Mötley Crüe frontman Vince Neil for the singer's solo debut *Exposed* and its subsequent tour.

Later in the nineties, Stevens participated in a project spearheaded by groundbreaking drummer Terry Bozzio, which also featured renowned bassist Tony Levin. The resulting group, Bozzio Levin Stevens, released two albums of improvisational progressive rock that did much to show how broad Stevens' musical palette had become. The group released *Black Light Syndrome* in 1997 and *Situation Dangerous* in 2002.

In 1999 Stevens released his second solo record, *Flamenco A Go-Go*, an album of infectious flamenco guitar over electronica rhythm tracks. 2002 saw him finally reuniting with his former partner Billy Idol for an episode of *VH1 Storytellers*. In 2005, he collaborated with Idol on *Devil's Playground*, an album in which the duo combined Idol's punk influences with much heavier rock, while leaving the pop and dance elements of their previous work behind. In 2008, Stevens released *Memory Crash*, an album of instrumental hard rock that showcased his rock guitar chops and featured a cover of Robin Trower's "Day of the Eagle" in collaboration with Doug Pinnick of King's X.

Discography: *Atomic Playboys* (Warner Bros., 1989); *Flamenco A Go-Go* (Ark 21, 1999); *Steve Stevens* (Wea International, 2000); *Memory Crash* (Magna Carta, 2008).

STRYPER (1982–90; 2003–PRESENT). Michael Sweet (vocals), Oz Fox (guitar), Tim Gaines (bass, Brad Cobb for several records and tours, now Tracy Ferrie), Robert Sweet (drums).

During the heyday of the Christian rock scene, most Christian rock bands stayed away from metal and its satanic influences and "rock and roll all night and party every day" ethos. Most bands however, did not have the prostelyzing power, or extreme bad taste in clothing, that the Christian band members in Stryper had. (Stryper's name stood for Salvation Through Redemption Yielding Peace Encouragement and Righteousness) Originally formed in the early eighties as Roxx Regime by the brothers Michael and Robert Sweet, the band started out as a secular metal band but were inspired by friend Ken Metcalf (who also toured with the band as a keyboard player and touring evangelist) in 1982 and decided to preach an evangelical Christian message via heavy metal.

The band, in their garish beelike costumes, was almost instantaneously successful. Their debut record, *Soldier's Under Command*, went gold and established Stryper as one of the most popular metal, much less the most popular Christian, bands in the world. Their next record, *To Hell with the Devil*, was even more successful, going platinum and establishing Stryper as a major touring act. However, balancing commercial success with an evangelical Christian message proved difficult for Stryper to manage, and their next record, *In God We Trust*, was a major hit but was criticized by many fans for abandoning the Christian theme for more pop-ready commercial-sounding songs such as "Always There for You." Deciding suddenly that the secular world might be more lucrative, Stryper changed directions and costumes for the *Against the Law* record, which featured no songs that were explicitly about God or religion. Naturally the Christian fan base reacted with outrage at what many evangelicals considered to be the band choosing mammon over God.

After releasing a greatest hits record, frontman Sweet departed, leading the band to dwindle to a halt and the band dissolved with members playing in various Christian bands. In 2003, the band reunited to play several shows, and after some successful tour, a new record was rereleased in 2005. Stryper continued to tour to acclaim from old stalwart fans, as well as new fans in the Christian music industry. Stryper may have been labeled an anomaly by the mainstream metal press, but many both inside and outside the evangelical community welcomed Stryper's message of hope and positivity.

It is unclear how many fans were converted, or even affected, by Stryper's lyrics, or by the free copies of the New Testament that the band gave out for free to the audience, but at their height of popularity millions of people, Christian and non-Christian, were buying Stryper records. While Stryper may not have been the most successful metal band, they stand out as a stark contrast to the numerous black metal bands who claim to represent the true metal underground.

Discography: *The Yellow and Black Attack* [EP] (Hollywood, 1984); *Soldiers Under Command* (Hollywood, 1985); *To Hell with the Devil* (Hollywood, 1986); *In God We Trust* (Hollywood, 1988); *Against the Law* (Hollywood, 1990); *Reborn* (Big3, 2005); *Live in Puerto Rico* (Immortal, 2007).

STUDS. Studs, like spikes, were often used to adorn wristbands as well as leather jackets. They were almost ubiquitous among certain hair metal bands, as well as some of the more serious or mythical bands such as Manowar but did have connotations to the gay community as many metal fans found out to their chagrin (many in the metal community are openly homophobic) when Rob Halford of Judas Priest famously came out as both gay and a member of the gay leather community. Today some throwback bands still decorate with studs, but not many. Also like spikes, studs were also used to inflict maximum damage while moshing, although some aficionados were so protective of their clothing that they wouldn't deign to go in the pit for fear of damaging their (sometimes very) expensive outfits.

ST. VITUS (1979–95). Scott Reagers (vocals, replaced by Scott "Wino" Weinriech, Christian Lindersson, then Reagers), Dave Chandler (suitar), Mark Adams (bass), Armando Acosta (drums).

St. Vitus were a sludge metal band, sometimes categorized as an early doom metal band, with connections to the punk scene, mainly through their affiliation with the legendary SST punk label led by Black Flag guitarist Greg Ginn. St. Vitus were probably named after the Black Sabbath song but may also have been a reference to the spastic disease-inspired dance from the Middle Ages. The band also toured extensively with punk bands such as Black Flag, leading to an interesting intermingling of audiences. The band gained an extra dose of power with the addition of former Obsessed guitarist Wino, who replaced original vocalist Reagers for the *Born Too Late* record.

Despite their popularity in the underground punk and metal scenes, St. Vitus never seemed to make an impact on the metal world and broke up for good in 1995, after a reunion of the original lineup with Reagles singing for the *Die Healing* record. Recently the albums were remastered and rereleased by Southern Lord Records, a label that knows a good slow doom band when they hear it. Despite their alliance with SST and Wino's acclaim in the underground and stoner metal communities, St. Vitus was a criminally neglected band and is ripe for discovery. The SST records are all worth buying, especially the ones with Wino.

Discography: *St. Vitus* (SST, 1984); *Hallow's Victim* (SST, 1985); *Born Too Late* (SST, 1986); *Mournful Cries* (SST, 1988); *V* (Roadrunner, 1990); *COD* (Nuclear Blast, 1992); *Die Healing* (Hellhound, 1995); *Little Motor Mouth* (Black Market Music, 2001); *Live* (Southern Lord Records, 2005).

SUICIDAL TENDENCIES (1982–94). Mike Muir (vocals), Grant Estes (guitar), Louiche Mayorga (bass), Mike Clark (guitar), Amery Smith (drums).

Suicidal Tendencies were/are one of the earliest hardcore punk bands to crossover to a heavy metal style and one of the few to so ardently embrace heavy metal and remain true to the overall metal sound well after the punk revival of the early nineties. The band was started as an allegedly gang-affiliated hardcore band from Venice Beach and put out what many consider to be one of the best hardcore albums of all time, *Suicidal Tendencies*, released in 1983, which contained the classic tracks "I Shot Reagan," "I Saw Your Mommy," and "Institutionalized," which became popular due to a clever video that received MTV airplay. The song was later used in the classic punk film *Repo Man*.

But by the second record and after several personnel changes, the band, led by lead singer and visionary Mike Muir, had decided to go in a crossover direction and the next record, *Join the Army*, with its metalesque cover (which has strong similarities to the art used on many Megaforce releases, including the first Storm Troopers of Death record) fit in nicely with the growing thrash movement. This album spawned a minor hit single with "Possessed to Skate." The next record, *How Will I Laugh*, saw the band complete their transformation into a thrash metal band.

Subsequent records were increasingly hit and miss and the band floundered for many years with Muir seeming to lose interest at times. The most egregious example of this was a pointless remake of the first album. Eventually with the introduction of future Metallica bassist Robert Trujillo, the band moved in a more funk direction, culminating in the Infectious Grooves side project with Muir, Trujillo, and Stephen Perkins of Jane's Addiction, which improbably became as popular as Suicidal Tendencies in some parts of the world. At this writing the band is still touring both as Infectious Grooves and as Suicidal Tendencies.

Discography: *Suicidal Tendencies* (Frontier, 1983); *Join the Army* (Caroline, 1987); *How Will I Laugh Tomorrow When I Can't Even Smile Today?* (Epic, 1988).

SUNN O))) (1998–PRESENT). Stephen O' Malley (guitars/other instruments), Greg Anderson (bass/guitar/other instruments).

Words cannot describe the low-end intensity of Sunn O))), who are among the most powerful and mysterious new metal bands around. Instead of concentrating on traditional songs, Sunn O))) play soundscapes of noise and feedback. This is while dressed in monastic robes, where the audience can only peek at the grim, heavily bearded two members, Stephen O'Malley and Greg Anderson, both previously of legendary underground bands such as Burning Witch, Khanate, Thor's Hammer, and Goatsnake.

After the demise of their previous bands, the two guitarists were ready to start a new band, but they were unsure of the more mainstream (for black metal) approach that many of their contemporaries took. Instead the two founded the now extremely influential Southern Lord Records (think about it for a second ...) and started to release their own material, staring with the 1999 *The Grimm Robe Demos* featuring some of the slowest and most brutal metal then released. Sadly, the original release did not sell many copies, and Sunn O))) had to build their success as slowly as their music. Soon fans were starting to pick up their releases just for the notoriety the band was making with their radical musical statements.

Sunn O))) are one of the most fascinating new metal bands out there and one that is constantly challenging and redefining the boundaries of what is considered metal and what is considered heavy. Despite the fact that they are a heavy metal band, Sunn O))) do not play metal, or sometimes not even music as it is commonly known, but rely on deep trancelike drones. Their influences are not only from the metal community but also from minimalist composers and musicians such as Steve Reich, Tony Conrad, and LaMonte Young. (Also in the mix are bits of Philip Glass, Sun Ra, the Melvins, Celtic Frost, and Dissection.) Sunn O))) play metal that is extreme, but a brand of metal that lacks traditional parts of metal songs, such as bass melody, harmony, and even structures to their songs. Instead a typical Sunn O))) record or concert might start with the band playing an A or C sharp chord held sometimes for minutes with endless waves of feedback, and of course, usually no drums, and only occasionally vocals. An example of this is when Malefic Guest starred on *The Black One*, in which he (according to legend) recorded his vocal tracks locked in a coffin. Julian Cope of Teardrop Explodes and Attila Csihar of Mayhem have also made guest appearances. The formula was altered on *Altar*, which was a full collaboration with Japanese noise metal punks Boris, where the drums, bass, and guitar of Boris combined with the seemingly endless held chords of Sunn O))) to create a blinding and brilliant wall of sustained and often painful noise. Some trivia: The band was named after a rare brand of vintage amplifier and for novices, the pronunciation of the band's name is simply "sun."

Discography: *The Grimm Robe Demos* (Southern Lord, 1999); *0/0 Void* (Southern Lord, 2000); *Flight of the Behemoth* (Southern Lord, 2002); *White 1* (Southern Lord, 2003); *The Libations of Samhain* (Bastet, 2003); *Veils It White* (Thin the Herd, 2003); *White 2* (Southern Lord, 2004); *Cro-monolithic Mixes for an Iron Age* (Southern Lord, 2004); *Live White* (Archive, 2004); *Black One* (Southern Lord, 2005); *Altar* [with Boris] (Southern Lord, 2006).

THE SWORD (2003–PRESENT). J. D. Cronise (vocals/guitar), Kyle Schutt (guitar), Bryan Richie (bass), Trivett Wingo (drums).

The Sword are yet another American metal band founded in Austin, Texas, who seem to play classic metal with a bit of an ironic smirk. Ben Snakepit from punk greats J. Church was in an early version of the band. The Sword demonstrate that paying attention to metal traditions, whether in a winking way (as in hipsters wearing vintage Iron Maiden shirts) or seriously is always a great career move.

Discography: *Age of Winters* (Kemado, 2006); *The Sword/Witchcraft* [split] (Kemado, 2007); *Gods of the Earth* (Kemado, 2008).

T

TAD (1988–99). Tad Doyle (vocals/guitar), Gary Thorstensen (guitar), Kurt Danielson (bass), Steve Weid (drums, replaced by Rey Washam, Josh Sinder, Mike Mongrain).

Tad were one of the best to what were called the "grunge" bands from the Pacific northwest and were best known for the raw aggressive guitar sound and for butcher Tad Doyle, whose girth rivaled that of Leslie West of the band Mountain. Although Tad were lumped in with the grunge explosion, they were essentially a skuzzy metal band in style and form. Like Soundgarden and Alice in Chains, they did not clearly fit into the commercial parameters of metal prevalent at the time. Tad's music was a little more adventurous and the Sub Pop records are well worth listening to. Tad was signed in the major label feeding frenzy after grunge broke, and after putting out a mediocre record for Atlantic, which quickly dropped the band, they floundered until breaking up in 1999. Tad was also the focus of a lawsuit when the woman on the cover of their *8 Way Santa* record sued after she had become a born-again Christian and was ashamed of the half-naked picture used on the cover.

Discography: *God's Balls* (Sub Pop, 1989); *Salt Lick/God's Balls* (Sub Pop, 1990); *8 Way Santa* (Sub Pop, 1991); Inhaler (Warner Brothers, 1993); *Live Alien Broadcasts* (Futurist, 1995); *Infrared Riding Hood* (East West, 1995).

TESLA (1985–96; 2000–PRESENT). Jeff Keith (vocals), Frank Hannon (guitar), Tommy Skeoch (guitar), Brian Wheat (bass), Troy Luccketta (drums).

With a straight-ahead rock style that owed as much to seventies-era hard rock as it did to the pop metal/hair metal that they found themselves in, Tesla purveyed a no-frills brand of melodic hard rock that won them a significant following during the group's late eighties and early nineties heyday.

Coming together in 1985 in Sacramento, California, Tesla consisted of vocalist Jeff Keith, guitarists Frank Hannon and Tommy Skeoch, bassist Brian Wheat, and drummer Troy Luccketta. Naming themselves after inventor Nikola Tesla, the unsung pioneer of early radio technology, the band secured a record deal with Geffen Records after a series of showcases in L.A. Their debut, *Mechanical Resonance*, released in 1986 sold a million copies thanks to the single "Modern Day Cowboy." Their follow-up, *The Great Radio Controversy*, released in 1989, was an even bigger hit. The album featured the hits "Heaven's Trail (No Way Out)" (a rocker) and the ballad "Love Song," which evoked the band's seventies roots with its straightforward sentiments. The album was the band's commercial breakthrough, reaching the top twenty and selling over two million copies.

The band followed up the album with a low-key affair, the *Five Man Acoustical Jam*, which saw them playing acoustic versions of their better-known tunes. Featuring a hit cover of the classic sixties tune "Signs" which hit the top ten, the album went platinum, and its acoustic concept provided the inspiration for the hit *MTV Unplugged* series that followed soon after.

With *Psychotic Supper* in 1991, Tesla had their fourth consecutive hit. In spite of all their success, the alternative trend in music was taking shape. Even though the band's straightforward style was not going out of vogue as quickly as that of their more clearly hair-metal band contemporaries, the change was coming and would affect Tesla as well. While 1994's *Bust a Nut* sold just under a million copies, its comparatively lackluster sales were an indication of the coming of grunge. And inside the Tesla camp, the group was wrestling with the more immediate problem of guitarist Tommy Skeoch's substance abuse issues, which led him to leave the band in 1995.

Although the band tried their hand at working as a four-piece, it was a failed experiment, and the group disbanded in 1996. In 2000, with Skeoch back in good health, the band reunited and released the double-live album *Replugged Live*. The band has remained active since that time, releasing an album of new material with 2004's *Into the Now* (after which Skeoch left the group once more), and an album of classic seventies covers in 2007 called *Real to Reel*. *Forever More*, their first full studio album featuring new guitarist Dave Rude, was released in 2008.

Discography: *Mechanical Resonance* (Geffen, 1986); *The Great Radio Controversy* (Geffen, 1989); *Five Man Acoustical Jam* (Geffen, 1990); *Psychotic Supper* (Geffen, 1991); *Bust a Nut* (Geffen, 1994); *Time's Makin Changes: The Best of Tesla* (Geffen, 1995); *Replugged Live* (Sanctuary, 2001); *Standing Room Only* [live] (Sanctuary, 2002); *Into the Now* (Sanctuary, 2004); *Real to Reel* (Electric Company, 2007); *Real to Reel, Vol. 2* (Tesla Electric Co, 2007); *Forever More* (Tesla Electric Co, 2008).

TESTAMENT (1985–PRESENT). Chuck Billy (vocals), Alex Skolnick (guitars, replaced by Glenn Avaelais, James Murphy, now Skolnick), Erik Peterson (guitar), Greg Christian (bass, replaced by Derek Ramirez, then Steve Giorgio), Louie Christian (drums, replaced by Paul Bostaph then John Tempesta, then John Dette, then Gene Hoglan, then Dave Lombardo).

Testament are a technically adept thrash heavy metal band from the Bay Area who were notable for many years for the presence of virtuoso guitarist Alex Skolnick, who later left them to play in Savatage and later to start a rewarding full-time career as a respected jazz musician. Testament also went through a bewildering collection of drummers, with seemingly every great metal drummer at one time or another, including Gene Hoglan from Death and Dave Lombardo from Slayer

Testament, the most under-rated early American thrash band. (Photofest)

sitting in. The classic lineup with Skolnick reunited in 2006 and in 2008 released a new album.

Discography: *The Legacy* (Atlantic, 1987); *The New Order* (Megaforce, 1988); *Practice What You Preach* (Megaforce, 1989); *Live at Eindhoven* (Megaforce, 1990); *Souls of Black* (Megaforce, 1990); *The Ritual* (Atlantic, 1992); *Returning to the Apocalyptic City* (Atlantic, 1993); *Low* (Atlantic, 1994); *Live at the Filmore* (Burnt Offering, 1995); *Demonic* (Fierce, 1997); *The Gathering* (Spitfire, 1999); *First Strike Still Deadly* (Spitfire, 2001); *Days of Darkness* (Snapper, 2004); *Live in London* (Spitfire, 2005); *The Formation of Damnation* (Nuclear, 2008).

THIN LIZZY (1969–84, 1996–2001, 2004–PRESENT). Phil Lynott (vocals/ bass, now John Sykes on vocals), Eric Bell (guitar, replaced by Gary Moore, Brian Robertson, then Moore again, Snowy White, John Sykes), Scott Gorham (guitar), Brian Downey (drums).

Thin Lizzy were an earth-shaking legendary band led by bassist and vocalist Phil Lynott and one of the few Irish heavy metal bands to chart and make it big. The band started in 1969 with Lynott, guitarist Eric Bell and drummer Brian Downey. Although only the rhythm section was a constant, Lynott's distinctive blues-based voice made Thin Lizzy extremely popular, with hit singles still played on radio today, such as "Jailbreak" and of course "The Boys Are Back in Town." However, earlier singles such as the powerful metal cover of the traditional Irish song "Whiskey in the Jar" proved that Lynott and Lizzy were no one-trick pony. Lynott sang of working-class frustration as only a true outsider could; being not only Irish, but black as well, Lynott was in a unique cultural place, and his songs reflected his ambivalence about mainstream society.

After the loss of several guitarists (the best being Gary Moore) Thin Lizzy were ready to call it quits with the *Thunder and Lightning* record, but Lynott didn't live long enough to enjoy the fruits of his new career, dying as a result of years of alcohol and heroin abuse in 1986 at the age of 36. Lynott, who had worked with various punk musicians and began to record new solo material, left at the prime of his career.

Sadly, and almost inevitably, the band is touring once again today, featuring Sykes and Gorham with a new bassist, drummer, and keyboard player, but without the spirit of Phil Lynott, who now has a statue of his likeness on Grafton Street in the heart of Dublin, the band lacks that spirit that motivated them for their all-too-brief career.

Discography: *Thin Lizzy* (Dream, 1971); *Shades of a Blue Orphanage* (Dream, 1972); *Vagabonds of the Western World* (Dream, 1973); *Night Life* (Mercury, 1974); *Fighting* (Mercury, 1975); *Jailbreak* (Mercury, 1976); *Johnny the Fox* (Mercury, 1976); *Bad Reputation* (Mercury, 1977); *Live and Dangerous* (Warner Brothers, 1978); *Black Rose: A Rock Legend* (Warner Brothers, 1979); *Chinatown* (Warner Brothers, 1980); *Renegade* (Warner Brothers, 1981); *Thunder and Lightning* (Warner Brothers, 1983); *Boys Are Back in Town: Live in Australia* (Nippon Crown, 1999); *One Night Only* (CMC International, 2000); *Transmissions* (Storming Music Company, 2008).

THOR (1976–PRESENT). Jon Mikl Thor (vocals), John Shand (guitar, replaced by numerous, including Steve Price), Terry McKeon (bass, replaced by many including Keith Zazzi), Bill Wade (drums, numerous others including Mike Favata), Pantera (backing vocals during eighties).

One of the great unsung metal heroes is a man that was probably known more for his larger-than-life image than for his music. Thor, of the band by the same name, could seem ridiculous, but his sense of humor and nose for a hook, along with his bulging muscles, guarantees him a place in metal history. Jon Mikl Thor started as a professional body builder (at one time winning Mr. Young Canada) before turning to the far more lucrative career as a professional stage performer, where his tricks, such as bending a steel bar in his teeth and blowing up a hot water bottle until it burst, led to some notoriety. Thor eventually discovered that he also could carry a tune, and soon he was appearing on stage singing. A notable performance on *The Mike Douglas Show* in which a limber Thor sang a Sweet cover while blowing up his trademark hot water bottle led to a record deal and the classic metal hybrid *Keep the Dogs Away*.

After the success of that album in the underground metal and punk scenes (John Holmstrom of *Punk* magazine fame was an early and ardent supporter), Thor began a series of grueling tours that saw him playing in major venues (usually in England or Canada; for reasons unknown, Thor never seemed to break in most of North America). Thor also found a lucrative new source of gigs playing at comic book conventions, where his outlandish stage outfits, complete with capes and huge fake spikes (a precursor to the later outfits that bands like Manowar and Saxon would wear) inspired a new generation of metalheads with songs such as "Anger (Is My Middle Name)" and "Lightning Strikes."

Over the next two decades Thor toured less frequently and his backing band went through numerous personnel changes as he turned more toward low-budget horror films where his muscular body served him well as a hero. Subsequent

Thor: A true rock and roll warrior. (Photofest)

records were spotty and sadly much of his career output is out of print, fetching high prices on eBay to this day. After being all but written off in the nineties, Thor returned to form with the *Thor Against the World* album in 2005, where a sympathetic production team helped Thor return to his early sounds, a sort of mixture of Sweet and muscular metal. A DVD release, *An-thor-ology*, was put out by Smog Veil in 2005 and is an indispensable look at one of the great underlooked and underpraised metal giants.

Thor may have seemed like a god with his outfits and stage show, but what few realized is that Thor was one of the key innovators in bringing excitement and showbiz glamour to the formerly sedate metal shows of yore. Although his work can be hard to locate, listeners should be advised that anything from the seventies and eighties, as well as the *Thor Against the World* record, are essential metal listening.

Discography: *Keep the Dogs Away* (Midsong, 1976); *Unchained* (Mongol, 1983); *Live in Detroit* (Raw Power, 1985); *Only the Strong* (Enigma, 1985); *Ride the Chariots* (Star USA); *Thunderstruck* (Star USA, 1998); *Triumphant* (Thor Toen, 2002); *Dogz II* (Igroove, 2003); *Beast Women from the Center of the Earth: A Rock Odyssey* (Thor Toen Antimatter, 2004); *Thor/Mata Ala Bestia* (Got Metal, 2005); *Thor Against the World* (Smog Veil, 2005); *Rock and Roll Nightmare* (Smog Veil, 2006); *Devastation of Musculation* (Smog Veil, 2006); *Into the Noise* (Sudden Death/Antimatter, 2008).

THRASH METAL. The term *thrash metal* refers to a sped-up version of heavy metal that is defined by beats played in much the same tempo as those played in the mid-eighties by hardcore punk. Although some critics argue that thrash metal refers essentially to the same music as speed metal, some metal fans and bands would be careful to make a distinction between the two terms (as well as other close terms such as black metal and grindcore). As hardcore punk and metal began to crossover in the mid- to late eighties, many hardcore punk bands began to play in a more metallic style and grow their hair out, and numerous metal bands began to speed up their sound in emulation of punk.

The idea of thrash metal was that some punk audiences who grew up on bands like Bad Brains wanted more bands that were as proficient as they were intense, and many metal fans began to crave the raw intensity and physical abandon that was common to hardcore punk shows at the time. It helped that many bands on either side of the fence, such as Metallica, were fans of bands on the other side of the divide, such as the Misfits and Black Flag, the Circle Jerks, Bad Brains, Minor Threat, and DI, and that the metal scene had grown to embrace harder music. Thrash was a key movement in metal and helped open the doors to new fans and new stylistic innovations.

TORA TORA (1988–92). Anthony Corder (vocals), Keith Douglas (guitar), Patrick Francis (bass), John Patterson (drums).

After getting their start by winning a battle of the bands competition in their native Memphis, Tennessee, Tora Tora hit the pop metal scene with a decidedly blues/boogie feel, not unlike Tesla, with their hit MTV video "Walkin' Shoes," off of their A&M album *Surprise Attack* in 1989. Although a follow-up, *Wild America,* was released in 1992, the band was a victim of record company restructuring and changing musical tastes and had broken up by 1994. In 2008, however, the four members reunited for a performance at the Rocklahoma music festival, though there was no indication whether the band would engage in any further musical activity together.

Discography: *Surprise Attack* (A&M, 1989); *Wild America* (A&M, 1992).

TRIBUTE BANDS. The metal scene, more than any other subset of rock and roll, seems to specialize in tribute bands, bands that lavishly re-create not only the music of certain bands but also their stage show. There are thousands of bands out there re-creating the music of bands who have broken up, as well as bands who are active. Sometimes these tribute bands are adept at mimicking not just the sound of the band but the sound of the band at a certain time period. One example of this is the sheer number who replicate the music of Kiss, particularly in their make-up years. Examples of this phenomenon include Aces High (a Kiss tribute band where all the members dress as Ace Frehley in his classic make-up and the much abused roadie is forced to dress as Vinnie Vincent!) as well as the classic Mini-Kiss, who consist of a tribute to Kiss where all the members are dwarves.

Other gimmick tributes include all-female versions of male bands, such as the popular Lez Zeppelin. Still others turn tributes into high art, with the band Beatallica mixing the songs of the Beatles with Metallica riffs, that it might make the average fan question whether they are doing Beatles songs, or unknown Metallica originals. One of the main points of the tribute band is to capture a band at its peak, and for many who do not want to pay $100 to see a band in nosebleed seats in a stadium it is a chance to see bands close-up and live. Many musicians in the tribute community pride themselves on reproducing the songs exactly as they were played, and some even have the permission of various bands to tour as tribute acts.

As many metal bands continue to get older, and original members die, in the future tribute bands may not simply be seen as a cheap knock-off, but as a way of exposing new music to a new generation of fans, much like how a symphony orchestra expertly re-creates the music of Bach or Mozart; someday a band recreating the music of Kiss or Carcass may be seen as perfectly normal.

TRIUMPH (1975–93; 2007–PRESENT). Rik Emmett (guitar/vocals), Mike Levine (bass), Gil Moore (drums/vocals).

While the Canadian power trio Triumph were often compared to their fellow Canadians Rush, due to their three-person format and high-pitched vocal range that singer-guitarist Rik Emmett and Rush's Geddy Lee shared, Triumph was a much more mainstream hard rock/metal band with far fewer prog-rock tendencies. Their melodic songwriting helped them to become one of the few Canadian hard rock outfits to make significant commercial headway outside of their own country.

Coming together in Toronto in 1975, the band got their start with a self-titled album on the smaller Attic label. Although the album wasn't a commercial success, it did get some airplay, particularly in Texas, where the band began to build a regional fan base. The album also got the attention of RCA Records, who signed the band, re-releasing the debut. The band's second album, *Rock & Roll Machine*, released in 1977, gave the band its first hit in their cover of Joe Walsh's "Rocky Mountain Way." They hit the road, earning a reputation as a strong live act and augmenting their trio-format with a massive light show and pyrotechnics.

Subsequent albums did progressively better commercially, and with 1981's *Allied Forces*, the band scored its first breakout hit with the single "Fight the Good Fight." Triumph would go on to release a string of moderately successful albums with most going gold, until 1988 when guitarist/vocalist Rik Emmett decided to leave the band for a solo career.

Levine and Moore attempted to carry on, recruiting new vocalist/guitarist Phil X and releasing the 1993 album *Edge of Excess*, but the band broke up shortly afterward. In 2007, nearly twenty years after Emmett had left the band, Triumph were reunited when they were inducted into the Canadian Music Industry Hall of Fame. With the ceremony breaking the ice between the members, they subsequently found themselves giving a performance at the 2008 Sweden Rock Festival, after which it was rumored that they would be gearing up for a full-scale reunion tour in 2009.

Discography: *Rock & Roll Machine* (RCA Victor, 1977); *Just a Game* (MCA, 1979); *Progressions of Power* (MCA, 1980); *Allied Forces* (MCA, 1981); *Never Surrender* (MCA, 1982); *Thunder Seven* (MCA, 1984); *Stages* [live] (MCA, 1985); *The Sport of Kings* (MCA, 1985); *Surveillance* (MCA, 1989); *Edge of Excess* (Victory Music, 1993); *In the Beginning* (RCA, 1995); *Cleveland 1981* (King Biscuit Flower Hour, 1996); *King Biscuit Flower Hour* (In Concert) (King Biscuit Flower, 1996); *Live at the US Festival* (TML, 2003); *Live: A Night of Triumph* (Rare, 2008).

TRIXTER (1989–95). Peter Loran (vocals), Steve Brown (guitar), P. J. Farley (bass), Mark "Gus" Scott (drums).

New Jersey's pop-metal rockers Trixter caught a lucky break when their self-titled debut hit in 1990. With videos for the songs "Surrender," "One in a Million," and "Give It to Me Good" getting heavy airplay on MTV, the album sold more than half a million copies. The band followed up their debut with 1992's *Hear!* and a collection of covers (*Undercovers*) in 1994, but neither album could replicate their earlier success and the band called it a day shortly afterward.

Discography: *Trixter* (Mechanic, 1990); *Hear!* (MCA, 1992); *Undercovers* (Backstreet, 2004).

TROUBLE (1984–PRESENT). Original lineup: Eric Wagner (vocals), Bruce Franklin (guitar), Rick Wartell (guitar), Ian Brown (bass), Jeff Olson (drums).

Innovators of doom metal and its hearkening back to Black Sabbath's and other '70s metal slower-paced approach, Chicago's Trouble earned something of a cult following, but never made the commercial inroads enjoyed by their faster-paced speed metal contemporaries.

Trouble released their self-titled debut in 1984, on the Metal Blade label. The album established their seventies-oriented style. Their Christian perspective also led to their being labeled a "white-metal" group. Their second album, *The Skull*, released in 1985, consolidated the band's reputation, but like the debut went against the tastes of the period and failed to stir much widespread interest.

After the weaker 1987 album *Run to the Light*, the band lost their deal with Metal Blade. 1990 saw the band get a reprieve when producer Rick Rubin signed the band to his Def American label and produced their next album, the self-titled *Trouble* in 1990. Earning the band the widespread critical attention they had long sought, the album was a shot in the arm for the band, and they embarked on an extensive tour in support of it. Another excellent album followed the next year with *Manic Frustration*, an album title that might well have described the band's feelings as Def American dropped the band after the album failed to make any significant inroads with the record-buying public.

Shortly after the release of one more album, 1995's *Plastic Green Head*, Trouble officially disbanded, with the band's members going off to a variety of separate projects. Finally, in 2007, after having sporadically reunited for various one-off performances, the band officially regrouped, releasing the album *Simple Mind Condition*.

Discography: *Psalm 9* (Metal Blade, 1984); *The Skull* (Metal Blade, 1985); *Run to the Light* (Metal Blade, 1987); *Trouble* (Def American, 1990); *Manic Frustration* (Def American, 1991); *Plastic Green Head* (CEN, 1995); *Warrior* (Sma, 2005, 2007); *Simple Mind Condition* (Escapi, 2008).

EDDIE TRUNK (1964–). Eddie Trunk is a heavy metal expert, DJ, and for many years also a VJ on VH1 Classic. In New York he hosts the popular *Eddie Trunk Rocks* show on Q104.3, where he demonstrates his vast knowledge of metal history as well as highlighting current bands on a regular basis. Trunk left VH1 in 2007 and now concentrates on his radio shows on both terrestrial radio and on the XM satellite station The Boneyard. Trunk also does interviews for the MSG network.

TSOL (1979–PRESENT). Metal lineup: Joe Wood (vocals), Marshall Rohner (guitar), Mike Roche (bass), Mitch Green (drums).

TSOL (True Sounds of Liberty) were one of the best and most violent of the Southern California hardcore bands of the early eighties. The original lineup featured vocalist Jack Grisham, bassist Mike Roche, guitarist Ron Emory, and drummer Mitch Todd Barnes. They played a successful balance of punk and what would eventually be called goth. The band was a success, but by the late eighties TSOL had gone through almost an entire turnover in members and by the time of *Revenge,* the band had reinvented itself as a Sunset Strip type metal band with the appropriate long hair, scarves, and metal paraphernalia.

After befriending Guns N' Roses the band completely transformed their music from dark punk to blues-based glam metal. The trouble was that TSOL was a very good punk band, but not a very convincing metal band. While many punk bands were also trying to cash in on the new metal scene, most of the metal fans who liked punk were more into the new thrash scene of Metallica, Slayer, and Megadeth, bands who had grown up listening to TSOL.

The band eventually broke up, but when the reunited original lineup started touring, they were faced with legal action by the band's last vocalist, Joe Wood, who still owned the legal rights to the band name. After touring under a variety of pseudonyms, the band was finally allowed to tour as TSOL (or True Sounds of Liberty) in 1999. The band broke up seemingly for good in 2007, but the ex-metal members may want to try again—why not?

Discography: *T.S.O.L.* [EP] (Posh Boy, 1981); *Dance with Me* (Frontier, 1981; Epitaph, 1996); *Weathered Statues* [EP7] (Alternative Tentacles, 1982); *Beneath the Shadows* (Alternative Tentacles, 1982; Restless, 1989; Nitro, 1997); *Change Today?* (Enigma, 1984; Restless, 1997); *Revenge* (Enigma, 1986; Restless, 1997); *Hit and Run* (Enigma, 1987; Restless, 1997); *Thoughts of Yesterday 1981–1982* (Posh Boy, 1988; Rhino, 1992); *TSOL Live* (Restless, 1988); *Strange Love* (Enigma, 1990; Restless, 1997); *Hell and Back Together 1984–1990* (Restless, 1992); *T.S.O.L./Weathered Statues* (Nitro, 1997); *Live '91* (Nitro, 1997); *Disappear* (Nitro, 2001); *Divided We Stand* (Nitro, 2003); *Who's Screwin' Who?: 18 TSOL Greatest Non-Hits* (Anarchy, 2005); TSOL/Slayer: *Abolish Government* EP 7 (Sub Pop, 1996); Cathedral of Tears: *Cathedral of Tears* EP (Enigma, 1984); Tender Fury: *Tender Fury* (Posh Boy, 1988); *Garden of Evil* (Triple X, 1990); *If Anger Were Soul, I'd Be James Brown* (Triple X, 1991); Jack Grisham/Mike Roche/Ron Emory/Todd Barnes: *Live 1991* (Triple X, 1991); Joykiller: *The Joykiller* (Epitaph, 1995); *Static* (Epitaph, 1996); *Three* (Epitaph, 1997); *Ready Sexed Go!* (Epitaph, 2003).

TWISTED SISTER (1978–87; 2001–PRESENT). Dee Snider (vocals), Jay Jay French (guitar), Eddie Ojeda (guitar), Mark "The Animal" Mendoza (bass), A. J. Pero (drums).

Inspired by the images of Kiss and the New York Dolls, New York City's Twisted Sister made a big splash in the hair metal era with the smash single "We're Not Gonna Take It." Although other releases would not meet with the same level of success, the band would go on to a much-loved and entertaining entity for a number of years in the 1980s before calling it quits and going their separate ways.

The group came together in the mid-1970s; by 1978 Twisted Sister consisted of guitarist Jay Jay French, vocalist Dee Snider, guitarist Eddie Ojeda, bassist Mark "The Animal" Mendoza, and drummer Tony Petri. After a handful of independent singles and an album on the independent Secret Records label, the band signed with Atlantic, releasing their 1983 album *You Can't Stop Rock 'n' Roll,* which was a modest success and paved the way to greater acceptance. The band's breakthrough would come with 1984's *Stay Hungry,* which featured their biggest single, "We're Not Gonna Take It," which was accompanied by a humorous video that enjoyed heavy rotation. Featuring an anthemic chorus about teenage rebellion, the song and video made the band stars—at least for a moment—and helped the album go platinum twice over.

Unfortunately, the band's follow-up, 1985's *Come Out and Play,* failed to replicate *Stay Hungry's* success, and after another poor showing with 1987's *Love Is for Suckers,* the band called it quits, with the members all pursuing separate projects. However, after a post–9/11 benefit reunion, the band has come together in a sporadic series of recordings and concerts, including the *Twisted Christmas* holiday album of 2006.

Discography: *Ruff Cutts* (Secret, 1982); *Under the Blade* (Secret, 1982); *You Can't Stop Rock 'N' Roll* (Atlantic, 1983); *Stay Hungry* (Atlantic, 1984); *Come Out and Play* (Atlantic, 1985); *Love Is for Suckers* (Atlantic, 1987); *Still Hungry* (Spitfire, 2004); *Twisted Christmas* (Razor & Tie, 2006); *Big Hits and Nasty Cuts: The Best of Twisted Sister* (Atlantic, 1992); *Live at Hammersmith* (CMC, 1994); *Early Works* (Spitfire, 1999); *Under the Blade* [WEA International] (Wea International, 1999); *Club Daze: The Studio Sessions, Vol. 1* (Spitfire, 1999); *Never Say Never: Club Daze, Vol. 2* (Spitfire, 2001); *Noble Savage* (Recall, 2002); *Club Daze, Vol. 2: Live in the Bars* (Spitfire, 2002); *The Essentials* (Warner Strategic, 2002); *We're Not Gonna Take It and Other Hits* (Rhino Flashback, 2003); *The Best of Twisted Sister* (Demolition, 2005).

TYPE O NEGATIVE (1990–PRESENT). Peter Steele (vocals/bass), Josh Silver (keyboards), Kenny Hickey (guitars), Sal Abruscato 1989–93, replaced by Johnny Kelly (drums).

Type O Negative were one of the most aggressive metal bands of the mid-nineties, led by frontman and bassist Pete Steele, they had to live up to the image of Steele's former band, the Mighty Carnivore. The music of Type O Negative is predictably hard and fast and loud (brutal may be too much to describe them) but they are a worthy successor to Carnivore. For a newcomer, buy *Bloody Kisses;* for the rest of you, buy them all.

Discography: *Slow, Deep and Hard* (RoadRacer, 1991); *The Origin of the Feces* (RoadRacer, 1992); *Bloody Kisses* (Roadrunner, 1993); *October Rust* (Roadrunner, 1996); *World Coming Down* (Roadrunner, 1999); *The Least Worst of Type O Negative* (Roadrunner, 2000).

U

UFO (1971–PRESENT). Classic lineup: Phil Mogg (vocals), Michael Schenker (guitar), Pete Way (bass), Andy Parker (drums), Paul Raymond (keyboards/guitar).

While never a huge draw in the States, UFO reached legendary status in Europe and remain one of the more solid metal acts of the seventies still active in the new millennium.

Debuting in 1971 with a "space rock" sound featuring extended song structures, UFO at first found little success in their native U.K., although they generated significant interest in Japan. After three albums, the band decided on a more straightforward rock direction and replaced their original guitarist, Mick Bolton, with a more rock-oriented player, eventually settling on Bernie Marsden (who would go on to become a founding member of Whitesnake).

Before the band would release their fourth album, however, a chance encounter brought them to the guitarist whose addition would help them enter the big leagues of seventies Euro-metal. On a gig in Germany, guitarist Bolton either went missing or was unable to make the trip due to a missing passport (the story seems to vary with the teller). At any rate, when UFO heard the support band on the gig at their soundcheck (the Scorpions), they were impressed by the 19-year-old guitarist playing lead. Asking him to fill in on the gig, they ultimately asked him to join the band on a permanent basis.

Schenker, for his part, would ultimately prove to be just what the band needed: a highly refined melodicism that permeated both his writing and his virtuosic lead playing, along with an incendiary guitar style that combined complex scale work with the passion of the blues. With Schenker aboard, the band crafted a unique rock style that was heavy, yet song-oriented and melodic.

Phenomenon (1974), the band's first with Schenker, was also their first in their new harder rocking incarnation and featured the future classics "Doctor, Doctor" and the guitar workout "Rock Bottom." While the album wasn't a huge seller, it established the band's new direction, one they would mine in the years to come. It also was the first of many albums featuring the enigmatic artwork of the art design group Hipgnosis.

Continuing with their melodic metal, UFO released *Force It* (1975) and *No Heavy Petting* (1976), and began to build their reputation in Europe and increasingly in the States. Their biggest breakthrough was the band's classic 1977 album *Lights Out*, which, in addition to the title track, featured the songs "Too Hot to Handle," "Alone Again Or," and "Love to Love," and garnered the band a good deal of critical acclaim. The album also featured the contributions of keyboardist/rhythm guitarist, whose dual talents effectively filled out and complemented the band's sound.

Lights Out was a watershed moment for the band, which, with an evolving quasi-glam image, would prove one of the most popular and influential heavy bands in Europe throughout the 1970s, ultimately serving as a major influence on the bands of the New Wave of British heavy metal that would emerge in the early eighties.

While the follow-up recording, 1978's *Obsession*, wasn't quite as impressive, it contributed to the band's upward mobility and featured the classic "Only You Can Rock Me." After the album's release, however, Schenker left the band, ultimately forming the Michael Schenker Group, after a short reunion with the Scorpions.

The band soldiered on, with Paul "Tonka" Chapman filling the guitar chair. The classic live album *Strangers in the Night* was released the following year and tellingly featured Schenker's playing, not Chapman's. While the band's next studio album, *No Place to Hide*, was a solid effort, it began the band's slide in popularity after Schenker's departure.

Mechanix (1982) was released the next year, but before long bassist Way had left the band to form Waysted. UFO then began a pattern that would follow for more than a decade, of partial reunions, and a revolving door of musicians collaborating with vocalist Mogg, and most often, Way. *Making Contact* was released in 1983 after which the band disbanded. They came together again for *Misdemeanor*, featuring U.S. guitarist Atomik Tommy M (McClendon), and quit again when the album failed to do well.

In 1995 Schenker joined up with the rest of the band's classic seventies lineup to release *Walk on Water*, which was something of a return to form for the band, albeit in a new musical era. Nonetheless, with a resurgent interest in classic rock, the band was able to mount a successful tour of the States and Europe in support of the album.

Afterward, the band split up again, coming back together for 2000's *Covenant* and then *Sharks* in 2002. Schenker was then replaced with American guitarist Vinnie Moore and the band released *You Are Here* (2004) and the live *Showtime* album in 2005. 2006 saw the release of *The Monkey Puzzle*.

Discography: *Flying* (Beacon, 1971); *UFO 1* (Rare Earth, 1971); *Phenomenon* (Chrysalis, 1974); *Force It* (Chrysalis, 1975); *No Heavy Petting* (Chrysalis, 1976); *Lights Out* (Chrysalis, 1977); *Obsession* (Chrysalis, 1978); *Strangers in the Night* [live] (Chrysalis, 1979); *No Place to Run* (Chrysalis, 1980); *The Wild, the Willing and the Innocent* (Chrysalis, 1981); *Mechanix* (Chrysalis, 1982); *Making Contact* (Ariola, 1983); *Misdemeanor* (Chrysalis, 1985); *Ain't Misbehavin'* (Metal Blade, 1988); *Live in Japan* (Alex, 1992); *TNT* (European Import, 1994); *Walk on Water* (Zero, 1995); *On with the Action* (Zoom Club/Windsong, 1998); *Live in London* (Delta, 2000); *Covenant* (Shrapnel, 2000); *Sharks* (Shrapnel, 2002); *You Are Here* (Steamhammer/SPV, 2004); *Showtime* [live] (Steamhammer/SPV, 2005); *The Monkey Puzzle* (SPV, 2006); *The Best of the Rest* (Chrysalis, 1987); *The Best of UFO 1974–1983* (EMI/Chrysalis, 2008).

UPPER CRUST (1995–PRESENT). Lord Bendover (vocals/guitar), Duc D'istortion (guitar), Count Basie (bass), Jackie Kickassis (drums).

Upper Crust dress like eighteenth-century French fops and play like AC/DC. The band, consisting of Lord Bendover ("perpetually at your service") on guitar and vocals, Count Basie on bass and vocals, the Duc D'istortion on guitar and vocals, and Jackie Kickassis on drums, plays what could be a one-note joke superbly, with songs that celebrate the virtues of being born with a silver spoon in one's mouth. The band started in Boston in the early eighties and soon began a long and noble career as the upper class of rock and roll, with hilarious and kick-ass songs as well.

Discography: *Let Them Eat Rock* (Upstart, 1995); *The Decline & Fall of the Upper Crust* (Emperor Norton, 1997); *Entitled* (Reptilian, 2000); *Once More Into the Breeches* (Emperor Norton, 2001).

URIAH HEEP (1970–80, 1982–PRESENT). Trevor Bolder (bass/vocals, 1977–1981; 1983–present), Mick Box (guitar/vocals, 1970–present), Russell Gilbrook (drums/vocals, 2007–present), Phil Lanzon (keyboards/ vocals, 1986–present), Bernie Shaw (lead vocals, 1986–present)

"If this group makes it I'll have to commit suicide. From the first note you know you don't want to hear any more ..."—Melissa Mills, *Rolling Stone* magazine, reviewing Uriah Heep's debut album in 1970.

Heavy metal did not have an easy birth. Perhaps more than any other genre of rock, the bands instrumental in developing it were belittled and ridiculed by mainstream critics from the start, with recognition of their influence and artistic genius grudgingly coming much later, including icons such as Led Zeppelin (whose debut album was initially dismissed by *Rolling Stone* magazine as "stainless steel shit"),

Uriah Heep, **masters of art rock and metal.** (Ilpo Musto/Rex Features)

Black Sabbath, and Deep Purple. Uriah Heep rank with them as among the most influential British founders of heavy metal and were similarly reviled by mainstream rock critics in the process. Heep went on to sell over 30 million albums worldwide from 1970 through the present, while the fate of the critic noted above is unrecorded.

Uriah Heep was founded in early 1970, when organist/guitarist/vocalist Ken Hensley was asked by record producer Gerry Bron to join Spice, a London-based band he was recording, on the recommendation of the band's bassist, Paul Newton. Newton had previously played with Hensley in a band called the Gods, which at various times had also included Mick Taylor (Rolling Stones), Greg Lake (King Crimson/ELP), and John Glascock (Jethro Tull). Spice consisted of David Byron (vocals), Mick Box (guitar), Paul Newton (bass), and Alex Napier (drums), and much of their music was based on American blues and jazz influences. Hensley brought in both a Beatlesque sense of melody and vocal harmonies and a heavy, organ-driven sound influenced primarily by Vanilla Fudge. The name of the band was taken from a character in the novel *David Copperfield* by Charles Dickens, at producer Bron's recommendation.

Heep's first album, *Very 'Eavy, Very 'Umble*, was a combination of their various influences, from the thunderous proto-metal opening track, "Gypsy" (reminiscent of Black Sabbath with a Hammond B3 organ added), to the acoustic "Come Away Melinda," to the straightforward jazz of the closing track, "Wake Up (Set Your Sights)." The rest of the album was largely a mélange of a band looking to find their direction (some tracks sound like Spice, some like the Gods), although all of the material is first-rate. During the recording, Alex Napier left the band, to be replaced by Nigel Ollson, who would leave after playing on one song ("Dreammare") to become Elton John's longtime drummer. Ollson was replaced by Keith Baker, whose playing is first heard on "Bird of Prey," which was substituted for the track "Lucy Blues" on the U.S. release of the first record (entitled *Uriah Heep*, and with a different cover).

The most significant impact of Heep's first album was not in the rotating drummers (often cited as the inspiration for the succession of drummers in the film *This Is Spinal Tap*) or even the material, as much as the performances. Vocalist David Byron established himself immediately as one of the most versatile singers in rock history; his ability to shift from a gentle ballad to a piercing, operatic scream in the same breath is almost unmatched, and the list of singers significantly influenced by him includes Ian Gillan, Freddie Mercury, Klaus Meine, Rob Halford, Bruce Dickinson, and King Diamond. Keyboardist Ken Hensley had a similar impact; his (often heavily distorted) Hammond B3 was cited by W.A.S.P.'s Blackie Lawless as "writing the book on heavy metal keyboards."

Most important were the backing vocals. Often incorporating three- to five-part harmonies, either supporting or engaging in counterpoint with the lead vocal, they became Uriah Heep's signature sound, leading to them sometimes being referred to as "The Beach Boys of Heavy Metal," and heavily influencing Queen, The Scorpions, Iron Maiden, Queensryche, Def Leppard, Saxon, and others.

Salisbury, their second album, was released in early 1971 and showed the band growing by leaps and bounds, with the prolific Hensley largely taking over the songwriting (which was to become a major point of tension down the line). Most prominent among the tracks were "Lady in Black," an acoustic number that continues to be a major hit in Continental Europe, and the title song, a complex,

16-minute epic featuring a 22-piece orchestra, and a lengthy guitar solo by Mick Box that many Heepsters (a term used by fans of the band to refer to each other) consider his finest performance, and which featured his prominent usage of the Vox "wah-wah" pedal that became the final important component of the band's overall sound.

Subsequent to the release of *Salisbury*, drummer Keith Baker left the band, citing their grueling tour schedule, and was replaced by Iain Clarke. The next album, *Look at Yourself*, released later in 1971, was even more of a quantum leap and possibly stands as the heaviest album of its era. The title track, featured in every live performance to this day, thunders like a runaway train, with three guest percussionists from the band Osibisa adding to the frenzy. Tracks like "I Wanna Be Free" and "Tears In My Eyes" are similarly energetic. Most important, the album contained the epic "July Morning," which, to use the cliché, is widely considered by Heepsters as the band's "Stairway to Heaven," and is still placed as the climax of every live show the band performs.

During subsequent months, bassist Paul Newton left the band, following a business dispute between his father, who had been the band's nominal manager, and producer Gerry Bron, who would manage the band for the next decade. Around the same time, Iain Clarke also departed. Lee ("The Bear") Kerslake, who had played with Hensley in both the Gods and a short-lived band called Toe Fat, would take up the sticks, while Mark Clark would join briefly on bass, staying long enough to co-write and sing lead on the bridge of "The Wizard," recorded as a single. He was replaced by New Zealand-born bass virtuoso Gary Thain, completing the "classic" Uriah Heep lineup of Box/Byron/Hensley/Kerslake/Thain, who would produce their career-defining (in the opinion of many Heepsters) works over the next three years.

Demons and Wizards, with cover art by Roger Dean, was recorded largely during breaks in the grueling tour schedule that manager Bron had established for the band, and was the first release by the "classic" lineup, in June 1972. In addition to the previously recorded "The Wizard," the songs included "Traveler in Time" (an homage to the BBC's "Doctor Who"), "Easy Livin'" (their first hit single and still probably their best-known song), the mysterious and ominous "Rainbow Demon," and two fantasy-oriented epics, "Circle of Hands" and "Paradise/The Spell," the latter clocking in at nearly 13 minutes.

Amazingly, the band managed to record a second album that year, *The Magician's Birthday*. Originally intended to be a full-blown concept album, it continued the mystical lyrical themes established by its predecessor, and featured another Roger Dean fantasy cover, depicting dueling magicians. Standout tracks were the opener, "Sunrise," filled with Heep's trademark vocal harmonies; "Blind Eye," a fast, largely acoustic song, which shifts interestingly between minor and major keys; "Rain," a gorgeous ballad showcasing Hensley's piano and Byron's voice; "Sweet Lorraine," an FM-radio hit; and the title track, a 10-minute multipart epic, featuring a guitar and drum duel from Box and Kerslake in the middle, as well as what may be a unique moment in rock history—a kazoo solo by Kerslake, during a rendition of the song "Happy Birthday To You."

With two seminal albums under their belt, and the lineup finally stable, Bron felt it was time to record a live album, and in January 1973, the band recorded the double LP *Uriah Heep Live*. Primarily featuring selections from the three most recent albums, along with a medley of 1950s classics, it is widely considered one of the definitive live albums of its era, frequently compared to Deep Purple's *Made in Japan*. Lavishly packaged, with a photo book in the gatefold, the band thumbed their noses at the critics by including a montage of some of the most negative reviews they could find. Certainly, by this point, they were "crying all the way to the bank."

At this stage, no one could have blamed the band for taking a rest, but they soon returned to the recording studio to produce 1973's *Sweet Freedom*. More straightforward lyrically than the previous two albums, it showcased Heep at their most confident and powerful. Highlights included the title track, an early "power ballad" with an almost "gospel" feel to Byron's vocal, the thunderous epic "Pilgrim," the dreamy, almost psychedelic "If I Had the Time," and "Stealin'," one of their biggest hits, and still played at every live performance, although some U.S. radio stations refused to play it at the time because of the (now tame) lyric "I done the rancher's daughter."

Unfortunately, along with success came rising tensions between members and personal demons. Hensley's domination of the band's songwriting led to the other members resenting what they saw as favoritism towards him by Bron. Worse, substance abuse problems were beginning to rear their ugly heads: Hensley had become addicted to cocaine, Thain to heroin, and Byron's drinking had spiraled out of control into full-blown alcoholism (although the entire band acquired a reputation as having a fondness for alcohol that continues to this day).

Wonderworld, recorded in 1974, saw the cracks in the façade start to become obvious. While largely a solid effort, it lacked the inspiration of the previous three studio albums, and communication had broken down to the point that guitarist Mick Box actually showed up at the studio the day after recording had been finished, because no one had told him the album was completed. The band's attitude was best summed up by a line from one of the album's highlights, "So Tired": "Yes I'm so tired of everybody staring at me. Yes I'm so tired, and I'm so uninspired—Please help me!" Other highlights included the title track, with a gorgeous vocal from Byron, "The Easy Road," an achingly beautiful ballad, and "The Shadows and The Wind," with a multipart counterpoint vocal section that clearly influenced Queen's *A Night at the Opera*.

While touring the U.S. in support of *Wonderworld*, bassist Gary Thain was electrocuted and nearly killed onstage in Dallas in September 1974. While Thain recovered sufficiently to rejoin the tour in mid-October, his health, always frail, and further impaired by heroin addiction, did not permit him to continue with the band, and he left (it is still unclear whether by mutual agreement or termination) in January 1975. Thain would be found dead of a heroin overdose on December 8 of that year (Ling 2002, 66). He was replaced by John Wetton (formerly of Family and King Crimson), and the band carried on with *Return to Fantasy*.

The album was a return to form for the band, with Wetton bringing a new energy and the writing becoming more sharply focused. While several songs are standouts, the title track (like "July Morning," composed by Hensley and Byron together) ranks among their very finest work and was brought back to the live set in the early 2000s as the opening song, much to the surprise and delight of Heepsters. The album reached number 7 on the British charts, the highest position of their career.

If 1974 was a difficult year for the band, 1976 would prove disastrous. Tensions had grown to the point that the band members actually insisted on five separate limos to take them three hundred yards from their hotel to a concert hall in Switzerland, and a row with manager/producer Gerry Bron led to the band deciding to self-produce their next album, *High and Mighty*. Almost entirely penned by Hensley, it showed that even the finest writers need an objective producer's ear to tell them when things aren't working. While some songs are gems, particularly "Weep in Silence," "Footprints in the Snow," "Misty Eyes," and "Confession," the album is also saddled with some of the worst material they ever recorded, especially "Woman of the World" and "Can't Stop Singing."

Fans were mystified at the alarming drop-off in quality from the previous comeback album. One weak album is recoverable. What followed arguably wasn't. David Byron's drinking had been out of control for some time, and his alcohol abuse, combined with his "rock star" ego, led to such outrageous behavior on his part (including cursing out a stunned audience in Philadelphia and kicking in plate glass doors at an arena in Spain) that Ken Hensley left the tour after the latter incident to fly back to England, and demanded of Gerry Bron "it's him or me." Bron, unwilling to lose the band's primary songwriter, capitulated, and Byron was fired in July 1976. Wetton, who was personally close to Byron, and who had been dissatisfied with the musical direction, resigned two weeks later (he would go on to front prog/pop band Asia in the 1980s).

Byron went on to form Rough Diamond with former members of Wings and Humble Pie. The group would last for one album, before Byron was sacked again for his drinking. He would attempt another comeback with the Byron Band, before suffering an alcohol-related seizure on stage at London's Marquee club, while singing "July Morning," in 1981. Another such seizure would kill him at age 38 in February 1985. (Ken Hensley, by then touring as a member of U.S. "Southern rock" band Blackfoot, was so shaken by the news of Byron's death that several years later he temporarily left the music business to address his own cocaine addiction and subsequently became a born-again Christian).

The band would audition several potential replacements for Byron, including Mott the Hoople's Ian Hunter and Deep Purple's David Coverdale, before offering the position to John Lawton, who had fronted German band Lucifer's Friend. The bass slot was filled by Trevor Bolder, who had played with David Bowie's Spiders From Mars. While Lawton and Bolder brought a fresh energy to the band, Heep arguably never fully recovered from the loss of Byron, a unique and charismatic frontman, whose dramatic and theatrical vocal delivery was one of the essential components of their sound. Many fans seemed to agree, and while Heep have had successes since 1976, they never again attained the level of popularity in the U.S. and UK that they had enjoyed with Byron.

Firefly, the first album with Lawton and Bolder, was released in 1977. With Bron back in the producer's chair, the material was much more focused, and both Lawton and Bolder turn in stellar performances, as if trying to prove themselves. Standouts include "Wise Man," a power ballad with an amazing vocal by Lawton, whose voice was more powerful (if less versatile and emotional) than Byron's; "Who Needs Me," a rare contribution by Lee Kerslake; and the title track, largely sung by Hensley. It was followed up later that year by *Innocent Victim*, which represented a significant change of direction; while containing riff-rockers like "Free 'n' Easy," and Heep's trademark mysticism in "Illusion," the centerpiece of the album was the outright pop song "Free Me," which became their biggest hit in Continental Europe.

Its follow-up, 1978's *Fallen Angel*, veered even more in a pop direction, alienating many longtime fans, and winning few new ones, although it contained a few excellent songs, such as the Kerslake-Hensley collaboration "Come Back to Me," and "I'm Alive," which would become Lawton's signature song.

By this point, Hensley had come to completely dominate the band, to the point where he insisted on a separate dressing room for himself at concerts. Tensions, exacerbated by his cocaine addiction (Ling 66), rose to the point that he demanded Lawton's firing, during the recording of a fourth album, which Bron accommodated. A disgusted Lee Kerslake quit shortly afterward; his enmity towards Hensley continued for decades. (Outtakes from the abortive fourth Lawton album have circulated for years as bootlegs, variously entitled *Five Miles* and *Ten Miles High*).

What followed ultimately resulted in the temporary dissolution of the band. Hensley wanted Peter Goalby from Trapeze to replace Lawton, while the rest of the band insisted on U.S.–born John Sloman, and Sloman was given the job. Filling in for Kerslake on drums was Chris Slade. The resulting album, 1980's *Conquest*, further mystified and dissatisfied not only the fan base, but also Hensley. Sloman didn't have a bad voice, but his soul and funk influences made it wildly unsuited for Uriah Heep, and Hensley was extremely unhappy with Sloman's live performances of the older material. Again, he delivered an ultimatum to Bron. This time, a disgusted Bron refused, and Hensley quit the band in September 1980, leaving it in a state of collapse. He was briefly replaced by Greg Dechert, but the handwriting was on the wall, and everyone in the band besides Box and Bolder left in early 1981. Mick and Trevor attempted to coax David Byron back into the fold; amazingly, Byron refused. Bolder then left to join Wishbone Ash, leaving Box as the sole member of the once-proud band.

1982 saw the unlikeliest of events: Uriah Heep re-formed, now with Mick Box as the bandleader. Lee Kerslake rejoined on drums (in the absence of long-time nemesis Hensley), bringing with him bassist Bob Daisley, whom he had played with on the first two Ozzy Osbourne solo albums while on hiatus from Heep. John Sinclair, who had toured with Heep as part of opening act Heavy Metal Kids, played keyboards, and the new vocalist (probably much to Hensley's chagrin) was none other than Peter Goalby. *Abominog*, their first release, was a surprising critical and commercial success; its contemporary sound placed it comfortably in the New Wave of British heavy metal genre (ironically enough, Heep now drew inspiration from bands that they had originally inspired), and the single from the album, "That's the Way That it Is," found its way into heavy rotation on U.S. radio stations. *Head First*, released in 1983, continued in the same vein, although it was less commercially successful. Unfortunately for the band, at this point, Bronze Records collapsed financially, ending their association with both their longtime label, and manager Gerry Bron. Stalwart Mick Box took over the band's management himself, a position he held until 2005. At around this time, Bob Daisley left as bassist, only to be replaced by his predecessor, Trevor Bolder, who has remained with the band to date.

1985's disappointing *Equator*, released on CBS subsidiary Portrait Records, found the band floundering for direction, with most of the record consisting of poor attempts at a contemporary "hair metal" sound; only "Night of the Wolf" is up to the band's usual standards. Worse, the record was poorly distributed, leading to the band touring to support a product that most fans didn't have access to. Goalby and Sinclair left, demoralized and exhausted.

They were replaced in 1986 by U.S.–born Steff Fontaine and Phil Lanzon, respectively. Lanzon was an inspired choice, who has remained with the band to this day. Fontaine's tenure proved the shortest of any member; following a disastrous U.S. tour in which he managed to get lost while taking a walk during a rehearsal break, and at one point found himself in L.A. while the band was ready to go onstage in San Diego (Ling 2002, 123). He was replaced by Canadian–born Bernie Shaw, who remains the band's frontman. Shaw proved ideal for the situation; his voice is versatile enough to perform songs from all eras of the band, including the Byron–era material, which had challenged the band's other singers, not so much because of its difficulty, but because of Byron's unique delivery.

1987 was a triumphant year for Uriah Heep. With their lineup now settled, they played ten sold-out shows in Moscow's Olympic Stadium, to a total of 185,000 fans, the first Western rock band to be invited to play in the Soviet Union. Unfortunately, their refound glory was to prove short lived. Signed to Legacy Records, a small label with few resources to promote the band, 1988's *Live in Moscow*, 1989's *Raging Silence*, and 1991's *Different World* were barely noticed by the record-buying public; indeed, many U.S. fans assumed that they had broken up during the 1980s. While they still retained significant popularity in Continental Europe, especially in Germany, which boasts several Uriah Heep "tribute" bands, their U.S. and UK audiences dwindled down to "cult" band size.

Sea of Light, recorded for German label CBH, followed in 1995. Widely considered one of the best albums of their career, it saw the band shedding the synthesizers and 1980s production that had marred their previous few efforts. Returning to their proto-metal and prog roots, *SOL* was their first record in years to actually sound like a Uriah Heep album, with Bernie Shaw's vocal delivery sounding uncannily like David Byron's in places. Highlights include "A Time of Revelation," "Universal Wheels," and Bolder's haunting acoustic ballad "Dream On." The album also saw Heep return to their visual roots, with a cover painting by Roger Dean. Unfortunately, the album was not even released in the U.S. until 1999, as Heep lacked an American distributor at the time, the situation only being rectified in 1998.

In addition to the release of *SOL*, 1995 was significant for the band in that it featured a brief reunion with John Lawton for a tour of South Africa, following Bernie Shaw undergoing surgery to remove nodes from his vocal cords.

Three years later, in 1998, again on a new label, Eagle Rock (Spitfire in the U.S.), the band released *Sonic Origami*, which would turn out to be their last studio effort for ten years. Continuing in the vein of its predecessor, *SO* clocked in at well over an hour in length, making it the equivalent of a "double" LP, the first such studio effort in Heep's history, and the quality of the material continued to improve: Mick Box and Phil Lanzon had developed into a formidable songwriting team, with Trevor Bolder also contributing strong compositions. Standouts on this record included the opening track, "Between Two Worlds," written about and dedicated to Gary Thain and David Byron, "Heartless Land," "Question," "Sweet Pretender," and the epic "The Golden Palace," featuring an orchestral backing. Unfortunately, again, a lack of promtional funds became an issue, and not only was the album largely ignored as a result, but the band was forced to cancel a planned U.S. tour at the last moment.

After *Sonic Origami*, Heep spent the next few years recording and releasing live albums (no less than seven between 2000 and 2005), the most significant being

Acoustically Driven (2001) and *The Magician's Birthday Party* (2002). The former was actually funded by online subscriptions and featured Heep reworking both classic and contemporary songs in a special one-time concert with various acoustic accompanists, including an uleiann piper, and special guest flautist Ian Anderson of Jethro Tull. (The concert was also significant in that it stands as the only show since the band's inception at which "Gypsy" was not performed).

The latter album, recorded live in concert in London in December 2001, featured the wildly unlikely one-time reunion of Heep with Ken Hensley, to a packed house of deliriously happy fans who had come from around the world to witness the event. Featuring several songs that had never before been performed live, including "Paradise/The Spell," and the entirety of "The Magician's Birthday," the evening reached a climax when John Lawton walked out on stage during the latter song to sing the part of the evil magician, completing the onstage reunion of the 1977–79 lineup. Both albums were also released as DVDs. After their first U.S. appearances in several years during 2001, the band managed to return to the U.S. in late 2002, appearing with Asia, Focus, and others; another live album, recorded in Trenton, New Jersey, and a DVD resulted from the trip. Two subsequent "Magician's Birthday Party" concerts led to the same CD/DVD combination, one of them again including John Lawton's participation, this time in a more prominent role.

Plans for a new studio LP had been announced for several years, without materializing, when in April 2005 the band made the surprising announcement that it had retained Simon Porter as their manager, Box relinquishing the position he had held since the mid-1980s. Porter aggressively pursued a new record contract for the band, and they were signed to Sanctuary Records in 2006, with an album planned for release in 2007. Unfortunately, these plans were derailed by the ill health of longtime drummer Lee Kerslake, and in early 2007, he was forced to leave the band he had played with for most of the past 35 years, to the disappointment of Heepsters, to whom he had long been a favorite. He was replaced by Russell Gilbrook, and the band began recording their long-awaited 21st studio album with producer Mike Paxman, due out this year. Nearly 40 years since their inception, through every from of adversity, the Uriah Heep story still appears to be far from over.

Discography: Given their multiple changes in record labels, and the several U.S. distributors used by Bronze Records, an almost bewildering collection of Heep anthologies (as well as several unofficial live albums, including *Live in Europe 1979*, *Live At Shepperton '74*, and *Live on the King Biscuit Flower Hour*) are available from various sources. The following list consists of recordings officially approved and released by the band, with their original U.S. label of release:

Very 'Eavy, Very 'Umble [*Uriah Heep* in U.S. release] (Mercury, 1970); *Salisbury* (Mercury, 1971); *Look at Yourself* (Mercury, 1971); *Demons and Wizards* (Mercury, 1972); *The Magician's Birthday* (Mercury, 1972); *Uriah Heep Live* (Mercury, 1973); *Sweet Freedom* (Warner Brothers, 1973); *Wonderworld* (Warner Brothers, 1974); *The Best of Uriah Heep* (Mercury, 1974); *Return to Fantasy* (Warner Brothers, 1975); *High and Mighty* (Warner Brothers, 1976); *Firefly* (Warner Brothers, 1977); *Innocent Victim* (Warner Brothers, 1977); *Fallen Angel* (Chrysalis, 1978); *Conquest* (Chrysalis, 1980); *Abominog* (Mercury, 1982); *Head First* (Mercury, 1983); *Equator* (Portrait, 1985); *Live in Moscow* (Legacy, 1988); *Raging Silence* (Legacy, 1989); *Different World* (Legacy, 1991); *Sea of Light* (released in 1995 in Europe and Japan, finally released in the U.S. on the Spitfire label in 1999); *Spellbinder*

Live (released in 1996 in Europe and Japan, released in the U.S. on the Spitfire Label in 1999); *Sonic Origami* (Spitfire, 1998); *Future Echoes of the Past* (Classic Rock Legends, 2000); *Acoustically Driven* (Classic Rock Legends, 2001); *Electrically Driven* (Classic Rock Legends, 2001); *Remasters* (Classic Rock Legends, 2001); *The Magician's Birthday Party* (Classic Rock Legends, 2002); *Live in the USA* (Classic Rock Legends, 2003); *Magic Night* (Classic Rock Legends, 2004); *Between Two Worlds* (Classic Rock Legends, 2005); *Wake the Sleeper* (Sanctuary, 2008).

V

STEVE VAI (1960–). One of the most recognizable guitarists on the rock scene over the last twenty years, Vai, along with his erstwhile teacher Joe Satriani, has only worked within established groups for short periods of time, instead having established a successful solo career of largely instrumental albums.

After graduating from the prestigious Berklee College of Music, Vai started his professional career in 1979 as a transcriber for Frank Zappa, going on to play guitar for Zappa's band for several years. Leaving Zappa in 1984, Vai released a pair of self-recorded albums, *Flex-Able* and *Flex-Able Leftovers*, which were Zappa–influenced, instrumental works.

Soon after, Vai took his impeccable chops and became something of a hard rock hired gun, first replacing Yngwie Malmsteen in the Graham Bonnett–led Alcatrazz, recording the 1985 album *Disturbing the Peace* with the band. Also in 1985, Vai turned in a delicious performance in the film *Crossroads*, playing the devil's guitarist whom Ralph Macchio's character has to play against in a guitar duel.

Vai's next stop was with former Van Halen frontman David Lee Roth, whose strategy after Van Halen was to enlist virtuoso players and let them strut their stuff. Vai and bassist Billy Sheehan didn't disappoint, pulling out all the stops in the studio, on stage, and in a series of seriously funny and entertaining videos for the album. As a result, Vai became a mainstream star, idolized by guitarists and guitar fans all over the world, a fan base that would go far in sustaining Vai later in his solo career. Vai stayed with Roth for two albums, 1986's *Eat 'Em and Smile* and 1988's *Skyscraper*, leaving just after the latter's release.

1988 was also the year that Vai became an endorser of the Japanese guitar company Ibanez, which released Vai's signature model guitar, the Jem 777, which he has played ever since. Later in the year, while working on his solo album, he was asked to join Whitesnake, who were at their peak of popularity, getting ready to follow up their massively successful 1987 *Whitesnake* album. Vai joined the band, playing on the 1989 album *Slip of the Tongue*. His solo album *Passion & Warfare* came out the same year and was a significant hit, going gold.

Leaving Whitesnake after completing the *Slip of the Tongue* tour, Vai assembled his own rock group featuring veteran musicians bassist T. M. Stevens, drummer Terry Bozzio, and singer Devin Townsend. The band, dubbed VAI, released a single album, 1993's *Sex & Religion*, which failed to meet Vai or the public's expectations, and the group disbanded shortly thereafter, with Vai going back to his solo career. He has continued to release solo albums ever since, and in the late nineties began the annual G3 guitar tour, which he co-headlines with Joe Satriani and a revolving third guitarist.

Discography: *Flex-Able* (Epic, 1984); *Passion & Warfare* (Epic, 1990); *Sex & Religion* (Epic, 1993); *Alien Love Secrets* (Epic, 1995); *Fire Garden* (Epic, 1996); *Flex-Able Leftovers* (Epic, 1998); *The Ultra Zone* (Epic, 1999); *The 7th Song: Enchanting Guitar Melodies* (Sony, 2000); *Alive in an Ultra World* (Epic, 2001); *Live Around the World* (Sony, 2001); *Real Illusions: Reflections* (WK, 2005); *Live Album* (Sony, 2007); *Sound Theories, Vols. 1–2* (Epic/Red Ink, 2007); *The Elusive Light and Sound, Vol. 1* (Favored Nations, 2002); *Mystery Tracks Archives, Vol. 3* (Favored Nations, 2003); *The Infinite Steve Vai: An Anthology* (Epic/Legacy, 2003); *Archives, Vol. 4* (Favored Nations, 2005); *Original Album Classics* (Sony/BMG, 2008).

VANDENBERG (1982–86). Adrian Vandenberg (guitar), Bert Heerink (vocals), Dick Kemper (bass), Joe Zoomer (drums).

Best known as the vehicle that first gave future Whitesnake guitarist Adrian Vandenberg his start, Dutch hard rockers Vandenberg purveyed a somewhat bland yet sometimes catchy melodic rock that gave them a substantial European following, yet failed to break big in the States. While "Friday Night," the lead single from the band's 1983 sophomore album *Heading for a Storm*, enjoyed a bit of American airplay, the band broke up after 1985's *Alibi*, when Adrian Vandenberg was tapped by David Coverdale to join the revamped lineup that would tour behind Whitesnake's self-titled 1987 breakthrough album.

Discography: *Vandenberg* (Atco, 1982); *Heading for a Storm* (Atco, 1983); *Alibi* (Atco, 1985).

VAN HALEN (1977–PRESENT). David Lee Roth (vocals, 1977–84, 2007–present), Eddie Van Halen (guitar), Alex Van Halen (drums), Michael Anthony (1977–2005), Sammy Hagar (vocals, 1985–?), Gary Cherone (vocals), Wolfgang Van Halen (bass, 2007–present)

Van Halen changed everything. The release of Van Halen's self-titled album in 1978—was it really in 1978?!—almost overnight changed the dominant paradigm in rock music. It's amazing to realize that before Van Halen was an eighties rock band, they were an eighties rock band, which is merely to say that heavy rock music in the eighties probably wouldn't have developed in quite the way that it did if Van Halen hadn't led the way out of the 1970s. As a whip-cracking guitarist, Eddie Van Halen cracked the loudest whip anyone had ever experienced, single-handedly (well, actually he used both hands) changing the way a whole generation of guitarists conceived of their instrument, what it should do, how it should look, and how it should sound. His highly developed two-handed tapping technique and innovative use of the whammy (tremolo) bar expanded the vocabulary of rock guitar in one fell swoop.

Van Halen ruled the roost with David Lee Roth in the early 1980s. (Photofest)

Van Hagar: Many fans thought the band was not quite the same without Diamond Dave (David Lee Roth). (© Pictorial Press Ltd / Alamy)

And frontman David Lee Roth drew as much inspiration from lounge singers and vaudeville performers as from Robert Plant. And as a band (whose sound was very much shaped by the sound of that guitar), Van Halen effortlessly fused pop sensibilities into the sturm and drang power of heavy metal in such a way that most who followed could only offer what can at best be described as "pop metal" in the band's wake. Ultimately, the genius of the original VH lineup was in their charismatic approach to changing the rules, which helped them to become one of the most popular bands of the late seventies and early eighties.

Van Halen began when Van Halen brothers guitarist Eddie and drummer Alex, who had been playing in the Pasadena-based trio Mammoth, joined forces with vocalist David Lee Roth. After Roth suggested adopting the brothers' surname for the band, they hired bassist Michael Anthony to fill out their ranks. The band soon became a fixture on the Hollywood rock scene playing their high-energy original music. One early admirer was Kiss bassist Gene Simmons, who flew the band to New York to record a series of demos. Eddie, having to use rented gear, had trouble getting the unique signature guitar tones that he had been developing back home, and the band was not enthused with the results.

Back in L.A., the band was spotted at a gig at the Starwood Lounge by Warner Record exec Mo Ostin and producer Ted Templeman who, in a moment out of a Hollywood fairy tale, offered the band a record contract. Recorded largely live by Templeman, the band's first self-titled album was released in 1978. The album soon became a hit, selling a million copies within the first six months of its release. The album was a powerhouse of modern rock without an ounce of filler on it, and the energy level was sustained on the whole album. It soon became *the* album to put on at a party. In fact, in addition to the band's serious musicianship, Roth's particular style of fronting the band, along with the band's general good-time vibe, led to their shows feeling like a party where everyone was invited. The album's one-two punch was found in the tracks "Eruption," which led into the band's cover of the Kinks' "You Really Got Me."

"Eruption" was the track, more than any other, that established Eddie Van Halen's reputation. The blistering, unaccompanied solo (save for its bombastic full band intro) was the sonic equivalent of "the world of guitar, according to Eddie." Achieving the fullest, richest tone of a cranked Marshall amp (later to be dubbed the "brown sound" by fans), Ed proceeded to rip into a series of improvised riffing that seamlessly led into the beautiful, baroque-sounding two-handed tapping flourishes that led more than one guitarist at the time to ask: "How is he doing that?!" As the solo climaxes and the last descending notes begin to fade, the track segues into the blistering power chords that start "You Really Got Me," and the band kicks in all their power. Not surprisingly, the band quickly became a powerful live attraction and toured heavily behind the album.

The band followed up their debut with *Van Halen II*, released in 1979. Again produced by Templeman, *VH II* contained the band's first hit single, "Dance the Night Away," which showed a much more melodic, pop side to the band. They also covered Linda Ronstadt's "You're No Good," which received a good amount of airplay.

Women and Children First followed in 1980 and continued the band's winning formula, with the track "And the Cradle Will Rock" receiving significant airplay. For the first time, the band headlined on their supporting tour. *Fair Warning* in 1981 was a darker record for the band, with a dangerous air about it, perhaps best captured on the opening track "Mean Street." More popular was the band's *Diver Down*, which had a decidedly more upbeat feel, and featured a number of cover tunes, most notably Roy Orbison's "Pretty Woman" and the Martha and the Vandellas classic "Dancin' in the Streets."

1984 saw, well, *1984*, the album that would take the band to a whole new level of success. Released on New Year's Day, the album contained the synthesizer-driven hit "Jump," which brought a new sound to the band's repertoire. The song was a number one smash and helped to take the album to the number two spot, the highest charting position a Van Halen album had gone to that point. The album continued three more hits in "I'll Wait," "Panama," and "Hot for Teacher."

Just as *1984* would remain a high-water mark for the band, it would also mark the end of an era, as tensions within the band, between Roth and the Van Halen brothers, came to a head. Roth had disapproved of Ed's playing on Michael Jackson's "Beat It," while Ed and Alex had grown tired of Roth's' comedic hijinks. Roth had experienced a good deal of success with his solo EP *Crazy from the Heat*, which had produced the hits "California Girls" and "Just a Gigolo/I Ain't Got Nobody." And when Roth's activities delayed the band's recording schedule, he was fired.

The band's choice of former Montrose frontman Sammy Hagar was on the surface an unlikely choice, given that the "Red rocker" was just the sort of serious rocker that Roth liked to parody. But given that the VH brothers were sick of Roth's humor, the choice made more sense. At the same time, as serious musicians, Ed and Alex's choice also made sense, in that Hagar was a skilled singer with a range and vocal technique that Roth hadn't possessed.

While the change upset many fans, the first album with Hagar did well. *5150*, released in 1986, ended up being a massive hit, fueled by the hit singles "Why Can't This Be Love," "Dreams," and "Love Walks In." Hagar's vocal style was much different from Roth's and actually fit the band's evolving sound, which, following the experiment of "Jump," involved a greater integration of keyboards. The next album with Hagar, 1988s *OU812*, was similarly successful, producing the hits "When It's Love" and "Finish What You Started." *For Unlawful Carnal Knowledge* continued the string of hit albums of the "Van Hagar" version of the band, and produced the hit "Right Now." 1993 saw the release of the band's first live album, *Right Here, Right Now.*

While the Hagar/Van Halen union had been commercially and creatively successful, tensions had grown, especially between the singer and the guitarist. Eddie had undergone rehab for alcoholism while Hagar remained a friend of the party. After the release of *Balance* in 1995, the band wanted to schedule a greatest hits collection, an idea that Hagar was not in favor of. After another difference of opinion over a song being recorded for the *Twister* soundtrack, the band began recording some new music (to be included in the greatest hits collection) without telling Hagar. When the singer heard about the collaboration with Roth he hit the roof.

Accounts differ regarding Hagar's exit from the group, with Eddie claiming he quit, and Hagar claiming he was fired. At any rate, Roth ended up recording two new tracks for the *Best of ...* collection and assumed he was back in the band. Unbeknownst to Roth, the position had allegedly been secretly offered to singer Mitch Malloy. But when the four original members of the band made a joint appearance on the *MTV Music Awards*, Malloy bowed out. After the awards show

Roth was out again and cried foul, saying that he had been tricked into recording the tracks under the false pretense of a reunion.

The best-of collection, entitled *Best of, Vol. 1*, was a hit, and ex-Extreme vocalist Gary Cherone was brought on board as the new frontman for the band. The resulting studio album, *Van Halen III*, while entering the charts at number 3, performed poorly, becoming the least successful album in the band's catalog. After a single tour, the band and Cherone parted ways.

More rumors of a reunion with Roth began to circulate, with the singer alleging on his website that he had been recording with the band. Shortly thereafter, it was announced that Eddie, a longtime smoker, was suffering from oral cancer, but that the prognosis for a full recovery was good. A short time later came the surprising announcement that Van Halen was parting ways with longtime label Warner Brothers. No new recording contract with any other labels was mentioned at the time.

After Eddie's treatment and recovery, the band reunited in 2004 for a tour that saw Sammy Hagar fronting the band again. After the tour, sessions were held with Hagar for a few new songs for the upcoming second volume of the band's greatest hits collection. Bassist Michael Anthony was conspicuous in his absence, with Eddie playing bass on the sessions.

In 2006, the band announced that Anthony had been fired from the band, with Eddie explaining to *Rolling Stone* magazine that since Anthony had been playing with Hagar, he couldn't be in two bands at the same time. Shortly thereafter, it was announced that Roth would indeed finally be returning to the band for an extended tour that would also feature Eddie's son Wolfgang taking Anthony's place on bass. While the tour was initially postponed while Eddie entered rehab again (Christie, 2008), and was mysteriously interrupted in early 2008, after a successful start in the fall of 2007; by June 2008, it was announced that the tour had thus far grossed over $93 million, making it the most successful Van Halen tour ever.

Discography: *Van Halen* (Warner Bros., 1978); *Van Halen II* (Warner Bros., 1979); *Women and Children First* (Warner Bros., 1980); *Fair Warning* (Warner Bros., 1981); *Diver Down* (Warner Bros., 1982); *1984* (Warner Bros., 1984); *5150* (Warner Bros., 1986); *OU812* (Warner Bros., 1988); *For Unlawful Carnal Knowledge* (Warner Bros., 1991); *Live: Right Here, Right Now* (Warner Bros., 1993); *Balance* (Warner Bros., 1995); *Van Halen III* (Warner Bros., 1998); *Best of Van Halen, Vol. 1* (Warner Bros., 1996); *Live in Pittsburgh '98* (Import, 1998); *Van Halen Box: 1986–1993* (WEA, 1999); *Van Halen Box: 1978–1984* (WEA International, 2000); *The Best of Both Worlds* (Warner Bros., 2004); *The Very Best of Van Halen* (WEA International, 2004); *Best of Van Halen: The Early Years* (Rhino, 2007); *Best of Van Halen 1978–1984* (Warner Bros., 2007).

VENOM (1997–PRESENT). Cronos (vocals/bass), Mantas (guitar, replaced by James Barnes, Alistair Clarke, Mykvys, now Rage), Abbadon (drums, replaced by Antton).

Venom are one of the key originators of the black metal movement and are largely responsible for its spread, especially in England and North America. Although there were lean years for Venom, the band continues to tour as a sort of living fossil, demonstrating who it was that inspired all of those kids to sign a contract with the devil and pick up a guitar all those years ago (or was that Robert Johnson?). Venom's legacy in terms of the history of black metal is indescribable.

The band was formed by Cronos (Conrad Lant) along with guitarist Mantas (Jeffrey Dunn) and drummer Abbadon (Anthony Bray), names taken to match the early satanic tilt of their lyrics. Venom, nominally a part of the New Wave of British heavy metal, can also be looked upon as the true fathers of the black metal scene. Their first record, the classic *Welcome to Hell*, hinted at the speed and power of the direction that Venom was moving in. By the time of the second record, *Black Metal*, the overall sound of black metal had been set. Venom had been inspired not only by Black Sabbath, from whom they cribbed the basic satanic vocabulary, but also by early punk rock, particularly hardcore, where the drums and guitars are sped up, sometimes beyond the technical capabilities of the band (Venom once did a show with legendary punks Black Flag, demonstrating the crossover appeal of the band.)

Mantas departed the band after *Possessed*, and the quality went downhill after that, although his replacements James Barnes and Alistair Clarke were more than competent. After a few years Mantas returned as Cronos left and a new lead singer Tony Dolan toured as Venom and recorded the forgettable *Prime Evil* and *The Wastelands*, which many fans do not consider to be "true" Venom records. Eventually the band reunited in the mid-nineties, but soon Mantas and Abbadon were gone again, and Cronos continued with new musicians, releasing the *Metal Black* record in 2006 as an indication that the band had returned to its roots. Although their career has been marred by personnel changes and spotty mid-period records, Venom is the most important band in the history of black metal and a key influence on thousands of other bands in the black and death metal scenes.

Discography: *Welcome to Hell* (Combat, 1981); *Black Metal* (Combat, 1982); *At War with Satan* (Combat, 1983); *Eine Kleine Nachtmusic* [live] (Dead Line, 1985); *Official Botoleg Live* (Magnum America, 1985); *Possessed* (Combat, 1985); *Calm Before the Storm* (AJK, 1987); *Prime Evil* (Maze/Kraze, 1989); *Temples of Ice* (Under One Flag, 1991); *The Book of Armageddon* (Combat, 1992); *The Waste Lands* (Under One Flag, 1992); *The Second Coming Live at Dynamo 1996* (Nuclear Blast, 1997); *From Heaven to the Unknown* (Snapper, 1998); *New, Live & Rare* (Deadline, 1998); *Cast in Stone* (Steamhammer UK, 1998); *Official Botoleg* (Thunderbolt, 1999); *Court of Death* (Receiver, 2000); Resurrection (Steamhammer, 2000); *Beauty and the Beast* (Dressed to Kill, 2000); *Kissing the Beast* (Sanctuary, 2002); *Under a Spell* (Teenile Dementia, 2003); *Witching Hour* (Demolition, 2003); *Metal Black* (Sanctuary, 2006); *Hell* (Noise, 2008).

VINNIE VINCENT. Vinnie Vincent's greatest claim to fame is that he was the first guitarist to replace original lead guitarist Ace Frehley in Kiss. Born Vincent Cusano, Vincent was given his stage name by Gene Simmons when Vincent joined the band in 1982.

Prior to joining Kiss, Vincent (as Cusano) had played in a variety of bands and done session work for Laura Nyro and Dan Hartman and had been a composer for the television show *Happy Days*. Meeting Kiss's Gene Simmons through a mutual friend, Vincent was soon asked to contribute songwriting and lead parts on the band's *Creatures of the Night* album when the band began experiencing problems with original guitarist Frehley. Once Frehley had exited the band, Vincent was asked to join. With "Ankh Warrior" face makeup (designed by Paul Stanley), Vincent joined the band for its tour in support of the *Creatures* album.

After the tour finished in 1983, Vincent joined the band for that year's *Lick It Up*, for which the band took off their makeup. Vincent contributed songwriting on much of the album, which after a string of commercially disappointing albums became the band's first in three years to go gold. Unfortunately, Vincent was unhappy about his salary with the band and departed before work on 1984's *Animalize* began.

Landing on his feet, Vincent soon emerged with the Vinnie Vincent Invasion, which released its eponymous debut in 1986. Featuring pop-oriented metal tunes and an over-the-top glam rock image, the band made something of a splash on MTV and released a second album, *All Systems Go*, in 1988. Shortly after the second release, Vincent's bandmates, singer Mark Slaughter and bassist Dana Strum, departed themselves to start their own band, Slaughter, and the invasion was over.

Vincent popped up again briefly in 1992, contributing writing to Kiss's *Revenge* album, but by 1997 had filed suit against the band for alleged nonpayment of royalties. Little more has been heard from Vincent since, apart from occasional appearances at Kiss conventions during the 1990s, although he released *Speedball Jamm* in 2004, featuring informally recorded unaccompanied shredding.

Discography: *Vinnie Vincent Invasion* (Chrysalis, 1986); *All Systems Go* (Chrysalis, 1988); *Speedball Jamm* (Vinnie Vincent, 2004).

VIRTUOSITY IN HEAVY METAL. In keeping with heavy metal's emphasis on power, instrumental virtuosity has long been a common feature of many heavy metal bands. Sociologist Deena Weinstein notes, too, that part of heavy metal's appeal, especially to male fans, is that many of the genre's musicians demonstrate physical mastery over their chosen instruments. In particular, this mastery is most clearly manifested in the performances of guitarists and somewhat secondarily in those of drummers. (While the performances of vocalists and bassists—the other two main elements of heavy metal—are often masterful, the quality of a vocalist's "instrument" is largely a matter of what they are born with, while bassists function in a largely supportive role and play at very low pitches, both of which serve to keep them out of the spotlight.)

Guitar Virtuosity. The first virtuoso guitarists were the blues players like Eric Clapton and Jeff Beck who used the space provided by the basic instrumentation (bass, drums, and guitar) of their bands, Cream and the Jeff Beck Group, to take their rock-infused blues guitar playing to new heights and volumes, as they led the way in defining the new heavy rock that they played.

Two major factors in guitar virtuosity have been technique and technology. For Clapton, Beck, and others of their generation (such as Jimmy Page of Led Zeppelin and Leslie West of Mountain), the new technology of bigger, louder, and more distorted amplifiers, combined with the easier playing and heavily sustaining Gibson Les Paul guitars, led to a new, more expressive style of lead guitar playing that involved more emotional vibrato styles and string-bending than that coming out of the previous American blues tradition.

As these early pioneers set a new standard for guitar playing, those who followed them would build on many of their playing techniques while at the same time incorporating new technological developments and outside influences. Jimi Hendrix was one of the first to take the virtuoso mantle from the bluesman, as he incorporated innovative uses of the Fender Stratocaster's "whammy bar" (vibrato arm) and fuzz pedals in his performance of a new "acid rock" style (even as he incorporated jazz and R&B chord voicings in his mellower work). Other guitar virtuosos in heavy metal have included Michael Schenker, who combined classical melodic style with heavy, blues-infused rock runs; Eddie Van Halen, who rewrote many of the "rules" of hard rock with his fretboard tapping and whammy bar exploits; Randy Rhoads with his composed, classical-styled solos; and Yngwie Malmsteen who combined a fascination with classical composers and performers like Niccolo Paganini and Mozart with a love for Jimi Hendrix and Ritchie Blackmore, to almost overnight establish the instrumental institution of shredding (a style of playing scales and arpeggios at blindingly fast speeds).

As time went on, the presence of a highly proficient guitarist has become a standard requirement for heavy metal success, and no heavy metal band worth its salt has been without a fret-shredding guitar hero at center stage.

Drum Virtuosity. While not as conspicuous as guitarists, heavy metal has its share of virtuoso drummers as well. Beginning at the same time in musical history, the first drum virtuosos in rock (jazz had had its share, especially in the swing era, with players like Gene Krupa and Buddy Rich) were such drummers as Ginger Baker of Cream and John Bonham of Led Zeppelin. As the volume levels of the guitar and bass amps went up, such drummers pioneered use of bigger drums and larger drum kits and hitting harder. Bonham, in particular, led the way in his use of large, resonant drums for a huge percussion sound. At the same time, he, like Baker, maintained a sense of swing derived from his jazz influences that would give Zeppelin a groove that transcended their seemingly bombastic style.

As heavy metal drummers have followed, the tradition of big-sounding drums has become a hallmark of the genre, and drummers themselves have become faster and more adept in driving the demanding rhythms of the genre. If anything, drummers in heavy metal have become more athletic, the better to drive the music. The tradition of Bonham, Deep Purple's Ian Paice, Emerson, Lake, and Palmer's Carl Palmer, Vanilla Fudge's Carmine Appice, among others, was then picked up and advanced by such players as Neil Peart of Rush, Tommy Aldridge of Whitesnake and Pat Travers Band, and Terry Bozzio, all of whom significantly advanced the state of the art in rock drumming.

With the coming of thrash and speed metal, heavy metal went even further in increasing the speed and stamina demonstrated by its drummers. Stefan Kaufman of Accept turned in one of the earliest thrash metal drumming performances on "Fast as a Shark" on the band's 1982 album *Restless and Wild*, a song widely acknowledged as being one of the first in the thrash style. Others like Metallica's Lars Ulrich, Greg Hall of Sacred Reich, Charlie Benante of Anthrax, and John Tempesta of Exodus helped to establish the drumming style of thrash, which involves incredibly high tempos and fast double-bass drum patterns. At this point in the development of heavy metal, any group that seeks to be taken seriously needs to have a drummer whose skin-pounding skills are at least approaching the virtuoso level to compete.

VISION OF DISORDER (1992–2002). Tim Williams (vocals), Matt Baumbach (guitar), Mike Kennedy (guitar), Mike Fleischman (bass), Brendon Cohen (drums).

Based out of Long Island, New York, Vision of Disorder played thrash–influenced brand of hardcore, featuring socially conscious lyrics, and won a large underground following before disbanding in 2002.

Initially put together in 1992 by guitarists Matt Baumbach and Mike Kennedy, the band was filled out by vocalist Tim Williams, drummer Brendon Cohen, and bassist Mike Fleischman. Fleischman left the band soon after its formation, and the band made the unusual decision to perform without a bassist. Their lack of a bass player notwithstanding, Vision of Disorder's high-energy live shows won them a strong following in their local hardcore scene, and led to Fleischman's return. In 1996, the band released its 7–inch debut EP, *The Still*, which consolidated their local standing and won them record company interest from the Roadrunner subsidiary Supersoul, who released their self–titled full–length debut later that same year. *Vision of Disorder*, built on the band's promise, combined a sometimes melodic, thrash–driven attack with lyrics that attacked the evils of modern society as the band perceived it.

The band returned in 1998 with *Imprint*, a tour de force of hardcore metal produced by Dave Sardy. A year later, the band released *For the Bleeders*, an album of older songs from their demo days that the band rerecorded. After releasing *From Bliss to Devastation* in 2001, the group disbanded after failing to achieve substantial commercial success, with guitarist Kennedy and vocalist Williams going on to form the metalcore outfit Bloodsimple. In the intervening years (2006 and 2008) the band has briefly reunited for a handful of shows, with a DVD of 2008 performances scheduled to be released in November 2008.

Discography: *Vision of Disorder* (Roadrunner, 1996); *Imprint* (Roadrunner, 1998); *For the Bleeders* (Go Kart, 1999); *From Bliss to Devastation* (TVT, 2001).

VIXEN (1980–91, 1998 2001–PRESENT). Janet Gardner (vocals/guitar, replaced by Jenna Piccolo), Jan Kuehnemund (guitar), Liza Carbe (bass, replaced by Pia Maiocco, Share Pedersen, Lynne Louise Lowrey), Laurie Hedlund (drums, replaced by Roxy Petrucci, Kat Kraft).

Vixen was one of the few all-female heavy metal bands that men appreciated not just for their looks but also for their prodigious chops, particularly guitarist Kuehnemund who formed the band back in 1980. Vixen played Los Angeles relentlessly and finally earned a record contract after appearing in the film *Hardbodies* and making a notable appearance in the classic metal documentary, *The Decline of Western Civilization, Part II: The Metal Years*. The hit single "Edge of a Broken Heart" led to Vixen claiming lucrative opening slots for acts such as Ozzy Osbourne, among others, before the band broke up due to the usual creative differences in 1991.

Vixen was also the subject of a VH1 special *Bands Reunited*, in which the original band got back together for a reunion show and where all of the animosity of the past seemed to be buried as the band played together. Although the VH1 special reunited the "classic" lineup of the band (the 1987–91 lineup of Gardner, Kuehnemund, Share Pedersen and Roxy Petrucci), today the band tours with Kuehnemund as the only original member.

Discography: *Vixen* (EMI, 1988); *Rev it Up* (EMI, 1990); *Tangerine* (CMC International, 1998); *The Works* (Pryma Axis, 2003); *Live and Learn* (Demolition, 2006); *Live* (Castle, 2007).

VOIVOD (1982–PRESENT). Denis "Snake" Belanger (vocals, replaced by Eric Forrest, then Belanger), Denis "Piggy" D'Amour (guitar), Jean-Yves Theriault (bass, then Eric Forrest, now Jason Newsted), Michael Langevin (drums).

Voivod had among the most unique sound of metal bands of the past twenty years, mixing metal with jazz and prog rock influences and creating a new sound that inspired many newer bands. The band formed in Canada in 1982 and soon established themselves as one of the weirdest and most experimental metal bands in history, putting out twisted metal records such as *Rrroooaaarrr* and the classic *Killing Technology*. Eventually the band went downhill when Belanger left and was replaced by Forrest for a while, but things improved when Forrest left and was replaced by Belanger and Jason Newsted (of Metallica) on bass.

The band called it quits in 2005 when guitarist Denis "Piggy" D'Amour died of cancer but have continued to release new material in subsequent years. Snake also contributed the instantly recognizable Voivod style artwork of the cover of the Dave Grohl–led Probot project on which Snake sang the song "Dictatosaurus."

Discography: *War and Pain* (Metal Blade, 1984); *Thrashing Rage EP* (Noise International/Combat, 1986); *Rrröööaaarrr* (Noise International/Combat, 1986); *Killing Technology* (Noise International/Combat, 1987); *Dimension Hatrôsss* (Noise International, 1988); *Nothingface* (Mechanic/MCA, 1989); *Angel Rat* (Mechanic, 1991); *The Best of Voivod* (Futurist/Mechanic, 1992); *The Outer Limits* (Mechanic/MCA, 1993); *Negatron* (Mausoleum/BMG, 1995); *Phobos* (Hypnotic, 1997); *Kronik* (Hypnotic, 2000); *Voivod Lives* (Ger. Century Media, 2000).

W

WARRANT (1989–PRESENT). Jani Lane (vocals), Erik Turner (guitar), Joey Allen (guitar), Jerry Dixon (bass), Steven Sweet (drums).

One of the last pop metal bands of the eighties to hit it big before the emergence of grunge and alternative rock put an end to the scene, Warrant emerged from same Sunset Strip rock scene that Guns N' Roses and Poison came from. After making a local splash with their derivative yet tuneful metal, the band signed with Columbia Records, releasing their debut, *Dirty Rotten Filthy Stinking Rich*, in 1989. The album spawned the hits "Down Boys," "Heaven," and "Sometimes She Cries," and helped the album go platinum. The band's videos for the singles also became favorites on MTV. The band's sophomore album, *Cherry Pie*, released the following year was another huge success, with the title track becoming a hit single and video. The vocalist shortly thereafter married model Bobbi Brown, who starred in the video.

The band's third album, *Dog Eat Dog*, released in 1992, was a relative disappointment, only going gold, and the band shared the fate of many of their pop-metal contemporaries as the genre suffered a general decline in popularity in the wake of alternative rock's emergence. Moving to the smaller label CMC International, the band released *Ultraphobic* in 1995, which sold much more modestly. The band's activities have been much more sporadic since, although they have benefited somewhat from the eighties nostalgia that has seen them tour somewhat successfully with other of their contemporaries in package tours.

Discography: *Dirty Rotten Filthy Stinking Rich* (Columbia, 1989); *Cherry Pie* (Columbia, 1990); *Dog Eat Dog* (Columbia, 1992); *Ultraphobic* (CMC International, 1995); *Belly to Belly* (CMC International, 1996); *Under the Influence* (Perris, 2001); *Born Again* (Deadline, 2006); Compilations: *The Best of Warrant* (Sony Legacy, 1996); *Warrant Live 1986–1997* (CMC International, 1997); *Most Wanted* (Mausoleum, 2004); *Extended Versions* [live] (BMG Special Products, 2005).

W.A.S.P. (1982–PRESENT). Blackie Lawless (vocals/bass), Chris Holmes (guitar), Randy Piper (guitar, replaced by Johnny Rod on bass as Lawless shifted to guitar, Stet Howland), Tony Richards (drums, Frankie Banali, Mike Duda).

W.A.S.P. are one of the longest-lasting eighties shock metal bands, best known for their over-the-top behavior and the clever and twisted lyrics of leader Blackie Lawless. The show was impressive for a while and Lawless even portrayed himself as a freedom of speech crusader, but the music was never much to being with. Guitarist Chris Holmes is notorious for a scene in the film *The Decline of Western Civilization, Part II: The Metal Years* in which he gets insensible while constantly drinking vodka in a swimming pool as his mother watches. Ultimately, W.A.S.P. is Alice Cooper without the songs, or much like Alice Cooper today, all show.

Discography: *Animal (Fuck Like a Beast)* (Restless, 1983); *W.A.S. P.* (Snapper, 1984); *The Last Command* (Snapper, 1985); *Inside the Electric Circus* (Snapper, 1986); *Live ... in the Raw* (Snapper, 1987); *The Headless Children* (Snapper, 1988); *Live Animal* (Enigma, 1990); *The Crimson Idol* (Snapper, 1993); *Still Not Black Enough* (Raw Power, 1996); *K.F.D.* (Castle, 1997); *Double Live Assassins* (CMC International, 1998); *Helldorado* (Snapper, 1999); *The Sting [live]* (Snapper, 2000); *Unholy Terror* (Metal-Is, 2001); *Dying for the World* (Metal-Is, 2002); *The Neon God Pt. 1* (Sanctuary, 2004); *The Neon God Pt. 2: The Demise* (Sanctuary, 2004); *Dominator* (SPV, 2007).

WATAIN (1998–PRESENT). Erik Danielsson (vocals), P. Forsberg (guitar), Set Teitan (guitar/bass), H. Jonsson (drums).

Watain are a Swedish black metal band (there must be something in the water there ...) that has consistently turned out some of the most twisted and evil music in the genre since forming in 1998. The lyrics contain fairly typical satanic imagery but the music is a combination of almost progressive instrumentation and brutal vocals. The best album is still the classic *Rabid Death's Curse*, but almost all of their material is essential for fans of well-done and well-produced black metal.

Discography: *Ritual Macabre: Live* (Sacrilegious Warfare, 2000); *Casus Luciferi* (Drakkar, 2006); *Rabid Death's Curse* (Drakkar, 2006); *Sworn to the Dark* (Seasons of Mist, 2007).

WHITE LION (1984–91; 2004–PRESENT). Mike Tramp (vocals), Vito Bratta (guitar), James LoMenzo (bass), Greg d'Angelo (drums).

New York's White Lion came together in the late eighties, formed initially by Danish singer Mike Tramp and guitarist Vito Bratta, with drummer Greg D'Angelo and bassist James LoMenzo joining shortly thereafter. Releasing their first album on the independent Grand Slamm label in 1984, they soon inked a contract with Atlantic and released *Pride* in 1987. The album featured a melodic, radio-ready pop metal sound that was anchored by Bratta's tasteful Eddie Van Halen-influenced guitar work (Bratta's use of fretboard tapping in particular was tasteful and innovative in its own right). *Pride* was a hit thanks to MTV's heavy rotation of the "Wait" video, which also highlighted Tramp's matinee idol good looks, and later, the release of the hit ballad "When the Children Cry." The album went double platinum and the band continued to grow its fan base on tours with Ozzy Osbourne, Aerosmith, and AC/DC.

Their follow-up, *Big Game*, released in 1989, failed to replicate the success of the debut, largely since it was a rushed affair, and despite the airing of two more videos on MTV, the album only sold a half a million copies. *Mane Attraction* in 1991 fared even worse, and the band broke up shortly thereafter as grunge and alternative proved more popular than pop metal to the contemporary audience.

In 2004, Tramp revived the name, putting together a new touring lineup and releasing a live album in 2005 and the studio effort *Return of the Pride* in 2008.

Discography: *Fight to Survive* (Grand Slamm, 1984); *Pride* (Atlantic, 1987); *Big Game* (Atlantic, 1989); *Mane Attraction* (Atlantic, 1991); *Return of the Pride* (Frontiers, 1992); *The Best of White Lion* (Atlantic, 1992); *The Ultimate White Lion* (Cleopatra, 2005); *The Definitive Rock Collection* (Atlantic/Rhino, 2007).

WHITESNAKE (1978–PRESENT). David Coverdale (vocals), Doug Aldrich (guitar), Reb Beach (guitar), Uriah Duffy (bass), Timothy Drury (keyboards), Chris Frazier (drums).

Beginning as a bluesy solo vehicle for former Deep Purple vocalist David Coverdale in the late seventies, Whitesnake would go on to evolve a more hard-rock style and reached their peak as million-selling superstars of MTV in the late eighties.

After leaving Deep Purple in 1976, vocalist David Coverdale released a string of three solo albums beginning with Whitesnake in 1977. In the process of touring and recording, Coverdale assembled a crack backup band featuring the bluesy guitarists Bernie Marsden and Micky Moody. Eventually he decided to give the band a name and took the title of his first solo album. From 1978 to 1982, the band put out a series of albums of soulful blues-based rock that well featured Coverdale's bluesy vocals. As the band developed, Coverdale took them in a harder rock direction enlisting former (latter day) Thin Lizzy guitarist John Sykes to write and play on 1984's *Slide it In*. The album became the band's first platinum album and was the first to do well in the U.S.

Now on the Geffen label, the band was stripped down to Coverdale, Sykes, Neil Murray on bass, and Ansley Dunbar on drums, for 1987's self-titled release. The album was a huge hit in large part to Coverdale's new collaborator Sykes. The songs were still blues based but much harder and heavier than anything else the band had attempted before, and tracks like "Crying in the Rain," and "Still of the Night" evoked Led Zeppelin in their production and Coverdale's vocals. Additionally, Sykes brought a huge and aggressively original and metallic sound to the guitars, which helped to give the tracks a larger-than-life quality. The album would become a huge hit, but unfortunately, Coverdale and Sykes had a falling out just before the album was completed and Sykes was fired before its release (going on to form and front the similar-sounding Blue Murder).

To tour and promote the album, Coverdale put together a whole new lineup of photogenic veterans including guitarists Adrian Vandenberg and Vivian Campbell (ex-Dio), bassist Rudy Sarzo (ex-Ozzy and Quiet Riot), and drummer Tommy Aldridge (ex-Pat Travers, Ozzy). With a series of MTV videos for the songs "Here I Go Again," "Still of the Night," and "Is This Love?" the album sold phenomenally well, going six-times platinum in the U.S., making Coverdale and the band superstars.

1989's *Slip of the Tongue* saw Steve Vai taking Vivian Campbell's place in the band, initially though, entering to fill in for Vandenberg, who had injured his hand. The album was a modest success, but a disappointment after the success of its predecessor. Lacking Sykes' writing input, it more significantly lacked his signature guitar tone that had defined the sound of the 1987 album, a sound that arguably rivaled Eddie Van Halen's early tone, both in its quality and in its pivotal role in defining the overall sounds of the respective bands.

After touring for *Slip of the Tongue*, Coverdale disbanded the group and went on to a collaboration with Jimmy Page in 1993. 1997 saw a brief reunion with Vandenberg for the album *Restless Heart*. The solo album *Into the Light* with guitarist Earl Slick followed in 2000.

Finally, in 2002, came a new lineup of crack musicians including drummer Tommy Aldridge, veteran guitarist Doug Aldrich, ex-Winger guitarist Reb Beach, bassist Marco Mendoza, and keyboardist Timothy Drury. Touring in the U.S. and Europe, the band proved to be one of the strongest Whitesnake lineups ever, and with Aldrich in particular proving to be a uniquely powerful guitarist, whose muscular yet fluid and soulful playing served the band well. After live CD and DVD releases in 2006, the band finally returned with the stellar studio release *Good to Be Bad* in 2008.

Discography: *Snakebite* (Geffen, 1978); *Trouble* (Geffen, 1978); *Lovehunter* (Geffen, 1979); *Live at Hammersmith* (Sunburst, 1980); *Live in the Heart of the City* (Geffen, 1980); *Live ... In the Heart of the City/Live at Hammersmith* (Geffen, 1980); *Ready an' Willing* (EMI, 1980); *Come an' Get It* (Geffen, 1981); *Saints & Sinners* (Geffen, 1982); *Slide It In* (Geffen, 1984); *1987* (EMI, 1987); *Whitesnake* (Geffen, 1987); *Slip of the Tongue* (Geffen, 1989); *Restless Heart* (EMI, 1998); *Starkers in Tokyo* [live] (EMI, 1998); *Live ... In the Shadow of the Blues* (Steamhammer UK, 2006); *Good to Be Bad* (Steamhammer, 2008); *Box Set* (Alex, 1992); *Whitesnake's Greatest Hits* (Geffen, 1994); *20th Century Masters—The Millennium Collection: The Best of Whitesnake* (Geffen, 2000); *Here I Go Again: The Whitesnake Collection* (Universal, 2002); *Best of Whitesnake* (EMI, 2003); *The Silver Anniversary Collection* (EMI, 2003); *The Early Years* (EMI, 2004); *Chronicles* (Geffen, 2005); *The Definitive Collection* (Geffen, 2006); *30th Anniversary Collection* (EMI, 2008).

WHITE ZOMBIE (1985–96). Rob Zombie (vocals/guitar), Jay Yuenger (guitar), Sean Yseult (bass), Ivan Deprume (drums, replaced by John Tempesta).

White Zombie were an American heavy metal band influenced by science fiction, old horror films, fifties trash culture, and a heavy dollop of twisted humor. Led by vocalist and guitarist Rob Zombie, the band started out fairly sedate on their first record, which sounds more like their Lower East Side origins than later efforts would, but by the time of their breakthrough into respectability on the *La Sexorcista* record, they had perfected the formula, and the video for "Thunderkiss 65," with its relentless repetitive guitar riff, soon made them MTV darlings, which the band was uniquely suited for with their image tailor-made for the video age. Their next record, *Astro Creep 2000*, also charted big with the hit song inspired by a line in the film *Bladerunner*, "More Human than Human."

However, Zombie, a control freak under the best of circumstances, took over the band completely, and by 1997 he had jettisoned the rest of the group and carried on under his name in a solo career for the past decade. Recently, Zombie has become better known to a new generation for his directing skills; he has so far directed three horror films: *House of a Thousand Corpses*, its sequel, *The Devil's Rejects*, and the pointless remake of the classic horror film *Halloween*. Zombie is a talented director, if given the right material, and may be more comfortable following his own idiosyncratic vision than making mainstream movies. Also it is hoped by his many fans that he resumes his music career, or reunites White Zombie in the future.

Discography: *Gods on Voodoo Moon EP* (Silent Explosion, 1985); *Psycho-Head Blowout* (Silent Explosion, 1987); *Soul-Crusher* (Silent Explosion, 1987; Caroline, 1988); *God of Thunder* (Caroline, 1989); *Make Them Die Slowly* (Caroline, 1989); *La Sexorcisto: Devil Music Volume One* (Geffen, 1992); *Astro-Creep: 2000* (Geffen, 1995); *Supersexy Swingin' Sounds* (Geffen, 1996).

WINO (1961–). Wino (Scott Weinrich) remains one of the heroes of the underground metal scene for his longevity and the various bands he has graced with his presence. Originally Wino was one of the few metal fans active in the early Washington, D.C., hardcore punk scene and his early band, the legendary doom rock band the Obsessed, along with his later involvement in bands such as St. Vitus, Spirit Caravan, Place of Skulls, and the Hidden Hand. Wino is one of the major unsung American underground metal heroes who has long pursued his musical vision, despite a consistent lack of commercial success or mainstream exposure.

WISHBONE ASH (1969–PRESENT). Andy Powell (guitar/vocals), Ted Turner (guitar/vocals, replaced by Laurie Wisefield, Jamie Crompton, Phil Palmer), Martin Turner (bass/vocals, replaced by John Wetton, Trevor Bolder, Mervyn Spence, Andy Pyle, many others), Steve Upton (drums, replaced by Ray Weston, Mike Sturgis, others).

Wishbone Ash are on the periphery of metal, along with bands such as Uriah Heep who seemed to fall more in the art rock camp at times. The band started as a project of guitarists Turner and Powell. Soon, the band was creating beautiful, atmospheric long songs with dueling guitar leads from Powell and Turner. After several classic records, including the medieval-themed *Argus*, the band began to go through internal turmoil, and various members began to come and go until the band was down to only two long-lasting members. An offer by IRS records founder Miles Copeland to re-form the original lineup led to the instrumental album *Nouveau Calls*, leading to a brief but effective reunion, until original drummer Upton retired from the band in 1990, followed in short order by Martin turner and Ted Turner a few years later.

In 1993, Powell formed a new version of the band with a revolving cast of session musicians, much like those touring fifties bands "featuring" one original member; to further confuse things, there is also a touring "Martin Turner's Wishbone Ash." Although there are many classics, fans of artistic metal are urged to seek out the early periods of the band, particularly their finest moment, *Argus*, although *Twin Barrels Burning* may be the most classically "metal" album the band has released.

Discography: *Wishbone Ash* (MCA, 1970); *Pilgrimage* (MCA, 1971) *Argus* (MCA, 1972); *Twin Barrels Burning* (Castle, 1982); *Nouveau Calls* (IRS, 1989).

WOODSTOCK 1999. One of the darker moments in metal history was the Woodstock reenactment known as Woodstock 1999. Although many critics were later to blame the harder bands, such as nu metal band Limp Bizkit, for the eventual riot and rapes that occurred, there may have been many other factors involved. The festival was held in Rome, New York, not Woodstock. The lineup included numerous popular music acts of the time including Limp Bizkit, Beastie Boys, Kid Rock, and Metallica. However, by the last day of the festival, tempers were running high in the audience. Poor planning in terms of shade and crowd hydration had led to many fans feeling frustrated at the organizers and angry at the obscene amounts being charged for food and water (as an example, a typical bottle of water cost $4).

There had already been several instances of crowd violence and abuse toward women, but by the time Limp Bizkit took the stage on Saturday night, the crowd had already become ugly. As Limp Bizkit played many in the crowd had already dismantled numerous stores and other temporary buildings and started small fires. During their set, Limp Bizkit played their usual brand of raw and aggressive rap-tinged nu metal, but many critics later saw the band's usual aggressiveness as an initiatory factor in the violence and rapes that later occurred. Many critics in particular pointed to the fact that the band's song "Break Things" was unusually incendiary, and after the set was over there had been a wave of vandalism and minor violence throughout the park.

This raises the question of how much is a heavy metal band responsible for the actions of their fans, and how much are the fans individually responsible, and how much blame should be laid on the promoters who clearly did not plan adequately for a festival of this kind. Several factors may indicate that the violence at Woodstock 1999 cannot necessarily be traced back to any one particular band, much less the music itself. In media and music research, the idea of the magic bullet theory, that things such as television programs and songs can directly cause response, is usually dismissed.

This is not to say that there is not a visceral crowd response to certain songs. Anyone that has attended a concert can attest to the fact that certain songs cause a greater crowd reaction, particularly when a mosh pit or stage diving is concerned. But to simply blame a band for the actions of a groups of mostly young fans, who were angered by lack of shade and high prices for food and water, not only dismisses the idea of personal responsibility but also ignores the many successful festivals such as Monsters of rock that have been held over the years with a minimum of violence and aggression reported. Ultimately, the lesson of Woodstock 1999 may not be that music incites crowds to reckless behavior but rather that large groups of people deprived of basic necessities may resort to criminal behavior. However, since Woodstock 1999 did result in numerous crimes and several rapes, the legacy of Limp Bizkit is still connected in the minds of many in the media with the violence that occurred at the festival. Still, many bands have been blamed unfairly for violence since the dawn of rock and roll, and sadly, it seems that this will continue to be an issue for the foreseeable future.

WYKYD SCEPTRE. Generic Metal stereotype (vocals/guitar), Generic Metal stereotype (guitar), Generic Metal stereotype (bass), Generic Metal stereotype (drums).

Wykyd Sceptre were a fake metal band created by *Mr. Show* comedians David Cross and Bob Odenkirk. In the sketch, which parodies the Mötley Crüe "party" tapes, fans are seen watching the Wykyd Sceptre party tape, which starts off

looking much like a regular heavy metal backstage video, before it becomes apparent that the male band members are having sex with each other. Despite the best
efforts of the record company to convince the band that they are in fact gay, the
band claims that they were just "partying" and end up insulting an openly gay
member of the record company when he tries to get them to say along with him
that *"we're* gay." At the end of the sketch, the record company is forced to market
the band to a Fire Island concert featuring an audience of gay men in leather, much
to the band's confusion, although the band does gain an important marketing partner when they endorse "King Royal" butt plugs. The sketch not only brilliantly
parodies the excesses of heavy metal but also suggests that the homoerotic imagery
of many metal bands is a disguise for sexual confusion of closeted band members
or fans Sadly, there are no official Wykyd Sceptre releases, but fans can find the
sketch on the collected DVDs of *Mr. Show* season 4, in the episode "Show Me
Your Weenis," or online.

Z

ZOLAR X (1973–81, 2004–PRESENT). Zory Zenith (vocals, replaced by Ygar Ygfarrist (guitar/vocals), Eon Flash (drums, synths), Qazar Quanotr (synths).

Zolar X were a proto metal band from Los Angeles who claimed to be from Venus. When the tales of the Sunset Strip and glam metal are told, one band usually is sadly, and tragically, forgotten. One of the key bands to help create the glam look and aesthetic in the early seventies was this band of (perhaps) dead-serious alien imitators, who spoke their own language and played the Sunset Strip to adoring fans, all the while dressed as extras from a *Star Trek* episode. The band played a combination of what is closest to glam rock, but with distinct art rock touches and some unworldly sounds that suggest either heavy drug use or that the band was involved in the electronic music scene during the sixties. The band's main peak was circa 1974–75, and by 1981 they had broken up. L.A. scene insiders praised the band and both punk and metal enthusiasts began to research the band, leading to Jello Biafra, formerly of the Dead Kennedys, to finally release a compilation of the known Zolar X music on his Alternative Tentacles records in 2004.

The band retuned to earth after a lengthy hiatus in space (and for lead singer Zory Zenith, in jail, where he remains today for a particularly brutal assault on an ex-girlfriend)(Myers) to enlighten the modern metal scene on the true Venusian virtues of the Sunset Strip.

Discography: *Timeless* (Alternative, Tentacles 2004); *X Marks the Spot* (Alternative, Tentacles, 2007).

ROB ZOMBIE (1966–). Multi-talented Rob Zombie (Robert Cummings) might well be considered a heavy metal renaissance man, if that's not too confining a way to put it. The one-time production assistant for *Pee Wee's Playhouse* has experienced a multitude of successes over the past two decades, from overseeing the rise of White Zombie and his own solo musical career, to writing and directing two feature films, as well as directing music videos, designing album artwork, to designing a ride for Universal Studios' theme perks. Central to all these activities has been his focus on fulfilling a musical vision that borrows from classic and industrial metal genres combined with the iconography of classic horror and exploitation films.

Zombie, whose real name is Robert Cummings, moved to New York in the mid-eighties from Massachusetts. He worked a series of creative day jobs—art director for a porn magazine, production assistant for *Pee Wee's Playhouse*—while developing and fronting the band White Zombie at night. Initially a noise rock band akin to Sonic Youth, White Zombie eventually evolved into a groove metal band and ultimately won a major label deal with Geffen Records in the early nineties. While the band moved toward greater mass appeal in their metal period, their albums were highly entertaining and creatively executed and featured the unique use of samples from such camp sources as Russ Meyer and cult horror films and television shows like *Batman.*

After the latter-day success of the White Zombie albums *La Sexorcisto: Devil Music, Vol. 1* and *Astro Creep: 2000*, in 1992 and 1995, respectively, Zombie was able to try his hand at a variety of creative endeavors, from animating a sequence in the feature film *Beavis & Butthead Do America*, to film directing. In addition, he released a solo album, *Hellbilly Deluxe* in 1998. In its first week, the album sold more than the previous White Zombie album had. Seeing the writing on the wall, Zombie disbanded the group to focus full-time on his solo career, taking most of the band's audience with him. To a large extent, after all, his new act mined very much the same territory—industrial groove metal featuring gothic cinematic horror themes—and he still had the Zombie name.

Hellbilly Deluxe paired Zombie with producer and guitarist Scott Humphrey. The sound that the two contrived was very similar to that of White Zombie, though it was even more heavily produced. In 1999 Zombie released *American Made Music to Strip By*, an album of remixes of tracks from *Hellbilly.*

In 2000, after having designed a horror display for a ride at Universal Studios theme perk, Zombie was given the green light by the studio to direct his script for *House of 1000 Corpses*. The studio, however, found the final cut of the film to be so gruesome that they backed out of the project, and Zombie had to seek another studio to release the film. Ultimately, the film was released through MGM.

In 2001, Zombie's second studio album, *The Sinister Urge*, was released, again a collaboration with Humphrey, it also featured appearances by a who's who of metal, including Ozzy Osbourne, Tommy Lee, and Slayer guitarist Kerry King. Zombie toured to support the record with a band comprised of John Tempesta, his old drummer from White Zombie, guitarist Mike Riggs, and bassist Blasko (Rob Nicholson), and the tour culminated with a Christmas tour with Osbourne at the end of 2001.

2005 saw the release of Zombie's second feature film, *The Devil's Rejects*, and the following year he released his third studio album, *Educated Horses*, on which he toned down some of the more gothic elements of his act and utilized a more natural vocal approach.

Zombie has continued to keep busy, serving as co-writer and director for the remake of the classic horror film *Halloween* in 2007, and releasing the live album *Zombie Live*. Another major tour with Ozzy Osbourne followed its release.

Discography: *Hellbilly Deluxe* (Geffen, 1998); *American Made Music to Strip By* (Interscope, 1999); *The Sinister Urge* (Universal, 2001); *Educated Horses* (Geffen, 2006); *Zombie Live* (Geffen, 2007); *Past, Present & Future* (Geffen, 2003).

Selected Bibliography

Alexander, Allison, and Cheryl Harris, eds. *Theorizing Fandom: Fans, Subculture and Identity.* Cresskill, NJ: Hampton Press, 1998.

Ambrose, Joe. *The Violent World of Moshpit Culture.* London: Omnibus Press, 2001.

Anderson, Kyle. *Accidental Revolution: The Story of Grunge.* New York: MacMillan, 2007.

Andersen, Mark, and Mark Jenkins. *Dance of Days: Two Decades of Punk in the Nation's Capital.* New York: Soft Skull Press, 2001.

Auslander, Philip. "Seeing Is Believing: Live Performance and the Discourse of Authenticity in Rock Culture." *Literature and Psychology* 44, no. 4 (1998): 1–26.

Berelian, Essi. *The Rough Guide to Heavy Metal.* New York: Rough Guides, 2005.

Blush, Steven. *American Hardcore: A Tribal History.* Los Angeles: Feral House, 2001.

Bogdanov, Vladimir, Stephen Thomas Erlewine, and Chris Woodstra. *All Music Guide to Rock: The Definitive Guide to Rock, Pop, and Soul* (3rd Edition). San Francisco: Backbeat, 2002.

Bourdieu, Pierre. *Distinction: A Social Critique of Taste.* Cambridge, MA: Harvard University Press, 1984.

"Burning Witch" accessed from the Southern Lord website on May 15, 2008, from http://southernlord.com/band_BNW.php

Burroughs, William S. *Nova Express.* New York: Grove Press, 1964

Christie, Ian. *Everybody Wants Some: The Van Halen Saga.* Hoboken: Wiley, 2008.

Cogan, Brian. *The Encyclopedia of Punk Music and Culture.* Westport, CT: Greenwood Press, 2006.

Davis, Stephen. *Hammer of the Gods: The Led Zeppelin Saga.* New York: Harper, 2008.

Davis, Stephen, and Aerosmith. *Walk This Way: The Autobiography of Aerosmith.* New York: Harper, 1983.

Des Barress, Pamela. *I'm with the Band: Confessions of a Groupie.* Chicago: Chicago Review Press, 2005.

Doyle, Michael. *A History of Marshall: The Illustrated Story of the Sound of Rock.* Milwaukee: Hal Leonard, 1993.

"D.R.I.: Crossover" accessed on May 12, 2008, from www.metal-observer.com/articles.php?lid=1&sid=1&id=9099.

Engleheart, Murray and Arnaud Durieux. *AC/DC: Maximum Rock & Roll: The Ultimate Story of the World's Greatest Rock-and-Roll Band.* New York: Harper, 2008.

Ernst, Erik. "Cooper Tees off on Alcoholism." Eposted August 21, 2007, http://www.jsonline.com/entertainment/musicandnightlife/29414304.html, accessed on February 4, 2009.

Ewen, Stewart. *All Consuming Images: The Politics of Style in Contemporary Culture.* New York: Basic Books, 1988.

Fish, Stanley. *Is There a Text in This Class?: The Authority of Interpretive Communities.* Cambridge, MA: Harvard University Press, 1980.

Freeman, Phil. "Godsmacked: '70's Heavy Metal Pioneers Sir Lord Baltimore Return with a New Sound and a New Master." *Village Voice,* February 14–20, 2007.

Frith, Simon. *Music for Pleasure: Essays in the Sociology of Pop.* New York: Routledge, 1988.

———. *Performing Rites: On the Value of Popular Music.* Cambridge, MA: Harvard University Press, 1996.

———. *Sound Effects: Youth, Leisure and the Politics of Rock and Roll.* New York: Random House, 1982.

Gencarelli, Thomas. "Reading Heavy Metal Music: An Interpretive Communities Approach to Popular Music as Education." Ph.D. diss., New York University, 1993.

Glasper, Ian. *Burning Britain: The History of UK Punk 1980–1984.* Norfolk, England: Cherry Red Books, 2004.

"Goblin Cock," on *SignOnSanDiego Entertainment Guide.* The San Diego Union-Tribune (2006). Retrieved on March 12, 2008, http://singonsandiego.com

Grossberg, Lawrence. "Reflections of a Disappointed Popular Music Scholar." In *Rock over the Edge,* ed. Roger Beebee, Denise Fulbrook, and Ben Saunders, 25–59. Durham, NC: Duke University Press, 2002.

Hamilton, Sean. "Hawkins in 'I Quit' Shocker." *The Sun,* October 11, 2006.

Harris, Chris. "Static-X guitarist Charged in Two Separate Assaults" from MTVnews.com. Retrieved on November 6, 2008, from www.mtv.com/news/articles/1497553/20050228/static_x

"Heavy Metal," www.phrases.org.uk/meanings/heavy-metal.html.

Hebdige, Dick. *Cut 'n' Mix: Culture, Identity and Caribbean Music.* London: Comedia, 1987.

———. *Subculture: The Meaning of Style.* London: Routledge, 1979.

Hiatt, Brian. "How Slayer Became Teen Idols," *Rolling Stone,* September 7, 2006, 20.

Hunter, Seb. *Hellbent for Leather: Confessions of a Heavy Metal Addict.* New York: Harper Perennial, 1984.

Khan Harris, Keith. "'Roots?' The Relationship Between the Global and the Local Within the Extreme Metal Scene." In *The Popular Music Studies Reader,* ed. Andy Bennett, Barry Shank, and Jason Toynbee, 128–36. New York: Routledge, 2006.

Klosterman, Chuck. *Fargo Rock City: A Heavy Metal Odyssey in Rural North Dakota.* New York: Touchstone, 2001.

Lisa, John. Interview with Brian Cogan. March 23, 2008.

Ling, David. *Wizards and Demons: The Uriah Heep Story.* Stratford-On-Avon, England: Classic Rock Productions, 2002.

Macomber, Sean. "Longhairs vs. Blue Helmets." From the American Spectator online, accessed on May 5, 2008, from www.spectator.org/dsp_article.asp?art_id=11697.

Marsh, David, and Swenson, John. *The New Rolling Stone Record Guide.* New York: Random House/Rolling Stone, 1983.

McNeil, Legs and Gillian McCain. *Please Kill Me: The Uncensored Oral History of Punk.* New York: Grove Press, 1996.

Mills, Melissa. "Uriah Heep." Retrieved on November 7, 2008, from www.rolling stone. com/artists/uriahheep/albums/album/150141/review/6067513/uriah_heep.

Morgan, 2008.

Moynihan. Michael, and Didrik Soderlind. *Lords of Chaos: The Bloody Rise of the Satanic Metal Underground.* Venice, CA: Feral House, 1998.

Mudrian, Albert. *Choosing Death: The Improbable History of Death Metal and Grindcore.* Venice, CA: Feral House, 2004.

Myers, Ben. "Zolar X: Glam's Forgotten Pioneers." Retrieved on November 6, 2008, from www.guardian.com/music/musicblog/2008/July/28/zolarxglam.

Negus, Keith. "Popular Music: In-between Celebration and Despair." In *Questioning the Media: A Critical Introduction,* ed. Roger Dowling and Ali Mohammadi, 379–93. Thousand Oaks, CA: Sage, 1995.

O'Donnell, Kevin. "Best Metal Band; Mastodon," *Rolling Stone,* May 1, 2008.

Peart, Neil. *Ghost Rider: Travels on the Healing Road.* Toronto: ECW, 2002.

Popoff, Martin. *Black Sabbath: Doom Let Loose: An Illustrated History.* Toronto: ECW, 2006.

Poulsen, Henrik Bech. *'77: The Year of Punk & New Wave.* London: Helter Skelter, 2005.

Radaway, Janice. *Reading the Romance: Women, Patriarchy and Popular Literature.* Chapel Hill: University of North Carolina Press, 1984.

Rushkof, Douglas. *Media Virus: Hidden Agendas in Popular Culture.* New York: Ballantine, 1994.

Sadler, Roger L. *Electronic Media Law.* Thousand Oaks: Sage, 2005.

Sanneh, Kelefa. "On the Road to Spread the Word of Good Old Fashioned Evil." *New York Times.* Retrieved on November 8, 2007, from www.nytimes.com/2007/11/08/arts/music

Sarig, Roni. *The Secret History of Rock: The Most Influential Bands You've Never Heard.* New York: Billboard Books, 1998.

"Slayer Axeman Kerry King Interviewed." Accessed on May 15, 2008, from www.metalunderground.com/interviews/details.cfm?newsid=24837.

Sixx, Nikki. *The Heroin Diaries: A Year in the Life of a Shattered Rock Star.* New York: Pocket Books, 2007.

Smith, Anthony Neil. *The Drummer.* New York: Two Dollar Radio, 2006.

Straugsbaugh, John. *Rock Till You Drop: The Decline from Rebellion to Nostalgia.* London: Verso, 2001.

Toynbee, Jason. "Making Up and Showing Off: What Musicians Do." In *The Popular Music Studies Reader,* ed. Andy Bennett, Barry Shank, and Jason Toynbee. New York: Routledge, 2006.

Tsitsos, William. "Rules of Rebellion: Slamdancing, Moshing and the American Alternative Scene." In *The Popular Music Studies Reader,* ed. Andy Bennett, Barry Shank, and Jason Toynbee. New York: Routledge, 2006.

Walser, Robert. "Eruptions: Heavy Metal Appropriations of Classical Virtuosity." In *The Subcultures Reader,* ed. Ken Gelder and Sarah Thornton. London: Routledge, 1997.

Weber, Barry. "Iron Maiden: Biography." All Music Guide Entry. http://www.allmusic.com/cg/amg.dll?p=amg&sql=11:3ifyxqe5ldae~T1.

Weiderhorn, Jon. "Metallica's James Hetfield Calls Stint in Rehab Challenging, Gratifying," *MTVNews,.com.* Retrieved on November 6, 2008, from www.mmtv.com/news/articles/1452494/2002022/metallica.jhtml.

Weinstein, Deena. *Heavy Metal: The Music and Its Culture.* New York: Da Capo Press, 2000.

Welch, Chris, Jeff Nicholls, and Geoff Nicholls. *John Bonham: A Thunder of Drums.* San Francisco: Backbeat, 2001.

Wohlrob, Ken. Interview with Brian Cogan, January 22, 2008.

———. Interview with Brian Cogan, May 8, 2008.

WEBSITES

www.Allmusic.com
www.trouserpress.com
Encyclopedaia Metallum, www.metal-archives.com
The Metal Observer, www.metal-observer.com
www.officialfilter.com
www.aliceinchains.com

Biography for AC/DC drummer Phil Rudd, www.drummersrepublic.com/drummers/
    acdc-drummer-phil-rudd-biography/
Biography for former bassist for Extreme, Paul Mangone, www.paulmangone.com/bio.htm

Index

Abigail, 130

Abominog, 246

Accept, 4, 7, 10–11, 19, 28, 55, 258; *Metal Heart*, 11

AC/DC, 11–14, 19, 25, 46, 52, 57, 66–67, 131, 135, 136–37, 198, 241, 262, 272, 274

Ace of Spades, 170

"Adam's Apple," 15

Adrenalize, 68

Aerosmith, 14–16, 45, 52, 88, 136, 165, 181, 262, 271

Against the Grain, 17

Agalloch, 17

Agents of Fortune, 40

Airheads, 17

Alabama Thunder Pussy, 18

Alcatrazz, 18, 151, 250

Alcohol, 13, 16, 19–20, 36, 68, 106, 118, 168, 180, 184, 232, 244–45

Alibi, 251

Alice in Chains, 21–22, 101, 229

Alive or Just Breathing, 129

Allied Forces, 235

Altar, 219

Altars of Madness, 79

Alternative Tentacles, 177

The Amalgamut, 94

The Amboy Dukes, 23, 97, 180

American Spectator, 157

Amon Amarth, 23, 159

Among the Living, 26

Amps, 24–25, 81–82, 258

Anaal Nathrakh, 25–26, 127

And Justice for All

Angel Dust, 89

Angel of Retribution, 125

Angel Witch, 26

Animal House, 11

Animal Magnetism, 209

Animalize, 134

Anthems for the Damned, 94

Anthrax, 10, 26, 27–28, 33, 109, 167, 210, 216, 220, 258

Anvil, 27, 159

Apocalyptic Raids, 112

Appetite for Destruction, 84, 106

April Wine, 27

Arch Enemy, 28, 38, 50, 216

Armored Saint, 26, 28

Around the Fur, 69

As the Palaces Burn, 139

Ashes of the Wake, 139

Asphalt Ballet, 29

At the Gates, 29, 38, 80

Atomic Playboys, 224

Autograph, 29

Avenged Sevenfold, 29–30

Awake, 101

Awaken the Garden, 92

Back for the Attack, 76
Back in Black, 13, 67
Back to Reality, 213
Backwaxed, 27
Bad News, 31
Badlands, 31
Badmotorfinger, 219
Ballbreaker, 13
Bang Tango, 31–32
Bark at the Moon, 183
Bathory, 32, 34–35
Battle Hymns, 152
The Battle Rages On, 65
Beast From the East, 76
Beatallica, 32, 234
Beavis & Butthead, 56
Beck, Jeff, 7
Beg to Differ, 190
Behemoth, 33, 69
Beneath the Remains, 210
The Beyond, 58
Biohazard, 33
Bite Down Hard, 46
Black Butterfly, 46
Black Flag's record company, 97
Black Label Society, 33–34
Black Light Syndrome, 224
Black Metal, 4–6, 17, 21, 23, 25, 29, 32,
    34–35, 48, 51–52, 54, 61–62, 69–71,
    75, 80, 85–86, 91–92, 101, 103, 109,
    112, 115, 130, 149, 155–56, 158, 163,
    166–67, 179–80, 190, 205–207, 210–
    11, 214, 217, 225, 234, 255–56, 262
Blackout, 209
Black Rain, 184
Black Sabbath, 3–4, 7–8, 25, 31, 34–37,
    50–51, 63, 71–73, 85, 89–90, 97, 104,
    110–11, 114, 120, 122–23, 153, 163,
    169, 183–84, 187, 196, 218, 220, 225,
    236, 242, 256, 273
Blashrykh Kingdom, 115
Blaze of Glory, 44
For the Bleeders, 259
Blessed Are the Sick, 166
Blitzkreig, 37;
    over Nüremberg, 39
Blizzard of Ozz, 183
Bloodstock, 38, 93
Blow My Fuse, 136
Blow Up Your Video, 13
Blue Cheer, 3–4, 8, 35, 38–39
Blue Murder, 39–40, 263
Blue Öyster Cult, 40, 73

Body Count, 41
Boggy Depot, 22
Bolin, Tommy, 41, 65
Bolt Thrower, 42–43, 80, 159, 186
Bon Jovi, 43–45, 52, 66, 68, 192, 43
Bon Jovi Fans Can't Be Wrong, 44
Bonded by Blood, 87
The Book of Taliesyn, 64
Boris, 45, 146, 219, 227
Born in America, 199
Bounce, 44
Bourdieu, Pierre, 5
Bow to None, 86
Boys in Heat, 46
Brave New World, 120
Breaker, 10
Bring 'Em Out Live, 95
Bring the Noise, 26
British Steel, 124
Britny Fox, 45–46
Broken Glass, 56
Buckcherry, 46
Budgie, 46
Bullet Boys, 47
Bump Ahead, 173
Burn, 65
Burning Red, 150
Burning Witch, 47, 99, 219, 227, 271
Burn My Eyes, 150
Burroughs, William S., 48, 271
Burzum, 34, 48, 80, 149, 155
Butch Cassidy and the Sundance Kid, 212

Cacophony, 49
Candlemass, 28, 49–50
Candyass, 182
Cannibal, 223
Cannibal Corpse, 50, 63, 159
Carcass, 28, 50, 54, 69, 79, 235
Caress of Steel, 202
Cathedral, 51, 79, 97, 174
Cat Scratch Fever, 181
Celtic Frost, 51–52, 112, 127, 190, 227
Cherry Pie, 261
Chimera, 155
Chinese Democracy, 105, 107
Christ Illusion, 215
Cinderella, 45–46, 52–53, 92–93, 177,
    188
Circus of Power, 53
Cirith Ungol, 53–54, 149
Clapton, Eric, 7
Cold Lake, 51

Coma of Souls, 137
Come Taste the Band, 42, 65
Concerto for Group and Orchestra, 64
Condition Critical, 193
"Cookie Monster" vocal style, 54
Cool Kids, 135
Cooper, Alice, 15, 20–21, 132, 153, 210–11, 262
"Cop Killer," 41
Corpsepaint, 54, 61, 91–92
Corrosion of Conformity, 54, 56–57, 109, 204
Crawdaddy, 4
Creatures of the Night, 256
Creem, 4
Crossover, 26–27, 41, 45, 54–57, 74, 77–78, 86, 88, 104, 116–17, 125, 154, 163, 167, 171, 187, 190, 204, 214, 220, 223, 226, 234, 256, 272
Crowbar, 56
Crumbsuckers, 55–56, 204
Crush, 44
Cryptic Slaughter, 56–57, 159
Cryptic Writings, 156
The Cult, 32, 57–58, 114, 200
Cult of Luna, 58, 177
Cultosaurus Erectus, 40

Dance of Death, 120
Dancin' on the Edge, 96
Dancin' Undercover, 197
Dangerous Curves, 96
Danzig, 59, 163, 190
Dark Angel, 60, 70
The Darkness, 60–61
Darkness Descends, 60
Darkthrone, 34, 54, 61
Dead Horse, 61–62
Dealing With It, 78
Death, 62
Death is this Communion, 114
Death Metal, 4, 6, 7, 23, 28, 33, 42–43, 50–51, 54, 61–63, 69–71, 74, 78–79, 89, 91, 100, 103–4, 123, 127, 137, 142, 147, 158, 166–67, 186–87, 189, 206, 210, 213–14, 216, 256, 273
Death on the Road, 120
Death Row, 11
Decline of Western Civilization Part II: 19, 63, 22, 259, 262
Deep Purple, 9, 40, 42, 63–66, 72, 85, 117, 151, 195–96, 207, 242, 244, 245, 258, 263
Defenders of the Faith, 124

Def Leppard, 61, 66–68, 137, 242
The Deftones, 69
Deftones, 68–69
Dehumanizer, 73
Deicide, 69, 79–80
Demolition, 125
Demon Alcohol, 20
Demos, 25, 43, 56, 69–70, 112, 227, 253
De Mysteriis Dom Sathanas, 155
Destroyer, 133
Dethklok, 70
Diary of a Madman, 183
Dimmu Borgir, 38, 70–71
Dining with Sharks, 39
Dio, 35–37, 65, 68, 71–73, 85, 110–11, 114, 149, 187, 195–96, 200, 216, 221
Dio, Ronnie James, 35–36, 65, 71–73, 85, 110, 111, 114, 187, 195, 200, 216
The Dirt 169
Dirty Rotten Filthy Stinking Rich, 261
Discharge, 57, 73–74, 78, 86, 103, 109, 174, 220
Dismember, 74
Dissection, 34, 75, 227
Distortion, 24
Disturbed, 75
Disturbing the Peace, 250
Dogman, 131
Dokken, 76–77
Don't Break the Oath, 158
Done With Mirrors, 16
Doomsday for the Deceiver, 95
Doomsday Machine, 28
Dopesmoker, 215
Down on the Upside, 219
Down to Earth, 184, 196
Draw the Line, 15
Dream Theater, 77, 200
Dreamtime, 57
DRI, 56–57, 77–78, 109, 159, 204
Dusk, 78
Dust, 78, 89
Dynamite Monster Boogie Concert, 195
Dynasty, 134

Eagles of Death Metal (EoDM), 79–80
Earache Records, 25, 51, 79, 103
Eat the Heat, 11
Edge of Excess, 235
Edward the Great, 120
Electric Guitars, 24, 80, 81, 82–84, 105

Elf, 71–72, 85, 111, 114, 195, 200
Emperor, 34, 85
Enemy of the Sun, 177
English Dogs, 85–86, 109
Enslaved, 86
Enthrone Darkness Triumphant, 70
EoDM. *See* Eagles of Death Metal
Equator, 246
Equilibrium, 56
Era Vulgaris, 192
Erase the Slate, 77
The Essential Iron Maiden, 120
Eternal Live, 213
Euphoria, 68
Europe, 11, 38, 39, 65, 76, 86–87, 103,
    112–13, 118, 137, 146, 150–52, 195,
    199, 209, 239–40, 242, 245, 247, 251,
    264
Excalibur, 25
Exodus, 87, 88, 216, 258
Extreme, 26, 50–51, 60, 62, 86, 88, 90–91,
    100–101, 103, 125, 127, 141, 149,
    159, 161, 166–67, 174–75, 186–87,
    189–90, 205, 217–18, 221, 224, 227,
    255, 272, 274
Eye for an Eye, 54

Fabulous Disaster, 87
Faith Hope Love, 131
Faith No More, 89–90
Fargo Rock City, 90, 272
Fashion and Metal, 90–92
Faster Pussycat, 92
Fates Warning, 92
Fear No Evil, 103
Fear of the Dark, 119
*Fenriz Presents ... the Best of Old School
    Black Metal*, 61
Festivals, 38, 60, 92–94, 130, 181, 206,
    266
Filter, 94
The Final Countdown, 87
Fire Down Under, 198–99
Fireball, 65
Firehouse III, 94
Firehouse, 94–95
First Glance, 27
The First Ten Years, 119
Fist Full of Metal, 26
Five Man Acoustical Jam, 230
Flesh and Blood, 188
Flex-Able Leftovers, 250
Flick of the Switch, 13

Flotsam & Jetsam, 95
Fly by Night, 202
Fly on the Wall, 13
Fly to the Rainbow, 209
Foghat Live, 95–96
Foghat, 95–96
FOPP, 218
Ford, Lita, 96, 200–201
Forged in Fire, 27
For Those About to Rock We Salute You,
    13
Forward into Battle, 86
Fu Manchu, 96–97, 138
Funeral, 97

Get a Grip, 16
Get Your Wings, 14–15
Ghost Rider: Travels on the Healing Road,
    203
Girls, Girls, Girls, 169
Girlschool, 46, 98–99, 171
Give Me Your Soul ... Please?, 130
GNR. *See* Guns N' Roses
Goatsnake, 99, 227
Goblin Cock, 100, 272
God Dethroned, 100, 159
Godflesh, 100
Godsmack, 101, 272
Good Acoustics, 94
Gorgoroth, 101, 149
The Great Radio Controversy,
    230
Great White, 102, 187
Gretchen Goes to Nebraska, 131
Grim Reaper, 103
The Grimm Robe Demos, 227
Grindcore, 50–51, 54, 74, 79, 100,
    103–4, 115, 147, 163, 166, 174,
    186–87, 216–17, 220, 223, 234,
    273
Grohl, Dave, 104, 172, 190, 191, 260
Grunge, 11, 21–22, 31–32, 44, 53, 68, 92,
    104–5, 131, 157, 159, 164, 169, 173,
    178, 192, 197, 208, 213, 218–19,
    229–30, 261, 263, 271
Guinness Book of World Records, 171
Guitar Hero, 8, 76, 89, 105, 148, 178,
    180, 207, 222, 258
Guns N' Roses (GNR), 15, 19, 46, 53, 58,
    70, 84, 92, 94, 102, 105–7, 108,
    177–78, 222, 237, 261
GWAR, 21, 107, 159, 173, 211,
    220

Hangover Music, 34
Hanoi Rocks, 108–9, 169, 178, 224
Happy Days, 256
Hard 'n' Heavy, 27, 67
Hardcore (Punk), 55–57, 74, 86, 97, 103, 109–10, 159–60, 162, 172, 177, 189, 220, 226, 234, 265
Hatebreed, 110
Haunting the Chapel, 214
Have a Nice Day, 44
Headbanger's Ball, 56
Headbanging, 10, 110
Headhunter, 137
Heading for a Storm, 251
Hear in the New Frontier, 192
Hear Nothing, See Nothing, Say Nothing, 74
Heartache, 129
Heartbreak Station, 52
Heaven and Hell, 36–37, 71–73, 110–11, 114, 172
Heaven and Hell, Live Evil, 36
Heavy Metal, 3–9;
    audience, 5–7;
    metal music beginnings, 4–5;
    musical roots of, 7–9;
    term, 3–4;
    theory, 5–9
Heavy Metal Kids, 111, 246
Heavy Metal Parking Lot, 111–12
Hell Awaits, 214
Hell Bent for Leather, 123
Hellbilly Deluxe, 269
Hellhammer, 51–52, 70–71, 112, 115, 155, 180
Helloween, 38, 112–13
Hemispheres, 203
The Heroin Diaries, 170
Hesher, 178
Highlights & Lowlives, 39
High Live, 113
High on Fire, 114, 182, 215
High Voltage, 12
Highway to Hell, 13
Hold Your Fire, 94
Hole in the Sun, 179
Holocaust, 114, 115
Holy Mountain, 70
Honkin' on Bobo, 17
Hooked, 102
The Horns, 114
Hot Wire, 136
Hotter Than Hell, 133
Houses of the Holy, 145

How Will I Laugh, 226
Hysteria, 68

Idol, Billy, 223
If You Want Blood You've Got It, 13
Imaginos, 40
I'm a Rebel, 10
Immortal, 115
Imprint, 259
In-A-Gadda-Da-Vida, 117
Incubus, 115–16
Indecent & Obscene, 74
Infectious Grooves, 116, 226
Innocent Victim, 245
Insane Clown Posse, 116, 125
In the Shadows, 158
In Through the Out Door, 146
In Trance, 209
Invasion of Your Privacy, 197
Iron Butterfly, 3, 35, 116–17
Iron Maiden, 5, 91, 112, 117–20, 123–24, 205, 208, 228, 242
Isis, 20, 45, 56, 109, 120

Jackyl, 121
Jerusalem, 182, 215
Jethro Tull and the Grammys, 121–22
John Wesley Harding, 123
Join the Army, 226
Judas Priest, 8, 10, 34, 73, 83, 112, 118, 122–25, 140–42, 170, 172, 208, 220, 225
Juggalos, 116, 125–26
Jugulator, 124
Just Push Play, 17

Kaizoku-Ban, 11
Kajzer, Jen, 127
Kamikaze, Diane, 127
Kat, 49, 127–28, 259
Keeper of the Seven Keys, Pt. 1, 112, 113
Keeper of the Seven Keys, Pt. 2, 112, 113
Keep the Dogs Away, 232
Keep the Faith, 44
Kid Rock, 128–29, 266
Kill 'Em All, 159
Killers, 118
Killing Is My Business ... And Business Is Good!, 156
Killing Machine, 123
Killswitch Engage, 129–30, 216

King Diamond, 49, 54, 104, 130, 158–59, 180, 187, 190, 199, 242
King's X, 130–31, 224
Kingdom Come, 212
Kiss, 11, 19, 32, 54, 73, 96, 107, 118, 130, 132–34, 153, 157, 183, 188, 199, 201, 207, 213, 234–35, 237–38, 253, 256–57
Kiss Unmasked, 134
Kittie, 135
Kix, 135–136
Kix Live, 136
KKK Bitch, 41
Korn, 50, 68, 85, 90, 101, 115, 136, 182, 190
Kreator, 54, 137, 216
Krokus, 137
Kyuss, 97, 99, 138, 154, 191

L'Amours, 139–40
Lamb of God, 56, 129, 139
The Last in Line, 71
Law & Order: Special Victims Unit, 41
The Laws of Scourge, 205
Leather, 90–91, 123, 140–42, 152, 160, 168, 170, 178, 196, 200, 205–6, 220, 221, 225, 267, 272
Led Zeppelin, 3–4, 8, 14, 19, 31, 34–35, 37, 40, 63, 67, 85, 102, 110, 142–46, 153, 165, 187, 201–2, 234, 241, 257–58, 263, 271
Leng Tch'e, 146–47
Let Them Eat Pussy, 176
Leviathan, 154
Lez Zeppelin, 147, 234
Life's a Bitch, 198
Limp Bizkit, 33, 50, 68, 90, 94, 101, 115, 129, 136, 147–48, 194, 265–66
A Little South of Sanity, 17
Live Bootleg, 16
Live in Budokan, 217
Live in Phoenix, 95
Live Sentence, 151
Living Colour, 131, 148
Lonesome Crow, 209
Long Cold Winter, 52
Look What the Cat Dragged In, 188
Lord of the Rings, 53, 101, 148, 149, 155, 101, 149
Lords of Chaos, 149, 180, 273
Lost Highways, 45
Love, 57
Love After Death, 32

Machine Head, 9, 65, 150, 200, 216
Magic & Madness, 53
Malmsteen, Yngwie, 9, 18, 49, 64, 88, 150–52, 209, 250, 258
Manic Frustration, 236
Manowar, 5–6, 152, 220, 225, 232
Manson, Marilyn, 21, 94, 153, 184, 187, 212
Marching Out, 151
Master of Puppets, 161
Master of the Rings, 113
Masters of Reality, 153–54, 192
Mastodon, 23, 92, 127, 154–55, 273
Matter of Life and Death, 120
Mayhem, 34–35, 48, 61, 70–71, 80, 94, 101, 155–56, 169, 180, 206, 215, 227
Mean Machine, 11
Megadeth, 27, 49, 124, 156–57, 210, 216, 220, 237
Melvins, 51, 56, 157, 215–16, 227
Mentally Murdered, 79
Mercyful Fate, 130, 158, 159, 172
Meshuggah, 158–59
Metal Blade, 95, 97, 131, 159, 236
Metal Church, 38, 159
Metal Hammer, 139
Metalheads, 55, 93, 109, 147, 160–61, 170, 232
Metal Health, 193
Metallica, 19, 27, 32, 69, 87, 95, 109–10, 114, 122, 124, 137, 156, 159, 160–63, 172, 190, 192, 195, 210, 220, 226, 234, 237, 258, 260, 266, 273
Metalocalypse, 70–71
Metalogy, 125
Metal on Metal, 27
"Metal Up Your Ass," 159–60
The Metal Years, 19, 63, 221, 259, 262
Method of Destruction (M.O.D.), 164, 217
Midnight Dynamite, 135–36
Midnight Madness, 179
The Midnight Special, 181
The Mike Douglas Show, 232
Misfits, 59, 87, 109, 163–64, 220, 234
Misogyny, 7
The Mob Rules, 36
M.O.D. *See* Method of Destruction
Money Talks, 57
The Monkey Puzzle, 240
Monster Magnet, 164
Montrose, 165, 179, 254
Monumension, 86
Moonlight and Valentino, 44

Moonsorrow, 166

Morbid Angel, 79, 166–67

Morbid Visions, 210

More Things Change, 150

Moshing, 167, 188, 221, 225, 273

Mötley Crüe, 10, 19, 108, 136, 167–70, 224, 266

Motorhead, 20, 55, 87, 90, 92, 98, 104, 109, 110, 137, 158, 170–72, 176, 190, 220

Moving Pictures, 203

Mr. Big, 172–73, 194

MTV Music Awards, 254

MTV Unplugged, 146

Mudvayne, 173

The Muppet Show, 211

Mushroom Head, 173

Music from "The Elder," 134

Naked Lunch, 48

Napalm Death, 42, 51, 54, 62, 69, 74, 79, 80, 100, 103, 104, 174–76, 186

Narita, 198

Nashville Pussy, 18, 176

Nature of the Beast, 28

Neil Diamond Parking Lot, 112

Neurosis, 58, 177

Never Turn Your Back on a Friend, 47

New American Gospel, 139

New Wave of British heavy metal (NWOBHM), 38, 198, 206

New Wave of British metal (NWOBM), 114

New World Disorder, 33

New York Dolls, 92, 108–9, 132, 141, 177–78, 237

Nickelback, 104, 129, 178–79

A Night at the Opera, 244

Night in the Ruts, 16

Night Ranger, 165, 179, 181, 183

Night Songs, 52

Nightmare on Elm Street III: Dream Warriors, 76

Nightmare on Elm Street 5: The Dream Child, 119

Nile, 179–80

Nine Lives, 17

The Nightcomers, 114

No One Rides For Free, 97

No Parole from Rock 'n' Roll, 18, 151

No Place for Disgrace, 95

No Prayer for the Dying, 119

No Rest for the Wicked, 184

Nodtveidt's idiocy, 75

Noise of Music's Sake, 80

Norwegian Black Metal, 61, 101, 115, 149, 180

Notorious Byrd Brothers, 4

Nouveau Calls, 265

Nova Express, 3

Nugent, Ted, 16, 19, 23, 33, 96, 180–81. See also Alcohol

Number of the Beast, 5, 118

NWOBM. *See* New Wave of British metal

NWOBHM. *See* New Wave of British heavy metal

Obedience Thru Suffering, 56

Objection Overruled, 11

Obsessed by Cruelty, 217

Om, 4, 182

On Through the Night, 67

On Your Feet or On Your Knees, 40

Once Bitten...., 102

One Live Night, 76

One Way Ticket to Hell ... and Back, 60

Open to the Public, 222

Open Up and Say ... Ahh!, 188

Operation: Mindcrime, 192

Orgy, 182

Osbourne, Ozzy, 9, 19–20, 31, 34–37, 63, 67, 72, 93, 96, 111, 124, 157, 169, 179, 183–84, 193, 196, 213, 246, 259, 262, 269

The Osbournes, 183–84

Out for Blood, 96

Out of the Cellar, 197

Out of the Night, 102

Out of the Silent Planet, 131

Out of This World, 87

Over the Years and Through the Woods, 192

Overdose, 22, 42, 65, 111, 169, 178, 184, 193, 218, 244

Overkill, 170, 172, 185

Painkiller, 124

Paper Money, 165

Pariah, 186, 206

Pearlman, Sandy, 4

Peel, John, 42, 50, 174, 186

The Peel Sessions, 174, 186

Pentagram, 187

Perfect Strangers, 65

Permanent Vacation, 16

Permanent Waves, 203
Permission to Land, 60
Persistence of Time, 27
Phantom of the Opera, 208
Physical Grafitti, 145
Piece of Mind, 119
Piercings, 91, 187
Pig Destroyer, 104, 187
Pink Bubbles Go Ape, 113
The Pit, 26, 83, 167, 188, 225
The Plague That Makes Your Booty Move, 116
Pleasure to Kill, 137
Poison, 21–22, 46, 53, 92, 93, 109, 173, 177, 188, 261
Poison the Well, 189
Pornograffitti, 88
Possessed, 7, 62, 148, 189, 222, 226, 254, 256
Pound for Pound, 27
The Power and the Gloryhole, 92
Power Mad, 113, 189
Power Play, 28
Powerage, 13
Powerman 5000, 189–90
Powerslave, 119
Predator, 11
Presence, 145
Primus, 189
Prisoners in Paradise, 87
Private Eyes, 42
Probot, 104, 172, 190, 260
Prong, 190
The Process of Elimination, 147
Psycho Café, 32
Psycho Circus, 134
Psychotic Supper, 230
Pump, 16
Punk, 232
Punk Statik Paranoia, 182
Push Comes to Shove, 121
Pyromania, 67

Quadrophenia and Breaking Glass, 111
Queens of the Stone Age, 79, 104, 138, 153, 154, 191
Queensrÿche, 192–93
Quiet Riot, 95, 183, 193, 263

Racer X, 124, 172, 194
Rage Against the Machine, 68, 194–95, 219
Raging Slab, 195

Rainbow, 18, 65, 71–72, 85, 111, 114, 151, 183, 195–96, 200, 209, 243
Raising Hell, 120
Ram It Down, 124
Rammstein, 197
Ratt, 76, 84, 93, 102, 135, 183, 197
Raven, 100, 140, 190, 198
The Razor's Edge, 13
The Real Thing, 89
Real to Reel, 230
Rebel Without a Cause, 141
Rebel Yell, 223
The Red Sea, 120
Reek of Putrefaction, 50, 79
Reign in Blood, 214
Remaking Vince Neil, 169
Restless and Wild, 10
Restless and Wild, 10, 258
The Return of Martha Splatterhead, 103
Revenge, 257
Revolver, 139
Ride the Lightning, 160
Riot, 147, 198–99, 266
Rising Force, 151
River City Revival, 18
Roadrunner Records, 150, 178, 199–200
Rocka Rolla, 123
Rock & Roll Machine, 235
Rock in Rio, 120
Rocks, 15
Rock Star, 125
Rock Star, 34
Rock You to Hell, 103
The Rods, 195, 200
Roll the Bones, 203
Rolling Stone, 132, 139, 154, 241
Rubin, Rick, 13
The Runaways, 96, 200–201
Running Wild, 98, 201
Run to the Light, 236
Rush, 137, 199, 201–203, 221, 235, 258, 262
Russian Roulette, 11

Sacrament, 139
Sacred Groove, 76
Sacred Heart, 71
Sacred Reich, 55, 204, 258
Sad Wings of Destiny, 123
Saigon Kick, 204
Salisbury, 243
Samson, 118, 205
Sarcófago, 205

Satan, 206

Satanic Rites, 112

Satanic Rock, 207

Satanicide, 91, 206

Satriani, Joe, 65, 207, 250, 251

Saturday Night Live, 152

Savatage, 207–8, 230

Scatterbrain, 208

Scorpions, 9–10, 72, 76, 199, 208–9, 239–40, 242

Scream Bloody Gore, 62

Screaming for Vengeance, 124

Screaming Love, 218

Scum, 174

Secret Treaties, 40

See You In Hell, 103

Sehnsucht, 197

Sepultura, 199, 205, 210, 218

Sesame Street, 54

Seven Churches, 189

Seventh Son of a Seventh Son, 119

Shades of Deep Purple, 63

Shadowlife, 76

Shark Sandwich, 221

Shock Rock, 20, 153, 210–11

Short Bus, 94

Shot in the Dark, 102

Shotgun Messiah, 211–12

Shout at the Devil, 168

Show No Mercy, 214

The Sickness, 75

Sign in Please, 29

Silver and Gold, 119

Silver Side Up, 179

Sin After Sin, 123

Singles, 104

Sir Lord Baltimore, 4, 212, 272

Sixx, Nikki, 19, 167–69; *Heroin Diaries*, 19

Skid Row, 10, 43, 212–13

Slaughter of the Soul, 29

Slaughter, 29, 56–57, 63, 95, 119, 159, 189, 213, 257

Slave to the Grind, 212

Slaves and Masters, 65

Slayer, 10, 27, 109–10, 124, 159, 180, 210, 213–15, 219–20, 230, 237, 269, 272–73

Sleep, 70, 79, 114, 182, 213, 215, 222

Slip of the Tongue, 39

Slipknot, 173, 200, 216

Slippery When Wet, 43

Smokewagon, 216

Sneap, Andy, 129, 216

S.O.D. *See* Stormtroopers of Death

Sodom, 217

The Soft Machine, 3, 48

Soilent Green, 104, 217–18

Soldier's Under Command, 224

Some Kind of Monster, 160

Somewhere in Time, 119

The Song Remains the Same, 145

Songs for the Deaf, 104, 191

Sonic Temple, 58

Sons of Northern Darkness, 115

Soulfly, 205, 210, 218

Soundgarden, 68, 104, 195, 218–19, 229

The Soundhouse Tapes, 117

The Sound of Perseverance, 62

South of Heaven, 215

South Side of Heaven, 219

Southern Lord Records, 99, 219, 226–27

The Spaghetti Incident, 107

Speak of the Devil, 183

Speak Your Peace, 57

Spectrum, 41, 65

Speed Metal Symphony, 49

Speed Metal, 27, 49, 55, 56, 109, 123–24, 150, 160, 163–64, 172, 188–89, 201, 220, 234, 236, 258

Speedcore, 57, 220

Spikes, 32, 91, 220–21, 223, 225, 232

Spinal Tap, 31, 37, 162, 173, 206, 221–22, 242

Spirit of the Wild, 181

Spiritual Healing, 62

Split, 79

Spread Eagle, 222

Squawk, 47

St. Vitus, 50, 109, 190, 215, 219, 225–26, 265

Stained Class, 123–24

Star Trek, 268

Static X, 223, 272

Stay Hungry, 238

Stevens, Steve, 223–24

Stiff Upper Lip, 13

Stiletto, 96

Still Alive, 53

Still Climbing, 53

Storm of the Lights Bane, 75

Stormbringer, 65

Stormtroopers of Death (S.O.D.), 164, 216–17

Strangers in the Night, 240

Stryper, 224–25

Studs, 91, 225
Subhuman Race, 213
Suicidal Tendencies, 116, 226
Sunn O))), 45, 48, 99, 219, 227
Sunrise on the Sufferbus, 154
A Sun That Never Sets, 177
Superunknown, 219
Surfing with the Alien, 207
Surf Nicaragua, 204
Survivors, 205
The System Has Failed, 156
"Sweet Emotion," 15
The Sword, 228

Tad, 104, 229
Taken by Force, 209
Tattooed Millionaire, 119
Tesla, 102, 229–30, 234
Testament, 60, 87, 114, 145, 208, 216,
    225, 230–31
Theatre of Pain, 168
Thin Lizzy, 19, 40, 117, 171, 231–32, 263
This Left Feels Right, 44
Thor, 166, 220, 227, 232–33
Thor Against the World, 233
Thrash Metal, 4, 10, 26, 59, 60, 62, 87,
    95, 103, 109, 112, 124, 137, 156,
    159, 163–64, 184–85, 189, 198, 204,
    210, 213–14, 216, 220, 226, 234,
    258
Thunder and Lightning, 232
The Time of the Oath, 113
Time Bomb, 46
Time Heals Nothing,
Titanic, 206
Title of Record, 94
TNT, 12
To Hell with the Devil, 225
*To Mega Therion and Into the
    Pandemonium*, 51
Too Fast for Love, 168
Too Much Too Soon, 177
To the Ends of the Earth, 86
Tora Tora, 234
Toys in the Attic, 15
Trampled Under the Hoof, 99
Tribute Bands, 32, 147, 234–35, 247
Trilogy, 151
Triumph, 112, 235
Triumph of Death, 112
Trixter, 236
Trouble, 19, 40, 75, 113, 161, 162, 199,
    236, 253

Trunk, Eddie, 127, 236–37
TSOL, 109, 177, 237
Twelve Shots on the Rocks, 109
Twice Shy, 102
Twisted Sister, 237–38
Twister, 254
The Two Towers, 48
Type O Negative, 238
Tyranny & Mutation, 40

UFO, 83, 111, 117, 209, 239–40
Ultimate Sin, 184
Ultramega OK, 218
Ultraphobic, 261
Under Jolly Roger, 201
Under Lock and Key, 76
Unleashed in the East, 124
The Unquestionable Truth Part 1, 148
Upper Crust, 241
Uriah Heep, 19, 111, 170, 183, 141,
    241–49, 265, 272, 273

Vai, Steve, 18, 84, 207, 250–51, 263
Vandenberg, 199, 251, 263, 264
Van Halen, 19, 22, 25, 47, 81, 83–84, 88,
    129, 165, 183, 209, 251–55, 258, 262,
    264, 271
Vanity/Nemesis, 51
Venom, 5, 34–35, 62, 104, 109, 112, 163,
    180, 190, 255–56
*Viides Luku:
    Havitetty*, 166
Village Voice, 132
Vincebus Eruptum, 39
Vincent, Vinnie, 134, 213, 234, 256–57
Virgin Killer, 209
Virtual XI, 120
Virtuosity in Heavy Metal, 257–58
Vision of Disorder, 258–59
Vixen, 201, 259
Voivod, 259–60

Wages of Sin, 28
Walking Into Clarksdale, 146
Wake Me When It's Over, 92
Walk on Water, 240
Walls of Jericho, 112
Warhammer, 42
The Warning and Rage for Order, 192
Warrant, 261
W.A.S.P., 19, 63, 220, 221, 242, 262
Watain, 262
Welcome to Bob City, 211

Whatever Doesn't Kill You ..., 39
When the Storm Comes Down, 95
Whiplash Smile, 224
Whipped, 92
White Lion, 262–63
White Pony, 69
White Zombie, 17, 190, 264–65, 268–69
Whitesnake, 39, 65, 68, 84, 199, 239, 250, 251, 258, 263–64
Who Do We Think We Are?, 65
Who Made Who, 13
Wild at Heart, 189
The Wild Bunch, 140
The Wild Life, 213
Willy, Uranium, 3
Wings of Tomorrow, 87

Wings, 15
Wino, 104, 190, 225–26, 265
Wishbone Ash, 117, 246, 265
With Odin on Our Side, 23
Wonderworld, 244
Woodstock 1999, 265–66
Worship Me or Die, 128
Wykyd Sceptre, 266–67

The X Factor, 119

Young Guns II, 44

Zolar X, 268, 273
Zombie, Rob, 268–69
Zooma, 146

About the Authors

WILLIAM PHILLIPS is an academic and scholar. He has written extensively on music, technology, and culture. He is currently at New York University, writing his Ph.D. on digital technology and music culture, where he teaches courses on media, communication, and culture. He also works on a variety of musical projects as a guitarist and producer out of his Brooklyn home recording studio.

BRIAN COGAN is a professor who has written extensively on music and popular culture as well as music criticism. He received his Ph.D. in Media Ecology in 2002 from New York University. He teaches at Molloy College and has taught at New York University and the College of Staten Island. Cogan is the author of Greenwood's *Encyclopedia of Punk Music and Culture* (2006).